T0270952

QUALITY STANDARDS, VALUE CHAINS, AND INTERNATIONAL DEVELOPMENT

Over the past decades, the world has witnessed an unprecedented growth in global value chains, associated with increasingly demanding quality standards. These trends lead to concerns about the impact of value chains on development and poverty and about the possible protectionist nature of quality standards in rich countries. This book offers the first integrated theoretical analysis of the economic and political factors that determine the level of quality standards, as well as their economic effects along the value chain. Using realistic assumptions motivated by empirical research, the theoretical framework in this book makes it possible to study the efficiency effects as well as the distributional consequences of one of the most striking evolutions affecting global trade and development today.

Johan Swinnen is Professor of Economics and Director of the LICOS Centre for Institutions and Economic Performance at the University of Leuven (KU Leuven). He is Senior Research Fellow at the Centre for European Policy Studies and Visiting Scholar at the Centre for Food Security and the Environment at Stanford University. Previously he was Lead Economist at the World Bank and Economic Advisor at the European Commission. He has published widely on political economy, institutional reform, trade, and global value chains. His books include *Political Power and Economic Policy, Global Supply Chains, Standards and the Poor, Foreign Direct Investment and Human Development, Private Standards and Global Governance*, and *From Marx and Mao to the Market*.

Koen Deconinck is a senior research affiliate at the LICOS Centre for Institutions and Economic Performance at KU Leuven. Previously he was a visiting researcher at OECD and at UC Davis. His research has been published in international journals such as *Business History,* the *American Journal of Agricultural Economics*, and *Food Policy*.

Thijs Vandemoortele currently works for Caterpillar Distribution Services Europe and is a senior research affiliate with the LICOS Centre for Institutions and Economic Performance at KU Leuven. Previously he was a visiting researcher at OECD and at UC Berkeley. His research has been published in *The World Trade Review, The World Economy*, the *European Review of Agricultural Economics*, and the *Review of Development Economics*.

Anneleen Vandeplas works as an economist for the European Commission and is a senior research affiliate with the LICOS Centre for Institutions and Economic Performance at KU Leuven. Previously she was visiting professor at the University of Hasselt and visiting researcher at the International Food Policy Research Institute (New Delhi). Her work has been published in international journals including the *World Bank Economic Review,* the *Journal of Development Studies*, the *Journal of Agricultural Economics*, and *World Development*.

Quality Standards, Value Chains, and International Development

Economic and Political Theory

JOHAN SWINNEN
University of Leuven and
Stanford University

KOEN DECONINCK
University of Leuven

THIJS VANDEMOORTELE
Caterpillar Distribution Services Europe and
University of Leuven

ANNELEEN VANDEPLAS
European Commission
and University of Leuven

CAMBRIDGE
UNIVERSITY PRESS

CAMBRIDGE
UNIVERSITY PRESS

University Printing House, Cambridge CB2 8BS, United Kingdom

One Liberty Plaza, 20th Floor, New York, NY 10006, USA

477 Williamstown Road, Port Melbourne, VIC 3207, Australia

4843/24, 2nd Floor, Ansari Road, Daryaganj, Delhi - 110002, India

79 Anson Road, #06-04/06, Singapore 079906

Cambridge University Press is part of the University of Cambridge.

It furthers the University's mission by disseminating knowledge in the pursuit of
education, learning and research at the highest international levels of excellence.

www.cambridge.org
Information on this title: www.cambridge.org/9781107025912

First published 2015

A catalogue record for this publication is available from the British Library

Library of Congress Cataloging in Publication data
Swinnen, Johan F. M., 1962–
Quality standards, value chains, and international development : economic and
political theory / Johan Swinnen, University of Leuven and Stanford University, Koen
Deconinck, University of Leuven, Thijs Vandemoortele, Caterpillar Distribution
Services Europe and University of Leuven, Anneleen Vandeplas, European
Commission and University of Leuven.
pages cm
Includes bibliographical references and index.
ISBN 978-1-107-02591-2 (hardback) – ISBN 978-1-107-68886-5 (pbk.)
1. Value. 2. International trade. 3. Economic development. I. Title.
HB201.S945 2015
330.01–dc23 2015009549

ISBN 978-1-107-02591-2 Hardback
ISBN 978-1-107-68886-5 Paperback

Contents

Preface and Acknowledgments

This book is global in its coverage and in its creation. Standards and value chains are rapidly spreading across the world, as we document in the book. While much of the creation of this book was centered in the LICOS Centre for Institutions and Economic Performance at the University of Leuven in Belgium, it was inspired by empirical research in various parts of the world and enhanced by discussions and collaborations with researchers from many institutions around the globe.

Our first encounter with the importance and the role of standards and value chains (or supply chains as we referred to them then) in development was in the transition world. In the early 1990s we witnessed an unexpected economic collapse in Eastern Europe and the former Soviet Union: output was falling and productivity was going down in country after country that embarked on the road to a market economy. The things that were going up were unemployment and poverty.

Then, rather suddenly, things turned around. One of the first sectors to turn around was the sugar sector in Slovakia. Following up on discussions at the Organisation for Economic Co-operation and Development (OECD) Expert Group on Transition we carefully analyzed the transformation of this sector and discovered the crucial role that the supply chain restructuring process and the introduction of various standards had on productivity and output.

These insights triggered us to embark on a large set of value chain studies, at LICOS and later at the World Bank. The empirical research started in Eastern Europe (with field research in, e.g., Poland, Hungary, Bulgaria, and Albania); later we extended our analyses to Asia (in China in collaboration with CCAP; in India in collaboration with the International Food Policy Research Institute [IFPRI]) and to Africa (e.g., in Madagascar, Senegal, Benin, and Ethiopia).

Our empirical findings and those of others suggested quite heterogeneous impacts and effects that were not captured or explained by traditional economic models. It became obvious after some time that our difficulties with interpreting the various findings were partially due to the absence of a good theoretical framework. We started developing conceptual frameworks to model the processes that we observed, derive hypotheses, and use these to improve our future empirical work and enhance the interpretation of existing empirical findings on value chains and standards.

In parallel a second set of theoretical work started, which was triggered by discussions on the trade implications of standards – and why certain standards are introduced. Economic analyses of standards and value chains take the standards as given and study their effects. However, the decision to introduce standards, be it by governments or the private sector, is of course an intriguing question in itself. Our research on the political economy of standards was also inspired by discussions on the reasons and effects of the proliferation of standards, including the Genetically Modified Organism regulations, in the European Union in the wake of a series of food safety crises in the late 1990s – and by our dissatisfaction with existing theoretical models that simply ignored the potential beneficial welfare effects of standards.

At some point during this research process the idea for this book emerged. We started trying to put together the different papers. At first we thought it would be a (relatively) simple compilation of our past and ongoing work. But we soon discovered that this would be unsatisfactory. The only effective way to do it was to truly compare the theories and models to integrate the analyses. We went back to the drawing board more times than we would like to remember. At times our project seemed lost or stalled amid that quagmire of other demands. But many colleagues kept reminding us that our project was worth pursuing. This kept our spirits up through the numerous revisions.

The book as it is in front of you now is an attempt to integrate these various pieces of research into a coherent set of models. It attempts to be innovative by presenting new material and to be comprehensive by summarizing and integrating earlier theoretical work. It explains how different models relate to each other and have been used to address different topics or different ways to analyze the same topic.

Although our names appear as authors on this book, the insights in it are based on many research collaborations with colleagues throughout the world. We owe thanks to many people. Unfortunately they are too numerous to name them all.

A few people, however, deserve mention in particular. Hamish Gow played a crucial role early on in helping us understand the impact of value chain transformation on productivity and output. Our theoretical work was given a crucial boost by research visits of Scott Rozelle and Jim Vercammen at LICOS in the mid-2000s. We learned much from case studies and field research by many colleagues, especially from Bart Minten, Miet Maertens, Liesbeth Dries, Nivelin Noev, Liesbeth Colen, Kristine Van Herck, Siemen van Berkum, and Matt Gorton.

Many discussions with Tom Reardon inspired and stimulated us to think harder. d'Artis Kancs and Tao Xiang played a crucial role in analyzing general equilibrium impacts. Colin Poulton and colleagues inspired us by their work on the trade-off between competition and coordination. Alexander Sarris and Eugenia Serova at FAO, Ken Ash and Frank Van Tongeren at OECD, Sara Savastano and David Zilberman at ICABR, and former colleagues of the World Bank's Eastern European and Central Asia Socially Sustainable Development Division (ECSSD) were an important source of encouragement to continue this research.

Our political economy work on standards benefited from collaborations with Jill McCluskey, Alessandro Olper, Gordon Rausser, John Beghin, Claire Delpeuch, Thomas Heckelei, Giulia Meloni, Justus Wesseler, and David Vogel.

Some of the chapters in this book are based on joint work with Scott Rozelle and Tao Xiang (Chapters 10 and 17), with Miet Maertens (Chapters 14 and 15), and with d'Artis Kancs and Jikun Huang (Chapter 17). Elfriede Lecossois, Martijn Huysmans, and Li Fan did a great job in helping to finish the final version of the manuscript.

We would also like to thank OECD, UC Berkeley, UC Davis, IFPRI, and Stanford University for providing (some of) us with stimulating environments to work on the manuscript. We thank the KU Leuven Research Fund (Centre of Excellence and Methusalem grants) and the Research Foundation–Flanders for their generous financial support.

Finally, we should thank Cambridge University Press for being so patient with us. The contract and the manuscript's structure changed several times before we were ready to deliver. Or, to put it in terms of our work: both sides insisted on high standards for the book and managed to avoid a breakdown of the contractual relationships in the value chain in view of high specific investments on both sides. We hope the self-enforcement of the relationship also means that sufficient value has been created for the readers.

Disclaimer: This book is based on research conducted before Anneleen Vandeplas joined the European Commission. Any opinions expressed in this book are those of the authors and do not necessarily reflect the views of their respective institutions.

1

Introduction

The past decades have witnessed an unprecedented restructuring of global markets, which included a rapid increase in trade, foreign investment, and the globalization of value chains. Changing consumer preferences in rich countries, rapid income growth and urbanization in emerging countries, together with technological developments and globalization have transformed the industrial organization and international location of production. One of the most important mechanisms underlying the globalization process lies in the transfer of advanced production capabilities to low-wage economies. These capabilities comprise an increase both in productivity and in product quality (Goldberg and Pavcnik, 2007; Grossman and Helpman, 2005). Leading economists have argued that the quality aspect is by far the more important element: poor productivity can be offset by low wage rates, but until firms attain some threshold level of quality, they cannot achieve sales in global markets and participate in modern value chains, however low the local wage level (Sutton, 2001).

1.1 The Rise of Standards

Not surprisingly, these changes have coincided with a global proliferation of "quality standards." These standards specify requirements on (characteristics of) the production process, the final product, the packaging of the product, and so on. They are increasing in number, in their global reach, and in what they cover, such as safety aspects (e.g., no small toy parts, nuclear equipment safety measures), environmental effects (e.g., organic products, low carbon dioxide emission), health concerns (e.g., low lead or pesticide residues), nutrition requirements (e.g., low fat), and social concerns (e.g., no child labor, fair trade). Standards are set by governments ("public standards") and by commercial organizations ("private standards").[1]

An illustration of this trend are the notifications submitted to the World Trade Organization (WTO) whenever member states introduce public standards and regulations that may restrict trade. Notifications to the WTO of sanitary and phyto-sanitary (SPS) and technical barrier to trade (TBT) measures have increased exponentially over the past fifteen years (see also Figure 5.1 in Chapter 5). In 2014, more than 17,000 notifications were submitted to the WTO (WTO, 2014a, b). In the past, most of these notifications originated with the United States and the European Union, but in recent years developing countries have caught up and now issue 60 percent of the SPS notifications. Systematic data on private standards are hard to find but indirect data can be used to gauge the parallel explosion of private standards, for example, by using data on standards such as Global Partnership for Good Agricultural Practice (GlobalG.A.P.), a standard used by the world's leading retailers for their suppliers of food and agricultural produce.[2] GlobalG.A.P. is now used in more than 100 countries and the number of GlobalG.A.P.-certified producers increased approximately tenfold over the past decade (GlobalG.A.P., 2014). In summary, empirical indicators show that in rich and poor countries alike both public and private standards are growing rapidly.

These standards have an increasingly far-reaching impact on economic development and international trade, operating through two main channels. First, increasing safety and quality requirements have effects beyond the imposing countries' borders, as these standards also affect imports and consequently have an impact on producers and traders in exporting nations. Second, global value chains are playing an increasingly important role in world markets, and the growth of these (often vertically coordinated) marketing channels is associated with increasing quality standards. Modern retailing companies increasingly gain market share in international and local markets and set standards for quality and safety wherever they are doing business, including in many poor countries with significant implications for local producers. The rising investment in processing and retailing in developing and emerging countries has in turn stimulated the

---

[1] In this book, we refer to the set of these characteristics with the general concept of "quality standards" or "standards." When we distinguish between various aspects, such as environmental standards versus safety standards, we make this explicit (as, e.g., in Chapter 6).

[2] The GlobalG.A.P. standard implies criteria for food safety; sustainable production methods; worker and animal welfare; and responsible use of water, compound feed, and plant propagation materials (www.globalgap.org).

demand for higher quality commodities from local suppliers (Figuié and Moustier, 2009; Minten and Reardon, 2008; Reardon et al., 2003).

1.2 The Debate

The rise of standards and value chains has triggered a vigorous debate on the impacts on international trade and development.

There are two broad lines of critiques, addressing both of the afore-mentioned channels. The first critique is that standards are (non-tariff) trade barriers. As international trade agreements such as the WTO have contributed to a global reduction in tariffs, countries have turned to new instruments to shield their domestic markets from foreign competition (Anderson et al., 2004; Augier et al., 2005; Brenton and Manchin, 2002; Fischer and Serra, 2000; Sturm, 2006). The second line of critique is that, even if developing and emerging countries can comply with the new standards, there are major distributional effects within these countries, mostly to the detriment of the poor. More specifically, it is argued that standards cause the exclusion of small, poorly informed, and weakly capitalized producers from participating in these "high-standard value chains."[3] Moreover, even if small producers could participate, these chains are said to be dominated by large multinational companies that extract the entire surplus through their superior bargaining power within the chains (Reardon and Berdegué, 2002; Unnevehr, 2000; Warning and Key, 2002).

However, there is considerable uncertainty and debate regarding the validity of these critical arguments on the impacts of these standards, and more generally the welfare implications of high-standards trade and global value chains (Swinnen, 2007).

First, regarding trade and the protectionist effects of standards, several authors argue that the simple "standards as protectionism" argument ignores the social benefits of standards in terms of consumer welfare, for example, by reducing asymmetric information, or by reducing externalities in society. Including these other effects of standards makes the impact of standards on trade and welfare much less obvious (Beghin et al., 2012;

---

[3] Several empirical studies indicate that small producers are excluded because of increasing standards (Gibbon, 2003; Key and Runsten, 1999; Kherralah, 2000; Maertens and Swinnen, 2009; Reardon et al., 2003; Schuster and Maertens, 2013; Subervie and Vagneron, 2013; Weatherspoon and Reardon, 2003). For example, evidence from Kenya, Zimbabwe, and Côte d'Ivoire suggests that horticulture exports are increasingly grown on large industrial estate farms, thereby excluding smallholder suppliers in the export supply chain (Dolan and Humphrey, 2000; Minot and Ngigi, 2004).

Beghin and Li, 2013; Sheldon, 2012; Swinnen and Vandemoortele, 2012).[4] Moreover, although quality and safety standards indeed make production more costly, at the same time they reduce transaction costs in trade, and can be "catalysts" for trade (Henson and Jaffee, 2007; Maertens and Swinnen, 2007). Standards can communicate the presence of desirable attributes or the absence of undesirable attributes that are otherwise difficult, costly, or even impossible to verify by consumers (Roe and Sheldon, 2007).[5]

In fact, despite the rapidly growing and tightening standards, global trade has increased sharply over the past three decades. Moreover, even for developing countries, the growth has been strong in sectors where standards have become (much) more restrictive and spread rapidly. This is, for example, the case in high-value (and high standards) food exports – which includes fruits, vegetables, seafood, fish, meat, and dairy products. In Asia and in Latin America, exports of such high-value food products increased from around 20 percent of agricultural exports in the 1980s to around 40 percent in recent years, with overall exports increasing significantly. The process is similar, albeit somewhat slower, in Africa (Swinnen and Maertens, 2014).

Second, regarding the impact of standards on inequality and poverty inside developing and emerging countries, although quality and safety standards indeed make production more costly, at the same time they increase the value of the products, potentially yielding higher profits (Maertens et al., 2012; Reardon and Farina, 2002; Swinnen and Vandeplas, 2011). Empirical studies also show that the introduction of standards induces important changes in the industrial organization of value chains, such as the growth of vertical coordination with potentially important implications for access to technology, capital, and crucial inputs for local suppliers (Dries et al., 2009; Gow and Swinnen, 1998).[6] The empirical literature thus suggests that smallholder participation in high standards global value chains is more

---

[4] Several authors have determined protectionism of standard-like measures conceptually; see, e.g., Baldwin (1970) and Fisher and Serra (2000), with some limitations highlighted in Marette and Beghin (2010). However, empirically determining whether a standard is a protectionist measure is a difficult empirical problem, as explained in detail in Beghin et al. (2015).

[5] In addition, minimum quality standards may increase welfare in a vertically differentiated market by reducing firms' pricing power. Standards may also solve problems related to network externalities. We briefly review this literature in Chapter 2.

[6] Minten et al. (2009) find that inclusion in a contract-farming scheme for high-standard vegetable export production in Madagascar improves farmers' access to new technologies and food security. Dries and Swinnen (2004, 2010) find that participation of small-scale farmers in contract-farming schemes in dairy value chains in Poland increases access to credit, technology, and farm investment. Similar results have been documented by Gow et al. (2000), Negash and Swinnen (2013), Noev et al. (2009), and World Bank (2005)2013.

widespread than what was initially predicted, or feared (Reardon et al., 2009; Swinnen, 2007).[7]

Finally, regarding the rent distribution within these value chains, recent empirical studies show quite different effects than predicted. Early empirical studies focused mostly on the exclusion issue (i.e., whether poor producers were marginalized by the introduction of standards). Only more recent studies actually measure welfare, income, or poverty. The studies that do measure welfare effects find positive effects for poor households in developing countries who may participate either as smallholder producers or through wage employment on larger farming companies (Andersson et al., 2015; Colen et al., 2012; Maertens and Swinnen, 2009; Maertens et al., 2011; Minten et al., 2009; Rao and Qaim, 2011; Rao et al., 2012;).[8] What is remarkable is that these strong benefits occur in several of these cases despite the fact that trade is organized by monopsonistic exporting companies.

1.3 Objective and Outline of the Book

As is clear from this review, the debate has been intense and the literature has contributed a rich set of studies with heterogeneous findings. The rapidly growing set of papers and books on these issues is mostly empirical in nature. To interpret the variation in findings and draw correct implications, a theory or conceptual framework is necessary. However, an integrated theoretical framework to analyze the economic and political interactions of standards, value chains, and international development, and to interpret the variation in empirical findings, has not yet been developed. Our book is an attempt to fill this gap. The book presents an integrated set of theoretical models and conceptual frameworks on economic and political aspects of standards, value chains, and international development.

---

[7] For example, Minten et al. (2009) show that in Madagascar most fresh fruit and vegetable production for exports is on very small farms, often on a contract basis with the agrifood industry, and with important positive effects on farmers' productivity. Similar results are found by studies in Asia (Gulati et al., 2007), in Eastern Europe (Dries and Swinnen, 2004; Dries et al., 2009), and in China (Wang et al., 2009).

[8] Maertens and Swinnen (2009) find that farmers' income doubles as a result of being included in the horticultural export chain in Senegal, and Dedehouanou et al. (2013) point out that participation in such contract farming schemes increases farmers' subjective well-being or happiness. Andersson et al. (2015), Rao and Qaim (2011), and Rao et al. (2012) find that the participation of smallholder vegetable farmers in high-standard supermarket channels in Kenya increases farm productivity and income by almost 50 percent. Minten et al. (2009) find that inclusion in a contract-farming scheme for high-standard vegetable export production in Madagascar improves poor households' food security.

The theoretical models and analyses are kept general to the extent possible, to make them broadly relevant. The implications of standards and value chains for trade and development have been actively debated for various economic sectors. Examples include textiles (Barrientos et al., 2011; Czubala et al., 2009; Evgeniev and Gereffi, 2008; Frederick and Gereffi, 2011), handicraft (LeClair, 2002), forestry (Stringer, 2006; Marx et al., 2012a), the automotive industry (Sturgeon et al., 2008, 2009), chemicals (Ackerman et al., 2007), nanotechnology (Dillemuth et al., 2011), and the agrifood sector (Reardon et al., 2003). Cross-sector reviews of the implications of standards and value chains can be found in, for example, Gereffi et al. (2005), Cattaneo et al. (2010), Heckelei and Swinnen (2012), Hoekman (2013, 2014), Marx et al. (2012b), and Vogel and Swinnen (2011).

Many of the empirical examples that we use in this book to illustrate and motivate the assumptions in the models and theoretical findings are from agriculture and the food industry, as these sectors have been most extensively analyzed empirically and the debate has been especially fierce in these sectors (Dolan and Humphrey, 2000; Reardon et al., 1999). One reason is that rich country food safety and quality standards, both from private and public sources, have tightened dramatically over the past decade, strongly affecting international trade and global value chains in these commodities (Jaffee and Henson, 2005). A second reason concerns the development implications of this evolution. As many of the world's poor are employed in agriculture, exports of agricultural commodities are seen as a very important potential source of pro-poor growth (World Bank, 2007). Third, many people are confronted with the effects as consumers of food (Beghin et al., 2015; Reardon and Timmer, 2012). But, as mentioned, we have tried to keep the models as general as possible and explained in detail where assumptions relate to specific sectors or conditions.

As we explained in Section 1.2, the debate has focused on two different critiques or areas of disagreement, and the structure of our book reflects these debates. After the introductory part (Chapters 1–3), the second part of the book (Chapters 4–9) focuses on how countries set standards. Given the importance of public standards (in particular in trade conflicts), we use a political economy approach to model the decision-making process around public standards. In an extension of the basic model, we also analyze interactions between private and public standards. The third part of the book (Chapters 10–17) then focuses on the effects of standards through value chains. We provide a theoretical framework to analyze the economic impacts of standards on efficiency and on equity, explicitly taking into account how value chains are reorganized in response to standards.

Before starting our political and economic analysis of standards, Chapter 2 discusses our approach to modeling standards. Chapter 3 develops a basic analytical framework to illustrate the impact of standards on equity and efficiency in the presence of asymmetric information. Such standards may generate efficiency gains by solving asymmetric information issues but may also involve implementation costs. The framework allows for standards to impact producers differently, creating differences in implementation costs. This basic model will show that standards involve rent redistribution from consumers to producers and that these rents may differ according to the producer's costs of implementing the standard.

The second part of the book (Chapters 4–9) analyzes the political economy of standards. Chapter 4 presents a political economy model of public standards. We use this model to derive the politically optimal public standard and to analyze different factors affecting that political equilibrium, including the level of economic development.

Chapter 5 extends the theoretical analysis of Chapter 4 to an open economy framework and explicitly integrates the impact of standards on international trade, how it may induce lobbying to use standards as non-tariff barriers – and what the political equilibrium is. The theoretical analysis compares the political outcome with the social optimum to identify under which cases "understandardization" or "overstandardization" results, and when standards are protectionist measures. The chapter includes a discussion of the rules of the WTO in relation to standards (e.g., agreements on SPS measures and on TBTs that make explicit reference to the issue of international standards).

Chapter 6 extends the political economy model of Chapter 5 to analyze the choice of different standards by integrating risk and externalities. This allows analyzing whether the nature of public standards (safety standards, quality standards, social and environmental standards) affects the politically optimal standard and the likelihood of trade conflicts. This extension shows that in general, public safety standards are set at higher levels because stronger consumption effects translate into larger political incentives for governments. The relationship between standards and protectionism is also affected by the nature of the standards.

Chapter 7 analyzes the interaction between public and private standards. Private company standards are increasingly important in addressing consumer concerns about safety, quality, social, and environmental issues. Often these private standards are more stringent than their public counterparts. The chapter presents a model that combines market power and political economy to explain this observation. A key outcome of the model is that if producers are able to exercise their political power to induce the government to set lower public standards, retailers may apply their market power to set their private standards at a higher level than the public ones.

Chapter 8 extends the static political economy models of the previous chapters into a dynamic model to analyze intertemporal implications. In this framework, minor differences in consumer or producer preferences can lead to important differences in standards and regulations over time, and temporary shocks to these preferences can have long-lasting effects on regulation. This analysis contributes to explaining cross-country differences in technology and environmental regulations. Chapter 9 studies the political economy of standards that include or exclude producers in value chains, such as occupational licenses or geographical indications. Such standards are often justified by referring to the need to protect quality, but the exclusion or inclusion of producers obviously has distributional effects. Our analysis incorporates possible negative effects on quality of an expansion, as well as cost sharing effects, and shows how the political outcome may either be too large or too small from a social welfare point of view.

The third part of the book (Chapters 10–17) focuses on the interaction among standards, value chains, and economic development. Chapter 10 develops a formal theory of the endogenous process of the introduction of quality and safety standards. Initial differences in income and capital and transaction costs are shown to affect the emergence and the size of the high standards economy. This theory shows that there is an important interaction between standards and production structures. Initial differences in the production structure are shown to influence the emergence of high-standards economic sectors and also which producers are included in the high-standards economy, and which are not. The nature of transaction costs – as well as the possibility of vertical coordination between producers and processors – also matter.

Chapter 11 focuses specifically on how small producers can be integrated in high-standards value chains through vertical coordination (a key characteristic globally observed) in a context of factor market imperfections and weak contract enforcement. The chapter analyzes how these characteristics affect surplus creation and rent distribution and how the process of development affects both. It also shows that, under some conditions, poor producers may, paradoxically, benefit more from vertical coordination at low levels of development.

Market power and competition policy in value chains have emerged as an important policy issue. With rapid consolidation in the global retail, agribusiness, and food industry (both in high-income countries and in emerging economies), the impact of concentration in global value chains on efficiency and rent distribution is an important issue. Chapter 12 extends the model of Chapter 11 to explore the impact of competition on global value chains, taking into account market imperfections and contract enforcement problems. One key finding is that although increased competition may benefit suppliers by improving contract conditions, at the same time contract enforcement may become more complicated.

In the wake of sharply rising food prices in 2007–2008, observers feared that although consumers faced higher prices, this would not lead to higher producer prices because of market power exercised along the value chain. In the empirical literature, imperfect price transmission is often interpreted as the exercise of market power by retailers or processors, and considered as disadvantageous to suppliers. Chapter 13 uses the model of Chapter 11 to show that if vertical coordination requires buyers to invest in suppliers, price transmission along the value chain is likely to be nonlinear, and weaker price transmission does not necessarily imply lower welfare for producers.

Chapter 14 analyzes the impact of commodity characteristics on the success of value chains to enhance efficiency and reduce poverty. Globally one observes the poor performance of low-standards staple crop value chains. At the same time, dynamic high-standards commodity sectors have emerged in which technology and capital are transferred to suppliers through contracts and interlinked market transactions with private companies. These high-standards sectors have contributed importantly to income mobility and poverty reduction in certain areas but have generally not reached a large part of the rural population, which mostly remains dependent on staple food production. The theoretical model of Chapter 11 is used to analyze how commodity characteristics and the type of standards are likely to affect the success of value chains.

Chapter 15 uses an extended version of the models developed in Chapters 11 and 12 to formally analyze how economic reforms (liberalization) affect production and income distribution when the emergence of standards and value chains is endogenously determined. Thirty years ago, a vast share of the poor and middle-income countries were heavily state controlled. Since then many have liberalized their economies. However, the growth effects of the liberalizations in the 1980s and 1990s differed strongly between regions in Africa, Asia, and Europe. Chapter 15 shows theoretically how endogenous institutional adjustments can affect the growth response to economic reforms. These insights are used to forward a series of explanations on the differences in performance across countries and commodities following liberalization.

Chapter 16 zooms in on the different types of investments or contracting costs buyers may need to cover in the context of vertically coordinated value chains. It shows that the efficiency and equity effects of these investments may differ strongly depending on the nature of the contracting cost, with important differences between, for example, search costs, training costs, monitoring costs, and input costs.

Finally, standards may have an impact on incomes and poverty through their effect on households producing for high-standards value chains or on households being employed in larger companies producing for the high-standards value chains. Chapter 17 explains how these labor market effects can be very important and discusses general equilibrium effects of the introduction of quality and safety standards, as well as how the effects can differ strongly depending on whether the growth of high-standards production systems is driven by exports or by domestic demand.

2

Modeling Standards

2.1 Introduction

A key issue is how to model standards. An extensive theoretical literature addresses the economics of regulation and standards. Standards typically have an impact on both efficiency and equity – a key issue in this book. Hence different groups in society may be affected differently and will therefore have different preferences. This has engendered a substantial literature on how standards are suboptimal instruments that transfer income from one group to another. Initially, the main focus of this literature was on competition and welfare effects of minimum quality standards. Examples are Bockstael (1984), Crampes and Hollander (1995), Leland (1979), Ronnen (1991), Valletti (2000), and Winfree and McCluskey (2005). Other types of standards such as labeling (e.g., Fulton and Giannakas, 2004; Roe and Sheldon, 2007) or environmental standards (e.g., Schleich, 1999) have been analyzed more recently.

Standards may solve market failures related to production and consumption externalities (Roberts et al., 1999; Schleich, 1999; van Tongeren et al., 2009). Externalities arise when one economic agent's actions have direct effects on other economic agents, which are not accounted for in the market's price system. For example, an upstream firm's river pollution imposes a negative externality on downstream firms using the river water as input, which may therefore need to install a costly purification plant without compensation by the upstream firm. This type of externality could be reduced by, for example, imposing a minimum abatement standard on the upstream firm.

Standards may also address market failures due to network externalities. In industrial sectors such as telecommunication and consumer electronics, compatibility between different products and firms is an important issue.

Compatibility standards that improve the interoperability between various products and firms may have considerable effects on competition and welfare (see, e.g., Farrell and Saloner, 1985; Jeanneret and Verdier, 1996; Katz and Shapiro, 1985).

Probably the most important motivation for the use of safety and quality standards is the existence of information asymmetries. In general, product characteristics can be divided into three categories: search, experience, and credence characteristics (Darby and Karni, 1973; Nelson, 1970). Search attributes can be ascertained in the search process prior to purchase (e.g., the color of an apple), whereas experience characteristics can be discovered only after purchasing and using the product (e.g., the apple's taste), and credence qualities cannot be evaluated in normal use (e.g., the amount of pesticide residue on the apple). Many newly demanded product attributes are experience or credence characteristics. Hence, they are not directly observable to consumers (Roe and Sheldon, 2007). As a result of this incompleteness or lack of information on the side of consumers, both categories of attributes may cause problems related to information asymmetries (Darby and Karni, 1973). As Akerlof (1970) has shown in his seminal article on the market for lemons, information asymmetries may lead to the underprovision of these product characteristics and to market failure.

Standards may reduce or resolve market failures caused by asymmetric information (Gardner, 2003; Thilmany and Barrett, 1997) and moral hazard (Shapiro, 1986).[1] Standards specify requirements with which the production

---

[1]   Other mechanisms and initiatives may reduce these information asymmetries and related market failures. First, producers may provide product information by labeling, thus transforming experience or credence attributes into search characteristics. The impact of product labeling has been analyzed extensively, e.g., by Fulton and Giannakas (2004), Giannakas and Yiannaka (2008), Lapan and Moschini (2004, 2007), Moschini et al. (2008), Roe and Sheldon (2007), and Veyssiere (2007). Second, reputation effects can provide producers with incentives to deliver products with consumers' preferred characteristics (Gardner, 2003; Shapiro, 1983). This is effective only if consumers can observe product characteristics after consumption, i.e., for experience qualities. In the case of credence characteristics – where the product's attributes remain hidden even after consumption – reputation mechanisms do not provide a solution (Baltzer, 2010). Moreover, reputation incentives are conditional on products being traceable to the individual producer. For example, Winfree and McCluskey (2005) show that in the case of experience goods without firm traceability, individual firms have an incentive to provide quality levels that are suboptimal. A third mechanism is to make producers liable for the characteristics of their products, i.e., "caveat vendor" instead of "caveat emptor." However, for experience qualities that have a long-delayed effect or for credence characteristics, vendor liability has limited impact on producers' incentives to provide sufficient levels of these characteristics (Leland, 1979). Fourth, in a business-to-business setting, quality-linked private contracting and vertical integration may lead to a better provision of quality characteristics (Gardner, 2003).

process or the final product must comply (Roberts et al., 1999). In this way, standards can guarantee to consumers the presence of positive, or absence of negative, experience and credence features. In this way, standards may improve on the market equilibrium in their absence. However, their effect is obviously conditional on the credibility of the standards. Credibility of standards may be enhanced by specific institutions, such as government control or verification by a third party (Baltzer, 2010).

The choice of how to model standards is therefore related to the cause of market failure that the standard intends to remedy: information asymmetries or various externalities. In the rest of this chapter we review some of the most common approaches to modeling standards and relate these approaches to specific market imperfections. We also explain how we use these different approaches in various chapters of this book. Table 2.1 gives an overview of the modeling approaches used in the different chapters of this book.

2.2 Standards and Asymmetric Information

Standards to address asymmetric information have been modeled in two ways. The first approach is through vertical differentiation. Standards that address market failures due to information asymmetries guarantee certain experience or credence characteristics that are often vertically aligned (Roe and Sheldon, 2007). The vertical differentiation approach to modeling consumer utility assumes that all consumers value the experience or credence characteristic (i.e., the standard), but that they differ in their willingness to pay for this attribute. In other words, if products with and without the standard would be offered at the same price, all consumers would buy the product with the standard, that is, with guaranteed experience or credence characteristics.

The vertical differentiation framework was introduced in the economic literature by Mussa and Rosen (1978), Spence (1975), and Tirole (1988), and has been applied by, among others, Baltzer (2010), Boom (1995), Crampes and Hollander (1995), Fulton and Giannakas (2004), Giannakas and Yiannaka (2008), Jeanneret and Verdier (1996), Lapan and Moschini (2007), Maxwell (1998), Moschini et al. (2008), Motta (1993), Roe and Sheldon (2007), Ronnen (1991), Valletti (2000), and Veyssiere (2007).

The second approach to model standards that remedy information asymmetries is by including a preference parameter in the consumer's utility function without specifying a particular functional form. Examples are Anderson et al. (2004), Lapan and Moschini (2004), Leland (1979), Swinnen and Vandemoortele (2008), and Winfree and McCluskey (2005).

Table 2.1. *Overview of the chapters*

Chapter	Asymmetric information	Externalities	Public or private?	Demand/utility	Continuous or binary?
3 Efficiency and Equity Effects of Standards	X		Public	General form	Continuous
4 The Political Economy of Standards and Development	X		Public	General form	Continuous
5 International Trade and Standards	X		Public	General form	Continuous
6 Risk, Externalities, and the Nature of Standards	X	X	Public	General form	Continuous
7 Endogenous Private and Public Standards in Value Chains	X		Private and Public	General form	Continuous
8 Butterflies and Political Economy Dynamics in Standard Setting	X		Public	Vertical differentiation	Binary
9 The Political Economy of Standards and Inclusion in Value Chains	X		Public	General form	Continuous

10	Standards, Production Structure, and Inclusion in Value Chains	X	Private or Public	Vertical differentiation	Binary
11	Standards, Market Imperfections, and Vertical Coordination in Value Chains		Private or Public	Not explicitly modeled	Binary
12	Market Power and Vertical Coordination in Value Chains		Private or Public	Not explicitly modeled	Binary
13	Price Transmission in Value Chains		Private or Public	Not explicitly modeled	Binary
14	Commodity Characteristics and Value Chain Governance		Private or Public	Not explicitly modeled	Binary
15	Economic Liberalization, Value Chains, and Development		Private or Public	Not explicitly modeled	Binary
16	Standards and Value Chains with Contracting Costs: Toward a General Model		Private or Public	Not explicitly modeled	Binary
17	General Equilibrium Effects of Standards in Value Chains	X	Private or Public	Vertical differentiation	Binary

In this book, we use the vertical differentiation framework in Chapters 8, 10, and 17. We use the second approach, without a vertical differentiation structure, in Chapters 3 to 7 to maintain a more tractable presentation of our analysis. A similar approach is used in Chapter 9. Finally, Chapters 11 to 16 do not explicitly model consumer demand, but the implicit consumer demand function underlying these models is consistent with both approaches described previously.

2.3 Standards and Externalities

Standards that aim at remedying consumption or production externalities are typically modeled by inserting an externality component in the consumer's utility function, the producer's profit function, or the social welfare function, depending on the type of externality under analysis (see, e.g., Fischer and Serra, 2000; Marette and Beghin, 2010; Schleich, 1999; Sturm, 2006; Tian, 2003; van Tongeren et al., 2009).

We use this externality approach in Chapter 6, where we compare different types of standards, including standards that address externalities.

2.4 Standards and Compliance Costs

It is generally assumed that standards involve some compliance costs for producers. The idea behind this assumption is that all standards can be defined as the prohibition to use a less costly technology. Examples are the prohibition of an existing technology (e.g., child labor) or of a technology that has not yet been used but that could potentially lower costs (e.g., genetical modification [GM] technology). Also, traceability requirements can be interpreted as a prohibition of less costly production systems that do not allow for tracing production.

Compliance costs are modeled in different ways. Some authors have assumed that standards involve fixed implementation costs, for example, Amacher et al. (2004), Boom (1995), Fischer and Serra (2000), Leland (1979), Maxwell (1998), Moschini et al. (2008), Motta (1993), Roe and Sheldon (2007), Ronnen (1991), Tian (2003), and Valletti (2000). Others assume that standards increase variable production costs, for example, Anderson et al. (2004), Baltzer (2010), Crampes and Hollander (1995), Fischer and Serra (2000), Fulton and Giannakas (2004), Giannakas and Yiannaka (2008), Lapan and Moschini (2004, 2007), Marette and Beghin (2010), Moschini et al. (2008), Motta (1993), Sturm (2006), Swinnen and

Vandemoortele (2008), Tian (2003), Winfree and McCluskey (2005), van Tongeren et al. (2009), and Veyssiere (2007).

In all chapters of this book, we follow the latter approach and assume that standards increase producers' variable production costs. In addition, in line with Amacher et al. (2004), we assume in Chapter 8 there is a fixed cost of switching between different levels of a standard.

2.5 Standards: Continuous or Not?

Both continuous and binary variables have been used to represent standards. The choice depends mainly on the underlying product characteristics that are guaranteed by the standard.

Standards that regulate the amount of an ingredient are usually modeled with a continuous variable. Examples in the literature that use a continuous variable are Anderson et al. (2004), Boom (1995), Crampes and Hollander (1995), Fischer and Serra (2000), Leland (1979), Marette and Beghin (2010), Motta (1993), Roe and Sheldon (2007), Ronnen (1991), Sturm (2006), Tian (2003), Valletti (2000), and Winfree and McCluskey (2005).

Standards are best represented by a binary variable when they determine whether an ingredient or a technology is allowed or not. Using a binary variable to model standards is common when analyzing producers' or governments' choices between different production technologies, and/ or the labeling of that choice, such as GM technology and geographical indications (GI) products labeling (see, e.g., Fulton and Giannakas, 2004; Giannakas and Yiannaka, 2008; Jeanneret and Verdier, 1996; Lapan and Moschini, 2004, 2007; Moschini et al., 2008; Veyssiere, 2007).

In this book we follow the literature in applying these two approaches. We apply binary variables to model standards in Chapters 10 to 17 and in Chapter 8, as Chapters 10 to 17 analyze the endogenous emergence of high-standards value chains in developing countries (e.g., subject to a standard) as compared to the persistence of low-standards value chains (e.g., not subject to a standard); and Chapter 8 analyzes governments' strategic technology choices through their implementation of public standards. In Chapters 3 to 7 we use continuous variables to model standards to capture the essential issues that arise when standards can be made more or less stringent to varying degrees. In Chapter 9, the government sets a standard determining which producers are included in the high-standards value chain. From the point of view of an individual producer, who is either included or not, this could be interpreted as a binary standard. From the point of view of the government's objective function, however, the standard is continuous.

2.6 Private and Public Standards

In this book we model both public standards (set by governments) and
private standards (set by private firms).[2] An important strand of the literature on standards has focused on the relation between trade and public
standards – and how standards are used to protect domestic interests from
foreign international competition. Examples are Anderson et al. (2004),
Baltzer (2010), Barrett and Yang (2001), Fischer and Serra (2000), Sturm
(2006), Sykes (1995), and Thilmany and Barrett (1997). The political economy issues related to this are discussed and analyzed in the first part of this
book. For this reason, in Chapters 4 to 6 and in Chapters 8 and 9 we assume
that governments impose public standards and we ignore private standards.

In Chapter 7 we address the possibility that firms (retailers in our case)
may strategically choose private standards in interaction with public standards. In Chapter 10 we analyze the endogenous emergence of standards in
response to changes in consumer demand. Although this could be due to
public standards through political economy mechanisms, our focus is on
the private sector and its standards.

In the rest of the book we take standards as exogenously given. Depending
on the situation they could be set by the government or the private sector.
For example, if producers in developing countries face high standards for
exports, these standards could be set by the importing country's private sector or by its government. However, if suppliers face a choice between different standards and value chains for domestic markets it is typically the case
that these result from private standards, as public standards usually imply
that producers have no such choice.

---

[2] We use a simple dichotomy between "private" and "public" standards, as is often done in
the literature. However, in reality the distinction between private and public standards
is often less simple. For example, public standards may rely on private certification and
private standards may have important public regulatory components. Also, the same standards may be public standards in one country and private in other countries. See Henson
and Humphrey (2010) for a more elaborate discussion.

3

Efficiency and Equity Effects of Standards

3.1 Introduction

A crucial aspect of standards is that they have both efficiency and equity effects, and that these effects may be influenced by various factors such as consumer preferences, implementation costs, and so forth. Standards may enhance aggregate welfare, but they may also be set at suboptimal levels, causing welfare losses. Moreover, the introduction of a standard may create winners and losers in society as its effects can differ for consumers and producers, and even within consumer and producer groups.

To illustrate these effects and to show how to derive them formally, we start by developing a closed-economy model to identify efficiency and equity effects of public standards that address problems of asymmetric information. In later chapters, we use this model to analyze the political economy of standards (Chapter 4), and we subsequently extend this model to an open-economy framework (Chapter 5), compare different types of standards (Chapter 6), and move from a setting with public standards only to a situation with both public and private standards (Chapter 7).

In our basic framework, standards generate efficiency gains by solving (or reducing) asymmetric information problems (see Chapter 2), but they also involve implementation costs. We show that under these assumptions, standards involve rent redistribution between consumers and producers. When there is variation in implementation costs, standards may affect producers differently according to the producer's type and the standard's implementation costs.

The chapter is organized as follows. We first introduce the basic closed-economy model. We then analyze the impact of a change in the public standard on aggregate consumer surplus, producer surplus, and welfare, for three different cases. In the first case (Section 3.3), there are no implementation costs related to the standard. The second case (Section 3.4) introduces these implementation costs and the third case (Section 3.5) analyzes the effects when implementation costs are different between different types of producers.

3.2 The Model

Consider the market for a "credence good," that is, a good with certain characteristics that cannot be determined by the consumer, either by search or experience, although consumers value the presence of these characteristics if positive, respectively their absence if negative (Darby and Karni, 1973; Nelson, 1970).

As discussed in Chapter 2, a standard that guarantees certain credence features of the product positively affects consumer utility as it reduces or solves informational asymmetries. Therefore a standard induces consumers to buy more of the product through an increased willingness to pay, ceteris paribus.

To model this, we assume a representative consumer utility function $u(x,s)$ where x is consumption of the good, and s is the level of the standard.[1] A higher s refers to a more stringent standard. Consumer utility is increasing and concave both in consumption ($u_x > 0$; $u_{xx} < 0$) and the standard ($u_s > 0$; $u_{ss} < 0$).[2] We assume that $u_{xs} > 0$, that is, that an increase in the standard leads to a higher marginal utility of consumption. The representative consumer maximizes consumer surplus Π^C by choosing consumption x:

$$\Pi^C = \max_x \left[u(x,s) - px \right] \qquad (3.1)$$

where p is the consumer price. The first-order condition (FOC) of this maximization problem is

$$\frac{\partial \Pi^C}{\partial x} = u_x(x,s) - p = 0 \qquad (3.2)$$

---

[1] Throughout the following chapters, the variable q denotes consumption and x production. Whenever the analysis concerns a closed economy, such that with market clearing $q = x$, we denote both consumption and production by x to simplify the notation.

[2] In the remainder of the chapter, subscripts denote partial derivatives to x or s, and superscripts refer to consumers C, producers P, or social welfare W.

Equation (3.2) implicitly defines the inverse demand function. Given our assumptions on the utility function, the inverse demand function is downward sloping, that is,

$$u_{xx}(x,s) < 0 \tag{3.3}$$

Moreover, a higher standard moves the inverse demand function upwards:

$$u_{xs}(x,s) > 0 \tag{3.4}$$

On the production side, we assume that a standard imposes some production constraint or obligation that increases production costs. To model this, consider a representative producer with cost function $c(x,s)$ that depends on output and the standard. The cost function is assumed to be increasing and convex both in production ($c_x > 0; c_{xx} > 0$) and the standard ($c_s > 0; c_{ss} > 0$). We further assume that $c_{xs} > 0$, that is, that a standard increases the marginal costs of production. Producers are price takers, maximizing their profits Π^P by setting output x:

$$\Pi^P = \max_{x}\left[px - c(x,s) \right] \tag{3.5}$$

The FOC of this maximization problem is

$$\frac{\partial \Pi^P}{\partial x} = p - c_x(x,s) = 0 \tag{3.6}$$

Equation (3.6) implicitly defines the inverse supply function. The inverse supply function is upward sloping, that is,

$$c_{xx}(x,s) > 0 \tag{3.7}$$

Moreover, a higher standard moves the inverse supply function upward:

$$c_{xs}(x,s) > 0 \tag{3.8}$$

At the market equilibrium, demand equals supply and

$$p^* = u_x(x^*,s) = c_x(x^*,s) \tag{3.9}$$

where x^* and p^* denote the market equilibrium. In equilibrium, aggregate consumer and producer surplus are respectively

$$\Pi^C = u(x^*,s) - p^* x^*$$ (3.10)

and

$$\Pi^P = p^* x^* - c(x^*,s)$$ (3.11)

Aggregate welfare is defined as the sum of aggregate consumer and producer surplus and equals

$$W(s) = u(x^*,s) - c(x^*,s)$$ (3.12)

3.3 No Implementation Costs

In our first case, producers are not directly affected by the standard because there are no implementation costs, so the inverse supply function is specified as

$$p = c_x(x)$$ (3.13)

with the market equilibrium at

$$u_x(x^*,s) = c_x(x^*)$$ (3.14)

Taking the total derivative of equation (3.14) with respect to the standard results in

$$u_{xs}(x^*,s) + \frac{dx^*}{ds} u_{xx}(x^*,s) = \frac{dx^*}{ds} c_{xx}(x^*)$$ (3.15)

Rewriting this expression shows that

$$\frac{dx^*}{ds} = \frac{u_{xs}}{c_{xx} - u_{xx}}$$ (3.16)

When the inverse supply and demand functions are properly behaving and demand is increasing in the standard, equation (3.16) demonstrates that $(dx^*/ds) > 0$. Logically, the market equilibrium output increases with a more stringent standard if consumers have a willingness to pay for the credence characteristic in the absence of implementation costs.

3.3.1 Impact on Consumers

The marginal impact of an increase in the standard on consumer surplus is

$$\frac{\partial \Pi^C}{\partial s} = \underbrace{u_s}_{>0} - x^* \underbrace{\frac{dp}{ds}}_{>0} = \underbrace{u_s}_{>0} - x^* \underbrace{\left(u_{xs} + \frac{dx^*}{ds} u_{xx} \right)}_{>0} \qquad (3.17)$$

The first term, u_s, is the (positive) *efficiency gain* of the more stringent standard, that is, the value that consumers attach to the reduced informational asymmetries. The second term, $x^* (dp / ds) = x^* [u_{xs} + (dx^*/ds) u_{xx}]$, is the *marginal increase in consumption expenditure*, and is also positive. This term consists of both the higher willingness to pay for a product with a higher standard ($u_{xs} > 0$) and the change in willingness to pay because of a marginal change in consumption dx^*/ds. The size of the latter change in willingness to pay is determined by the slope of the inverse demand function u_{xx}. Their combined effect on expenditure is positive.[3] Intuitively, consumption expenditures increase because of an increase in the equilibrium output as well as an increase in the equilibrium price.

Figure 3.1 illustrates this effect on consumer surplus in the case where a change in the standard leads to a parallel upward shift in demand by a distance u_{xs}. The light gray area shows the increase in consumer surplus u_s while the vertically shaded area shows the increase in expenditures $x^* u_{xs}$ if the equilibrium quantity x^* remained constant. In this case, consumer surplus is unchanged. However, an increase in the equilibrium quantity dx^*/ds leads to a lower increase in consumption expenditures. The dark gray area shows this effect. The height of this area equals $(dx^*/ds) u_x$; the total effect on consumer surplus is thus $u_s - x^* [u_{xs} + (dx^*/ds) u_{xx}]$, as indicated in equation (3.17).[4]

As equation (3.17) makes clear, the standard's marginal impact on consumer surplus is ambiguous. If the efficiency gain is larger than the marginal change in consumption expenditures, consumer surplus increases with the standard and vice versa.

Ceteris paribus, the magnitude of the efficiency gain u_s depends on whether a higher standard induces demand to shift upward in parallel

---

[3] This can be seen by using $dx^*/ds = u_{xs}/(c_{xx} - u_{xx})$ to rewrite the marginal increase in consumption expenditure as $x^* [(u_{xs} c_{xx})/(c_{xx} - u_{xx})]$, which is positive since $u_{xs} > 0$ and $c_{xx} > 0$.

[4] Because we are looking at the marginal effect of a standard, the change in s is infinitesimal and hence the triangle with base dx^*/ds and height $(dx^*/ds) u_x$ is negligible.

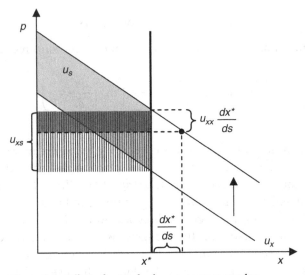

Figure 3.1. Effect of a standard on consumer surplus.

(as in Figure 3.1) or to rotate clockwise or counterclockwise. Figure 3.2 demonstrates how a clockwise rotation in demand affects consumer surplus. Showing for simplicity a case in which equilibrium quantity remains unchanged, the clockwise rotation increases the utility gain u_s as indicated by the diagonally shaded area.[5] The net gain in consumer surplus is thus more positive when the standard induces a clockwise rotation of demand, because the change in willingness to pay *at the margin* (which determines the consumer price and hence the marginal increase in consumption expenditure) is then smaller than the increase in the *average* willingness to pay (which constitutes the efficiency effect).

To see the determinants of the marginal increase in consumption expenditure, we can rewrite this term as

$$x^* \frac{dp}{ds} = x^* \left[\frac{-\varepsilon_p^D u_{xs}}{\varepsilon_p^S - \varepsilon_p^D} \right] \tag{3.18}$$

---

[5]   Similar graphs can be made to illustrate the effects of a counterclockwise rotation of demand and/or a decrease in equilibrium quantity on consumer surplus, or to demonstrate the effects of a change in standards on producer surplus.

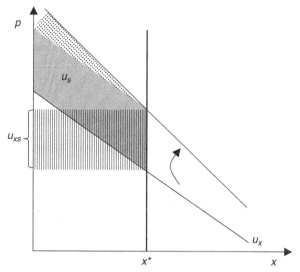

Figure 3.2. Clockwise rotation in demand.

where $\varepsilon_p^S = [1/c_{xx}(x^*)][c_x(x^*)/x^*]$ is the price elasticity of supply and $\varepsilon_p^D = [1/u_{xx}(x^*,s)][u_x(x^*,s)/x^*]$ is the price elasticity of demand. The magnitude of the increase in consumption expenditure thus depends on the supply and demand price elasticities. The more inelastic supply is (ε_p^S low), the larger is the increase in consumption expenditure. Similarly, if demand is more elastic ($|\varepsilon_p^D|$ high), then the increase in consumption expenditure is larger.

In summary, as both terms on the right-hand side of equation (3.17) have opposing effects, the sign of $\partial \Pi^C/\partial s$ is undetermined. Hence an increase in the public standard may either increase or decrease consumer surplus, depending on how the demand curve rotates if the standard increases, and on the price elasticities of supply and demand.

3.3.2 Impact on Producers

The marginal impact of a more stringent standard on producer profits, in the absence of implementation costs, equals

$$\frac{\partial \Pi^P}{\partial s} = x^* \frac{dp}{ds} = x^* \left(c_{xs} + \frac{dx^*}{ds} c_{xx} \right) > 0 \tag{3.19}$$

where the right-hand side is the *marginal increase in producer revenue*. Given the assumption of a closed economy, this is equal to the marginal increase in consumption expenditure $[x^*(dp/ds)]$. Equation (3.19) shows that the marginal increase in producer revenues consists both of the direct effect of the upward shift of marginal costs ($c_{xs} > 0$) and the indirect effect of a movement along the marginal cost curve due to a change in output $[(dx^*/ds)\,c_{xx}]$.

The marginal impact on producer surplus is always positive in the absence of implementation costs. Because the revenue gain for producers equals the increase in consumption expenditure, it follows from equation (3.18) that the revenue gain for producers is larger when supply is more inelastic (ε_p^S low) and demand more elastic ($\left|\varepsilon_p^D\right|$ high).

More importantly, equations (3.17) and (3.19) show that an increase in the standard creates *rent redistribution* $x^*(dp/ds)$ between consumers and producers whereby rents are shifted from consumers to producers. This rent redistribution is always positive.

3.3.3 Impact on Aggregate Welfare

Finally, the effect of a change in the public standard on aggregate welfare is

$$\frac{\partial W}{\partial s} = u_s > 0 \tag{3.20}$$

which is equal to the efficiency gain, and is unambiguously positive. In summary, this analysis shows that in the absence of implementation costs, a more stringent public standard is welfare improving thanks to the efficiency gain u_s, but creates at the same time rent redistribution from consumers to producers. Hence producers always gain in the absence of implementation costs, and consumers may either gain or lose depending on the relative magnitude of the efficiency gain and the marginal increase in consumption expenditure.

3.4 Implementation Costs

In the second case, we assume – more realistically – that there are implementation costs related to the standard. We therefore use the inverse supply function $p = c_x(x,s)$ with $c_{xs}(x,s) > 0$. Taking the total derivative of the market equilibrium in equation (3.9) results in

$$u_{xs}\left(x^{*},s\right)+\frac{dx^{*}}{ds}u_{xx}\left(x^{*},s\right)=c_{xs}\left(x^{*},s\right)+\frac{dx^{*}}{ds}c_{xx}\left(x^{*},s\right) \qquad (3.21)$$

which can be rearranged to give

$$\frac{dx^{*}}{ds}=\frac{u_{xs}-c_{xs}}{c_{xx}-u_{xx}} \qquad (3.22)$$

In contrast to equation (3.16), the sign of equation (3.22) is undetermined. The marginal impact of the standard on the equilibrium output is positive if the upward shift in demand u_{xs} is larger than the upward shift in marginal costs c_{xs} and vice versa.

3.4.1 Impact on Consumers

The marginal impact of an increase in the standard on consumer surplus is still given by equation (3.17), although the effect of the standard on equilibrium output $\left(dx^{*}/ds\right)$ is now given by equation (3.22). Using the elasticity notation of equation (3.18), the marginal impact on consumer surplus can therefore be written as

$$\frac{\partial \Pi^{C}}{\partial s}=\underbrace{u_{s}}_{>0}-x^{*}\underbrace{\left[\frac{\varepsilon_{p}^{S}c_{xs}-\varepsilon_{p}^{D}u_{xs}}{\varepsilon_{p}^{S}-\varepsilon_{p}^{D}}\right]}_{>0} \qquad (3.23)$$

where, as before, ε_{p}^{S} and ε_{p}^{D} are the price-elasticities of supply and demand. Again, an increase in the standard may either increase or decrease consumer surplus. As before, the first term on the right-hand side of equation (3.23) is the (positive) efficiency gain of the more stringent standard. Analogously, the second term is the marginal increase in consumption expenditure, which is again positive. However, this term is larger than in the first case if one starts from the same initial equilibrium x^{*}. This is easily inferred from comparing equation (3.18) with the corresponding term in (3.23). The driver of this higher marginal increase in consumption expenditure is the increase in marginal costs due to the standard, which leads to a larger price increase. Hence, consumers gain less (or lose more) from an increase in the public standard when the standard involves implementation costs.

3.4.2 Impact on Producers

The marginal impact of an increase in the standard on producer profits is

$$\frac{\partial \Pi^P}{\partial s} = \underbrace{x^* \left(c_{xs} + \frac{dx^*}{ds} c_{xx} \right)}_{>0} - \underbrace{c_s}_{>0} \tag{3.24}$$

The first term on the right-hand side is again the (positive) marginal increase in producer revenue, equal to the marginal increase in consumption expenditures. The second term, c_s, is the *implementation cost* of the standard, which has a negative impact on producer surplus. Equation (3.24) shows that the impact on producer profits may now be either positive or negative, depending on the relative size of the marginal increase in producer revenue and the implementation cost.

Departing from the same initial equilibrium, x^*, it is undetermined how equation (3.24) compares to equation (3.19). On the one hand, the implementation cost in equation (3.24) has a negative effect on producer surplus; on the other hand, the marginal increase in producer revenue is larger than in equation (3.19). The latter effect implies that there is more rent redistribution from consumers to producers in the case with implementation costs. In other words, the extra costs of a standard are not borne solely by producers, but also partially passed on to consumers by a larger rent redistribution.

Analogously to our discussion of consumer surplus in the previous section, the net effect on producer surplus depends on how the supply curve rotates when the standard increases. Ceteris paribus, if the effect is a counterclockwise rotation, the cost increase *at the margin* will be larger than the *average* cost increase. Because the equilibrium price is determined by marginal cost, this would result in a net increase in producer surplus, ceteris paribus.

3.4.3 Impact on Aggregate Welfare

The impact on aggregate welfare is now ambiguous, with

$$\frac{\partial W}{\partial s} = u_s - c_s \tag{3.25}$$

Equation (3.25) shows that the impact on total welfare depends on the relative efficiency gain and implementation cost of the standard. Assuming the necessary conditions are in place to ensure global concavity, the socially optimal level of the standard, s^*, is given by

$$u_s\left(x^*,s^*\right)=c_s\left(x^*,s^*\right) \tag{3.26}$$

That is, the socially optimal standard balances the marginal efficiency gain for consumers with the marginal implementation cost for producers. At the same time, equations (3.23) and (3.24) show that also the socially optimal standard involves rent redistribution from consumers to producers that is larger than in the absence of implementation costs; but according to equation (3.26) this rent distribution does not affect total welfare.

3.5 Different Implementation Costs for Different Producers

How do differences in implementation costs influence the results? Assume now that there are N producers, indexed $j \in \{1,\dots,N\}$, who may have different production costs (both related to quantity and the standard) and hence different supply functions.[6] The market equilibrium is identified by the following $N+1$ equations:

$$p^* = u_x\left(x^*,s\right) = c_{xj}\left(x_j^*,s\right) \ \forall j \in \{1,\dots,N\} \tag{3.27}$$

$$x^* = \sum_{j=1}^{N} x_j^* \tag{3.28}$$

Taking the total derivative of equations (3.27) and (3.28) with respect to the standard results in

$$\frac{dp^*}{ds} = u_{xs}\left(x^*,s\right) + \frac{dx^*}{ds}u_{xx}\left(x^*,s\right) \tag{3.29}$$

$$\frac{dp^*}{ds} = c_{xs,j}\left(x_j^*,s\right) + \frac{dx_j^*}{ds}c_{xx,j}\left(x_j^*,s\right) \tag{3.30}$$

and

$$\frac{dx^*}{ds} = \sum_{j=1}^{N} \frac{dx_j^*}{ds} \tag{3.31}$$

---

[6] As Salop and Scheffman (1983) demonstrated, a producer that faces significantly lower production costs than its competitors may gain monopoly power vis-à-vis the competitive fringe by setting a price below the competitive one, or even drive the competition out of the market. We abstract from such more extreme cases.

Equation (3.29) shows that the marginal effect of the standard on the equilibrium price consists of the direct effect of the standard on the marginal willingness to pay (u_{xs}) and the indirect effect through a change in total output dx^*/ds. As shown in equation (3.31), the change in total output is the sum of output changes of individual producers, dx_j^*/ds. In turn, the output change of individual producers is determined by equation (3.30) and depends on how the costs of the individual producer change compared to the price effect.

3.5.1 Impact on Consumers

The marginal impact on consumer surplus is the same as before, namely

$$\frac{\partial \Pi^C}{\partial s} = u_s - x^* \frac{dp^*}{ds} = u_s - x^* \left(u_{xs} + \frac{dx^*}{ds} u_{xx} \right) \tag{3.32}$$

and can again be either positive or negative depending on the relative sizes of the efficiency gain u_s and the marginal increase in consumption expenditures, which now equals the *aggregate* rent redistribution to producers.

3.5.2 Impact on Producers

The marginal impact on the profits of an individual producer is

$$\frac{\partial \Pi_j^P}{\partial s} = \underbrace{\frac{dp^*}{ds} x_j^*}_{>0} - \underbrace{c_{s,j}}_{>0} \tag{3.33}$$

Its sign is undetermined and depends on the relative sizes of the *marginal increase in individual producer revenue* (dp^*/ds) x_j^* and the *producer-specific implementation cost* $c_{s,j}$. As shown in equation (3.29), the price effect dp^*/ds is determined by the *aggregate* change in output; with a large number of producers, dp^*/ds will therefore be unrelated to changes in output in an individual producer.

In the aggregate, the marginal impact on producer profits is

$$\frac{\partial \Pi^P}{\partial s} = \underbrace{\frac{dp}{ds} \sum_{j=1}^{N} x_j^*}_{>0} - \underbrace{\sum_{j=1}^{N} c_{s,j}}_{>0} \tag{3.34}$$

The marginal impact on aggregate welfare is found by combining equations (3.32) and (3.34):

$$\frac{\partial W}{\partial s} = \underbrace{u_s}_{>0} - \underbrace{\sum_{j=1}^{N} c_{s,j}}_{>0}$$

(3.35)

which can be either positive or negative. The first term is the *efficiency gain* of the standard, and the second term is the *aggregate implementation cost*. Hidden within this welfare result is, however, the rent redistribution $x^*(dp^*/ds)$ from consumers to producers.

Equations (3.24) and (3.25) are the same as respectively equations (3.34) and (3.35) if implementation costs are identical across all producers. However, standards may involve different implementation costs for different producers. For example, if a standard imposes the use of a specific input factor that one producer can source costlessly while other producers must incur an implementation cost, the impact of an increase in this standard has different impacts on producers' profits (e.g., the input factor "land" in geographical indication regulations). The aggregate implementation cost may still be the same as in case 2, but distributed heterogeneously among producers.

To clarify the effects of these potentially different implementation costs, assume there are two producers, A and B, with respective cost functions $c_A(x_A)$ and $c_B(x_B,s)$. In other words, producer A does not incur implementation costs while producer B does. Following equation (3.30), it must be that

$$\frac{dp^*}{ds} = \frac{dx_A^*}{ds} c_{xx,A}\left(x_A^*\right) = c_{xs,A}\left(x_B^*,s\right) + \frac{dx_B^*}{ds} c_{xx,B}\left(x_B^*,s\right) > 0$$

(3.36)

Assuming that the initial equilibrium output is the same for both producers ($x_A^* = x_B^*$) and that their respective supply curves have the same slope at this equilibrium ($c_{xx,A}\left(x_A^*\right) = c_{xx,B}\left(x_B^*,s\right)$), it must be that $(dx_A^*/ds) > (dx_B^*/ds)$. It also follows that $dx_A^*/ds > 0$ while the sign of dx_B^*/ds is undetermined. Hence the impact of the more stringent standard on output is positive for producer A whereas output of producer B increases less, or even decreases. From equation (3.33), it is obvious that

$$\frac{\partial \Pi_A^P}{\partial s} = \frac{dp^*}{ds} x_A^* > 0$$

(3.37)

and

$$\frac{\partial \Pi_A^P}{\partial s} > \frac{\partial \Pi_B^P}{\partial s} = \underbrace{\frac{dp^*}{ds}}_{>0} x_B^* - \underbrace{c_{s,B}}_{>0} \tag{3.38}$$

Hence, the impact of more stringent standards on producer A's profits is always positive (as in case 1) and larger than the impact on profits of producer B, which may be either positive or negative (as in case 2). If the implementation cost of producer B is sufficiently large, it may be that producer B's profits decrease with the more stringent standard, while producer A's profits increase. Thus, the standard gives rise to a rent distribution from consumers to producers (as in case 1 and case 2) but potentially also to a rent distribution between different producers.

Finally, note that our analysis here implicitly assumes that all producers continue to operate regardless of the level of the standard. In reality, as a standard changes, some producers may no longer find it profitable to produce. This cutoff will again depend on producer-specific costs and gives rise to entry and exit in the industry. We look at such "inclusion effects" in more detail in Chapters 9 and 10.

3.6 Conclusion

The analysis in this chapter demonstrates the efficiency and equity effects of public standards in a closed economy. If the efficiency gain for consumers exceeds the implementation cost for producers, social welfare increases. However, standards cause a rent distribution between consumers and producers. As a result, the effects of a standard on consumer surplus and on producer surplus may be different from the effects on social welfare. The magnitude of the rent distribution effect depends on how the standard affects demand and supply, and on elasticities. Moreover, when producers differ in terms of implementation costs, standards will also cause rent distribution among producers.

Because of the distributional effects of standards, various groups in society have a vested interest in trying to influence governments' decision processes on standards. This political economy aspect of standards will be central to the analyses in Part II of this book – the political economy of standards. Chapter 4 builds on the analysis of this chapter to study the political economy of standards in a closed economy. In Chapter 5, the model is expanded to study standards in an open-economy framework. Chapter 6 looks at standards that resolve various externalities, while Chapter 7 studies the interaction between public and private standards. In Chapter 8, we look at standards in a dynamic context. In Chapter 9, we study the political economy of standards that determine the inclusion of producers in a high-standards value chain.

Although this chapter clearly identifies the potential equity and efficiency effects of standards, we have not imposed any regulatory details or institutional structure to the model. Such factors may have an important influence on the effects. In Part III of this book we analyze some of the income and development effects in more detail, when we take the institutional organization of standards in value chains explicitly into account. This includes, among others, various types of transaction costs, factor market imperfections, and endogenous vertical coordination in the value chains.

4

The Political Economy of Standards
and Development

4.1 Introduction

As demonstrated in Chapter 3, the introduction of standards typically impacts both efficiency and rent distribution between different groups in society. This, in turn, is likely to induce lobbying by interest groups to influence government decision making on public standards. As we show in this chapter, this may lead to "overstandardization" or "understandardization," depending on the relative political pressures, much like taxes and subsidies are used in other areas of public policy and public finance.

One can thus expect to observe variations in public standards setting across countries. However, the observed variations in standards do not seem to be random. There appears to be a positive correlation between public standards and the level of economic development. An important question is what causes this correlation. The most straightforward explanation is that rich consumers (countries) prefer higher standards (e.g., Wilson and Abiola, 2003). Although this is undoubtedly an important element, in this chapter we show that the impact of development on the government's choice of standards is more complex and depends on several factors – including, besides consumer preferences, compliance costs, enforcement problems, and institutions of information provision that may influence (consumer) perceptions.

The political economy approach in this chapter, as well as in subsequent ones, is based on the seminal "protection for sale" framework of Grossman and Helpman (1994) but applied to standard setting.[1] We develop a

---

[1] Our approach is related to an extensive literature on the political economy of public regulations. The political economy of regulation has a long tradition, with seminal contributions by Downs (1957), Olson (1965), Stigler (1971) and Becker (1983). Recent surveys of these literatures include Acemoglu and Robinson (2006), Coen et al. (2011), Dewan and Shepsle (2008a, b); Persson and Tabellini (2000; 2003); Rausser et al. (2011), and Weingast and Wittman (2006).

political economy model of public standards in which both producers and consumers are actively and simultaneously lobbying. In this chapter, we apply our model to a closed economy to analyze the essential features of the political economy equilibrium. In Chapter 5, we extend the model to study the political economy of standards in an open economy, and to derive the conditions under which standards can be categorized as protectionist instruments.

We start by developing a model of the economy (Section 4.2) where standards benefit consumers because standards guarantee that the product satisfies certain characteristics preferred by the consumer. Production costs are increasing in the level of the public standard. As in Chapter 3, producers or consumers may gain or lose from a change in the standard. With these potential welfare effects, we derive the political incentives and the political equilibrium (Section 4.3). We then analyze how the equilibrium is affected by several political and economic characteristics (Section 4.4). We show that either over- or understandardization may result (Section 4.5).

In the final sections of the chapter we focus explicitly on the impact of economic development on the political equilibrium. We show that there may be a "pro-standard coalition" in rich countries and an "anti-standard coalition" in poor countries (Section 4.6), which provides an explanation for the observed correlation between public standards and economic development. In Section 4.7 we discuss how institutions of information provision (such as commercial mass media) may influence perceptions on the impact of standards and thus the political equilibrium, and how this may also contribute to differences in standards with economic development.

4.2 The Economy and the Social Optimum

As in Chapter 3, we consider the market for a credence good, where a standard which guarantees certain quality or safety features increases consumers' utility, ceteris paribus. Our specification of demand follows that of Chapter 3. On the production side, we assume that production is a function of a sector-specific input factor that is available in inelastic supply. All profits made in the sector accrue to this specific factor. We assume that the costs of a representative producer are given by

$$c(x,s) = k(x,s) + \tau(s)x \tag{4.1}$$

where $k(x,s)$ denotes production costs, and $\tau(s)x$ denotes transaction costs. Standards may increase the production costs $k(x,s)$ because of the obligation to use a more expensive production technology $(k_s > 0)$. Standards may also increase the transaction costs $\tau(s)$ because of control and enforcement costs related to the standard $(\tau_s > 0)$.[2] This implies that the costs increase with higher standards $(c_s > 0)$ for $s \geq 0$. We will refer to c_s as the implementation cost of a standard, encompassing production and transaction costs. We assume, as in Chapter 3, that producers are price takers. The inverse supply function is then given by

$$p = c_x(x,s) = k_x(x,s) + \tau(s) \tag{4.2}$$

As in the previous chapter, both consumers and producers may either gain or lose from a change in the standard.

The marginal effect of a standard on consumer surplus was derived in equation (3.17). Aggregate consumer surplus increases with the standard if the efficiency gain u_s is larger than the marginal increase in consumption expenditure $(dp/ds)\,q$. Likewise, the marginal effect of a standard on producers' profits $\Pi^P(s)$ is given by equation (3.24). Producers gain with an increase of the standard if the marginal increase in producer revenues $(dp/ds)\,x$ exceeds the implementation cost c_s.

We again define social welfare $W(s)$ as the sum of producer profits and consumer surplus in this sector, that is,

$$W(s) \equiv \Pi^C(s) + \Pi^P(s). \tag{4.3}$$

The socially optimal standard $s^* \geq 0$ maximizes this sum.[3] The corresponding first-order condition is $(\partial W/\partial s) = (\partial \Pi^C/\partial s) + (\partial \Pi^P/\partial s) = 0$, or

$$\frac{\partial W}{\partial s} = u_s - \frac{dp}{ds}q + \frac{dp}{ds}x - c_s = 0. \tag{4.4}$$

(subject to $s^* \geq 0$). In the context of a closed economy as studied in this chapter, domestic consumption equals domestic production $(q = x)$, and the first-order condition reduces to

$$\frac{\partial W}{\partial s} = u_s - c_s = 0. \tag{4.5}$$

---

[2] We implicitly assume that control and enforcement costs are borne by producers.
[3] Throughout this and the following chapters, we assume that the relevant cost functions are sufficiently convex in the standard such that the social welfare function, and the government objective function introduced in the text that follows, is concave in s so that the first-order condition determines a global maximum.

As in equation (3.26), the first-order condition for the social optimum equates the marginal efficiency gain for consumers with the marginal implementation cost for producers. Importantly, although we know that standards lead to rent transfers between consumers and producers, these do not show up in equation (4.5) and hence do not influence the socially optimal standard. Finally, equation (4.5) may imply either a strictly positive optimal standard s^*, or the absence of a standard ($s^* = 0$), depending on the benefits to consumers and costs to producers.

4.3 The Political Structure and Political Optimum

Consider a government that maximizes its own objective function which, following the approach of Grossman and Helpman (1994), consists of a weighted sum of contributions from lobbies and social welfare. Similar to Grossman and Helpman (1994), we restrict the set of policies available to politicians and only allow them to implement a public standard. We assume that both producers and consumers are politically organized and that they lobby simultaneously. This assumption differs from Anderson et al. (2004), Cadot et al. (2004), and Grossman and Helpman (1994). We believe it is not realistic to assume that consumers are not organized – or do not effectively lobby – on issues related to product standards. There is substantive evidence that consumers and producers lobby governments on issues of public standards.[4]

The "truthful" contribution schedule of the specific-capital owners is equal to the function $C^P(s) = \max\{0; \Pi^P(s) - b^P\}$, in which the constant b^P represents the share of profits that producers do not want to invest in lobbying the government.[5] One could also interpret this constant b^P as a minimum threshold, a level of profits or surplus below which producers believe the return from lobbying is less than its cost. Similarly, the "truthful" contribution schedule of the consumers is of the form $C^C(s) = \max\{0; \Pi^C(s) - b^C\}$, with $\Pi^C(s)$ the aggregate consumer surplus as defined earlier. The constant

---

[4] In reality, consumer lobbying occurs not only through consumer organizations but also through political parties representing consumer interests. See also Gulati and Roy (2007) on lobbying of both producers and consumers with respect to environmental standards.

[5] The common-agency literature (e.g., Bernheim and Whinston 1986) states that a truthful contribution schedule reflects the true preferences of the interest group. In our political economy model this implies that lobby groups set their lobbying contributions in accordance with their expected profits and how these are marginally affected by the standard. We refer to Appendix A.1 for a proof of the truthfulness of the contribution schedules in our model.

b^C can be interpreted in the same way as in the contribution schedule of the specific-capital owners.

The government's objective function $\Pi^G(s)$ is a weighted sum of the contributions of producers (weighted by α^P), the contributions of consumers (weighted by α^C), and social welfare, where α^P and α^C represent the relative lobbying strength:

$$\Pi^G\left(s\right)=\alpha^P C^P\left(s\right)+\alpha^C C^C\left(s\right)+W\left(s\right) \tag{4.6}$$

The government chooses the level of the public standard to maximize its objective function (equation (4.6)). Each possible level of this standard corresponds to a certain level of producer profits and consumer surplus, and hence also to a certain level of producer and consumer contributions. This is driven by the functional form and the truthfulness of the contribution schedule. The government receives higher contributions from producers (consumers) if the imposed standard creates more profits (consumer surplus) for producers (consumers). Conversely, the government receives less producer or consumer contributions if the standard decreases respectively profits or consumer surplus. Therefore maximizing the contributions from producers (consumers) by choosing the level of standard is equivalent to maximizing their profits (consumer surplus). The government thus chooses the level of the standard that maximizes the weighted sum of producer profits, consumer surplus, and social welfare. The politically optimal standard, $s^\#$, is therefore determined by the following first-order condition, subject to $s^\# \geq 0$:[6]

$$\frac{\partial \Pi^G}{\partial s}=\left(1+\alpha^P\right)\left[x^\#\frac{dp}{ds}-c_s\right]+\left(1+\alpha^C\right)\left[u_s-x^\#\frac{dp}{ds}\right]=0 \tag{4.7}$$

where $x^\#$ denotes aggregate consumption and production in the political optimum and $p^\#$ the equilibrium price.

The first term in equation (4.7) captures the marginal impact of a public standard on producers' profits weighted by their lobbying strength $(1+\alpha^P)$. As we explained earlier this marginal impact may be positive or negative. The second term represents the weighted marginal impact of a public standard on aggregate consumer surplus, which may also be positive or negative.

If producers and consumers have the same lobbying strength ($\alpha^P = \alpha^C$), equation (4.7) reduces to equation (4.5) defining the social optimum. In

---

[6]   See Appendix A.2. Because we are restricting ourselves to the closed economy case in this chapter, we here use the symbol x to denote consumption and production ($q = x$).

that case, the term $x^\#$ (dp/ds) capturing the rent transfer between producers and consumers would cancel out. When producers and consumers have differing lobbying strengths, however, the political equilibrium will generally differ from the social optimum. In that case, the rent transfer $x^\#$ (dp/ds) does affect the standard set by the government. To analyze the political equilibrium, we first discuss how the different variables in equation (4.7) affect the political equilibrium. We then compare the political equilibrium more explicitly to the social optimum.

4.4 Determinants of the Political Optimum: Comparative Statics

Optimality condition (4.7) implicitly defines $s^\#$ as a function of several variables, such as the relative lobbying strength of producers vis-à-vis consumers (α^P, α^C), the efficiency gain (u_s), implementation costs (c_s), and the marginal price effect (dp/ds). The impact of the exogenous variables on the optimal standard can be formally derived through comparative statics. We refer to Appendix A.3 for the formal derivations and restrict ourselves here to the presentation and discussion of the effects.

First, it is obvious from condition (4.7) that a change in the political weights α^P and α^C, capturing exogenous differences in the political influence of lobby groups, affects $s^\#$. When the political weight of a lobby group increases exogenously, it implies that its contributions are more effective in influencing the decisions of the government. However, the sign of the effect on $s^\#$ depends on the marginal benefit of $s^\#$ for the interest groups. For instance, an increase in α^P leads to a higher standard $s^\#$ (i.e., $(ds^\#/d\alpha^P)>0$) if and only if producers would gain from increasing the standard beyond $s^\#$, that is, if $(\partial\Pi^P/\partial s)>0$ at $s^\#$. In this case the government sets the optimal standard at a higher level if α^P increases, and vice versa. The same holds for increases in α^C.

Second, an exogenous change in the efficiency gain u_s – for example, because of higher consumer preferences for standards – affects the politically optimal standard $s^\#$. A higher efficiency gain leads to higher consumer surplus and higher contributions in favor of a public standard, which lead to a higher public standard.

Third, the implementation cost of the standard affects the politically optimal standard. Higher implementation costs (c_s) reduce the benefits of a standard for producers, ceteris paribus. This leads to a lower standard as producers reduce their contributions for the public standard.

Fourth, the marginal price effect of a public standard (dp/ds) clearly plays a major role in determining the political equilibrium through the rent transfer terms in equation (4.7). Notice that a higher price increase may increase or decrease the politically optimal standard, depending on other factors. On the one hand, a higher price reduces consumer benefits and their contributions. On the other hand, it increases profits and contributions of producers.

In a closed economy, the size of the price effect depends on the specifics of demand and supply, as demonstrated in Chapter 3. In particular, as in equation (3.17) the price effect can be written as

$$\frac{dp}{ds} = u_{xs} + \frac{dx^*}{ds} u_{xx}.$$ (4.8)

The change in price thus depends on the direct increase in the marginal willingness to pay due to the higher standard (u_{xs}) and the indirect effect of a movement along the demand curve due to a change in equilibrium quantity $(dx^*/ds)\, u_{xx}$. As shown in equation (3.22), the change in equilibrium quantity is given by $(dx/ds) = (u_{xs} - c_{xs})/(c_{xx} - u_{xx})$ and can be either positive or negative. The price effect is thus given by

$$\frac{dp}{ds} = \frac{c_{xx}u_{xs} - u_{xx}c_{xs}}{c_{xx} - u_{xx}} > 0.$$ (4.9)

As we discussed in Chapter 3, the price effect is always positive, and so is the associated rent transfer. However, the magnitude of the effect relative to the consumers' efficiency gain and the producers' implementation cost cannot be determined a priori. As a result, standards may move in either direction for a given price effect, depending on the relative benefits and the political weights of the different lobby groups.

Fifth, the nature of the implementation costs makes a difference. Following equation (3.24), the effect of a standard on producer profits can be written as

$$\frac{\partial \Pi^P}{\partial s} = x^* \left(c_{xs} + c_{xx} \frac{dx^*}{ds} \right) - c_s.$$ (4.10)

As discussed in Chapter 3, this effect will tend to be larger if the cost function rotates upward with a counterclockwise rotation, as in that case marginal costs (which determine the equilibrium price) increase faster than average costs (c_s). Using equation (4.1), we can rewrite this effect as

$$\frac{\partial \Pi^P}{\partial s} = \left(k_{xs} + \tau_s + k_{xx} \frac{dx^*}{ds} \right) x^* - k_s - \tau_s x^* = \left(k_{xs} + k_{xx} \frac{dx^*}{ds} \right) x^* - k_s.$$ (4.11)

Hence, the marginal change in transaction costs τ_s does not affect producer profits directly, but only through its indirect effect on dx^*/ds. The reason is that this type of costs increase average production costs by the same amount as marginal costs, so that they are passed on to consumers in the form of higher prices. The only channel through which transaction costs affect profits is through dx^*/ds, that is, the degree to which higher prices reduce demand. By contrast, the marginal change in production costs $k_s(x,s)$ does affect producer profits directly. If production costs rotate upward in a counterclockwise rotation (or, put differently, if they induce diseconomies of scale), they will increase marginal costs by more than average costs and hence improve producer profits, ceteris paribus. Thus, if standards lead to diseconomies of scale, they will improve producer profits and reduce consumer welfare, which in turn affects the political equilibrium through changes in their relative lobbying contributions. Ceteris paribus, production costs thus potentially affect the lobbying effort of producers to a larger degree than transaction costs.

Sixth, an important general implication from this discussion is that either consumers or producers may lobby in favor or against a standard, and that the political equilibrium may be affected by various factors.

4.5 Over- and Understandardization

To assess whether public standards are set at suboptimal levels in the political process, we can compare the first-order condition for a social optimum (equation 4.5) with the first-order condition determining the political equilibrium (equation 4.7). The politically optimal standard $s^{\#}$ equals the socially optimal standard s^* only if $\alpha^P = \alpha^C$ in the political equilibrium, and/or in the trivial case where both $\partial\Pi^P/\partial s$ and $\partial\Pi^C/\partial s$ equal zero at s^* so that the preferred standards of producers and consumers coincide.

If the above condition is not fulfilled, that is, if α^P and α^C are different in the government's objective function, the political equilibrium will not coincide with the social optimum. However, the divergence may go in either direction. Both "overstandardization" $\left(s^{\#} > s^*\right)$ and "understandardization" $\left(s^{\#} < s^*\right)$ may result from the lobbying process.

If producers are more influential than consumers $(\alpha^P > \alpha^C)$, overstandardization $\left(s^{\#} > s^*\right)$ results when producers' profits increase with a higher standard $[(\partial\Pi^P/\partial s) > 0]$ at s^* and in understandardization otherwise. In this case the overstandardization creates higher profits for producers than in the social optimum. This is more likely when the standard's price effect dp/ds is large and when the implementation cost c_s is small.

On the other hand, if $\partial\Pi^P/\partial s < 0$ at s^*, the resulting understandardization reduces the negative effect of the standard on producers' profits, and producers benefit from understandardization.

In a similar fashion, when consumers are more influential than producers ($\alpha^P < \alpha^C$) overstandardization occurs when $\partial\Pi^C/\partial s > 0$ at s^*, and understandardization when $\partial\Pi^C/\partial s < 0$ at s^*.

Hence, we see that at the political equilibrium the public standard $s^\#$ may be either too high or too low from a social welfare point of view. Influential lobby groups may push for both more stringent or less stringent standards depending on the relative magnitude of the price effect compared to the implementation cost (for producers) or the efficiency gain (for consumers).

4.6 Development and Pro- and Anti-Standard Coalitions

We can now use these results to explain the empirically observed positive relationship between standards and economic development. It is often argued that this relationship simply reflects consumer preferences. While our model confirms that preferences (in the form of the efficiency gain u_s) play a role, it also suggests a more complex set of causal factors that affect the relationship between development and the political economy of public standards. Our analysis suggests several reasons for the wide variety in standards across the world, in particular between developing ("poor") and developed ("rich") countries.

Define I as the country's per capita income, that is, its level of economic development, and z as an indicator of the quality of the institutions in the country. Studies find that the quality of institutions (including institutions for enforcement of contracts and public regulations) correlates positively with development $(dz/dI) > 0$ (North, 1990). If we abstract from possible economies or diseconomies of scale induced by changes in the standard, the impact of development on the politically optimal level of the public standard $s^\#$ can be derived as

$$\frac{ds^\#}{dI} = \frac{ds^\#}{du_s}\frac{\partial u_s}{\partial I} + \left(\frac{ds^\#}{d\tau_s}\frac{\partial \tau_s}{\partial z} + \frac{ds^\#}{dk_s}\frac{\partial k_s}{\partial z}\right)\frac{dz}{dI} \qquad (4.12)$$

The first term is positive because higher income levels (I) are typically associated with higher consumer preferences for quality and safety standards as reflected in higher efficiency gains u_s in equation (4.7), that is, $(\partial u_s / \partial I) > 0$. Because the effect on aggregate consumer surplus of a public standard is higher for higher u_s, consumer contributions are higher in rich countries than in developing countries, and this results in a higher politically optimal standard level in rich countries $(ds^\# / du_s) > 0$.

This is consistent with international survey evidence on consumer preferences for genetic modification (GM) standards. Consumers in rich countries are generally more opposed to GM than those in poor countries. Consumers in rich countries have less to gain from biotech-induced farm productivity improvements compared to consumers in developing country who have much to gain from less expensive food (McCluskey et al., 2003). This argument is also consistent with empirical observations that consumers from developed countries have generally higher preferences for other applications of biotechnology, such as medical applications (Costa-Font et al., 2008; Hossain et al., 2003; Savadori et al., 2004), which have more (potential) benefits for richer consumers.

The second and third terms in equation (4.12) capture how the quality of institutions affects the relationship between development and the political economy of public standards. The impact of standards on both production and transaction costs depends on the quality of a country's institutions z.

The second term is positive (with $(dz/dI) > 0$). A higher quality of institutions implies that enforcement and control costs of standards (i.e., the increase in transaction costs with higher standards) are lower such that $\partial \tau_s / \partial z < 0$ in our model. The politically optimal standard is decreasing in transaction costs $(ds^\# / d\tau_s < 0)$; hence, this is another channel through which development induces higher standards.

The third term is also positive. Although poor countries, with low wages and less urban pressure on land use, may have a cost advantage in the production of raw materials, better institutions of rich countries lower the marginal increase in production costs caused by standards $(\partial k_s / \partial z < 0)$. A lower increase in production costs could result from higher education and skills of producers, better public infrastructure, easier access to finance, and so forth. These factors induce a higher public standard as $ds^\# / dk_s < 0$.

In combination, the factors discussed earlier are likely to induce a shift of the political equilibrium from low standards to high standards with development. If we define a "coalition" as both groups having the same preferences, that is, either $s = 0$ (anti-standards) or $s > 0$ (pro-standards), then the mechanisms identified here may result in a pro-standard coalition of consumers and producers in rich countries. Consumers may derive large efficiency gains from a standard, whereas producers incur only moderate increases in transaction and production costs. The resulting rent transfer between consumers and producers may then be sufficient to more than compensate producers for the higher costs associated with the standards, while still being small enough to leave a net benefit to consumers. In contrast, an anti-standard coalition may be present in poor countries if consumers are more concerned with low prices than with high quality (leading to small efficiency gains from a higher standard) while the implementation costs for producers (both in terms of production costs and transaction costs) may be large. Formally, a pro-standard coalition thus exists when $u_s > x \, (dp/ds) > c_s$ at $s = 0$, and vice versa for an anti-standard coalition.

4.7 Information, Development, and Perceptions of Standards

So far, we have assumed that consumers have rational expectations and unbiased perceptions of standards. However, studies claim that perceptions of the public may differ importantly from expert opinions on a diversity of issues (e.g., Flynn et al., 1993; Savadori et al., 2004). If so, it is clear that biased perceptions can be an important factor in the political economy of public standards.

Several studies find that consumer perceptions are functions of the level of consumer trust in government regulators, attitudes toward scientific discovery, and media coverage (Curtis et al., 2004; Kalaitzandonakes et al., 2004; Loureiro, 2003). For example, a reason for the differences in perceptions across countries explored by Curtis et al. (2008) is the different organization and structure of the media in rich and poor countries. Mass media is the main source of information for consumers to form attitudes regarding many issues, including GM food (Hoban and Kendall, 1993; Shepherd et al., 1998). Commercial media is more likely to highlight potential risks associated with biotechnology in its reporting (McCluskey and Swinnen, 2004). The increased cost of media information in developing countries leads to lower media consumption and to a proportionately stronger reduction in risk reporting. In addition, government control of the media is stronger in poor countries. This may lead to a more positive coverage of new technologies such as biotechnology, which in turn may contribute to more favorable perceptions of GM food and biotechnology among consumers in these less developed countries. The public is most negative toward GM food in most of the developed countries, especially in the European Union (EU) and Japan. The United States is an exception, as consumers are largely ambivalent about GM food. In less developed countries (LDCs) consumer attitudes toward GM food are less negative and in many cases positive (see Curtis et al., 2008 for a review of the evidence). Therefore, the media structure and information provision is likely to induce a more pro-standard attitude in rich countries than in poor, as increased access to media increases attention to risks and negative implications of low standards.

An additional related element is how the rural/urban population structure affects perceptions. McCluskey et al. (2003) and recent research by Jikun Huang and Scott Rozelle in China find that people associated with agriculture are much more in favor of GM crops than urban consumers. It is likely that consumers who are associated with agriculture have a better idea of the amount of pesticides used on non-GM crops than urban consumers, and hence of the benefits from GM food (such as insect-resistant crops). As developing countries have a higher proportion of rural residents, this may contribute to explain the differences in preferences.

Hence, both perception factors may reinforce the effects of consumer preferences and quality of institutions in inducing a positive relationship between standards and development.

4.8 Conclusions

In this chapter we have developed a formal model of the political economy of public standards. We use our theoretical model to derive the political optimum and to analyze the different factors that have an influence on this political equilibrium. The relative political weights of the respective interest groups influence the politically optimal public standard, and the direction and magnitude of these effects depend on the standards' relative benefits to the different interest groups. Lower efficiency gains and higher implementation costs related to the standard decrease the level of the public standard while a higher price increase related to the standard may increase or decrease the politically optimal standard.

We also examined the positive relationship between standards and economic development. Higher income levels lead to more stringent standards because of higher consumer preferences for quality, less costly enforcement, and lower production costs related to standards. In combination these factors may result in a pro-standard coalition of consumers and producers in rich countries and an anti-standard coalition in poor countries. Differences in information structures between rich and poor countries may reinforce these differences in standards.

While the analysis in this chapter has focused on a closed economy, standards can affect international trade, and have often been considered

protectionist instruments. The effects of standards on trade, and the political
economy of standards in an open economy, are the subject of the next chapter.

4.9 Appendix

A.1 Proof of the Truthfulness of the Contribution Schedules

Define L as the set of active lobby groups, that is, $L = \{P, C\}$, $s^\#$ as the politically optimal standard, and $C^{l\#}$ as the optimal contribution schedule for
lobby group l. Following Lemma 2 of Bernheim and Whinston (1986)
and Proposition 1 of Grossman and Helpman (1994), the equilibrium
$\left(\{C^{l\#}\}_{l\in L}, s^\#\right)$ is a subgame-perfect Nash equilibrium of the standard-setting
game if and only if

(a) $C^{l\#}$ is feasible for all $l \in L$;

(b) $s^\#$ maximizes $\sum_{l\in L} \alpha^l C^{l\#}(s) + W(s)$;

(c) $s^\#$ maximizes $\Pi^j(s) - C^{j\#}(s) + \sum_{l\in L} \alpha^l C^{l\#}(s) + W(s)$ for every $j \in L$;

(d) for every $j \in L$ there exists an s^j that maximizes $\sum_{l\in L} \alpha^l C^{l\#}(s) + W(s)$
     such that $C^{j\#}(s^j) = 0$.

From condition (c) we derive the first-order condition

$$\frac{\partial \Pi^j(s^\#)}{\partial s} - \frac{\partial C^{j\#}(s^\#)}{\partial s} + \sum_{l\in L}\alpha^l \frac{\partial C^{l\#}(s^\#)}{\partial s} + \frac{\partial W(s^\#)}{\partial s} = 0 \text{ for all } j \in L. \quad (4.13)$$

Maximization of the government's objective function (condition b) requires
the first-order condition

$$\sum_{l\in L}\alpha^l \frac{\partial C^{l\#}(s^\#)}{\partial s} + \frac{\partial W(s^\#)}{\partial s} = 0. \quad (4.14)$$

Taken together, conditions (4.13) and (4.14) imply

$$\frac{\partial C^{l\#}(s^\#)}{\partial s} = \frac{\partial \Pi^l(s^\#)}{\partial s} \text{ for all } l \in L. \quad (4.15)$$

Condition (4.15) proves that all contribution schedules are locally truthful
around $s^\#$. This implies in our political economy model that lobby groups
set their contributions in accordance with their expected profits and how
these are marginally affected by the standard.

A.2 Proof of the First-Order Condition

Production: Producers maximize profits by choosing the optimal production level x. With $\Pi^P = px - c(x, s)$ this results in the first-order condition $\partial \Pi^P / \partial x = p - c_x(x, s) = 0$; hence

$$p = c_x(x, s). \tag{4.16}$$

Expression (4.16) defines the optimal behavior of producers in the equilibrium and implicitly defines x as a function $x = x(p, s)$. Deriving $\Pi^P(s)$ with respect to s, and making use of the envelope theorem and condition (4.16) results in

$$\frac{\partial \Pi^P}{\partial s} = \frac{dp}{ds} x + p \frac{dx}{ds} - c_s - c_x \frac{dx}{ds} = \frac{dp}{ds} x - c_s. \tag{4.17}$$

Consumption: Consumer surplus is equal to $\Pi^C(s) = u(q, s) - pq$ where $q = q(p, s)$ denotes consumption. Deriving $\Pi^C(s)$ with respect to s results in

$$\frac{\partial \Pi^C}{\partial s} = u_s - \frac{dp}{ds} q, \tag{4.18}$$

For the closed economy case studied in this chapter, $q = x$.

Government: The government's objective function is $\Pi^G(s) = \alpha^P C^P(s) + \alpha^C C^C(s) + W(s)$ in which the political weights α^i are exogenously given. We have that $(\partial \Pi^G / \partial s) = \alpha^P (\partial C^P / \partial s) + \alpha^C (\partial C^C / \partial s) + (\partial W / \partial s)$. From the functional form and the truthfulness of the contribution functions we have that $\partial C^P / \partial s = \partial \Pi^P / \partial s$ and $\partial C^C / \partial s = \partial \Pi^C / \partial s$ around the politically optimal $s^\#$ (see equation 4.15). Because total welfare is the sum of consumer and producer welfare, we find that $\partial W / \partial s = \partial \Pi^P / \partial s + \partial \Pi^C / \partial s$ so that $\partial \Pi^G / \partial s = (1 + \alpha^P) \partial \Pi^P / \partial s + (1 + \alpha^C) \partial \Pi^C / \partial s$ around the optimum. The government maximizes its objective function with respect to s (i.e., $\partial \Pi^G / \partial s = 0$) subject to $s \geq 0$. Using the expressions (4.17) and (4.18) and the fact that in a closed economy consumption equals production ($q = x$) we then obtain the result that

$$\frac{\partial \Pi^G}{\partial s} = (1 + \alpha^P) \left[x^\# \frac{dp}{ds} - c_s \right] + (1 + \alpha^C) \left[u_s - x^\# \frac{dp}{ds} \right] = 0, \tag{4.19}$$

This first-order condition determines the resulting standard under the condition that $s^\# \geq 0$; in any other case $s^\# = 0$. In equation (4.19), $x^\#$ denotes output in the political equilibrium.

A.3 Comparative Statics

Comparative statics analyses on $s^\#$ applies only when $s^\# > 0$ in condition (4.19). For cases in which condition (4.19) results in $s^\# = 0$, comparative statics results are trivial and equal to zero. Condition (4.19) implicitly defines $s^\#$ as a function of several variables. Hence, for some variable ω:

$$\frac{ds^\#}{d\omega} = -\frac{\partial^2 \Pi^G / \partial s \partial \omega}{\partial^2 \Pi^G / \partial s^2}. \tag{4.20}$$

From our assumptions on the convexity of $c(x,s)$ in s, it follows that $\partial^2 \Pi^G / \partial s^2 < 0$. Hence the sign of $ds^\# / d\omega$ is the same as the sign of $\partial^2 \Pi^G / \partial s \partial \omega$.

Political weight of producers α^P:
$(\partial^2 \Pi^G / \partial s \partial \alpha^P) = x^\# (dp / ds) - c_s$ which is equal to $\partial \Pi^P / \partial s$ at $s^\#$. Therefore $ds^\# / d\alpha^P$ has the same sign as $\partial \Pi^P / \partial s$ at $s^\#$.

Political weight of consumers α^C:
$(\partial^2 \Pi^G / \partial s \partial \alpha^C) = u_s - x^\# (dp/ds)$ which is equal to $\partial \Pi^C / \partial s$ at $s^\#$. Therefore $ds^\# / d\alpha^C$ has the same sign as $\partial \Pi^C / \partial s$ at $s^\#$.

Efficiency gain u_s:
$\partial^2 \Pi^G / \partial s \partial u_s = (1 + \alpha^C)$. This expression is positive, and hence $ds^\# / du_s > 0$.[7]

Implementation cost c_s:
$\partial^2 \Pi^G / \partial s \partial c_s = -(1 + \alpha^P)$. This expression is negative, and hence $ds^\# / dc_s < 0$.

---

[7] Strictly speaking, both the efficiency gain u_s and the implementation cost c_s are themselves functions, and not exogenous parameters. For our present purposes, however, we can interpret both as representing effects that are independent from the other derivatives of the utility and cost functions. Although this involves a slight abuse of notation, the interpretation is intuitive and nonproblematic.

International Trade and Standards

5.1 Introduction

We now extend the closed economy model of Chapters 3 and 4 to an open economy model to analyze the impact of international trade on the political economy of public standards. Standards play an increasingly important, and controversial, role in international trade. This is reflected in the enormous increase of notifications of new Sanitary and Phyto-sanitary (SPS) measures to the World Trade Organization (WTO; see Figure 5.1). Member countries have to notify the WTO of new SPS measures when these measures have a significant effect on trade. As Figure 5.1 illustrates, SPS notifications have increased almost 100 times in a fifteen-year period (1995–2010) and the rise is continuing.

The rapid increase in standards that affect trade has raised concerns about the potential protectionist nature of public standards. The recent growth in the number and form of public standards has been interpreted by many trade economists as a political economy response to the constraints being imposed by international trade agreements on traditional trade restrictions (Anderson et al., 2004; Fischer and Serra, 2000; Sturm, 2006). Already in 1970, Baldwin (1970: 2) wrote that: "[t]he lowering of tariffs has, in effect, been like draining a swamp. The lower water level has revealed all the snags and stumps of non-tariff barriers that still have to be cleared away." And the recent rise of standards is often interpreted in this perspective: as the use of tariffs is increasingly curbed by WTO and other trade agreements, new forms of non-tariff barriers (NTBs) emerge (OECD, 2001; Sturm, 2006). In this interpretation public standards are just a new form of NTBs and "protection-in-disguise" (Vogel, 1995).[1]

---

[1] For literature related to the effects of standards as barriers to trade, see, e.g., Barrett (1994), Barrett and Yang (2001), Schleich (1999), Suwa-Eisenmann and Verdier (2002), Sykes (1995), and Thilmany and Barrett (1997).

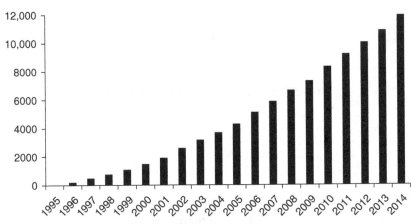

Figure 5.1. Cumulative number of SPS notifications to the WTO.
Source: WTO SPS Information Management System (2014). Data shown refer to regular notifications by date of communication to the Central Registry of Notifications.

For example, Fischer and Serra (2000) argue that standards are biased against imports and favor domestic producers. Bredahl et al. (1987) illustrate this with the United States' implementation of a larger minimum size requirement on vine-ripened tomatoes – mainly imported from Mexico – than on green tomatoes produced in Florida. Anderson et al. (2004) argue that governments raise genetically modified (GM) food standards as protection against imports.[2] Fulton and Giannakas (2004) point out that producers prefer GM labeling when they have low returns on GM food. In their infamous example, Otsuki et al. (2001) claim that a European Union (EU) standard on aflatoxins reduced health risk by approximately 1.4 deaths per billion a year, while decreasing African exports of cereals, dried fruits, and nuts to Europe by 64 percent.[3] Krueger (1996) concludes that, although it is not possible to generalize about labor standards' effects, many economists still argue that international labor standards are protectionist instruments.[4]

However, this trade-protection interpretation of public standards appears to conflict with some basic empirical observations. Many public standards, such as EU GM regulations, are introduced following demands by

[2] See also Baltzer (2011), who argues that domestic producers always favor more restrictive GM standards because of positive border costs.

[3] However, the conclusions of Otsuki et al. (2001) were disputed in later work by Xiong and Beghin (2013).

[4] In an earlier contribution, Bockstael (1984) argues that the same holds for domestic quality standards. She argues that these are mainly redistributive instruments and do not enhance welfare – they protect certain producer interests.

consumers, not producers. In fact, in many cases producers have opposed their introduction. If public standards would be merely protectionist instruments, producers would support their introduction and consumers would oppose them. Tian (2003) demonstrates that an increase in the minimum required "environmental friendliness" of imported goods is not necessarily protectionist in effect as it may hurt domestic firms and increase imports. In the framework of Marette and Beghin (2010) a standard is anti-protectionist when foreign producers are more efficient than domestic producers at addressing consumption externalities by the standard.

These observations are in line with insights from the literature on the economics of quality standards. For example, Boom (1995), Ronnen (1991), and Valletti (2000) all find positive effects of minimum quality standards on consumers' welfare, but mixed effects on overall welfare. Leland (1979) shows that, in general, the effect of a minimum quality standard on welfare is ambiguous. In a vertical product differentiation framework Ronnen (1991) shows that minimum quality standards increase welfare under Bertrand competition between firms, while Valletti (2000) finds that welfare decreases but under Cournot competition.

Our objective in this chapter is to analyze if or when public standards are protectionist instruments. We apply the political economy model developed in Chapter 4 to the case of a small open economy, and compare the political equilibrium with the social optimum to derive conditions under which public standards can be considered "protectionism."[5] As in Chapter 4, we find that the politically optimal public standards may be either too high ("overstandardization") or too low ("understandardization") – a situation that is similar to other forms of trade policy such as import tariffs or export taxes or subsidies (Grossman and Helpman 1994; Krugman 1987). However, contrary to common assumptions, we show that overstandardization is not necessarily protectionist, whereas understandardization may in fact be protectionism in disguise.

Before moving to the formal analysis, it is important to first clarify some key elements and terms in the relationship between trade and

[5] As already explained in Chapter 4, our approach is related to an extensive literature on the political economy of public regulations and of protectionist interventions in international trade (see references there). Much of the applied work on political economy and lobbying is in the domain of trade policy regulation and protection. Important contributions were made by Bhagwati (1982); Grossman and Helpman (1994, 1995); Hillman (1982); Hillman and Ursprung (1988); Krueger (1974); and Magee et al. (1989). Surveys of these literatures include Gawande and Khrishna (2003); Grossman and Helpman (2001); Hillman (1989); Rodrik (1995); and, applied to international agriculture and food policy, Anderson et al. (2013) and Swinnen (2008).

standards. In the literature "protectionism" mostly means "producer protectionism." However, as we showed in Chapters 3 and 4, standards may have different effects on producers or consumers, which implies that standards may benefit (or "protect") either producer or consumer interests. As with tariffs and trade restrictions, standards may either harm or benefit producers. For this reason, and contrary to what other studies suggest, there is no ex ante reason to see standards as producer protectionism. We show that, although almost all standards affect trade, there is no simple relation between "trade distortions" and "producer protection."

The rest of this chapter is organized as follows. We first develop a model of a small open economy with public standards and show the impacts of standards on prices and on consumer and producer surplus (Section 5.2). We identify conditions under which standards reduce trade, that is, act as "trade barriers"; or enhance trade, that is, act as "trade catalysts" (Section 5.3). In Section 5.4, we develop a political economy model, based on that of Chapter 4, and derive the political equilibrium. We then evaluate the validity of the "standards-as-protection" argument (Section 5.5). In Section 5.6, we discuss implications of our findings in relation to different approaches to international agreements on standards. We also describe the rules of the WTO in relation to standards – the Agreements on SPS measures and on TBT – which make explicit reference to the issue of international standards.

5.2 The Impact of Standards in a Small Open Economy

5.2.1 Standards in a Small Open Economy

To gain some insight into the potential effects of standards on trade, we extend the model in Chapter 4 to the case of a small open economy. For a small open economy, the world price $p(s)$ is taken as given. Domestic consumption q is then implicitly defined by equation (3.2) as

$$p = u_q(q, s) \tag{5.1}$$

Domestic production x is implicitly defined by equation (3.6) as

$$p = c_x(x, s) \tag{5.2}$$

We assume that globally a continuum of markets exists for every possible variety $s \in [0, +\infty)$. Domestic standards then "select" a variety to be produced and consumed locally. Foreign producers in sector s have a cost function similar to that of domestic producers (given by equation (4.1)), that is,

$$c^{F}\left(x^{F},s\right)=k^{F}\left(x^{F},s\right)+\tau^{F}\left(s\right)x^{F} \tag{5.3}$$

In this formulation, x^{F} refers to the production of an individual foreign producer. As was the case in Chapter 4, these costs are increasing in the standard $(k_{s}^{F}>0,\tau_{s}^{F}>0)$. We assume that the world market is characterized by free entry, so that for each variety s the world price equals average costs:

$$p(s)=\frac{c^{F}\left(x^{F},s\right)}{x^{F}} \tag{5.4}$$

Under this assumption, foreign output adjusts by entry and exit of producers, not by a change in x^{F}, which denotes the minimum efficient scale of production (i.e., the point where average costs are minimized). As a result, the supply function of foreign producers is perfectly elastic at $p(s)$. As different quality levels s correspond with different cost levels, there will thus be a continuum of prices $p(s)$ increasing in s.

To illustrate these assumptions, consider a small country that can set a standard regulating the level of growth hormones allowed in beef. For simplicity, assume that the standard can either allow or ban hormones. Both "hormone" and "non-hormone" beef are produced on the world market, but "non-hormone" beef is more expensive given higher production costs. If both "hormone" and "non-hormone" beef are allowed in the small country, and consumers cannot distinguish between the two varieties, then the domestic market price will depend on the world price for hormone beef, which is set by the average costs of foreign producers to produce the lower cost hormone beef. However, if the small country imposes a "non-hormone" standard, the relevant world price depends on the average costs of foreign producers to produce the non-hormone beef. These costs are higher, and therefore the relevant world price is higher.

5.2.2 Impact of Standards on Prices

We can now determine how the world price changes with a change in the standard s. Because foreign producers are price takers, the price for a given s equals marginal cost:

$$p(s)=c_{x}^{F}\left(x^{F},s\right) \tag{5.5}$$

The price effect dp/ds can then be written as

$$\frac{dp}{ds} = c_{xs}^{F} + c_{xx}^{F} \frac{dx^{F}}{ds} \qquad (5.6)$$

In this expression, the term dx^{F}/ds does not refer to a change in output for a given producer. Rather, the term denotes how the minimum efficient scale changes as standards change. Since this point is determined by the intersection of the marginal cost curve and the average cost curve, dx^{F}/ds can be found by applying the implicit function theorem on $c_{x}^{F}(s) = [c^{F}(x^{F},s)]/x^{F}$. It follows that

$$\frac{dx^{F}}{ds} = \frac{c_{s}^{F}}{c_{xx}^{F}x^{F}} - \frac{c_{xs}^{F}}{c_{xx}^{F}} \qquad (5.7)$$

Plugging this into equation (5.6), we find that

$$\frac{dp}{ds} = \frac{c_{s}^{F}}{x^{F}} \qquad (5.8)$$

That is, the change in world price is given by the direct effect of a standard on total costs c_{s}^{F} divided by the minimum efficient scale x^{F}. Intuitively, this corresponds to the increase in average costs, keeping output constant.

5.2.3 Impact of Standards on Producer and Consumer Surplus

In an open economy setting, the impact of a standard on consumer surplus is given by

$$\frac{\partial \Pi^{C}}{\partial s} = u_{s} - \frac{dp}{ds} q. \qquad (5.9)$$

As in Chapter 4, an increase in the standard results in an efficiency gain (u_{s}) but also leads to an increase in consumer expenditures due to an increase in prices (dp/ds) q. The impact on producer surplus is given by

$$\frac{\partial \Pi^{P}}{\partial s} = \frac{dp}{ds} x - c_{s}. \qquad (5.10)$$

A higher standard thus leads to an increase in revenues due to the higher price [(dp/ds) x], but also results in implementation costs (c_{s}), as in Chapter 4.

5.3 Standards as Catalysts or Barriers to Trade

To see how standards affect international trade, we consider the impact of a change in the standard on imports $m \equiv q - x$. A change in s leads to a change in consumption given by

$$\frac{dq}{ds} = -\frac{1}{u_{qq}}\left(u_{qs} - \frac{dp}{ds}\right) \tag{5.11}$$

Likewise, a change in s leads to a change in production given by

$$\frac{dx}{ds} = \frac{1}{c_{xx}}\left(\frac{dp}{ds} - c_{xs}\right) \tag{5.12}$$

The effect on imports is then given by

$$\frac{dm}{ds} = \frac{dq}{ds} - \frac{dx}{ds} = \left(\frac{c_{xs}}{c_{xx}} - \frac{u_{qs}}{u_{qq}}\right) - \frac{dp}{ds}\left(\frac{1}{c_{xx}} - \frac{1}{u_{qq}}\right) \tag{5.13}$$

Notice that the sign of expression (5.13) may be positive or negative. If the sign is negative, then standards are "trade barriers," that is, they reduce trade $(dm/ds < 0)$. However, the sign can also be positive, and then imports increase and standards work as "catalysts to trade" $(dm/ds > 0)$. As equation (5.13) shows, standards are catalysts to trade if an increase in the standard leads to a strong increase in marginal costs for domestic producers (c_{xs}) and a strong increase in the marginal utility of consumption (u_{qs}) for a given world price (recall that $u_{qq} < 0$). A given increase in price dp/ds will reduce imports more if the slope of the domestic supply and demand curves are small (c_{xx} and u_{qq} small), as in that case a given price increase leads to a larger expansion of production and a larger reduction in domestic consumption.

The effect of a standard on imports can thus be decomposed in a direct effect (due to the effect of a standard on marginal costs of domestic producers and marginal utility of domestic consumers) and a price effect, reflecting an adjustment along the domestic supply and demand curves to the change in world price as a result of the higher standard. As this analysis shows, only in very special circumstances would standards not affect trade; this case occurs when the effect on domestic production exactly offsets the effect on consumption.

5.4 The Political Equilibrium

As in Chapter 4, we assume that the public standard-setting process is influenced by contributions from lobby groups. Modifying the model of Chapter 4 to take into account international trade, the government's first-order condition determining the public standard $s^{\#} \geq 0$ is now given by

$$\frac{\partial \Pi^{G}}{\partial s} = \left(1 + \alpha^{P}\right)\left[x^{\#}\frac{dp}{ds} - c_{s}\right] + \left(1 + \alpha^{C}\right)\left[u_{s} - q^{\#}\frac{dp}{ds}\right] = 0 \qquad (5.14)$$

where $x^{\#}$ and $q^{\#}$ denote respectively domestic production and consumption in the political equilibrium. The factors that influence the political equilibrium in a closed economy continue to play a role in a small open economy. In particular, the interpretation of the role of the relative lobbying strength of producers and consumers (α^{P} and α^{C}), the efficiency gain u_{s}, the implementation cost c_{s}, and the price effect dp/ds still apply. However, we can study the relationship between trade and the politically optimal standard in more detail.

First, trade affects the net impact of standards on producers and consumers and hence the political contributions and their relative influence. For a given level of consumption q, with lower domestic production x and larger imports $m \equiv q - x$, the effect of standards on aggregate producer profits is smaller and hence producers' contributions and influence on policy lower. In the extreme case without domestic production ($x = 0$), only consumer interests affect government policy. Formally, the political equilibrium condition then equals the optimality condition for consumers. Vice versa, for a given level of domestic production more imports and higher consumption levels imply that the effects on total consumer surplus are larger and therefore consumer contributions and their influence on policy higher.

Second, standards may affect the comparative advantage in production between domestic and foreign producers. Using our derivation of the price effect in equation (5.8) the marginal effect of a standard on domestic producer profits can be written as

$$\frac{\partial \Pi^{P}}{\partial s} = x\frac{dp}{ds} - c_{s} = x\left(\frac{c_{s}^{F}}{x^{F}} - \frac{c_{s}}{x}\right) = x\left[\left(\frac{k_{s}^{F}}{x^{F}} - \frac{k_{s}}{x}\right) + \left(\tau_{s}^{F} - \tau_{s}\right)\right] \qquad (5.15)$$

A higher domestic standard increases profits for domestic producers if the average costs of foreign producers (keeping output constant) increase by more than those of domestic producers $\left(c_s^F / x^F - c_s / x\right)$. Equation (5.15) decomposes this effect into two separate cost effects. Standards may affect the *production costs* of foreign and domestic producers differently, that is, $(k_s^F / x^F) \neq (k_s / x)$. This is the argument used by Anderson et al. (2004) to explain why EU producers lobby against GM food: they argue producers in countries such as the United States and Brazil have a comparative production cost advantage in the use of GM technology and that it is therefore rational for EU producers to support (rather than oppose) cost increasing standards to ban GM food.

Standards may also affect comparative advantages through differences in *transaction costs*, that is, if $\tau_s^F \neq \tau_s$. The relative impact of standards on production costs and transaction costs may be quite different for foreign and domestic producers. Countries with high production costs (importers) may be more efficient at implementing or complying with standards. In such cases, standards may shift the cost advantage (in terms of the final cost of the product) from foreign to domestic producers. As a consequence, such comparative cost advantage in transaction costs (see, e.g., Baldwin, 2001; Salop and Scheffman 1983 for examples) leads to higher producer contributions in favor of the standard, rather than against it (i.e. $\tau_s^F > \tau_s$).[6] Vice versa, when $\tau_s^F < \tau_s$ domestic producers contribute less in favor of the standard.

Finally, standards may have an impact on (other) countries' terms of trade if the standard-imposing country is a large economy importing a significant share of the world market (Baldwin, 2001). For example, when a large country's imports decrease due to a standard, this depresses the world price of the unregulated product, thus deteriorating the terms of trade of countries that export the unregulated product (while ameliorating the terms of trade for importing countries). The standard's price effect in the large standard-imposing country is then not as pronounced as in the small country case.

Notice that, although these factors do concern the relationship between standards and trade, they do not say anything about standards being trade distorting or protectionist measures.

---

[6] Although we do not formally model instrument choice here, if the government has the choice between different standards that induce the same effect on consumption, a government would be inclined to enforce a standard that is less costly for the domestic sector, or to forbid the use of a technology in which the domestic sector has a comparative disadvantage. Fischer and Serra (2000) argue therefore that governments tend to use minimum standards that are biased against imports.

5.5 When Are Standards Protectionist?

As discussed in the introduction, it is commonly assumed that high standards are used as protectionist measures. However, the analysis in the preceding sections makes it possible to offer a more nuanced view. To assess whether public standards are set at suboptimal levels we use the same framework to identify optimal policy as is used in evaluating tariffs in traditional trade theory, that is, by comparing to the socially optimal trade policy. The political equilibrium is said to be suboptimal when the politically optimal tariff $t^{\#}$ differs from the socially optimal tariff t^*. In a small open economy, this analysis leads to the well-known result that the socially optimal tariff level is zero and free trade is optimal. By consequence, any positive tariff level constrains trade, is harmful to social welfare, and is by definition protectionist.

Similarly, we can compare the politically optimal standard $s^{\#}$ defined by equation (5.14) with the socially optimal standard s^* in a small open economy. The optimal standard is found by maximizing domestic welfare (see equation 4.4):[7]

$$\frac{\partial W}{\partial s} = u_s - c_s - (q-x)\frac{dp}{ds} = 0. \tag{5.16}$$

In addition to the efficiency gain for consumers and the implementation cost for domestic producers, domestic welfare depends on how the expenditures on imports (or the revenues from exports) change as a result of the price effect.

A first implication of equation (5.16) is that, in contrast with the socially optimal tariff t^*, in a small open economy the socially optimal standard s^* may be strictly greater than zero, even if this leads to a reduction in trade. Trade flows may change by the imposition of the standard, but this change is socially optimal, that is, it increases domestic welfare.[8]

More generally, comparing equation (5.13) representing the effect of standards on imports with equation (5.15) or (5.16) shows that there is no

---

[7] This is consistent with the standard definition in the international trade literature: the socially optimal policy maximizes domestic welfare. Interestingly, Fischer and Serra (2000) define the socially optimal standard as a measure that maximizes domestic welfare as if all producers were domestic. However, because in our model profits of foreign producers are not affected by a change in domestic standards, our definition of the social optimum is equivalent to the definition of Fischer and Serra (2000).

[8] This is, for example, consistent with the theoretical analysis of Lapan and Moschini (2004), who find that a standard prohibiting the sale of GM products in Europe may enhance European welfare.

simple relationship between the trade effects of a standard and its effects on producer profits or social welfare. As a result, one needs to be careful in defining the term "protectionism," which we use here to refer to the effects on producer profits, regardless of the effects on imports. A public standard is thus said to be protectionist if it results in producer profits that are larger than at the socially optimal standard, which by definition implies that the protectionist standard hurts consumer welfare. However, the protectionist standard may result in higher or lower trade volumes. For instance, a higher standard may increase consumer expenditures by more than the efficiency gain (thus hurting consumer welfare), raise the revenues of domestic producers by more than the implementation cost (thus increasing producer profits), and at the same time increase imports.

Analyzing public standards in an open economy thus requires looking at three different dimensions. A first dimension is whether there is over- or understandardization compared to the socially optimal standard. A second dimension is whether the public standard is protectionist, that is, whether the public standard results in higher domestic producer profits at the expense of domestic consumers. A third dimension is whether the public standard increases or reduces trade volumes, that is, whether the standard acts as a catalyst or a barrier to trade, as discussed earlier.

The analysis of which factors contribute to overstandardization $(s^{\#} > s^{*})$ or understandardization $(s^{\#} < s^{*})$ is similar to that in Chapter 4. Both in the closed economy case of Chapter 4 and the open economy case studied here, the political optimum coincides only with the social optimum if $\alpha^{P} = \alpha^{C}$ or in the trivial case where producers and consumers prefer the same standard.

If $\alpha^{P} > \alpha^{C}$, the public standard will differ from the socially optimal standard in a way that benefits producers (see Table 5.1). In particular, protectionist overstandardization $(s^{\#} > s^{*})$ results when producers' profits increase with a higher standard $(\partial \Pi^{P} / \partial s > 0)$ at s^{*}. If $\partial \Pi^{P} / \partial s < 0$ at s^{*}, the resulting protectionist understandardization (assuming that $s^{*} > 0$) reduces the negative effect of the standard on producers' profits. Since domestic producers benefit from this under-standardization, it serves as protection in disguise.

By contrast, if $\alpha^{P} < \alpha^{C}$ the politically optimal standard will give more weight to consumer interests. This results in overstandardization when $\partial \Pi^{C} / \partial s > 0$ at s^{*} and in understandardization when $\partial \Pi^{C} / \partial s < 0$ at s^{*}. Since at the social optimum $\partial \Pi^{P} / \partial s$ and $\partial \Pi^{C} / \partial s$ have opposite signs, overstandardization and understandardization both hurt domestic producers in this case. Although suboptimal, the politically optimal standard $s^{\#}$ is

Table 5.1. *Protectionist characteristics of standards with different political weights*

Domestic producers	$\alpha^P > \alpha^C$	$\alpha^P < \alpha^C$	Consumers
$\left.\dfrac{\partial \Pi^P}{\partial s}\right|_{s^*} > 0$	Protectionist overstandardization	Nonprotectionist understandardization[a]	$\left.\dfrac{\partial \Pi^C}{\partial s}\right|_{s^*} < 0$
$\left.\dfrac{\partial \Pi^P}{\partial s}\right|_{s^*} < 0$	Protectionist understandardization[a]	Nonprotectionist overstandardization	$\left.\dfrac{\partial \Pi^C}{\partial s}\right|_{s^*} > 0$

[a] *Assuming $s^* > 0$.*

then not "protectionist"; even though trade distortions may result, these do not protect domestic producers.

Finally, because standards may act as barriers or catalysts for trade (as shown by equation 5.13), any of the four outcomes in Table 5.1 may result in higher or lower trade volumes.

5.6 Implications for International Agreements on Standards

As shown in the previous section, domestic interest groups may influence their governments to set (producer) protectionist standards. Empirical evidence shows that such disguised protectionism does take place (see, e.g., Bredahl et al., 1987 for an illustration). Governments may try to prevent such regulatory capture among others by negotiating international agreements on standards in the margin of international trade agreements (Maggi and Rodríguez-Clare, 1998; 2007; Matsuyama, 1990; Staiger and Tabellini, 1987).

International trade agreements act as external commitment devices to tie the hands of member governments against the influence of domestic interest groups, in such a way helping governments that suffer credibility problems with respect to their domestic constituencies. Yet, trade agreements that only regulate traditional trade measures (such as tariffs), without including standards and other non-tariff measures, are necessarily incomplete and therefore ineffective commitment devices (WTO, 2012). International agreements on standards can prevent policy substitution that replaces heavily regulated measures (e.g., tariffs) with less regulated ones (e.g., standards) that aim at the same protectionist objective (Bagwell and Staiger, 2001; Copeland, 1990; Ederington, 2001).

However, the complexity and opacity of many standards and non-tariff barriers poses several challenges, not only for domestic regulators but also for international trade negotiators (WTO, 2012). Considerable uncertainty may exist about a standard's impact on trading partners' economies, and may preclude writing efficient agreements (Battigalli and Maggi, 2003). In addition, observing compliance across borders may turn out to be difficult, which is problematic for the enforcement of international agreements.

There are different approaches in international agreements on standards. "Shallow" agreements leave substantial autonomy to national governments in setting standards, and mainly require nondiscrimination of foreign goods (WTO, 2012). "National treatment" and "mutual recognition" are examples of shallow integration. In contrast, "deep" agreements include rules on domestic policies and standards that go beyond the removal of border barriers to promote trade liberalization, addressing among others (domestic) commitment issues.[9] The principle of "harmonization" is an example of deep integration.

The principle of "national treatment" – which is the WTO's main approach – requires that standards do not discriminate between domestic and foreign sources of supply. Member governments of "national treatment" agreements are obliged to treat foreign products at least as favorably as similar domestic products. The principle's advantage is its simplicity and broadness. As any trade agreement is an incomplete contract, simple and broad rules may be more efficient than specific provisions (Battigalli and Maggi, 2003; Horn et al., 2010). The disadvantage is that it may be too general: "national treatment" is effective only when there exists a similar domestic product, and the principle constrains governments' ability to target externalities that are present only in the consumption of foreign products (Horn, 2006).

The "mutual recognition" principle – central in the EU's approach – stipulates that goods being marketed according to the standards and regulations of any member state of the international agreement can also be marketed in any other member state (Schmidt, 2007). The principle implies that if differences between similar products legally sold in different member countries arise, the products are assumed to achieve the same legitimate goals (Costinot, 2008). Therefore, under "mutual recognition," governments retain sovereignty over their own standards, but cannot (or can only to a limited extent) impose these standards on imports from other member states. Compared to "national treatment," an advantage of "mutual recognition" is that foreign producers do not need to incur additional compliance costs to meet the importing country's standards (Chen and Mattoo, 2008).

---

[9] The terms "shallow integration" and "deep integration" were initially coined by Lawrence (1996).

However, a disadvantage of "mutual recognition" is that in the case of (negative) local consumption externalities, governments will set their standards too low because they do not account for the externalities generated by their exports to foreign markets. In contrast, under "national treatment," governments would set their standards too high because they do not take foreign producers' compliance costs into account. Costinot (2008) therefore concludes that "mutual recognition" is more efficient than "national treatment" when traded goods carry low levels of local consumption externalities.

The third principle, "harmonization," is the most ambitious one and aims at establishing common standards across different jurisdictions. Its efficiency depends on the tradeoff between the benefits of being able to address cross-border policy spillovers and the costs related to differences in policy preferences across countries (Oates, 1972). Typically, harmonization of standards is efficient whenever cross-border policy spillovers are large and/or policy preferences across countries are not important (WTO, 2012). Whether "harmonization" enhances international trade in comparison to "mutual recognition" depends on several factors. Homogeneous standards turn products into better substitutes, thus reducing home-bias, lowering consumers' information costs, and increasing their confidence in imported products – all factors that stimulate trade. However, when demand for imports is driven by "love for variety," or producers face asymmetric compliance costs across different countries, harmonization may reduce trade. In addition, Chen and Mattoo (2008) argue that "harmonization" may increase compliance costs for firms outside the agreement. With "mutual recognition," firms external to the agreement may choose which member country's standards to comply with, thus minimizing its compliance costs.

5.6.1 The WTO SPS and TBT Agreements

The general mandate of the WTO, as established in the 1947 General Agreement on Tariffs and Trade (GATT) agreement, is to remove barriers to international trade based on the principle of nondiscrimination.[10] The principle translates into three concepts: "like products," "national treatment," and the "most-favored nation" principle (Hobbs, 2010). The concept of "like products" prohibits the implementation of measures (such as technical regulations) based on process or production methods – trade measures should be based on products' end use. The concept of "national

---

[10] For a complete overview of the history and principles of the WTO SPS and TBT agreements, we refer readers to Baldwin (2001), Stephenson (1997), and Sykes (1995).

treatment" requires that regulations are applied equally to domestic and imported products, and the "most-favored nation" principle imposes equal treatment for goods from all GATT members.

However, Article 20 of the GATT agreement allows exceptions necessary to protect public morals or deceptive practices; to protect human, animal, or plant life or health; and to conserve exhaustible natural resources (Hobbs et al., 2002).[11] Article 20 also introduces the "sham" principle (Sykes, 1995): exceptions based on Article 20 should not be disguised restrictions to international trade.

The 1979 Tokyo Round resulted in the Standards Code, which extended the general GATT 1947 principles explicitly to standards, but that applied only to the Code signers (Organisation for Economic Co-operation and Development [OECD] members plus some developing countries – Baldwin, 2001). The Standards Code introduced the "least-restrictive-means" principle, which resulted in some specific obligations, for example, to use performance standards instead of design requirements, and to use international standards where possible. Importantly, this encouragement to use international standards does not mean that these constitute a floor or a ceiling on national standards. However, the Code did introduce the obligation to explain any deviation from international standards if requested – what Baldwin (2001) refers to as an extension of the "sham" principle to the "shame" principle. Finally, the Standards Code also included the "transparency" principle to reduce the negative trade impact of standards. It requires an advance notice-and-comment period for regulations with potentially large trade effects, that new standards have to be published promptly, and that an information clearinghouse for standards should be present.

The 1994 Uruguay Round eventually established the TBT Agreement. The TBT Agreement covers all technical requirements, voluntary standards and the procedures to ensure that these are met (i.e., conformity assessment procedures), except when these are SPS measures as defined by the SPS Agreement (see later). The most important contribution of the TBT agreement is that since then, the core principles of the general GATT agreement and the Standards Code (nondiscrimination, "sham," least-restrictive-means, transparency) apply to all WTO member states, and to process standards and conformity assessment procedures.[12] In addition, the TBT Agreement introduced the "Code of Good Practice," with which

---

[11] Yet, Blandford and Fulponi (1999) and Grethe (2007) argue that application of Article 20 to ethical issues related to (food) production (e.g., animal welfare) is ambiguous.

[12] Josling et al. (2004) argue, however, that the TBT Agreement provides only limited guidance on the legitimacy of process-based regulations.

it encourages subnational and nongovernmental standard organizations to adopt the main TBT Agreement principles.

The 1994 Uruguay Round split regulations on food standards off from the TBT Agreement into the SPS measures Agreement. According to the SPS agreement, an SPS measure is any measure applied

- To protect animal or plant life or health within the territory of the member from risks arising from the entry, establishment, or spread of pests, diseases, disease-carrying organisms, or disease-causing organisms;
- To protect human or animal life or health within the territory of the member from risks arising from additives, contaminants, toxins, or disease-causing organisms in foods, beverages, or feedstuffs;
- To protect human life or health within the territory of the member from risks arising from diseases carried by animals, plants, or products thereof, or from the entry, establishment, or spread of pests; or
- To prevent or limit other damage within the territory of the member from the entry, establishment or spread of pests.

The SPS Agreement differs from the TBT Agreement on two important points. First, the SPS Agreement is weaker than the TBT Agreement in terms of nondiscrimination. The SPS Agreement recognizes the fact that, because of differences in, for example, climate, existing pests or diseases, and so on, it is not always appropriate to impose the same SPS measures on products coming from different countries. However, the SPS Agreement does require that SPS measures should be based on "sufficient scientific evidence," by basing measures either on scientific risk assessment or international standards.[13] The SPS Agreement recognizes three international standard-setting bodies (aka "the three sisters"), namely the Codex Alimentarius Commission, the Office Internationale des Epizooties, and the Secretariat of the International Plant Protection Convention.

Second, the SPS Agreement does not contain a Code of Good Practice as in the TBT Agreement. This is highly important given the recent proliferation of private standards, which are frequently more stringent than public or international standards (see also Chapter 7). In principle, the SPS Agreement applies to all SPS measures that may affect trade, and is not explicitly limited to measures adopted by governmental authorities.

---

[13] Note that this "sufficient scientific evidence" is not required by the TBT Agreement, as TBT regulations may be introduced to meet a variety of legitimate objectives such as national security, the prevention of deceptive practices, and so forth.

However, some provisions refer explicitly to the rights and obligations of "members." Therefore, some argue that private food standards fall within the scope of the SPS Agreement, while others argue that private standards should be kept out of the WTO (Wouters and Geraerts, 2012). In contrast, under the TBT Agreement, members have to take reasonable measures to ensure that nongovernmental bodies accept and comply with the Code of Good Practice. Hence, the TBT Agreement does govern private (TBT) standards. Wouters and Geraerts (2012) therefore propose to introduce a similar Code of Good Practice in the SPS Agreement.

5.7 Conclusions

In this chapter, we identify the key factors that characterize the relationship between trade and standards and its effects. Trade affects the net impact of standards on domestic producers and consumers and hence their political contributions. Standards may also affect the comparative production cost advantage between countries, which may lead to either higher or lower standards. Similarly, the relative (domestic versus foreign) transaction (enforcement and control) costs of standards affect the politically optimal standard.

Our model provides an analytical framework to determine whether standards serve as protection in disguise, or not. We show that standards may be "barriers" to trade but also "catalysts" to trade, and that both "under-" or "overstandardization" may occur, depending on a variety of factors. Our findings imply that the effects of specific standards should be analyzed carefully before categorizing them as protectionist instruments.

In the last section, we discussed different approaches to international agreements on standards. We also described an example of such international agreements on standards: the WTO SPS and TBT agreements.

6

Risk, Externalities, and the Nature of Standards

6.1 Introduction

In Chapters 4 and 5 we derived the politically optimal level of standards and showed that the politically optimal choice of standards is affected by various factors including efficiency gains for consumers, implementation costs for producers, as well as levels of development, the media, a standard's effect on comparative advantage, and the ability of institutions to enforce standards.

An important question is whether these results are sensitive to the nature of standards. As discussed in Chapter 2, there is a variety of standards and, by consequence, a variety of ways of modeling standards. Studies in the literature have typically used a general concept of "standards" (as in our own analysis in Chapters 4 and 5) or analyzed a specific case (such as genetic modification [GM] regulations). Yet the issue whether the results depend on the nature of standards may be an important question, in particular if one considers the increasing importance of standards in trade conflicts. Some of the main conflicts in international trade policies relate to safety regulations, such as the bovine growth hormone case, the GM food case, and the (in)famous aflatoxin case. However, other types of standards, such as social and ethical standards, also affect trade. The growing influence of quality, environmental, and social standards on trade has caused Pascal Lamy, when he was Director-General of the World Trade Organization, to publicly warn that this proliferation of "green" and other standards could complicate trade negotiations (Minder, 2007). For all these reasons it is important to examine whether the nature of standards affects the political choice of the standard and how it may distort trade.[1]

---

[1] Empirical evidence in this field is scant. There are some ad hoc reports and case studies (Fulponi, 2007; Henson, 2004) but, as far as we know, there is no systematic evidence on how different types of standards affect production and trade.

The objective of this chapter is therefore to analyze how the nature of standards affects the political economy of standards. The model in this chapter builds on the analytical framework developed in Chapters 4 and 5, but is extended to model explicitly the effects of different types of standards. An important contribution of this chapter is that it explicitly integrates risk and externalities in a political economy setting.

The chapter is organized as follows. The next section extends the model of Chapters 4 and 5 to analyze the impact of different standards on consumers – taking risk considerations into account – and producers. We integrate the interests of consumers and producers in a political economy model in which the government sets standards and is influenced by contributions from lobby groups, and discuss the resulting political equilibrium. We then classify different types of standards and compare them in terms of political optimum, and discuss the relation between the nature of standards and trade conflicts.

6.2 Classification of Standards

A three-way categorization of standards, based on Brom (2000), distinguishes between safety standards (SS), quality standards (QS), and social and environmental standards (SES).

The first category of standards is safety standards. According to Brom (2000), this is the type of standards that matters to all consumers. The main purpose of safety standards is to provide consumers with safe products. Examples are the limitation of pesticide residues on vegetables and, more generally, the prohibition of harmful substances in any product. We assume that safety standards have an effect on producer profits and the expected utility of consumers.

The second category is quality standards. These standards ensure certain product quality characteristics to the consumers. These product characteristics do not include safety, but rather concern consumer preferences about other aspects of nutritional quality, taste, color, size, and so forth. These standards may be linked to personal life style choices (e.g., vegetarians). As with safety standards, we assume that these quality standards affect producer profits and consumers' expected utility.

The third category covers public standards that regulate social and environmental issues (SES) based on the ethical values of a society. Examples of SES include the prohibition of using child labor and the limitation of carbon dioxide emission in the production process. We assume that these SES have no direct effect on expected consumer utility (i.e., they do not reduce risk), but affect consumers through a "warm glow" effect (see, e.g., Andreoni, 1989; Besley and Ghatak, 2007). As with safety standards and quality standards, standards concerning social and environmental issues affect producer profits because of cost-increasing requirements concerning production practices.

In our theoretical analysis, we will use these three categories of standards. This categorization is a theoretical construct useful for our analysis as it allows us to trace the impact of different effects. In reality, however, many standards have characteristics from more than one category of standards. Consider organic food standards for example (see, e.g., Lusk and Briggeman, 2009). Consumers may consider food labeled as organic as safer because pesticides are not used in the production of organic food (a safety standard in our classification), but also as more tasteful (a quality standard in our classification). In addition, society may benefit from reduced pesticide use (an SES in our classification).[2] However, for the purpose of this chapter the mutually exclusive classification adopted is useful. Obviously, it is important to take these considerations into account when applying this analytical framework for empirical research.

6.3 The Model

To model these three types of standards explicitly, we follow the approach of Swinnen and Vandemoortele (2008) by incorporating direct consumer effects, externalities, and risk considerations in the model of Chapters 4 and 5.

We assume that the consumer surplus of a representative consumer is given by

$$\Pi^C = Eu(q,s) + \lambda\gamma(s) - pq \qquad (6.1)$$

[2] This classification issue is also one of the main causes for the lack of data concerning the number of food standards. Only some limited and incomplete information on the amount of different food standards is available. For example, the Codex Alimentarius, an initiative of the World Trade Organization (WTO) and the Food and Agriculture Organization (FAO) of the United Nations which has been set up to harmonize national standards, contains more than 290 product standards. The Agricultural Marketing Service (AMS), which belongs to the United States Department of Agriculture (USDA), reports that currently more than 360 minimum quality standards and grades relating to agricultural produce are in force in the United States. However, standards in both systems contain many substandards that can be related to food safety, food quality, or social and environmental issues. This makes the quantification and categorization of public food standards difficult, if not impossible.

The first component of expression (6.1), $Eu(q,s)$, is the *expected utility* of consuming q units of the good with standard s. The application of expected utility in relation to product characteristics is based on the literature on product warranties (see, e.g., Cooper and Ross, 1985; Emons, 1988; Elbasha and Riggs, 2003). We assume that there are two possible outcomes. If the product contains the characteristics desired by the consumer, utility of consumption is $u(q)$, which is assumed to be increasing and concave in consumption $(u_q > 0, u_{qq} < 0)$.[3] However, if the good has inferior characteristics, consumers incur a disutility of consumption, $h(q)$, which is increasing and convex in q $(h_q > 0, h_{qq} > 0)$. The probability of the latter outcome is $\rho(s)$ which is decreasing and convex in s $(\rho_s < 0, \rho_{ss} > 0)$, with a higher s referring to a more stringent standard. Hence a higher standard reduces the probability that the product has inferior characteristics.

The probability of the presence of inferior characteristics as perceived by consumers may differ from (expert opinions on) the actual probability (Flynn et al., 1993; Ritson and Mai, 1998; Savadori et al., 2004). We therefore define μ as the variable that measures bias in consumer risk perception, where μ takes values different from unity if consumer risk perception is biased. To summarize, the expected utility of consumption is represented by

$$Eu(q,s) = (1 - \mu\rho(s))u(q) - \mu\rho(s)h(q)$$
$$= u(q) - \mu\rho(s)[u(q) + h(q)] \tag{6.2}$$

As is clear from expression (6.2), expected utility can be decomposed in the utility of a "good" outcome $u(q)$ minus the *perceived risk*, which consists of the perceived risk probability $\mu\rho(s)$ and the magnitude of the adverse consequences $u(q) + h(q)$. Such two-dimensional specification of risk is consistent with, among others, Pennings et al. (2002), Peter and Ryan (1976), and Yeung and Morris (2001).

In addition to the expected utility component, consumer surplus as defined in equation (6.1) also contains the term $\lambda\gamma(s)$, which denotes the consumers' perceived private benefit from being aware that their consumption does not have a negative effect on the environment or the welfare of other individuals. The effect is similar to the "warm glow effect" of Andreoni (1989) and Besley and Ghatak (2007). This positive warm glow effect of the standard is denoted by $\gamma(s)$, which is increasing and concave

---

[3] By imposing a concave utility function, we assume that consumers are risk averse (see also Elbasha and Riggs, 2003; Mas-Colell et al., 1995; Pennings et al., 2002).

in the public standard $\left(\gamma_s > 0, \gamma_{ss} < 0\right)$. Examples of standards that create such a warm glow effect are standards that prohibit the use of child labor or enhance biodiversity. λ measures the bias in consumer perception of the warm glow effect and is defined similarly to μ, although μ and λ are not necessarily equal. By maximizing consumer utility, the inverse demand function can be derived:

$$p = u_q - \mu\rho(s)\left[u_q + h_q\right] \tag{6.3}$$

The marginal effect of a standard on consumer surplus is given by

$$\begin{aligned}
\frac{\partial \Pi^C}{\partial s} &= Eu_s + \lambda\gamma_s - \frac{dp}{ds}q \\
&= -\mu\rho_s\left[u(q) + h(q)\right] + \lambda\gamma_s - \frac{dp}{ds}q
\end{aligned} \tag{6.4}$$

A higher standard leads to an efficiency gain through expected utility Eu_s as well as through the "warm glow" effect $\lambda\gamma_s$. The efficiency gain through expected utility operates through the reduction in the probability of a bad outcome, given by ρ_s. Consumer welfare increases if the sum of the risk reduction effect and the warm glow effect outweigh the increase in expenditures, $(dp/ds)\,q$.

Apart from this formulation of consumer surplus and demand, the model has the same structure as in Chapter 5. Social welfare is therefore given by

$$W(s) = u(q) - \mu\rho(s)\left[u(q) + h(q)\right] - p(q - x) - c(x, s) \tag{6.5}$$

Given our specification of consumer surplus in equation (6.1), it is now straightforward to derive the government's first-order condition as in Chapter 5. The politically optimal standard s^* is determined by the following first-order condition, subject to $s^* \geq 0$:

$$\begin{aligned}
\frac{\partial \Pi^G}{\partial s} &= \left(1 + \alpha^P\right)\left[x^* \frac{dp}{ds} - c_s\right] \\
&+ \left(1 + \alpha^C\right)\left[-\mu\rho_s\left[u(q) + h(q)\right] + \lambda\gamma_s - q^* \frac{dp}{ds}\right] = 0
\end{aligned} \tag{6.6}$$

6.4 The Nature of Standards and the Political Optimum

We now use the classification of the three types of standards of Section 6.2 to analyze the impact of the nature of standards on the political optimum. First, the positive marginal risk reduction effect $-\mu\rho_s[u(q) + h(q)]$ applies only to types of standards that directly affect consumers by reducing the risk of consuming a good with inferior product characteristics. In our classification of standards this is the case for SS and QS, but not for SES. The marginal warm glow effect $\lambda \gamma_s$ is zero for safety standards and quality standards. In the case of SES, the marginal risk reduction effect is zero, but the marginal warm glow effect is positive.

Second, we assume that the disutility $h(q)$ of consuming goods with inferior *safety* characteristics is larger than the disutility of consuming goods with inferior *quality* characteristics. Because of the larger negative impact of the potential safety hazard, an increased safety standard will have a larger effect on direct consumer utility than an increased quality standard, ceteris paribus. Although we are not aware of any formal statistical tests comparing consumer reactions to changes in safety and quality of products, substantial empirical evidence does suggest that consumer reactions are stronger in cases of food safety issues. In several cases of (perceived) food safety crises, strong consumer reactions have been documented. For example, after the outbreak of the bovine spongiform encephalopathy (BSE; "mad cow disease") in 1996 in the United Kingdom, meat consumption in France declined dramatically (Latouche et al., 1998). Similarly, with the dioxin crisis in Belgium in 1999 consumer reactions were dramatic (Swinnen et al., 2005; Verbeke and Ward, 2001). Our assumption is also in line with the result of Lusk and Briggeman (2009) that consumers rate food safety as the most important food value compared to other values related to food quality such as nutrition and taste. In our model these differences in valuation of characteristics are captured by the differences in disutility $h(q)$ from consuming less safe products and products of low quality; the disutility of consuming a contaminated apple is arguably larger than the disutility of consuming an apple that is less tasty. As a result, the marginal risk reduction effect of a safety standard will be stronger than that of a quality standard, ceteris paribus.

These different effects of types of standards will obviously play a role in the political economy of public standards. These are captured by the different terms in the first-order condition of the government (equation (6.6)), which determines the politically optimal public food standard. The political optimum of the different standards will thus depend on (1) the (exogenous) relative lobby weights of the different political groups (captured by the relative values of α^P and α^C); (2) the lobby contributions of the different groups, which reflect (differences in) the impact of the different standards; and (3) whether the various standards differentially affect other variables such as the consumer perception variables.

A first result is that public safety standards will be higher than public quality standards. To see this, note that neither safety standards nor quality standards induce any warm glow effect, so that $\lambda\gamma_s$ in equation (6.6) is zero and the equilibrium for safety standards and quality standards is determined by the other terms. Assuming that the costs of implementing safety and quality standards are the same, the net impact on domestic producers is identical. With the marginal risk reduction $-\mu\rho_s[u(q)+h(q)]$ of safety standards being stronger than that of quality standards, it follows that the political equilibrium standard will be higher for safety standards than for quality standards, that is, $s^\#(SS) > s^\#(QS)$.

A second result is that a comparison of the political optimum of safety or quality standards with SES cannot yield an unconditional result without more detailed information on how much the different standards marginally affect expected consumer utility and the warm glow effect. If the implementation costs of safety standards, quality standards and SES are the same, producers are "neutral." Hence, whether safety or quality standards would be set higher than SES by the government depends on the effects of the different standards on respectively the risk of inferior product characteristics $-\mu\rho_s[u(q)+h(q)]$ (for safety or quality standards) and the marginal warm glow effect $\lambda\gamma_s$ (for SES).

Third, if perceptions are biased this obviously also affects the outcome. For example, if consumers perceive safety hazards to have a higher probability of occurrence than quality problems (i.e., if $\mu(SS) > \mu(QS)$) this would reinforce the earlier result that $s^\#(SS) > s^\#(QS)$ and further increase the gap between the levels of safety standards and quality standards.[4] Although there is little evidence on these issues, Ansell and Vogel (2006) argue that exaggerated negative perceptions are particularly important in food scares. If so, this would lead to a further relative increase of food safety standards compared to other food standards. Alternatively, if consumers perceive the risk effects correctly ($\mu = 1$ for safety and quality standards) but perceive the environmental impact of standards as more positive than they actually are ($\lambda > 1$), this would increase the level of SES relatively to quality standards and safety standards.

Finally, one can further refine our classification of standards. For example, within the class of quality standards one can distinguish between different quality characteristics that are affected by the standard. Nelson (1970) and Darby and Karni (1973) identify three types of quality characteristics, namely

---

[4]   Related to this, see, e.g., Pennings et al. (2002) on the differences in consumer risk perceptions concerning food safety issues in beef consumption.

search, experience, and credence characteristics. Search characteristics can be evaluated prior to purchase. Hence, a quality standard would not reduce any informational asymmetry or risk of buying a product with inferior quality characteristics (see also Bockstael 1984). In this case, the marginal risk reduction $-\mu\rho_s[u(q)+h(q)]$ is zero. In contrast, a quality standard may reduce informational asymmetries and increase expected utility if it concerns experience characteristics (quality characteristics that are known after consumption) or credence characteristics (quality characteristics that cannot be verified by consuming the product). As a consequence, politically optimal quality standards related to experience and credence characteristics will be higher than quality standards related to search characteristics. The politically optimal level of quality standards will thus depend on the type of quality characteristics and informational asymmetries that the quality standard reduces.

6.5 The Nature of Standards and Trade Conflicts

In Chapter 5 we studied the trade effects of standards, as well as the conditions under which the political process leads to over- or understandardization and when such deviations from the social optimum would be protectionist. The analysis developed in Chapter 5 applies to the standards discussed in this chapter too.

However, the issue we are particularly concerned with in this chapter is whether one type of standard is more likely to serve as a protectionist instrument than others. First, as we discussed previously, there is some limited evidence that the bias in perceptions differs between standards. In particular, exaggerated negative risk perceptions of safety problems and their impact on consumer welfare (and thus exaggerated positive effects of safety standards) may be higher than such biases in perceptions for quality standards. In this case, politically optimal safety standards would be higher than their social optimum. For example, many argue that negative European consumer reactions to GM food are based on biased risk perceptions of the impact of GM technology on food safety. Note, however, that this observation in itself does not provide evidence for the argument that safety standards will differ more from their social optimum than other food standards, as opposition to GM food is only partially related to the "food safety" aspect of GM food. Perceptions on environmental and quality aspects of GM food are important as well and it is not obvious whether these perceptions are less or more biased than those on the food safety aspect.

Furthermore, whether a relatively stronger bias in food safety risk perceptions would effectively imply (stronger) protection for domestic producers depends on other characteristics of the economy. For example, as discussed in Chapter 5, if domestic producers and foreign producers are equally affected by a safety standard then this standard is not protectionist. However, in case higher safety standards would effectively counteract a comparative disadvantage of domestic producers then the standard could be considered as protectionist. The latter case is related to the argument of Anderson et al. (2004), who argue that trade policies excluding GM foods from the EU market are hurting foreign producers as this technology would reinforce their comparative advantage.

A second element in the analysis of whether various standards affect trade differently relates to the power of the different lobbies. If one of the lobby groups has a relatively larger weight this would lead to a divergence of the politically optimal standard towards a level of the standard preferred by that particular lobby group. However, there is no ex ante reason why these weights should differ for varying types of standards. Moreover, different lobby weights for varying types of standards would lead to differences in trade protection only under certain conditions, as explained earlier.

Finally, notice that one of the main findings of the previous section, that is, that due to the consumption effects the level of a safety standard would be higher than the level of a quality standard in the political equilibrium, does not necessarily imply that there would be more protectionism with safety standards than with quality standards. If the political equilibrium for both types of standards coincides with the social optimum there is no over- or understandardization for either standard; the higher levels of the safety standard then simply reflect higher socially optimal levels. Safety standards would only be associated with (more) protectionism than quality standards if the lobby weight of domestic producers (α^P) is higher than the lobby weight of consumers (α^C), and under specific conditions of relative implementation costs.

6.6 Conclusions and Implications

In this chapter we have analyzed whether the nature of standards affects the level of the politically optimal standard and the likelihood of trade conflicts. Specifically, we have examined whether safety standards are different from other standards, such as quality standards or social and environmental standards.

An important result is that, in an environment with only public standards, safety standards will be set at higher levels than quality standards because the former, ceteris paribus, have a larger marginal effect on consumer welfare. The relative level of social and environmental standards compared to safety or quality standards depends on the specific characteristics of the different standards which determine how the standards affect consumer welfare.

Our analysis shows that the relation between the type of standard and protection is conditional on other factors. For example, if domestic producers have relatively more political influence – in combination with a set of production-side conditions that imply that more stringent standards provide benefits to domestic producers over foreign importers – one should expect safety standards to be relatively more important trade protectionist instruments than quality standards. Another example is when risk perceptions of consumers are biased. If risk perceptions are biased in such a way that they reinforce the perceived impact of standards on consumers, consumer lobbying will be more intensive and this may lead to the implementation of a trade distorting standard, but again conditional on a set of structural conditions on the supply side.

An overall conclusion from this analysis is that the relationships between the nature of standards, public decision making concerning standards, and the trade effects of standards are complex.

Endogenous Private and Public Standards
in Value Chains

7.1 Introduction

Chapters 4 to 6 developed a political economy approach to explaining public standard setting. An implicit assumption in those chapters is that private firms are unable to credibly communicate the quality characteristics of products, so that the market was governed only by public standards. However, private standards, introduced by private companies, are increasingly important in the global market system (Fulponi, 2007; Henson, 2004; Henson and Hooker, 2001). Retailers and producers often introduce private standards in the same domains as in which the government imposes public standards, such as safety, quality, and social and environmental aspects of production, retail, and consumption.

The literature provides several explanations why companies may impose private standards in the absence and in the presence of public standards (see Section 7.2 for a review). However, the explanations in the literature do not explain well why companies may set private standards significantly higher than public standards but not very different from their competitors. Yet this is what is observed in reality, for example, in rapidly spreading standards such as GLOBALG.A.P. (see later).

To explain this we extend the model of Chapter 4 to incorporate a richer value chain structure. More specifically, in our analyses in this book so far, like in most of the literature, we considered two-agent models with "producers" and "consumers." However, focusing only on these two groups ignores important structural features of modern value chains. The "producer" side of the value chain is often characterized by a large number of small "producers" (such as farms) and a few companies (such as processing companies or retail chains) which sell products to consumers and often exercise market power (Sexton et al. 2007). In reality, many private standards are set by retailers – not by producers.[1] Therefore we explicitly introduce a monopolist retailer that may set a private standard to regulate the same product characteristics as the government's public standard and show that this has important consequences for the analysis of private standards.[2] In addition to the retailer's private standard, we assume there is a public standard that is determined in a political game in which producers and the retailer have political power to influence the government's standard-setting process.

Our analysis shows that if the retailer can impose most of the costs of a higher standard on producers, the optimal retailer standard will be higher than the optimal standard for producers. Producers thus lobby for a lower public standard, but retailers impose a higher private standard. The joint determination of the politically determined public standard and privately determined private standard depends on a variety of factors, such as the retailer's market power, producers' political influence, the standard's efficiency gains, implementation costs, and rent transfers from the retailer to producers. Side payments from producers to the retailer may align the retailer standard more with producer interests.

The chapter is structured as follows. We first briefly review key contributions in the literature (Section 7.2). In Section 7.3, we specify the different players in our model and determine the market equilibrium. Section 7.4 analyzes how a standard affects the equilibrium. We determine the retailer's optimal private standard, and model the government's decision-making process on public standards in Section 7.5. We also compare the retailer's optimal private standard and the government's optimal public standard under different conditions. Next, in Section 7.6 we allow for side payments by producers to influence the retailer. The concluding section discusses extensions.

7.2 Private and Public Standards: Insights from the Literature

Retailers and producers can have a variety of motives to implement private standards in the absence of public standards. First, private standards may

---

[1] In the U.S. beef industry, for instance, fast food restaurants and retail chains are responsible for the drive toward more stringent traceability standards (Golan et al., 2004). One notable exception are geographical indications, where quality standards are set by producer organizations (Mérel and Sexton, 2012). We study the political economy of geographical indications in Chapter 9.

[2] We denote the third party as the "retailer," but this market player may be any intermediary between producers and consumers, for example, a processing firm. For our analysis, the third party's relevant characteristics are that it acts as an intermediary between producers and consumers, and that it has some market power in exercising its function.

reduce consumers' uncertainty and information asymmetry about product characteristics such as safety, quality, and social and environmental aspects, thus increasing consumer demand. For example, Kirchhoff (2000) shows that firms may voluntarily reduce pollution to attract "green" consumers if firms are able to signal their pollution abatement, for example, through a private standard. A similar argument can be made for business-to-business transactions in which the buyer is not a consumer but a private company. In such contexts, private standards make it possible to ensure and communicate product attributes about production, quality, and so forth that may facilitate firms to gear their activities to one another.

Second, firms may use private standards as strategic tools to differentiate their products, thus creating market segmentation and softening competition. A basic result from the vertical differentiation literature is that firms are able to reduce price competition and raise their profits by differentiating the (vertical) quality attribute of their products (see, e.g., Mussa and Rosen, 1978; Spence, 1976a; Tirole, 1988). Such quality differences can be signaled by setting a private standard.[3]

Third, as demonstrated by Von Schlippenbach and Teichmann (2012), firms may use private standards strategically to improve bargaining power over their suppliers. Their analysis shows that if suppliers cannot adjust product quality in the short run, retailers may either undercut or surpass other retailers' standards to weaken their suppliers' outside options and bargaining power. The authors show that such strategic differentiation by retailers results in welfare losses compared to the social optimum and that in such a setting a minimum quality standard can be welfare improving.

However, private companies regularly set standards that coexist with, and often exceed, public standards. Empirical evidence shows that 70 to 80 percent of retailers assess their own private standards slightly or significantly higher than public standards (see Figure 7.1). Animal welfare is an area in which private standards often exceed public standards.[4] Food safety

---

[3] Several other authors have shown that in a vertically differentiated market a minimum quality standard imposed by the government (a public standard) may raise welfare, depending on the type of competition between producers (see, e.g., Boom, 1995; Crampes and Hollander, 1995; Leland, 1979; Ronnen, 1991; Valletti, 2000; Winfree and McCluskey, 2005). If the minimum quality standard is not prohibitively high such that it does not exceed the highest quality voluntarily supplied by producers, firms differentiate their quality levels: some produce at the minimum quality level while others produce at a higher quality level. The latter firms can signal their higher quality by setting a private standard that is more stringent than the public minimum quality standard (see, e.g., Arora and Gangopadhyay, 1995).

[4] McDonald's, for instance, imposes more stringent standards for the treatment of animals than what is prescribed by law, and several U.S. producer groups such as the American

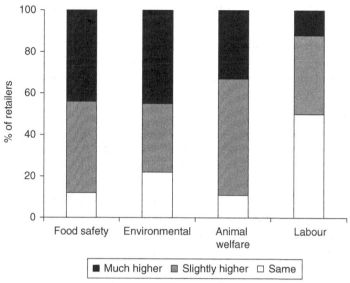

Figure 7.1. Retailers' self-assessed standards compared to those of government. *Source*: Fulponi (2007).

and quality is another typical area. Fulponi (2006) reports that 85 percent of the retailers maintain food safety and quality standards that are more stringent than public standards, for example, by imposing stricter norms for possible allergens or contaminants.

Concerning genetically modified organisms (GMOs), Vigani and Olper (2013) show that a majority of retailers in Europe are committed to selling GMO-free food, thus implementing a standard stricter than required by EU regulations.

Two theories may offer an explanation for this observation, that is, why most retailers set their private standards at higher levels than what is required by law. First, firms may try to strategically preempt costly political action through voluntary private standards (Lutz et al., 2000; Maxwell et al., 2000; McCluskey and Winfree, 2009). The political economy model of Maxwell et al. (2000) shows that high private standards may preempt public standards if consumers' costs of getting politically organized are sufficiently high. In the explanation of McCluskey and Winfree (2009), public

Meat Institute and the United Egg Producers issue voluntary guidelines on animal welfare (Mitchell, 2001). Fulponi (2006) notes that even though animal welfare is protected by both EU and national regulation, the majority of large European retailers report that their animal welfare requirements are higher than those imposed by national legislation.

standards are imposed (even though preempted by private standards) but at equal or higher levels than private standards.

Second, the vertical differentiation literature argues that those retailers who set their private standard at a higher level than the public minimum quality standard aim at differentiating themselves from other retailers that sell at the minimum quality standard, thus raising profits by reducing competition. Although this may be an appropriate description of some markets (e.g., organic food), the standard vertical differentiation framework seems less appropriate for analyzing the phenomenon that organizations such as the British Retail Consortium (BRC) or the Global Partnership for Good Agricultural Practice (GlobalG.A.P.) introduce private standards that are more stringent than public standards, and that these relatively stringent private standards are adopted by almost all retailers in European countries.[5] Retailers thus seem to implement private standards that are simultaneously higher than the existing public standards but not significantly different from the standards adopted by their rivals. One possible explanation would be that consumers have come to regard the stricter private standard as the de facto minimum (e.g., because of a lack of trust in the lower public standard), in which case retailers have no choice but to adopt the stricter private standard as if it were a minimum quality standard. This seems to be the case for standards such as the "dolphin-safe" tuna fish, a voluntary standard that nevertheless is adopted by all players in the U.S. market (Smith, 2009). However, although this explanation may hold true for some highly visible products and some characteristics, stricter private standards seem too pervasive to be attributable to such consumer perceptions alone.

In this chapter we provide an additional explanation for the observation that private standards may be set at higher levels than their public counterparts – even when implementation costs and consumer benefits do not differ between public and private standards. Our analysis shows that an intermediary with market power may set its private standard at a higher level than the government's optimal public standard if the retailer is able to shift the burden of the private standard's implementation cost to producers. While producers lobby for a lower public standard, the retailer uses its market power to impose a higher private standard.

---

[5] Another important example is the Global Food Safety Initiative (GFSI), a benchmarking organization in which leading retailers collaborate in harmonizing private standards for food safety and/or sustainability (Fulponi, 2007).

7.3 The Model

We again consider a market setting where consumers are ex ante uncertain about some characteristics of the product, so that standards may improve on the market outcome by guaranteeing the presence or absence of those characteristics. We assume that private and public standards have intrinsically the same effects, that is, that their impacts on consumer utility and production costs are not different, ceteris paribus, such that differences in levels of public and private standards are not attributable to intrinsic differences between public and private standards. We limit our analysis to a closed-economy model to refrain from potential standards-as-barriers-to-trade issues.

7.3.1 Consumers

Our assumptions on consumer utility and demand follow those introduced in Chapter 3. The utility function of a representative consumer is $u(x,s)$ where x is consumption of the good, and s is the (public or private) standard. In addition to the assumptions on $u(x,s)$ introduced in Chapter 3, we assume $u_{xxx} = 0$ to simplify the exposition.[6] As in equation (3.2), the inverse demand curve is given by

$$p = u_x(x,s) \qquad (7.1)$$

7.3.2 Producers

We again follow the assumptions of Chapter 3 regarding producers. Thus, we consider a representative producer with a cost function $c(x,s)$ that depends on output and the (public or private) standard. For simplicity, we also assume that $c_{xxx} = 0$.[7] Producers are price takers. However, because we now introduce an intermediary between producers and consumers, the decisions of producers depend on the *wholesale price* w, instead of on

---

[6] This assumption implies that the demand curve is linear. Although this does not fundamentally affect our results, this assumption simplifies the exposition. The third derivative of the utility function does not have a straightforward intuitive meaning in our setting and it is not clear a priori whether this derivative should be negative or positive. Assuming u_{xxx} to be zero is thus a reasonable simplification.

[7] As with the analogous assumption for utility, this assumption implies that the supply curve is linear, which simplifies our exposition without fundamentally altering the results.

the retail price p as in previous chapters. Producers thus maximize their profits Π^P by setting output x:

$$\Pi^P = \max_x \left[wx - c(x,s) \right] \qquad (7.2)$$

The first-order condition (FOC) of this maximization problem is

$$\frac{\partial \Pi^P}{\partial x} = w - c_x(x,s) = 0 \qquad (7.3)$$

Equation (7.3) is the analogue of equation (3.6) and defines the inverse supply function, with the same properties as in Chapter 3. In the remainder of the analysis we assume that production costs are sufficiently convex and consumer utility sufficiently concave in s to ensure global maxima.

7.3.3 The Retailer

We assume that output is sold by producers to consumers through one intermediary agent – a monopolist retailer. The retailer's handling costs are normalized to zero. The monopolist retailer sets consumer and producer prices such that, under optimal price-taking behavior of consumers and producers, consumption and output equal at a level that maximizes the retailer's profits Π^R. This is equivalent to maximizing the retailer's profits with respect to quantity x using the inverse demand and supply functions (7.1) and (7.3), which represent the optimal price-taking behavior of consumers and producers and thus define consumer and producer prices for a given quantity. Formally, the retailer's profits are

$$\Pi^R = \max_x \left(p(x,s) - w(x,s) \right) x \qquad (7.4)$$

where $p(x,s) - w(x,s) = u_x(x,s) - c_x(x,s)$ is the retailer's margin.

7.3.4 The Market Equilibrium

The FOC of the retailer's profit maximization is

$$\frac{\partial \Pi^R}{\partial x} = u_x - c_x + x\left(u_{xx} - c_{xx} \right) = 0, \qquad (7.5)$$

and hence the equilibrium quantity $x^*(s)$, for a given level of the standard s, is

$$x^*(s) = \frac{u_x - c_x}{c_{xx} - u_{xx}} \tag{7.6}$$

Equation (7.6) is not a closed-form solution because the right-hand side depends on x. The denominator is always positive because the cost function is convex and the utility function concave in x. The numerator is positive if $u_x > c_x$, or equivalently if $p > w$. This condition – which we assume to hold throughout the chapter – ensures a positive retailer margin and profits.

7.4 The Impact of a Standard

Before determining the optimal public and private standards and how they compare, we analyze the effect of a marginal change in the standard (whether public or private) on the market equilibrium, the interests of the different market players, and social welfare. Using the implicit function theorem, the impact of a marginal change in the standard on the equilibrium quantity $x^*(s)$ is

$$\frac{dx^*}{ds} = \frac{1}{2}\frac{u_{xs} - c_{xs}}{c_{xx} - u_{xx}} + \frac{1}{2}x^*\frac{u_{xxs} - c_{xxs}}{c_{xx} - u_{xx}} \tag{7.7}$$

Comparing with equation (3.22), which expressed the effect of a standard on quantities in a perfectly competitive environment, it is clear that the role of the retailer as intermediary changes the impact of a change in the standard on equilibrium quantity. Equation (7.7) shows that this impact consists of two effects. An increase in the standard leads to an upward shift in the inverse demand and supply functions (since $u_{xs} > 0$ and $c_{xs} > 0$) – the first term in equation (7.7) captures the net effect of these shifts on the equilibrium quantity. An increase in the standard may also affect the slopes of the inverse demand and supply functions ($u_{xxs} \neq 0$ and/or $c_{xxs} \neq 0$). The second term in equation (7.7) represents the effect on the equilibrium quantity of the change in slopes – in other words, the second term refers to rotations in demand and supply. If $u_{xxs} < 0$ an increase in the standard rotates the inverse demand function clockwise, while with $c_{xxs} > 0$ an increase in the standard rotates the inverse supply curve counterclockwise.

When $u_{xxs} = c_{xxs} = 0$, an increase in the standard only leads to parallel upward shifts in both demand and supply, which translate into parallel shifts upward by the same distance of the retailer's marginal revenue and cost functions. If the marginal revenue function shifts upward more than the marginal cost function ($u_{xs} > c_{xs}$), equation (7.7) shows that the retailer responds to a higher standard by increasing the traded quantity.

When u_{xxs} or c_{xxs} are different from zero, the rotation of the functions influences the effect of a standard on equilibrium quantity. For instance, the second term in equation (7.7) shows that a stronger counterclockwise rotation of the supply function ($c_{xxs} > 0$) will lead to a smaller positive (or more negative) output response.

In summary, equation (7.7) shows that the standard's marginal impact on the equilibrium quantity may be positive or negative. The equilibrium quantity increases with a more stringent standard if the upward shift in the inverse demand function u_{xs} is larger than the upward shift in the inverse supply function c_{xs} and this effect is not offset by the rotation of demand and supply. In particular, if demand rotates clockwise ($u_{xxs} < 0$) while supply rotates counterclockwise ($c_{xxs} > 0$), the effect of a standard on output will be less positive (or more negative) for given values of u_{xs} and c_{xs}.

Next, we derive the standard's marginal impact on the different market players' interests using the envelope theorem. As before, the marginal change in consumer surplus $\Pi^C(s)$ is

$$\frac{\partial \Pi^C(s)}{\partial s} = u_s - \frac{dp}{ds}x^* = u_s - x^*\left(u_{xs} + \frac{dx^*}{ds}u_{xx}\right) \qquad (7.8)$$

Likewise, the marginal change in producer profits $\Pi^P(s)$ is

$$\frac{\partial \Pi^P(s)}{\partial s} = \frac{dw}{ds}x^* - c_s = x^*\left(c_{xs} + \frac{dx^*}{ds}c_{xx}\right) - c_s \qquad (7.9)$$

The marginal change in the retailer's profits $\Pi^R(s)$ is

$$\frac{\partial \Pi^R(s)}{\partial s} = x^*\left(u_{xs} - c_{xs}\right) \qquad (7.10)$$

The factor $u_{xs} - c_{xs}$ is the marginal change in the retailer's margin and may be positive or negative, depending on the relative shifts of the inverse demand and supply functions. Hence the standard's marginal impact on the retailer's profits may be positive or negative. More specifically, the term $x^* u_{xs}$ represents the marginal increase in the retailer's revenues because of the upward shift of the inverse demand function. As consumers' willingness to pay is higher for a product with a more stringent standard, a higher standard allows the retailer to set a higher consumer price for a given level of consumption x^*. The higher consumer price results in higher revenues for the retailer but also in higher consumption expenditures for consumers. We therefore define $x^* u_{xs}$ as the *rent transfer* *from consumers to the retailer* due to a higher standard. Similarly, the term $x^* c_{xs}$ is the marginal increase in the retailer's expenditures due to the upward shift in the inverse supply function. With a higher standard, the retailer pays a higher producer price for a given level of output x^* to compensate producers for their higher marginal production costs. The higher producer price results in higher expenditures for the retailer and in higher producer revenues. Hence, we define $x^* c_{xs}$ as the *rent transfer from the retailer to producers* because of a stricter standard. Equation (7.10) thus shows that the retailer's profits increase with a higher standard if the rent transfer from consumers is larger than the rent transfer to producers and vice versa.

We can now also analyze the standard's marginal impact on social welfare $W(s)$, which is defined as the sum of consumer surplus, producer profits, and retailer profits:

$$W(s) = \Pi^C(s) + \Pi^P(s) + \Pi^R(s) \tag{7.11}$$

The marginal change in social welfare is

$$\frac{\partial W}{\partial s} = u_s - c_s - x^* (u_{xx} - c_{xx}) \frac{dx^*}{ds} \tag{7.12}$$

and equals the direct welfare effects, that is, the efficiency gain u_s minus the implementation cost c_s, plus an additional welfare gain (loss) if the equilibrium quantity increases (decreases). Therefore social welfare may increase or decrease with a higher standard, depending on the relative size of these factors. Comparing (7.12) to equation (3.25), we thus see that the existence of an intermediary with market power adds a third term that depends on the markup of the retailer. Using equation (7.6) this third term can be written as $-x^* (u_{xx} - c_{xx})(dx^*/ds) = (u_x - c_x)(dx^*/ds) = (p - w)(dx^*/ds)$. If the retailer has no market power, $p = w$ and equation (7.12) reduces to equation (3.25). If the retailer has some market power, $p > w$ so that a positive output effect of the standard increases social welfare, ceteris paribus. Intuitively, the retailer is both a monopolist and a monopsonist, buying and supplying a suboptimal quantity. If a higher standard induces the retailer to procure and deliver higher quantities, this has a positive effect, all else equal.

In summary, it follows that all market players may gain or lose from a change in the standard, and that this change involves rent transfers between the different market players. Likewise, social welfare may either increase or decrease with a change in the standard, depending on the relative size of the efficiency gain, the implementation cost, and the different rent transfers.

7.5 Optimal Public and Private Standards

We analyze the optimal standard-setting behavior of both the retailer and the government. In line with most of the literature on minimum quality standards, we assume that the government moves first in setting its public standard.[8] We solve the game by backward induction and determine first the retailer's optimal private standard for a given level of the public standard. Then we determine the government's optimal public standard to finally compare the level of the retailer's optimal private standard s^R to the level of the government's optimal public standard $s^\#$.

7.5.1 The Retailer's Optimal Private Standard

Being the only intermediary agent between producers and consumers, the retailer is able to unilaterally impose a private standard. The retailer maximizes profits by imposing a private standard, given the market equilibrium in equation (7.6) that results from the retailer's own optimal price-setting behavior and the consumers' and producers' optimal price-taking behavior. Using equation (7.10), the retailer's optimal private standard s^R is determined by the following FOC, subject to $s^R \geq s^\#$:[9]

$$x^*\left(s^R\right)\left(u_{xs} - c_{xs}\right) = 0 \qquad (7.13)$$

Equation (7.13) shows that $u_{xs}x^*\left(s^R\right) = c_{xs}x^*\left(s^R\right)$ at s^R, which indicates that the rent transfer from consumers to the retailer equals the rent transfer from the retailer to producers at s^R. The retailer sets its private standard at a level where marginal revenues equal marginal expenditures from increasing the private standard. In addition, abstracting from the trivial case where $x^*\left(s^R\right) = 0$, equation (7.13) implies that $u_{xs} = c_{xs}$ at s^R, that is, that the retailer sets its optimal private standard such that the shift in the inverse demand function is equal to the shift in the inverse supply function.

---

[8]   Lutz et al. (2000) and McCluskey and Winfree (2009) assume that firms are the first movers in the standard-setting process, whereas other work on minimum quality standards (such as Boom, 1995; Leland, 1979; Ronnen, 1991; Valletti, 2000) typically assume the government to be the first mover in setting minimum quality standards.

[9]   This condition reflects that the standard that effectively regulates the market is $s = \max\{s^\#; s^R\}$. As second mover, the retailer has no incentive to set a private standard lower than the public one, $s^\#$, even if the retailer's optimal private standard is lower than the public standard. Hence, the retailer sets its private standard either at a higher level than or equal to the government's public standard (which is given at this stage), or the retailer refrains from setting a private standard.

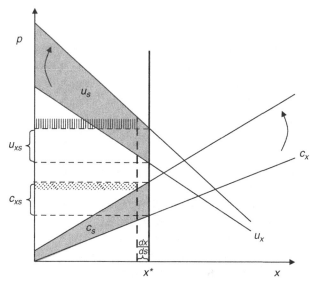

Figure 7.2. Social welfare and the retailer's optimal standard.

In general, the retailer's optimal private standard s^R does not coincide with the optimal standard for consumers and/or producers. The retailer standard s^R is optimal for consumers only if at s^R the standard's marginal effect on consumer surplus is zero. Equation (7.8) indicates that this occurs only if at s^R the efficiency gain u_s equals the marginal increase in expenditure $[u_{xs} + (dx^*/ds)\, u_{xx}]x^*(s^R)$. Likewise, s^R is optimal for producers only if at s^R the marginal increase in producers' revenues $[c_{xs} + (dx^*/ds)\, c_{xx}]x^*(s^R)$ equals the implementation cost c_s. Hence, only under very specific circumstances – depending on the efficiency gain, implementation cost, and the different rent transfers – the interests of consumers and/or producers coincide with the retailer's interests. In any other case, the interests of the various market players differ.

Likewise, equation (7.12) shows that the retailer's optimal private standard s^R equals the socially optimal standard s^* if and only if $u_s - c_s = x^*(u_{xx} - c_{xx})(dx^*/ds)$ at s^R. This is illustrated in Figure 7.2, which shows changes in social welfare for an infinitesimal increase in the standard starting from the retailer's optimal standard s^R. At the retailer's optimal standard, $u_{xs} = c_{xs}$; that is, the upward shift in demand equals the upward shift in supply at the equilibrium output level x^*. In the case drawn here, the demand curve rotates clockwise ($u_{xxs} < 0$) while supply rotates counterclockwise ($c_{xxs} > 0$) so that $dx/ds < 0$. Social welfare changes by $u_s - c_s - x^*(u_{xx} - c_{xx})(dx/ds)$. As drawn, the decrease in quantity leads to an increase in consumption expenditures (given by the vertically shaded area) as consumers move up on the demand curve. The increase in consumption expenditures equals $x^{*}u_{xx}$ (dx/ds). The decrease in quantity also leads to a decrease in producer revenues (given by the diagonally shaded area) as producers move down the supply curve. This decrease is given by $x^{*}c_{xx}$ (dx/ds). Only if $u_s - c_s$ is exactly equal to this combined effect would the retailer's optimal standard coincide with the social optimum. If $u_s - c_s$ is greater, the retailer's standard is too low from a social welfare perspective; if $u_s - c_s$ is smaller, the retailer's standard is too high.

The cause for the potential welfare suboptimality of the retailer's optimal private standard is that the retailer does not incorporate the direct utility and cost effects (u_s and c_s) into its profit maximizing behavior. The retailer only cares about maximizing the net rent transfer whereas the welfare calculus does take the net direct effects into account.

Importantly, even if the retailer's optimal private standard would be socially optimal, it need not be optimal for consumers and producers separately. Since s^R is optimal for the retailer, $\partial \Pi^R / \partial s \big|_{s^R} = 0$; if s^R is also socially optimal it must be that $\partial W / \partial s \big|_{s^R} = \partial \Pi^C / \partial s \big|_{s^R} + \partial \Pi^P / \partial s \big|_{s^R} = 0$ and hence $\partial \Pi^C / \partial s \big|_{s^R} = -\partial \Pi^P / \partial s \big|_{s^R}$. Only if both of the latter derivatives are zero do the optimal standards coincide; that is, even if the private standard were socially optimal, it would not necessarily be optimal for both consumers and producers at the same time.

7.5.2 The Government's Optimal Public Standard

We now analyze the public standard-setting behavior of a government that is interested in both interest group contributions and social welfare. For this purpose we build on the political economy model of public standards developed in Chapter 4. Without loss of generality, we assume that producers and the retailer are politically organized into separate interest groups that lobby simultaneously, but that consumers are not organized.[10]

The "truthful" contribution schedules of the producers and retailer are of the form $C^{\ell}(s) = \max\{0, \Pi^{\ell}(s) - b^{\ell} \mid s \geq s^R\}$ with $\ell = P, R$.[11] b^{ℓ} is a constant,

---

[10] Our assumption that consumers are not organized is not essential to the results, as we demonstrate in the Appendix, but it simplifies the exposition.

[11] The contribution schedules are conditional on $s \geq s^R$ to reflect that the standard which effectively regulates the market is $s = \max\{s^{*}; s^R\}$. Contributions in favor of a public standard lower than the optimal private standard have no effect on the standard that regulates the market (s^R), and thus have no impact on the interest groups' profits. Hence contributions in the interval $s < s^R$ would not be truthful and therefore the contribution schedule

a minimum level of profits the interest groups do not wish to spend on lobbying. The government's objective function $\Pi^G(s)$ is a weighted sum of the interest group contributions, weighted by α^ℓ, and social welfare, where α^ℓ represents the relative lobbying strength of the interest groups:

$$\Pi^G(s) = \sum_\ell \alpha^\ell C^\ell(s) + W(s) \tag{7.14}$$

The government chooses the level of the public standard to maximize its objective function (7.14).[12] The government's optimal public standard $s^\#$ is therefore determined by the following FOC, subject to $s^\# \geq s^R$:

$$\alpha^P \left[x^\# \left(c_{xs} + \frac{dx}{ds} c_{xx} \right) - c_s \right] + \alpha^R \left[x^\# \left(u_{xs} - c_{xs} \right) \right]$$
$$+ u_s - c_s + x^\# \left(u_{xx} - c_{xx} \right) \frac{dx}{ds} = 0 \tag{7.15}$$

Equation (7.15) implicitly defines $s^\#$ as a function of the lobbying strengths of the different interest groups α^ℓ, the efficiency gain u_s, the implementation cost c_s, the rent transfers $x^\# u_{xs}$ and $x^\# c_{xs}$, and the marginal change in producer revenues $x^\# [c_{xs} + (dx/ds) c_{xx}]$, all evaluated at $s^\#$.

7.5.3　A Comparison of the Retailer's Optimal Private Standard to the Government's Optimal Public Standard

We now compare the government's optimal public standard $s^\#$ to the retailer's optimal private standard s^R and analyze which factors determine their relative levels. Because production costs are sufficiently convex and consumer utility sufficiently concave in s to ensure that both Π^G and Π^R are concave in s, it suffices to determine the sign of the standard's marginal impact on the government's objective function at s^R, $\partial \Pi^G(s)/\partial s|_{s^R}$. Because of concavity, if $\partial \Pi^G(s)/\partial s|_{s^R} > 0$ then $s^R < s^\#$ and vice versa. Inserting into equation (7.15)

---

is restricted to $s \geq s^R$. However, because the government moves first in setting its public standard, this restriction of the contribution schedules does not imply that the government is not able to set a public standard in the interval $s < s^R$.

[12] Because the retailer is a monopolist, strong interactions between the government and the monopolist may exist. In the extreme case that the retail sector is a "state monopoly" and that the government is only concerned with the state monopoly's profits (i.e., the monopolist retailer's profits), the public standard would be set at the retailer's optimal private standard and the government's optimal public standard would coincide with the retailer's optimal private standard. Our assumption that the monopolist has some positive political power α^R – which could be large – is less extreme.

the results of equation (7.13) that $u_{xs} = c_{xs}$ at s^R, the expression for the standard's marginal impact on the government's objective function at s^R is

$$\left.\frac{\partial \Pi^G(s)}{\partial s}\right|_{s^R} = \underbrace{u_s - c_s + x^*(s^R)(u_{xx} - c_{xx})\frac{dx}{ds}}_{(1)} + \alpha^P \left[\underbrace{x^*(s^R)\left(c_{xs} + \frac{dx}{ds}c_{xx}\right) - c_s}_{(2)} \right],$$

$$(7.16)$$

which may be positive or negative. Part (1) of equation (7.16) equals the marginal social welfare effect of the standard at s^R (see equation (7.12)), and may be positive or negative. Part (2) represents the standard's marginal impact on producer profits at s^R. Part (2) may be positive or negative as well. Hence, *a priori*, it is not determined which of the two standards is more stringent. The retailer's optimal private standard may be higher or lower than the government's optimal public standard. We are particularly interested in the case where equation (7.16) is negative, that is, when the retailer's optimal private standard is more stringent than government's optimal public standard ($s^\# < s^R$), and which factors affect this.[13]

The key factors that lead to private standards being more stringent than public standards are summarized by equation (7.16). First, the marginal change in producers' revenues $x^*(s^R)[c_{xs} + (dx/ds)\,c_{xx}]$ plays an important role. If this term is smaller, the standard's marginal impact on producer profits at s^R (part (2) of equation (7.16)) is smaller such that equation (7.16) is more likely to be negative, and $s^\# < s^R$. A low value means that producers receive a smaller compensation for a higher standard. Ceteris paribus, producers thus bear a larger share of the implementation cost. The producers' interest group then lobbies in favor of a lower public standard and equation (7.16) is more likely to be negative, that is, $s^\# < s^R$.

Second, when producer profits are marginally decreasing in the standard at s^R, that is, when part (2) in equation (7.16) is negative, a larger political power of the producers' interest group α^P increases the likelihood

---

[13] Naturally, these same factors – in opposite direction – lead to the reverse situation where the retailer's optimal private standard is less stringent, that is, $s^R < s^\#$. However, this situation is not relevant since a private standard is redundant if less stringent than the public standard. Either the retailer sets its private standard at a higher level, or the retailer refrains from setting a private standard. As a consequence, the same factors as the ones we discuss (but in opposite direction) explain the absence of private standards in specific markets.

that equation (7.16) is negative and $s^\# < s^R$. In this case, producers lobby in favor of a public standard that is lower than the retailer's optimal private standard, and their larger political power means they can lobby more successfully, ceteris paribus, so that they are able to reduce the level of the government's optimal public standard.

Third, the size of the efficiency gain matters. If u_s is smaller, the marginal social welfare effect at s^R (part (1) of equation (7.16)) is smaller and equation (7.16) is more likely to be negative such that $s^\# < s^R$. A lower efficiency gain induces the government to set a lower public standard because of social welfare considerations, while the retailer does not take social welfare effects into account.

Fourth, the size of the implementation cost c_s affects both social welfare and producer profits. Equation (7.16) is more likely to be negative with a higher implementation cost, such that $s^\# < s^R$. The intuition behind this result is that a higher implementation cost causes the government to set a lower public standard, not only because of social welfare considerations but also because the producers' interest group lobbies in favor of a lower public standard. In contrast, the retailer is not concerned with social welfare effects, so that the retailer's optimal private standard is not affected by a change in the implementation cost. As a result of producer lobbying, a change in the implementation cost c_s has a larger impact on equation (7.16) than a similar change in the efficiency gain u_s (but in opposite direction), ceteris paribus.

Under these conditions, it is more likely that the retailer sets its optimal private standard at a higher level than the government's optimal public standard. Hence these factors may explain the observation that in some sectors, private standards are more stringent than public ones[14].

7.6 Extension: Side Payments

So far we have assumed that producers cannot directly influence the retailer's private standard-setting behavior. However, if producers are able to form into an interest group that influences the government's public standard-setting process through contributions, it is also conceivable that

---

[14] For instance, in a discussion of voluntary traceability standards in the U.S. food system, Golan et al. (2004) conclude that the extent and depth of these systems varies across industries, depending on varying costs, product characteristics, and industry organization. Traceability standards are higher in the fresh fruit and vegetables industry, as fresh produce needs to be boxed early in the supply chain, which implies that traceability imposes only minor additional costs on producers compared to other industries.

they engage in direct negotiations with the retailer to influence the retailer's private standard-setting behavior. In general, as discussed earlier, producers' interests do not coincide with the retailer's interests. Therefore, if the retailer's private standard would be more stringent than the public one, producers may make side payments to convince the retailer of setting a private standard that is more aligned with the producers' interests.[15] This section analyzes how side payments from producers to the retailer may affect the results of our model, that is, how the level of the retailer's optimal private standard compares to the level of the government's optimal public standard when side payments are possible.

To analyze the impact of these side payments, we need to make some additional assumptions. We assume that, after the public standard has been set by the government, the producers' interest group offers the retailer a truthful side payment schedule that specifies how much producers are willing to pay the retailer for each potential level of the private standard. The producers' truthful side payment schedule is of the form $\Omega(s) = \max\left\{0, \Pi^P(s) - \Pi^P(\max\{s^\#, s^R\}) \,|\, s \geq s^\#\right\}$.

The schedule implies that producers are willing to make side payments equal to at most the difference between their profits under a private standard s and their profits under the standard that regulates the market in the absence of side payments, that is, $\max\{s^\#, s^R\}$, where s^R and $s^\#$ are defined by respectively Equations (7.13) and (7.15). The side payments are restricted to the interval $s \geq s^\#$ because, given that the market is regulated by the most stringent standard, side payments for a private standard that is lower than the public standard $(s < s^\#)$ would have no impact on producers' profits, and would not be truthful.

Taking into account the producers' potential side payments, the retailer now maximizes $\Pi^R(s) + \Omega(s)$ when setting its private standard. The retailer's optimal private standard with side payments s^Ω is then determined by the following FOC, subject to $s^\Omega \geq s^\#$:[16]

$$x^*\left(s^\Omega\right)\left(u_{xs} + \frac{dx^*}{ds}c_{xx}\right) - c_s = 0 \qquad (7.17)$$

---

[15] Our formal treatment ignores the question of how side payments are implemented in practice. For instance, the retailer and the producers might sign a contract stipulating the private standard, the producer price, and a lump-sum side payment made by the producers. Such two-part tariffs are a common feature of vertical relationships in developed economies (see e.g., Rey and Vergé 2008). For simplicity, we assume producers' compensation to the retailer takes the form of a payment similar to the contributions made to politicians.

[16] The standard that effectively regulates the market is now $s = \max\{s^\#; s^\Omega\}$, and again the retailer has no incentive to set a private standard that is lower than the public one.

Equation (7.17) is equivalent to maximizing the joint surplus of the retailer and the producers. Hence, when setting a private standard with potential side payments, the retailer also takes the standard's marginal impact on producer profits into account. By making side payments to the retailer, producers obtain that the retailer internalizes the effect of a private standard on producer profits in its private standard-setting behavior.

As a consequence, these side payments may also have an impact on how the levels of the government's optimal public standard and the retailer's private standard compare to one another. Before we compare these levels, we first determine the government's optimal public standard $s^{\#}$ in the presence of side payments. To account for the potential side payments, the truthful contribution schedules of the producers and the retailer are adjusted to respectively $C^{P}(s) = \max\{0, \Pi^{P}(s) - \Omega(s^{\Omega}) - b^{P} \mid s \geq s^{\Omega}\}$ and $C^{R}(s) = \max\{0, \Pi^{R}(s) + \Omega(s^{\Omega}) - b^{R} \mid s \geq s^{\Omega}\}$.

The government's optimal public standard $s^{\#}$ is then determined by the following FOC, subject to $s^{\#} \geq s^{\Omega}$:

$$\alpha^{P}\left[x^{\#}\left(c_{xs} + \frac{dx}{ds}c_{xx}\right) - c_{s}\right] + \alpha^{R}\left[x^{\#}\left(u_{xs} - c_{xs}\right)\right]$$
$$+ u_{s} - c_{s} + x^{\#}\left(u_{xx} - c_{xx}\right)\frac{dx}{ds} = 0 \qquad (7.18)$$

Because the interest group's contribution schedules are truthful, that is, because the interest groups set their lobbying contributions in accordance with how their expected profits are *marginally* affected by the public standard, the side payments have no impact on the government's optimal public standard and the FOC in equation (7.18) is the same as without side payments in equation (7.15).

As earlier, to determine whether the retailer's optimal private standard with side payments is stricter than the government's optimal public standard, we need to determine the sign of the standard's marginal impact on the government's objective function at s^{Ω}, that is, $\partial \Pi^{G}(s) / \partial s \big|_{s^{\Omega}}$. If $\partial \Pi^{G}(s) / \partial s \big|_{s^{\Omega}} < 0$ then $s^{\#} < s^{\Omega}$, and vice versa. The expression for the standard's marginal impact on the government's objective function at s^{Ω} is

$$\underbrace{u_{s} - c_{s} + x^{*}\left(s^{\Omega}\right)\left(u_{xx} - c_{xx}\right)\frac{dx}{ds}}_{(1)} + (\alpha^{P} - \alpha^{R})\underbrace{\left[x^{*}\left(s^{\Omega}\right)\left(c_{xs} + \frac{dx}{ds}c_{xx}\right) - c_{s}\right]}_{(2)} \quad (7.19)$$

which may be positive or negative. Part (1) of equation (7.19) is the standard's marginal impact on social welfare at s^Ω, and can again be positive or negative. Part (2) of equation (7.19) represents the standard's marginal impact on producer profits at s^Ω which may also be positive or negative. The retailer's optimal private standard with side payments s^Ω may thus be higher or lower than the government's optimal public standard $s^\#$.

To examine how side payments affect the retailer's optimal private standard, it suffices to analyze whether producer profits are marginally increasing or decreasing in the retailer's optimal private standard *without* side payments, s^R. With side payments, the retailer's optimal private standard s^Ω maximizes the joint surplus of producers and the retailer, that is, $\partial\Pi^P/\partial s|_{s^\Omega} + \partial\Pi^R/\partial s|_{s^\Omega} = 0$. If the joint surplus is marginally increasing at s^R, then $s^R < s^\Omega$; if the joint surplus is marginally decreasing at s^R, then $s^\Omega < s^R$. However, since s^R is optimal for the retailer, $\partial\Pi^R/\partial s|_{s^R} = 0$. Hence, the joint surplus of producers and retailers is marginally increasing at s^R if and only if producer profits are marginally increasing at s^R and vice versa. The retailer's private standard thus moves in the direction preferred by producers.

The intuition behind the previous result is that if producer profits are marginally increasing at s^R, producers have an incentive to make side payments such that the retailer sets a higher private standard ($s^R < s^\Omega$). If $s^\# < s^R$, then the private standard with side payments is further away from the public standard ($s^\# < s^R < s^\Omega$). On the other hand, if $s^R < s^\#$, that is, if the retailer does not impose a private standard in the absence of side payments, producers' side payments may induce the retailer to set a private standard at a higher level than the public one, that is, $s^R < s^\# < s^\Omega$.

Conversely, if producer profits are marginally decreasing at s^R, and if the private standard without side payments is more stringent than the public standard ($s^\# < s^R$), producers have an incentive to make side payments to the retailer to lower its private standard. These side payments reduce the level of the private standard set by the retailer ($s^\Omega < s^R$) and the private standard is set closer to the government's optimal public standard. If the side payments are sufficiently large, they may even prevent the retailer from setting a private standard. In that case, the standard that governs the market is the public standard $s^\#$, and retailers receive side payments equal to $\Pi^P(s^\#) - \Pi^P(s^R)$. If side payments would not be allowed, the standard that governs the market would be s^R since $s^\# < s^R$.

In summary, side payments bring the retailer's private standard closer in line with producer interests. The private standard with side payments s^Ω will be higher than s^R if producer profits are marginally increasing at s^R, and lower if producer profits are marginally decreasing at s^R. Depending on circumstances, side payments may even reduce the private standard below the public standard, or may lead to the emergence of a private standard higher than the public standard where no such private standard existed before.

7.7 Conclusions

Private standards are frequently more stringent than their public counterparts. This phenomenon has been explained as the result of vertical differentiation or strategic standard setting to preempt public standards. This chapter provides an additional explanation. Modern supply chains often consist of a large number of small producers supplying an intermediary with considerable market power. Under certain conditions, these producers may use their political power to lobby for lower public standards, while the intermediary may use its market power to impose a higher private standard.

Several factors may cause the private standard to be more stringent than the public one. If producers receive a smaller compensation for an increase in the standard (which implies, ceteris paribus, that they bear a larger share of the implementation costs) and if producers have more political power, or if the utility gain to consumers of a higher standard is lower and/or if the implementation costs to producers are larger, the public standard is more likely to be lower than the retailer's private standard.

Producers could offer side payments to induce the retailer to bring its private standard more in line with producer interests. These side payments do not affect the public standard, but they do change the retailer's optimal private standard. Side payments will increase the private standard if producers want a higher standard than the retailer and vice versa.

In our analysis, we have assumed that the intermediary is a monopolist on the consumer side and a monopsonist on the producer side. It is straightforward to extend our analysis to the case where the retailer is a price taker on the consumer side but has monopsony power on the producer side, or the case where the retailer has market power over consumers but not over producers. In both cases, if the retailer is able to impose a private standard, our results remain valid.[17]

It is less straightforward to extend the analysis to an oligopoly/oligopsony (instead of a monopoly/monopsony). There are a number of analytical

[17] Under the assumption that the retailer has no market power on either side, the results of the model would be equivalent to assuming the absence of any intermediary. The analysis would then follow that of Mérel and Sexton (2012), who study the optimal quality standard for a producer organization managing a geographical indication. Using specific functional forms for demand and costs, they show that the producer organization has an incentive to oversupply quality. Their analysis confirms the implications of our model applied to the same context.

challenges. Multiple intermediaries would vertically differentiate to reduce competition on the consumer side. To study this, specific assumptions are needed about the structure of demand (e.g., using the standard vertical differentiation framework of Mussa and Rosen 1978) and about the type of competition (e.g., Bertrand vs. Cournot competition) between intermediaries. The present analysis by contrast has the benefit of using only minimal assumptions about functional forms. Moreover, if different intermediaries set different quality levels, producers must choose with which intermediary to interact. As different quality levels imply different costs, this might give rise to a segmentation of producers similar to the segmentation of consumers on the demand side.[18] The political game to determine the public standard would become more complex as a result.

7.8 Appendix

This appendix demonstrates that our assumption of politically unorganized consumers is not essential to our results. If we were to assume that consumers are organized and have a relative lobbying strength of α^C, the government's FOC would be

$$\alpha^P \frac{\partial \Pi^P \left(s^\#\right)}{\partial s} + \alpha^C \frac{\partial \Pi^C \left(s^\#\right)}{\partial s} + \alpha^R \frac{\partial \Pi^R \left(s^\#\right)}{\partial s} + \left[\frac{\partial W \left(s^\#\right)}{\partial s}\right] = 0 \quad (7.20)$$

Using equation (7.11) this can be rewritten as

$$\tilde{\alpha}^P \frac{\partial \Pi^P \left(s^\#\right)}{\partial s} + \tilde{\alpha}^R \frac{\partial \Pi^R \left(s^\#\right)}{\partial s} + \left[\frac{\partial W \left(s^\#\right)}{\partial s}\right] = 0 \quad (7.21)$$

where $\tilde{\alpha}^P = (\alpha^P - \alpha^C)/(1 + \alpha^C)$ and $\tilde{\alpha}^R = (\alpha^R - \alpha^C)/(1 + \alpha^C)$ denote the lobbying strength of respectively producers and retailers relative to consumers.

The intuition is that the government maximizes a weighted sum, so what matters is not the *absolute* weight assigned to different lobbying groups but rather the *relative* weights. It is therefore always possible to normalize the lobbying weights. One could thus interpret α^P and α^R as the relative lobbying strength of producers and retailers relative to consumers.

---

[18] In the model of Von Schlippenbach and Teichmann (2012) the duopolist retailers do not compete on quality; at most, their outputs are horizontally differentiated but not vertically. Thus, their model only looks at the producer side of the market. Moreover, while they show that a minimum quality standard can improve welfare, this standard is not set endogenously as in our model.

Butterflies and Political Economy
Dynamics in Standard Setting

8.1 Introduction

The models used in the previous chapters in this book were all static in nature. However, in many cases regulation and standards are introduced when preferences change (e.g., evolving social norms), environmental conditions change (e.g., climate change), or when new technologies become available (e.g., nuclear energy, genetic modification). These changes induce new policy questions to either allow new technologies or not or to try to change behavior in response of environmental and social concerns, or not. Some of these questions may be satisfactorily addressed by static models: comparing the impact of two sets of preferences may relate to differences between countries or differences at different points in time. However, the dynamics of the changes may imply issues that cannot be (easily) captured by a static model. What if some of these changes are temporary: Will they result in changes in standards? And, if so, will these standards be temporary as well, or will they last?

As an illustration, it is often argued that a series of food safety crises at the end of the 1990s in Western Europe[1] had a major impact on food standards and value chain regulations – as, for example, reflected in the 2002 General Food Law of the European Union. The crises triggered widespread media coverage, strong consumer reactions, and rapid responses from politicians and regulators. It is claimed that the impact of these public reactions, part of which were temporary, had a major influence on a series of standards that affect European food systems and value chains today, including the regulation of genetically modified (GM) food (McCluskey and Swinnen, 2011; Swinnen et al., 2010). Another, but related, example is the use of the

[1] This includes the outbreak of mad cow disease in 1996, swine fever in 1997, the dioxin crisis in 1999, and foot-and-mouth disease in 2001.

"precautionary principle" in policymaking. As David Vogel (2003) explains, this principle guided much of U.S. regulatory policy in the 1960s and 1970s, itself induced by widely publicized regulatory failures such as the 1962 thalidomide scandal, while the principle was not used in Europe. However, after the food safety crises of the 1990s in Europe and political changes in the United States, the situation is reversed. The precautionary principle is now guiding EU policymaking much more than that of the United States.

The possibility that small or temporary differences in initial conditions lead to large changes in outcomes is reminiscent of the "butterfly effect," as described by Smith (1991, p. 247): "A small blue butterfly sits on a cherry tree in a remote province of China. As is the way of butterflies, while it sits it occasionally opens and closes its wings. It could have opened its wings twice just now; but in fact it moved them just once – and the minuscule difference in the resulting eddies of air around the butterfly makes the difference between whether, two months later, a hurricane sweeps across southern England or harmlessly dies out over the Atlantic." Hence, the question is whether the dynamics of changes in, among others, preferences and technology may cause differences in standards and regulation, even among similar countries, and even when temporary shocks ("butterflies") have disappeared. To analyze this question, this chapter develops a dynamic political economy model of standards, in this case applied to technology regulation, by building on the previous chapters on the political economy of public standards. Our framework combines arguments about differences in consumer preferences and producer protectionism in a dynamic setting to explain why small differences in preferences between similar countries may lead to persistent differences in technology regulation, even after preference differences have disappeared (i.e., policy hysteresis).

Introducing dynamic elements in the political economy theory yields several additional results. First, our formal model shows that there exists a critical level of consumer preferences below which no technology regulation is imposed. Hence small variations in consumer preferences may determine whether a country imposes technology regulation or not. If consumer preferences are identical between countries and constant over time, countries adopt the same technology regulation and stick to the status quo independent of which technology regulation was initially imposed.

Second, when consumer preferences are different between countries and constant over time, different technology regulations may be imposed, and these differences may persist because of producer interests that change over time. If a government chooses to allow a technology, it continues to allow that technology independent of what the other government decides. If a government, however, chooses to ban that technology, it may continue to do so in the long run depending on the relative impacts of both regulatory options on consumers and producers, and their political power. A larger political power of producers leads to a larger range of situations in which the technology is banned in the long run, even though consumers prefer allowing it. In these situations producer interests are translated into *policy persistence*.

Third, we show that even a temporary difference in consumer preferences between countries, a "butterfly," may create a difference in technology regulation that may persist after the difference in consumer preferences has disappeared. We show that this *hysteresis*[2] in technology regulation is driven by producer protectionist motives.[3]

This chapter is structured as follows. In the next section we develop a general and dynamic political economy model of standards (applied to technology regulation). The following three sections apply this model to three different cases. In the first case, consumer preferences are identical between countries and constant over time. In the second case, consumer preferences are different between countries and constant over time. In the third case (the "butterfly" case), consumer preferences are only temporarily different between countries. We discuss the implications of our model and extend the model in several directions.

8.2 A Dynamic Political Economy Model of Standards

While the underlying analytical framework in this chapter builds on the analysis of Chapters 4 and 5, the complexity involved in a dynamic political

---

[2] Hysteresis is defined as "permanent effects of a temporary stimulus" (Göcke, 2002) and originates from physics and magnetism (Cross and Allan, 1988). See Göcke (2002) for an overview of various concepts of hysteresis as applied in economics.

[3] This chapter is related to research on hysteresis in socioeconomic behavior and policy. For example, Dixit (1989a) shows that output price uncertainty leads to investment hysteresis for certain ranges of entry and exit costs, and Dixit (1989b) and Baldwin and Krugman (1989) demonstrate that exchange rate fluctuations create similar hysteresis in firms' export decisions. Hysteresis is also shown to exist in labor markets where firing and hiring costs lead to persistence in unemployment (e.g., Belke and Göcke, 1999; Lindbeck and Snower, 1986). Our model is different from these contributions, both in the source of variation (small consumer preference variations) that triggers technology investment (or not), and in the hysteresis effect (persistence in technology regulation due to producer protectionism). Our chapter is also linked to research on path dependence in technical standards and technical lock-in by historical events (Arthur, 1989). This type of lock-in is driven by network externalities, increasing returns to adoption, or learning by doing. See, e.g., Cowan (1990), David (1985), Farrell and Saloner (1985), and Puffert (2002) for some historical cases.

economy approach makes it necessary to impose more structure regarding technologies and consumer preferences.

We assume two identical open economies $v = A, B$ with symmetric transportation costs (which could be small, but positive). In both countries we consider the same sector in which one product is produced and consumed. Two production technologies can be applied to create this product. The technologies differ in their cost efficiency, and consumers have some aversion to the "cheap" technology. All consumers rank products manufactured with the cheap technology as being of lower quality than products produced with the "expensive" technology, but are heterogeneous in their willingness to pay for this quality difference. One example is child labor – which is cheap – but consumers object to its use. Another example is the installation of expensive catalytic converters that, as preferred by consumers, reduce carbon dioxide emissions. A last example is conventional farming that uses non-GM seed versus biotechnology that applies GM seed. Using biotechnology is cheaper (Falck-Zepeda et al., 2000; Lapan and Moschini, 2007), but consumers have some aversion to GM products (Curtis et al., 2004). The applied production technology is a "credence" feature of the product: consumers cannot verify which technology has been used, even after consumption of the good (Roe and Sheldon, 2007).

8.2.1 Technology Regulation and Standards

In every period $t = 1, 2$, each country's government has to decide whether to approve the cheap technology or not by setting a standard s_t^v. We assume that there are only two possible levels (high and low) of this standard, that is, $s_t^v \in \{s_L, s_H\}$ with $s_H > s_L$, where s_L refers to a baseline safety and/or quality requirement satisfied by both technologies (see also Moschini et al., 2008). If the government sets $s_t^v = s_H$, the cheap technology is prohibited in country v at time t.

As in Chapter 5, we assume that the standard applies to all products *consumed or produced* in the country. That is, the standard applies to domestic producers whether they produce for the home or foreign market, and to all foreign producers who export to this country.[4] We assume that only the government can guarantee consumers that a good has been produced with the expensive technology. This implies that, in contrast to the analysis in Chapter 7, a producer who produces according to s_H is not able to credibly advertise his

---

[4] A standard could in theory apply to production only, to consumption only, or to imports only. The assumption that the standard applies to both production and consumption (and hence also imports) simplifies the analysis.

good as a high-standards product in a country where the government allows the use of the cheap technology (s_L), although the producer is allowed to sell his product on that market $(s_H > s_L)$.[5]

8.2.2 Producers

We assume that production is a function of a sector-specific input factor that is available in inelastic supply. All profits made in the sector accrue to this specific factor. In line with Besley and Ghatak (2007), we assume that there are more than three firms active in each country and that firms compete on prices. Aggregate producer profits at time t in country v are

$$\Pi_t^{P,v}\left(s_t^v\right) = \max_{p_t^v}\left\{x_t^v\left[p_t^v - c_{x,t}^v\left(s_t^v, s_{t-1}^v\right)\right] + L\right\}, \tag{8.1}$$

where p_t^v is the price of the good; x_t^v is the quantity produced; $c_{x,t}^v\left(s_t^v, s_{t-1}^v\right)$ is the marginal cost; and L is the sector-specific factor owners' total labor income, realized in some other sector(s).[6] Following Amacher et al. (2004) and consistent with Dixit (1980), Dong and Saha (1998), and Spence (1977), we use a specific form for the marginal cost function:

$$c_{x,t}^v\left(s_t^v, s_{t-1}^v\right) = b\left(s_t^v\right)^2 + a\left(s_t^v - s_{t-1}^v\right)^2, \tag{8.2}$$

where a and b are positive parameters. The first term, $b\left(s_t^v\right)^2$, represents the "cost of quality." As is typical in the vertical differentiation literature, it is a quadratic term: the marginal cost function is increasing and convex in the level of the standard (see, e.g., Ronnen, 1991; Valletti, 2000). The technology allowed under s_H is more expensive than under s_L: $b\left(s_H\right)^2 > b\left(s_L\right)^2$. The second term, $a\left(s_t^v - s_{t-1}^v\right)^2$, represents the "investment cost," which is an increasing and convex function of the difference between the standard of the current period and the standard of the previous period. If governments switch regulation between periods, producers need to adjust to the new regulation and incur a one-period increase in their marginal cost. This cost component can be interpreted as a capacity investment along the lines of Dixit (1980) and Spence (1977), which depends on the current and previous periods' regulations. All other production costs are normalized to zero.

---

[5] Because we assume Bertrand competition with more than three active firms per country (Section 8.2.2), this assumption is not essential to our results. However, it substantially reduces notational complexity and allows us to keep the analysis tractable.

[6] See also Grossman and Helpman (1994). This labor income ensures that producers' welfare is positive and their lobbying contributions credible.

We assume that $bs_L > a(s_H - s_L)$ to ensure that producing under the low-cost technology s_L is always cheaper than under the expensive technology s_H, even when producing under s_L involves an investment cost of switching from s_H to s_L.[7]

8.2.3 Consumers

In contrast with previous chapters, the analysis in this chapter requires us to impose a specific structure on consumer preferences. We impose a vertical differentiation representation of heterogeneous consumer preferences based on Mussa and Rosen (1978), Spence (1976a), and Tirole (1988). The underlying assumption is that if products with both technologies were available at the same price, all consumers would choose the high-standard product. Individuals consume at most one unit of the good and their preferences are described by the following utility function:

$$U_i = \begin{cases} \phi_i s_t^v - p_t^v & \text{if consumer } i \text{ buys the good with standard } s_t^v \text{ at price } p_t^v \\ 0 & \text{if consumer } i \text{ does not buy} \end{cases}$$

(8.3)

where ϕ_i is consumer i's preference parameter.[8] Consumers with higher ϕ_i have a higher willingness to pay for a product of higher quality, that is, with a more stringent standard s_t^v. The parameter ϕ_i thus captures the degree to which consumers care about quality. Consumers with $\phi_i < p_t^v / s_t^v$ do not consume the product. We assume that ϕ_i is uniformly distributed over the interval $\left[1 - \phi_t^v, \phi_t^v\right]$ with $\phi_t^v \geq 1$ and $i \in \{1, \dots, M\}$, where M is the number of consumers, which we assume to be constant over time and identical between countries. The aggregate demand function

$$Q_t^v\left(p_t^v, s_t^v\right) = M\left(\phi_t^v - p_t^v / s_t^v\right),$$

(8.4)

is presumed to be positive at market equilibrium. Consumer surplus in country v at time t is

---

[7] Given that the expensive technology was in use before, producing with the expensive technology costs bs_H^2, whereas producing with the cheap technology requires investment and costs $bs_L^2 + a(s_H - s_L)^2$. The former costs are larger than the latter if $(s_H + s_L) > a(s_H - s_L)$, which is true under our assumption.

[8] Our approach of modeling standards is common in the literature on vertical differentiation and GM technology (see, e.g., Fulton and Giannakas, 2004; Moschini et al., 2008) and consistent with the standard approach in the literature on minimum quality standards (see, e.g., Jeanneret and Verdier, 1996; Ronnen, 1991; Valletti 2000).

$$\Pi_t^{C,v}\left(s_t^v\right) = M \int_{p_t^v / s_t^v}^{\phi_t^v} \left(\phi_i s_t^v - p_t^v\right) d\phi_i$$

$$= \frac{M s_t^v}{2}\left(\phi_t^v - \frac{p_t^v}{s_t^v}\right)^2 \tag{8.5}$$

8.2.4 The Government

As in previous chapters, the government maximizes a weighted sum of contributions from interest groups and social welfare. Social welfare $W_t^v(s_t^v)$ is defined as the sum of producer profits and consumer surplus:

$$W_t^v\left(s_t^v\right) \equiv \Pi_t^{P,v}\left(s_t^v\right) + \Pi_t^{C,v}\left(s_t^v\right). \tag{8.6}$$

Interest groups offer contributions to the government conditional on the policy chosen by the government. For simplicity, we assume that only producers are politically organized, and that an interest group cannot contribute to a foreign government.[9] The government's objective function, $\Pi_t^{G,v}\left(s_t^v\right)$, is

$$\Pi_t^{G,v}\left(s_t^v\right) \equiv \alpha^P C_t^{P,v}\left(s_t^v\right) + W_t^v\left(s_t^v\right), \tag{8.7}$$

where $C_t^{P,v}\left(s_t^v\right)$ is the "truthful" contribution schedule of the producers' interest group (see Chapter 4); and α^P represents its relative lobbying strength. Because the government's regulatory choice is dichotomous, this truthful contribution function need only to comprise two numbers (see Grossman and Helpman, 1995), that is, the contributions associated with allowing the cheap technology, $C_t^{P,v}\left(s_L\right)$, or banning it, $C_t^{P,v}\left(s_H\right)$. We therefore define the truthful contribution function of the producers' interest group as $C_t^{P,v}\left(s_t^v\right) \equiv \Pi_t^{P,v}\left(s_t^v\right)$.

8.2.5 Time Framework

We assume that agents do not take future periods into consideration when making decisions, that is, they have a "myopic planning horizon" (Göcke, 2002).[10]

---

[9] This assumption makes the derivation simpler but is not essential for the results. Consumer interests still play a role but through the social welfare function in the government's objective function (see the Appendix of Chapter 7).

[10] An alternative assumption would be that agents have perfect foresight, so that agents' decisions in period 1 are affected by their expectations of the optimal behavior of all agents

Each period consists of several sequential moves that take place simultaneously in both countries. At the beginning of each period, agents take stock of the existing technologies. The producers' interest group then proposes its contribution schedule to the government that chooses the standard. On policy selection, producers make the necessary investments if the level of the standard has altered between periods. Finally, products are produced and sold, and the producers' interest group makes its political contributions.

A government maintains the existing standard if and only if

$$\Pi_t^{G,\nu}\left(s_t^\nu = s_{t-1}^\nu\right) \geq \Pi_t^{G,\nu}\left(s_t^\nu \neq s_{t-1}^\nu\right), \tag{8.8}$$

In the remainder of this chapter, we assume that only the expensive technology is available before period 1, and that therefore, by default, governments in both countries initially set their standard to s_H. This resembles a situation in which the expensive technology is a conventional existing technology, and the cheap technology is an innovation that becomes available in period 1.[11]

In the next sections, we analyze the governments' regulatory choices under different scenarios: (1) a baseline case when consumers in both countries have identical preferences, and these preferences are constant over time; (2) the case in which consumer preferences are constant over time but differ between countries; and (3) a temporary difference in consumer preferences (a "butterfly").

8.3 Case (1): Constant and Identical Consumer Preferences between Countries

Consider the case where consumers in both countries have constant and identical preferences, $\phi_1^A = \phi_2^A = \phi_1^B = \phi_2^B$. Under our assumptions, both

---

in period 2. However, under this alternative assumption of perfect foresight it would not be possible to analyze sudden "black swan" events, that is, events that are unexpected but have potentially large consequences, as agents would expect and foresee such events. Hence, although our assumption of myopic agents may be a rather extreme one, it allows us to analyze this particular type of events. The analysis under the alternative assumption of perfect foresight would be more complex and would generate some additional potential equilibria, but the model's outcomes with myopic agents would still hold albeit for a smaller range of parameter values.

[11] This resembles the case of biotechnology regulation. Oppositely, for issues such as child labor or carbon dioxide emissions, the expensive technology is an innovation that becomes available in period 1. In these cases the default option is to allow the cheap technology and conditions for regulatory hysteresis can be obtained in the same analytical framework as presented here. We discuss this in more detail at the end of Section 8.5.

countries are identical and with Bertrand competition and positive trade costs, there is no international trade. Thus, it suffices to look at one country.

Period 1

The cheap technology becomes available. If the government prohibits its use $\left(s_1^\nu = s_H\right)$, marginal costs remain $c_{x,1}^\nu(s_H) = b(s_H)^2$. If the government allows the cheap technology $(s_1^\nu = s_L)$, firms need to incur switching costs, so that the marginal cost is $c_{x,1}^\nu(s_L) = b(s_L)^2 + a\Delta^2$, where $\Delta \equiv s_H - s_L$. Under the assumption of Bertrand competition with more than three producers in each country, the market price equals the marginal cost of domestic producers, $p_1^\nu = c_{x,1}^\nu$, and $\Pi_1^{P,\nu}(s_H) = \Pi_1^{P,\nu}(s_L) = L$. Hence, producers are indifferent to the level of the standard in period 1. In particular, if switching costs are incurred, these are passed on to consumers.

As price equals marginal cost, consumer surplus $\Pi_1^{C,\nu}$ is equal to $\left(Ms_H/2\right)\left(\phi_1^\nu - bs_H\right)^2$ if only the expensive technology is allowed, and $\left(Ms_L/2\right)\left(\phi_1^\nu - bs_L - a\Delta^2/s_L\right)^2$ if the cheap technology is allowed. Consumers prefer to ban the cheap technology if $\Pi_1^{C,\nu}(s_H) \geq \Pi_1^{C,\nu}(s_L)$, or equivalently, if

$$\phi_1^\nu \geq \tilde{\phi}_1^{C,\nu} = \frac{1}{\left(\sqrt{s_H} - \sqrt{s_L}\right)}\left[b\left(s_H^{3/2} - s_L^{3/2}\right) - a\frac{\Delta^2}{\sqrt{s_L}}\right], \qquad (8.9)$$

where $\tilde{\phi}_1^{C,\nu}$ is the consumers' critical preference value in country ν and period 1.[12] If consumers' concern for quality is below this critical preference value, they prefer allowing the cheap technology.

As producers are indifferent, the government follows consumers' interests and the government's threshold $\tilde{\phi}_1^{G,\nu}$ coincides with $\tilde{\phi}_1^{C,\nu}$. Thus, the government prohibits the cheap technology if and only if

$$\phi_1^\nu \geq \tilde{\phi}_1^{G,\nu} = \frac{1}{\left(\sqrt{s_H} - \sqrt{s_L}\right)}\left[b\left(s_H^{3/2} - s_L^{3/2}\right) - a\frac{\Delta^2}{\sqrt{s_L}}\right]. \qquad (8.10)$$

Hence, given equal consumer preferences between countries, a threshold $\tilde{\phi}_1^{G,\nu}$ exists such that if consumers' concern for quality ϕ_1^ν is strictly lower than $\tilde{\phi}_1^{G,\nu}$, country ν's government allows the cheap technology and

---

[12] Consumer surplus is convex in ϕ_t^ν so $\Pi_t^{C,\nu}(s_H) = \Pi_t^{C,\nu}(s_L)$ has two solutions in ϕ_t^ν. Throughout this chapter, our analysis is restricted to the domain $\phi_t^\nu \geq \phi^{\min} = b(s_H + s_L) + a\Delta$, where higher consumer preferences for quality lead to larger consumer surplus differences between high and low standards.

the politically optimal standard is $s_1^v = s_L$. If ϕ_1^v is higher than $\tilde{\phi}_1^{G,v}$, the politically optimal standard is $s_1^v = s_H$ and the government prohibits the cheap technology. This "knife-edge" result shows that a minor difference in consumer preferences can lead to important differences in technology regulation.

A larger marginal "cost of quality," represented by parameter b, results in a larger threshold $\tilde{\phi}_1^{G,v}$, that is, $(\partial \tilde{\phi}_1^{G,v}/\partial b) > 0$, and thus in a larger range of consumer preferences ϕ_1^v for which the cheap technology is allowed. This is intuitive: for larger b the additional "cost of quality" of producing with the expensive technology is larger. It will be optimal to ban the cheap technology only if consumers have a correspondingly greater concern for quality, which is reflected in a higher threshold $\tilde{\phi}_1^{G,v}$.

By contrast, a higher switching cost between regulations (represented by a larger value of a) reduces the government's threshold $\tilde{\phi}_1^{G,v}$ $(\partial \tilde{\phi}_1^{G,v}/\partial a < 0)$.

With higher switching costs, consumers pay relatively more for the low standards product and are thus less in favor of allowing the cheap technology. This is represented by a lower threshold $\tilde{\phi}_1^{G,v}$ and thus a smaller range of consumer preferences ϕ_1^v for which the government will allow the cheap technology ($s_1^v = s_L$).

Period 2

The political equilibrium in period 2 is to maintain the regulations set in period 1. If the cheap technology was prohibited in period 1, the government will continue to prohibit it; if the cheap technology was allowed, the government will continue to allow it in period 2.

To see this, first consider the case where the cheap technology was prohibited in period 1 ($s_1^v = s_H$). The situation in period 2 is exactly the same as in the previous period, since in both periods $s_{t-1}^v = s_H$ and consumer preferences are constant. The government's threshold in period 2 is therefore the same as in period 1, $\tilde{\phi}_2^{G,v} = \tilde{\phi}_1^{G,v}$. Given our assumption of constant consumer preferences, $\phi_2^v = \phi_1^v$, and it follows that $\phi_2^v \geq \tilde{\phi}_2^{G,v}$. Hence, if the political equilibrium is to prohibit the cheap technology in the first period, the ban on the cheap technology remains in the second period, that is, $s_2^v = s_H$.

Second, suppose that $\phi_1^v < \tilde{\phi}_1^{G,v}$ such that the cheap technology was allowed ($s_1^v = s_L$) and producers invested in the cheap technology in period 1. Even though the cheap technology is of lower quality, consumers were sufficiently attracted by the lower prices to induce the government to allow the cheap technology in period 1. However, in period 2, producers no longer need to incur the cost of switching from the expensive to the cheap technology. Prices in period 2 will therefore be even lower than in period 1, and consumers will be even more supportive of the cheap technology. More formally, given our assumption of Bertrand competition, producers are in period 2 again indifferent to the level of the standard and the government's decision is determined only by consumer welfare. The consumers' critical preference value (and therefore the government's threshold) changes with respect to period 1 as a result of the lower price of the cheap technology. In addition, production with the expensive technology is now more costly because cost to switch back to the expensive technology would need to be incurred. The government's threshold in period 2 is then

$$\tilde{\phi}_2^{G,v} = \tilde{\phi}_2^{C,v} = \frac{1}{\left(\sqrt{s_H} - \sqrt{s_L}\right)}\left[b\left(s_H^{3/2} - s_L^{3/2}\right) + a\frac{\Delta^2}{\sqrt{s_H}}\right]. \qquad (8.11)$$

Comparing equations (8.10) and (8.11) shows that $\tilde{\phi}_2^{G,v} > \tilde{\phi}_1^{G,v}$, and given constant consumer preferences, we find that $\phi_2^v < \tilde{\phi}_2^{G,v}$. Hence, if the cheap technology is allowed in the first period and consumer preferences are constant, the political equilibrium is to continue allowing the cheap technology in the second period, that is, $s_2^v = s_L$.

Our dynamic political economy model thus shows that, if consumer preferences are identical between countries and constant over time, governments impose the same regulation in each period; once a government has imposed a certain regulation, it endorses the status quo. Moreover, minor differences in consumer preferences can cause different technology regulations which persist over time.

8.4 Case (2): Constant and Different Consumer Preferences between Countries

Without loss of generality, we assume that country A's consumers have higher preferences for quality than country B's consumers. Preferences remain constant over time: $\phi_1^A = \phi_2^A > \phi_1^B = \phi_2^B$.

Period 1

The analysis of the political equilibrium in period 1 is similar to that of case (1). The cheap technology becomes available in both countries.

Prohibiting that technology means marginal costs remain unchanged at $c_{x,1}^{v}(s_H) = b(s_H)^2$, while approving it requires switching costs so that the marginal cost becomes $c_{x,1}^{v}(s_L) = b(s_L)^2 + a\Delta^2$.

Producers are again indifferent to the level of the standard, since even if country A and B would end up with different regulations, producers would only supply their own market. As in case (1), the market price in each country then equals the marginal cost of the domestic producers, $p_1^{v} = c_{x,1}^{v}$, and $\Pi_1^{P,v}(s_H) = \Pi_1^{P,v}(s_L) = L$. To see why producers only supply their own market, first note that if the standards in both countries are the same, the situation is exactly as in case (1), with transport costs preventing trade. When standards are different between both countries, however, trade will still not occur. If country A has the more stringent standard ($s_1^{A} = s_H$ and $s_1^{B} = s_L$), producers in country B cannot export to country A because their products do not meet the more stringent standard in country A. On the other hand, producers in country A are using the more expensive technology. Because they are unable to credibly advertise their products as "high standards" on country B's market, producers in country A have a cost disadvantage and hence cannot compete on country B's market. Producers thus only supply their domestic markets, which implies that $\Pi_1^{P,v}(s_H) = \Pi_1^{P,v}(s_L) = L$, and hence that producers are indifferent to the level of the standard in period 1.

Because the situation is the same as in case (1) for both countries, the consumers' critical preference value $\tilde{\phi}_1^{C,v}$ is still given by equation (8.9) for $v = A, B$. From our assumption that $\phi_t^{B} < \phi_t^{A}$ follow three potential orderings of consumer preferences. First, if $\phi_1^{B} < \phi_1^{A} < \tilde{\phi}_1^{C,v}$, country A and country B permit the cheap technology in both periods. Likewise, if $\tilde{\phi}_1^{C,v} < \phi_1^{B} < \phi_1^{A}$, country A and country B prohibit the cheap technology in both periods. The analysis of these two cases is identical to that of case (1).

However, if $\phi_1^{B} < \tilde{\phi}_1^{C,v} < \phi_1^{A}$, country A's consumers prefer banning the cheap technology ($\phi_1^{A} > \tilde{\phi}_1^{C,A}$) while country B's consumers are in favor of allowing it $\left(\phi_1^{B} < \tilde{\phi}_1^{C,B}\right)$. We focus on this situation. As producers are indifferent between the two technologies, the government's threshold is $\tilde{\phi}_1^{G,v} = \tilde{\phi}_1^{C,v}$ for $v = A, B$. Hence, country A's government bans the cheap technology ($s_1^{A} = s_H$), while country B's government allows it ($s_1^{B} = s_L$). This difference in regulation is due to different consumer preferences, and the differences in consumer preferences need not be large to result in different regulations.

Period 2

Assuming the different preferences in country A and country B lead to different regulations in period 1, in period 2 the marginal costs associated with the two technologies are different between the countries. The choice between the two technologies now becomes a strategic decision. We first analyze country B's political equilibrium for each regulation selected by country A, and then analyze country A's political equilibrium.

The political equilibrium in country B is to maintain the status quo of allowing the cheap technology ($s_2^B = s_L$), regardless of the decision made by country A in period 2. Suppose that country A maintains its ban such that $s_2^A = s_H$. Both producers and consumers in country B then prefer to keep allowing the cheap technology. If country B keeps using the cheap technology, its producers have a cost advantage over country A where the more expensive technology is used. In contrast, if country B switches to a higher standard ($s_2^B = s_H$), both countries are using the more expensive technology but country A has a cost advantage, as country B's producers need to invest in switching technologies whereas country A's producers do not.[13] Hence, country B's producers are driven out of their own market with $s_2^B = s_H$, and therefore favor $s_2^B = s_L$. Country B's consumers also prefer allowing the cheap technology. With the cheap technology, country B's domestic market price is $p_2^B = b(s_L)^2$, while under a ban on the cheap technology the domestic market price increases to $p_2^B = b(s_H)^2$ because the price is then determined by the marginal costs of using the expensive technology in country A. With these prices, the consumers' critical preference value for country B in period 2, $\tilde{\phi}_2^{C,B}$, is

$$\tilde{\phi}_2^{C,B} = \frac{1}{\left(\sqrt{s_H} - \sqrt{s_L}\right)}\left[b\left(s_H^{3/2} - s_L^{3/2}\right)\right]. \tag{8.12}$$

Comparing equations (8.12) and (8.9), we see that $\tilde{\phi}_1^{C,B} < \tilde{\phi}_2^{C,B}$. Because consumer preferences are constant ($\phi_1^B = \phi_2^B$), and since country B was already allowing the cheap technology ($\phi_1^B < \tilde{\phi}_1^{C,B}$), it follows that $\phi_2^B < \tilde{\phi}_2^{C,B}$ so that country B's consumers prefer to allow the cheap technology in period 2 as well. As a result, because both country B's producers and consumers favor allowing the cheap technology, it is in the interest of country B's government

---

[13] This requires that transportation costs are smaller than the difference between $c_{x,2}^A(s_H)$ and $c_{x,2}^B(s_H)$. We assume that transportation costs are sufficiently small and do not introduce them algebraically.

to endorse this status quo (i.e., $s_2^B = s_L$) if country A maintains its ban on the cheap technology ($s_2^A = s_H$).

Suppose, however, that country A switches regulations and allows the cheap technology in period 2, such that $s_2^A = s_L$. In this case, country B will again prefer to maintain the status quo of allowing the cheap technology, as producers are indifferent and consumers prefer the cheap technology.

Country B's producers are indifferent regarding the standard. Under $s_2^B = s_L$, country B's producers competitively dominate country A's producers on prices since producers in country A incur switching costs: the marginal costs are given by $b(s_L)^2$ in country B but by $b(s_L)^2 + a\Delta^2$ in country A. The market price in both countries is then $p_2^y = b(s_L)^2$. Although producers in country B now export to country A, price competition implies that this does not result in extra profits. On the other hand, if country B would switch to a higher standard ($s_2^B = s_H$), country B's domestic market is protected from imports by a more stringent standard $\left(s_2^B > s_2^A\right)$. Producers in country B incur switching costs but these are passed on to consumers and profits are again unaffected. Hence, if country A allows the cheap technology ($s_2^A = s_L$), producers in country B have the same profit level regardless of what standard is adopted in country B: $\Pi_2^{P,B}(s_H) = \Pi_2^{P,B}(s_L) = L$.

Country B's consumers are, however, not indifferent, as the quality levels and corresponding market prices are different for $s_2^B = s_L$ and $s_2^B = s_H$. If country B continues to allow the cheap technology, consumers benefit from lower prices than in period 1 as the investment cost has already been incurred by country B's producers. On the other hand, if country B imposes the expensive technology, producers in country B pass on their switching costs to consumers. The consumers' critical preference value, $\tilde{\phi}_2^{C,B}$, is then given by equation (8.11), which is higher than in period 1 (equation (8.9)): $\tilde{\phi}_2^{C,B} > \tilde{\phi}_1^{C,B}$. Because consumer preferences are constant ($\phi_1^B = \phi_2^B$) and because consumers preferred the cheap technology in period 1 ($\phi_1^B < \tilde{\phi}_1^{C,B}$), it follows that $\phi_2^B < \tilde{\phi}_2^{C,B}$. Country B's consumers thus still prefer allowing the cheap technology. Because country B's producers are indifferent, the government of country B follows consumers' preferences. Thus, if country A allows the cheap technology in period 2, the political-economic optimum in country B is to keep allowing the cheap technology ($s_2^B = s_L$).

To summarize, the optimum for country B's government is to continue its policy of allowing the cheap technology, that is, $s_2^B = s_L$, irrespective of country A's regulation in period 2. There is policy persistence: once country B's government has chosen to allow the cheap technology, it endorses the status quo in future periods and supports the cheap technology, irrespective of the behavior of the other country's government.

Given this result, to evaluate country A's strategic response we only need to consider the case where $s_2^B = s_L$. This strategic response is not straightforward. Although producers in country A always endorse the status quo, consumers may or may not favor switching to the cheaper technology.

If country A maintains its ban on the cheap technology ($s_2^A = s_H$), its producers are protected from imports by a more stringent standard since $s_2^A > s_2^B$. Given price competition, $p_2^A = b(s_H)^2$ and $\Pi_2^{P,A}(s_H) = L$. On the other hand, if country A now allows the cheap technology ($s_2^A = s_L$), country A's producers are at a disadvantage compared to country B. The marginal cost of country A's producers is $c_{x,2}^A(s_L) = b(s_L)^2 + a\Delta^2$ because they need to invest in switching, while country B's producers already made this investment and produce at $c_{x,2}^B(s_L) = b(s_L)^2$. In that case, country A's producers see their profits reduced to $\Pi_2^{P,A}(s_L) = L - aM\Delta^2[\phi_2^A - bs_L]$ as a result of cheaper imports from country B.[14] Accordingly, country A's producers always endorse the status quo in period 2, since

$$\Pi_2^{P,A}(s_H) - \Pi_2^{P,A}(s_L) = aM\Delta^2[\phi_2^A - bs_L] > 0. \qquad (8.13)$$

By contrast, country A's consumers do not necessarily favor the status quo in period 2. If the ban on the cheap technology is maintained ($s_2^A = s_H$), consumers buy high standards at a high price, and their consumer surplus is given by $\Pi_2^{C,A}(s_H) = (Ms_H/2)(\phi_2^A - bs_H)^2$. If the cheap technology is allowed ($s_2^A = s_L$), consumers buy cheaper but lower quality imports and their consumer surplus is $\Pi_2^{C,A}(s_L) = (Ms_L/2)(\phi_2^A - bs_L)^2$. Hence

$$\Pi_2^{C,A}(s_H) - \Pi_2^{C,A}(s_L) = \frac{Ms_H}{2}(\phi_2^A - bs_H)^2 - \frac{Ms_L}{2}(\phi_2^A - bs_L)^2, \quad (8.14)$$

which may be positive or negative and equals zero at the consumers' critical preference value $\tilde{\phi}_2^{C,A}$, that is,

$$\tilde{\phi}_2^{C,A} = \frac{1}{\left(\sqrt{s_H} - \sqrt{s_L}\right)}\left[b\left(s_H^{3/2} - s_L^{3/2}\right)\right]. \qquad (8.15)$$

Comparing values (8.15) and (8.9) reveals that $\tilde{\phi}_1^{C,A} < \tilde{\phi}_2^{C,A}$. Hence, there is now a wider range of preferences for which the cheap technology would be chosen by consumers. Intuitively, in period 2 the low standards good can be

[14] This rests on the implicit assumption that country A's producers remain active in their domestic market, for example, due to exit costs that are larger than $M\Delta^2[\phi_2^A - bs_L]$. To ensure credible contributions from the producers' interest group, we assume that L is large enough such that $\Pi_2^{P,A}(s_L)$ is positive.

imported from country B at a lower price than in period 1 when it was still more expensive due to the switching costs. This makes the low standards good more attractive to country A's consumers.

There are two possible situations depending on the level of country A's consumer preferences, ϕ_2^A. First, if $\tilde{\phi}_1^{C,A} < \tilde{\phi}_2^{C,A} < \phi_2^A$, country A's consumers still favor the status quo in period 2, that is, $s_2^A = s_H$. As a result, it is optimal for country A's government to maintain $s_2^A = s_H$ as country A's producers also endorse the status quo.

In the second situation, $\tilde{\phi}_1^{C,A} < \phi_2^A < \tilde{\phi}_2^{C,A}$, country A's consumers are in favor of allowing the cheap technology in period 2, in contrast to the first period. In this situation, a coalition switch takes place between period 1 and 2. Producer interests have changed from being indifferent to favoring s_H, while consumer interests have changed from favoring s_H to favoring s_L. Producers and consumers now have opposing interests. Which regulation is then optimal for country A's government depends on the relative differences in producer profits and consumer surpluses between the two regulatory options, and the relative weight α^P of producers' contributions in the government's objective function. Inserting equations (8.13) and (8.14) into equations (8.6) and (8.7) gives

$$\Psi \equiv \Pi_2^{G,A}\left(s_H\right) - \Pi_2^{G,A}\left(s_L\right)$$
$$= \left(1 + \alpha^P\right) a M \Delta^2 \left[\phi_2^A - b s_L\right] + \frac{M s_H}{2}\left(\phi_2^A - b s_H\right)^2 - \frac{M s_L}{2}\left(\phi_2^A - b s_L\right)^2 \quad (8.16)$$

The government's threshold $\tilde{\phi}_2^{G,A}$ is defined as the value of ϕ_2^A for which $\Psi = 0$. To see how the government's threshold compares to the critical preference value of consumers, note that the second and third term of equation (8.16) together are identical to equation (8.14), which by definition equals zero at $\tilde{\phi}_2^{C,A}$. Because the first term is positive, it follows that $\Psi > 0$ at $\phi_2^A = \tilde{\phi}_2^{C,A}$. Finally, Ψ is increasing in ϕ_2^A (for $\phi_2^A > \phi^{min}$). Combining these three findings, it follows that

$$\tilde{\phi}_2^{G,A} < \tilde{\phi}_2^{C,A}. \quad (8.17)$$

This inequality implies that for a certain range of consumer preferences, $\phi_2^A \in [\tilde{\phi}_2^{G,A}, \tilde{\phi}_2^{C,A})$, lobbying by the producers' interest group is sufficiently powerful to induce country A's government to uphold the regulatory status quo even though consumers prefer to allow the cheap technology. For $\phi_2^A \in [\tilde{\phi}_1^{C,A}, \tilde{\phi}_2^{G,A})$, the producers' interest group fails in pushing its agenda and the optimal decision for country A's government is to allow the cheap technology.

The value of $\tilde{\phi}_2^{G,A}$ depends on the political power of the producers' interest group, α^P. From equation (8.16) it follows that Ψ is increasing in α^P. Using the implicit function theorem, it can be shown that

$$\frac{d\tilde{\phi}_2^{G,A}}{d\alpha^P} < 0. \tag{8.18}$$

The government's threshold $\tilde{\phi}_2^{G,A}$ thus decreases if the political power of producers increases. If the producers' interest group has more influence on the government, the range $[\tilde{\phi}_2^{G,A}, \tilde{\phi}_2^{C,A})$ for which the government chooses to endorse the status quo expands. In the special case where α^P is sufficiently high such that $\tilde{\phi}_2^{G,A} \leq \tilde{\phi}_1^{C,A}$, country A's government always prohibits the cheap technology since $\tilde{\phi}_1^{C,A} < \phi_1^A = \phi_2^A$.

Our dynamic political economy model shows that differences in consumer preferences between countries may lead to differences in technology regulation. These regulatory differences may persist over time, however, not only because of the differences in consumer preferences but also for reasons of producer protectionism. This is driven by the investment cost that induces producers in both countries to switch from being indifferent in the first period to supporting the status quo in the second period. If a government initially chooses to allow the cheap technology, its optimal policy is the regulatory status quo no matter what the other government decides. If a government chooses to ban the cheap technology, it prefers the regulatory status quo depending on the relative impacts on consumers and producers of both regulatory options, and the political power of the producers' interest group. A larger political power of the producers' interest group leads to a larger range of circumstances where the status quo is maintained, even though consumers oppose it. Different technology regulations are initiated by differences in consumer preferences, but persistence in these regulatory differences is motivated by producers' interests.

8.5 Case (3): A Temporary Difference in Consumer Preferences

In this section, we show that even if the difference in consumer preferences is only temporary and potentially small (a "butterfly"), hysteresis in technology regulation and long-lasting regulatory differences between countries may emerge. To this end, we assume that country A initially has higher consumer preferences than country B ($\phi_1^A > \phi_1^B$) but in period 2 consumer preferences are identical ($\phi_2^A = \phi_2^B$). We consider two potential scenarios. In the first scenario, country A's consumer preferences fall to the level of those in country B, which have remained constant ($\phi_1^B = \phi_2^B$). In the second scenario, country B's consumer preferences rise to the level of those in country A, which have remained constant $\left(\phi_1^A = \phi_2^A\right)$.

Scenario 1: $\phi_1^A > \phi_1^B = \phi_2^B = \phi_2^A$

We focus on the interesting case where $\phi_1^B < \tilde{\phi}_1^{C,v} < \phi_1^A$, with $\tilde{\phi}_1^{C,v}$ as in equation (8.9). In period 1, country A's government thus prohibits the cheap technology while country B's government allows it. This is the case even if the difference between ϕ_1^A and ϕ_1^B is only minor.[15]

In period 2, country A's consumer preferences fall to the level of those in country B ($\phi_2^A = \phi_2^B = \phi_1^B < \tilde{\phi}_1^{C,v}$). A potential cause for this shift could be that country A's consumers learn from country B's positive experiences with the cheap technology. As in case (2), the political-economic equilibrium in country B is to unconditionally uphold the status quo of allowing the cheap technology whereas country A's political-economic equilibrium depends on the political power of the producers' interest group. If α^P is sufficiently high such that $\tilde{\phi}_2^{G,v} < \phi_2^A$, the producers' interest group lobbies successfully to maintain the ban on the cheap technology although consumers prefer to allow it ($\phi_2^A \le \tilde{\phi}_1^{C,v} \le \tilde{\phi}_2^{C,v}$).

If, however, the producers' interest group is politically weak (low α^P) such that $\phi_2^A \le \tilde{\phi}_2^{G,v}$, the government allows the cheap technology. Table 8.1 summarizes the first scenario.

This scenario shows that if the producers' interest group in country A has sufficient political power, both countries end up having different technology regulations, even though consumer preferences are identical in period 2. The "butterfly," the temporary difference in consumer preferences, triggers different initial regulatory choices and investment that lead to a coalition switch in country A as consumer and producer interests change. Although consumers prefer the cheap technology, country A's producers lobby successfully to uphold the status quo in period 2, which protects them from cheaper imports. The temporary difference in consumer preferences leads to initial differences in regulation, but the producer protectionist motives cause hysteresis and long-lasting differences in technology regulation.[16]

---

[15] In terms of chaos theory, the situation in period 1 is a *hypersensitive* one (Smith, 1991), meaning that other states arbitrarily close to the hypersensitive one could eventually lead to highly divergent dynamical behavior.

[16] In the classification of Göcke (2002), this hysteresis effect is a form of "non-ideal relay hysteresis," which is part of the group "microeconomic hysteresis." This group shares the common feature that a certain critical value must be passed to induce persistent hysteresis effects.

Table 8.1. *A temporary difference in consumer preferences:*
Scenario 1 with $\phi_1^A > \phi_1^B = \phi_2^B = \phi_2^A$

t	A	B	s_t^v
1	$\phi_1^A \geq \tilde{\phi}_1^{C,v}$	$\phi_1^B \leq \tilde{\phi}_1^{C,v}$	$s_1^A = s_H$ $s_1^B = s_L$
2	$\phi_2^A < \tilde{\phi}_2^{C,v}$	$\phi_2^B < \tilde{\phi}_2^{C,v}$	$s_2^A = \begin{cases} s_H \text{ if } \tilde{\phi}_2^{G,A} \leq \phi_2^A \ (\alpha^P \text{ high}) \\ s_L \text{ if } \tilde{\phi}_2^{G,A} > \phi_2^A \ (\alpha^P \text{ low}) \end{cases}$ $s_2^B = s_L$

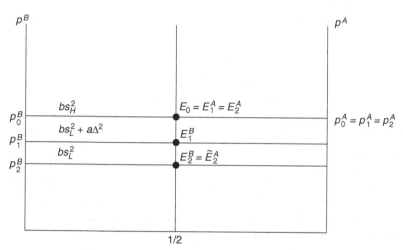

Figure 8.1. Interests at stake of country A's producers to maintain the status quo in technology regulation.

In Figure 8.1 we illustrate the interests of country A's producers in upholding the status quo where for simplicity world demand is assumed constant and equal to 1. The default situation is that initially only the expensive technology is available, that is, $s_0^v = s_H$, $p_0^A = p_0^B = bs_H^2$, and the equilibrium is at E_0. In period 1, because of the temporary difference in consumer preferences, country B allows the cheap technology while country A prohibits it ($s_1^B = s_L$ and $s_1^A = s_H$). The marginal cost and price are lower in country B, although country B's producers incur an investment cost ($p_1^B = bs_L^2 + a\Delta^2 < bs_H^2 = p_1^A$). Because of the different regulations and marginal costs, the markets are separated and the equilibrium is different for each country (E_1^A and E_1^B). In period 2, country B sticks unconditionally to the status quo such that its marginal cost and price decrease further $\left(p_2^B = bs_L^2 < p_1^B\right)$, and its equilibrium is at E_2^B. If country A would also allow the cheap technology, country A's producers would produce at marginal cost $bs_L^2 + a\Delta^2$. These are higher than in country B because the latter do not need to switch and have gained a first-mover advantage in the cheap technology. In that case, country A's equilibrium would be at $\tilde{E}_2^A$ and country A's producers would suffer a decrease in profits equal to $a\Delta^2/2$ in the figure. If, however, country A upholds its status quo, country A's equilibrium is at E_2^A, the markets remain separated, and country A's producers do not suffer a decrease in profits. Hence successful lobbying by country A's producers leads to hysteresis in technology regulation and long-lasting regulatory differences.

Scenario 2: $\phi_1^B < \phi_1^A = \phi_2^A = \phi_2^B$

In scenario 2, country B initially has lower preferences than country A, but in period 2 these preferences increase to the level in country A. A potential cause for this shift could be that in period 1 the cheap technology caused damage in country B which altered country B's consumer preferences (and confirmed consumers' concerns in country A).

Analogously to equation (8.16), we can define government B's threshold in period 2 as $\tilde{\phi}_2^{G,B}$ with $\tilde{\phi}_2^{G,B} > \tilde{\phi}_2^{C,v}$ and $(d\tilde{\phi}_2^{G,B}/d\alpha^P) > 0$. These properties imply that if the producers' political power is sufficiently strong in country B, the status quo in technology regulation is maintained ($s_2^B = s_L$) for an additional range of consumer preferences $\phi_2^B \in [\tilde{\phi}_2^{C,v}, \tilde{\phi}_2^{G,B})$.[17]

Table 8.2 summarizes the second scenario. Assume that in period 1, $\phi_1^B < \tilde{\phi}_1^{C,v} < \tilde{\phi}_2^{C,v} < \phi_1^A$ (where the critical preference values are defined by respectively equations (8.9) and (8.15)). Country A will then ban the cheap technology in period 1 ($s_1^A = s_H$) while country B allows it ($s_1^B = s_L$). In period 2, consumer preferences increase in country B so that $\phi_2^B = \phi_2^A = \phi_1^A$. As we assume $\phi_1^A = \phi_2^A > \tilde{\phi}_2^{C,v}$, country A's government continues banning the cheap technology ($s_1^A = s_H$). In country B, consumers would now also prefer a stricter standard since $\phi_2^B > \tilde{\phi}_2^{C,v}$. However, whether country B's government bans the cheap technology or maintains the status quo depends on the political power of the producers' interest group in country B. If

---

[17] Since we assumed in the previous cases that $\phi_t^B < \tilde{\phi}_1^{C,v}$ and found that $\tilde{\phi}_1^{C,v} < \tilde{\phi}_2^{C,v}$, the range $\phi_2^B \in [\tilde{\phi}_2^{C,v}, \tilde{\phi}_2^{G,B})$ was never relevant. This explains why we did not introduce $\tilde{\phi}_2^{G,B}$ before.

Table 8.2. *A temporary difference in consumer preferences: Scenario 2 with $\phi_1^B < \phi_1^A = \phi_2^A = \phi_2^B$*

t	A	B	s_t^v
1	$\phi_1^A > (\tilde{\phi}_2^{C,v} >)\tilde{\phi}_1^{C,v}$	$\phi_1^B > \tilde{\phi}_1^{C,v}$	$s_1^A = s_H$ $s_1^B = s_L$
2	$\phi_2^A > \tilde{\phi}_2^{C,v}$	$\phi_2^B > \tilde{\phi}_2^{C,v}$	$s_2^A = s_H$ $s_2^B = \begin{cases} s_H \text{ if } \tilde{\phi}_2^{G,B} \le \phi_2^B \ (\alpha^P \text{ low}) \\ s_L \text{ if } \tilde{\phi}_2^{G,B} > \phi_2^B \ (\alpha^P \text{ high}) \end{cases}$

producers have sufficient political power (high α^P) such that $\phi_2^B < \tilde{\phi}_2^{G,B}$, the status quo is endorsed although consumers prefer the expensive technology. If α^P is low such that $\tilde{\phi}_2^{G,B} \le \phi_2^B$, the producers' interest group in country B is unsuccessful at pushing for the status quo, and the cheap technology is prohibited.

This scenario demonstrates that if the producers' interest group has sufficient political power in country B, its government continues allowing the cheap technology although consumers want to ban it, and the regulatory difference between the countries persists although consumer preferences are identical from period 2 onward. The temporary difference in consumer preferences triggers different regulatory choices and investment in period 1. Because country A's producers kept using the more expensive technology, country B's producers would be at a competitive disadvantage if they switched back to the more expensive technology in period 2. By lobbying to uphold the status quo in technology regulation, country B's producers protect themselves from this competitive disadvantage. Hence also in the second scenario, the temporary difference in consumer preferences leads to different initial regulations, but it is again a producer protectionist motive that causes hysteresis in technology regulation and long-lasting differences in regulation between countries.

In conclusion, our dynamic political economy model shows that in the second period producers in both countries favor technology regulation that excludes foreign imports, due to technology-specific investments (or the absence of these investments) that were triggered by a temporary difference in consumer preferences in the first period. The model shows that persistent differences in technology regulation may occur because governments cater to domestic producers' interests, creating hysteresis in technology regulation.

These results are not driven by the assumption that the default option is the expensive technology, that is, that $s_0^v = s_H$, as in the case of biotechnology regulation. Our results hold also for issues where the default option is to allow the cheap technology, that is, $s_0^v = s_L$, for example, for child labor and carbon dioxide emissions. It is possible to show that also under this alternative default option a critical preference value exists above which consumers prefer the expensive technology. Subsequently, under very similar assumptions that consumer preferences are different between countries, the government of the country with the highest consumer preferences would switch to the expensive technology while the other country's government would stick to the cheap one. It can then be shown that, for constant consumer preferences, the government that initially switches to the expensive technology always endorses the regulatory status quo in the long run, independent of the other country's regulation. The government that initially allows the cheap technology may also support the regulatory status quo, even though its consumers may wish to ban the cheap technology, when its producers have sufficient political power. Producers in that country would lobby to continue allowing the cheap technology to protect themselves from imports from the country that adopted the expensive technology. Hence, also under this different default option, producer lobbying could lead to policy persistence and long-run differences in technology regulation. Similar results of hysteresis in technology regulation can be obtained when differences in consumer preferences are only temporary.

8.6 Extensions to the Model

It is possible to extend our model in several directions. First, we have assumed that consumer preferences in the second period are independent from regulation in the first period, that is, that $\phi_2^v = \phi_1^v + f(s_1^v)$ with $f(s_1^v) = 0$. However, it is not unlikely that consumer preferences are affected by previous regulation, for example because the (lack of) experience with the new technology may alter consumer preferences. Extending the model by assuming that $f(s_H) > 0$ and $f(s_L) < 0$ would reinforce our results. For example, consider case (2) where consumer preferences are higher in period 1 in country A, and where consequently the cheap technology is banned in country A but not in country B $(s_1^A = s_H; s_1^B = s_L)$. The assumption that $\phi_2^v = \phi_1^v + f(s_1^v)$ with $f(s_H) > 0$ and $f(s_L) < 0$ implies that in period 2 consumer preferences in country A increase, whereas in country B consumer preferences decrease. It is straightforward that also under these assumptions, once country B's government has chosen to allow the cheap technology, it endorses the status quo in future periods and supports the cheap technology irrespective of the behavior of the other country's government. Moreover, as then $\phi_2^A > \phi_1^A$, the range of situations where $\tilde{\phi}_2^A > \tilde{\phi}_2^{G,A}$ and $s_2^A = s_H$ would increase, thus extending the range where policy persistence in country A's technology ban occurs.

Another extension relates to the source of country differences. Hysteresis in differences in technology regulation may be caused by other factors than temporary differences in consumer preferences. For example, producers located in an environment favorable to technological innovation may have a comparative advantage in investing in a new technology. A temporary investment advantage can be modeled by assuming that country B's producers incur a lower investment cost than country A's producers in period 1 $\left(a_1^B < a_1^A\right)$. This temporarily lower investment cost may also lead to (persistence in) different technology regulations. Assume that consumer preferences for quality ϕ_t^v are constant and identical between countries. The lower value of a_1^B leads to a higher value of $\tilde{\phi}_1^{C,v}$ in both countries (see equation (8.9)) as also country A's consumers could benefit from the lower investment cost by importing the low standards good. With $\phi_t^v < \tilde{\phi}_1^{C,v}$, country B's government would allow the cheap technology, as country B's producers would be indifferent. Country A's producers would, however, oppose the cheap technology because they would be competitively dominated if the cheap technology were allowed, because $a_1^A > a_1^B$. Therefore country A's producers would lobby in favor of prohibiting the cheap technology, and $\tilde{\phi}_1^{G,A} < \tilde{\phi}_1^{C,v}$. If the political power of country A's producers would be sufficiently high such that $\tilde{\phi}_1^{G,A} < \phi_1^v$, country A's government would prohibit the cheap technology in the first period. The analysis of period 2, when $a_2^A = a_2^B$, is then similar to case (2). Hence a temporary difference in investment costs may also lead to an initial difference in technology regulation which results in hysteresis in (differences in) technology regulation due to producer lobbying.

A third extension could be to specify the different subgroups that are aggregated in the group of "producers." In reality there exists considerable heterogeneity, both horizontally and vertically. For example, horizontally, there are different types of "producers" who may vary in productivity and ability to apply different technologies. Vertically, the supply chain consists of different agents. As discussed in Chapter 7, these agents may have conflicting interests with respect to regulation. Depending on how these different agents in the supply chain interact, the distribution of market power in the supply chain, and the political power of the different agents, different outcomes may result. Separating out these different interest groups substantially complicates the analysis and is left for future research.

Finally, we have represented technology regulation by a one-dimensional and dichotomous standard, while in reality governments have a broad range of policy instruments at their disposal. For example, we have not allowed for labeling policies that would give consumers the opportunity to choose (see, e.g., Fulton and Giannakas, 2004; Golan et al., 2001; Moschini, 2008). In the case of some technologies, governments may also impose maximum use levels. Regulation may also distinguish between technology that is used for industrial use or for human consumption. Of course, these various regulations may have different effects on different actors in the market, and interest groups may prefer one type of regulation over another.

8.7 Conclusions

This chapter advances a dynamic political-economic model of regulation, in which two countries' governments decide which of two technologies to allow in each of two periods. One technology allows producing at lower marginal costs, but consumers have some (heterogeneous) aversion to it. Switching between technologies involves a one-time marginal cost increase. First we have demonstrated the existence of a critical (consumer) preference value above which the cheap technology is prohibited. A small variation in consumer preferences may thus determine whether a country bans a technology or not.

Second, our dynamic model showed that if consumer preferences are constant and identical between countries, countries adopt the same technology regulation and stick to the status quo independent of the initial technology regulation.

Third, constant but different consumer preferences between countries may lead to different technology regulations in the first period, depending on how the countries' consumer preferences are positioned with respect to the critical preference value. If different technologies are adopted in the first period, the government that initially allows the cheap technology always endorses the status quo in the long run, independent of the other country's regulation. The government that initially prohibits the cheap technology may also support the status quo in the long run, even though consumers may wish to change, because producers' interests switch around. Producers are initially indifferent but because of the switching cost they suffer a competitive disadvantage in applying the cheap technology. Therefore they lobby to maintain the ban on the cheap technology to protect themselves from cheaper imports from the country that adopts the cheap technology, and succeed if their political power is sufficiently strong. Hence producer lobbying, not consumer preferences, leads to policy persistence and long-run differences in technology regulation.

Fourth, the previous results may also hold when the difference in consumer preferences is only temporary. A temporary difference in consumer preferences may trigger different initial regulations, and thus different investments. In the next period, producers in both countries favor technology regulation that excludes foreign imports, due to technology-specific investments (or the absence of these). Hence, despite identical consumer preferences in the long run, regulatory differences may be long-lasting because governments respond to pressures of domestic producers, creating hysteresis in technology regulation. We have demonstrated that similar results may be obtained from temporary differences in company strategies that result in different investment costs.

The main cause of this regulatory persistence is the cost of switching between different technologies. This implies that in order to induce a change in technology regulation, one needs to ensure that producers can adjust their production technology without losing profits to foreign imports. This reduces producers' incentives to lobby in favor of a status quo in technology regulation, and would remove differences in regulation between countries, all else equal.

9

The Political Economy of Standards
and Inclusion in Value Chains

9.1 Introduction

As demonstrated in Chapter 3, standards may have heterogeneous effects on different groups of producers. Chapter 7 analyzed this for the "vertical" case where different actors along the value chain had potentially opposing interests. In this chapter, we extend the analysis of heterogeneous effects of standards to the "horizontal" case where standards allow only a subset of all companies or households to be included at a certain stage in the value chain. Examples of such standards include occupational licenses (Kleiner, 2000), the practices of the medieval guild systems (Ogilvie, 2014), or geographical indications (GI), collective labels backed by government regulation to certify the geographical origins of a product (Moschini et al., 2008).[1] GI regulations delineate the area for which the label applies, thus including or excluding producers on the basis of their location. In all these cases, the standard explicitly determines which producers are included in the value chain.

The selection of a subset of producers in a value chain can also occur as the result of private standards, as we discuss in Chapter 10. However, the case analyzed here concerns the selection of a subset of producers by the government. In some cases, the *implementation* of the public standard may depend on nongovernmental bodies. Occupational licensing, for instance, often happens through a nongovernmental licensing board, but

---

[1] GIs are used for a wide variety of products and the number of GIs has been growing steadily. In parallel with the growing importance of GIs, academics have explored the economics of GIs, with some positing welfare gains as a result of the resolution of asymmetric information problems (e.g., Moschini et al., 2008) and others claiming that GIs can be used as tools for extracting rents from consumers, for example, by systematically oversupplying quality (Mérel and Sexton, 2012). These results are consistent with the efficiency and equity effects of standards identified in Chapter 3.

members of this board are typically political appointees, and the exclusion of non-licensed producers is only effective because it is sanctioned by government (Kleiner, 2000).

Such exclusionary public standards are often justified by reference to an indirect positive effect on quality. To the extent that such a positive quality effect exists, the standard may thus have efficiency effects. However, obviously, the explicit inclusion or exclusion of producers causes distributional issues, which will in turn influence the political process of deciding on the size of the population of "insiders."[2] A crucial question is therefore how large the population of insiders should be, and how the political process determines the actual population.

This chapter develops a political economy model to analyze such issues. Our analysis makes four assumptions. First, the decision over the size of the population of insiders is taken by government bodies that may be influenced by various interest groups. Second, the group of insiders organizes some common activities that lead to both variable and fixed costs. Examples would be common marketing or training activities. An expansion of the population of insiders then means that fixed costs can be spread over a larger number of insiders, thus reducing the cost for the original insiders. Third, the expansion of the population may have a negative effect on (actual or perceived) quality. Fourth, we assume that demand is not perfectly elastic, so that an expansion of the population of insiders leads to a decrease in prices for all insiders.

Following the approach of Chapter 4, we model the political decision over the size of the population of insiders as the maximization of a weighted objective function by the government, with different weights representing different degrees of political influence. We show the conditions under which the political equilibrium would be closer or further away from the social optimum. A general conclusion is that the politically determined population may be either too large or too small from a social welfare perspective.

This chapter is organized as follows. After discussing the general setup and deriving the effects of a change in the population on the welfare of

---

[2] The history of the Champagne GI offers a clear example. In the early twentieth century, when the Champagne region was officially delimited for the first time, there were major disputes over the precise definition of the area. The original proposal included only villages in the Marne department, while producers in the neighboring Aube department claimed that they should also be included. The disagreement led to bitter conflicts, eventually erupting into violence in 1911 (Simpson, 2011). In recent years, the expansion of the Champagne area is again on the agenda. Given that vineyards in Champagne can fetch prices of €1 million per hectare or more compared to prices of around €4,000 per hectare outside the region, there is clearly much at stake (Stevenson, 2008).

consumers and of included and excluded producers, we determine the socially optimal size of the population of insiders and show how it depends on the relative size of the negative "quality" effect and the positive "output" effect of an expansion on consumer welfare, as well as on the magnitude of variable costs related to the common activities undertaken by the insiders. We then apply the political economy framework of Chapter 4 to derive the political equilibrium. To compare the social optimum with the political equilibrium, we consider several possible cases of influence of interest groups, studying the case where the government maximizes aggregate producer welfare (treating "insiders" and "outsiders" as equal), as well as the cases where the government maximizes only "insider" welfare or (for illustrative purposes) the unlikely case where the government maximizes only "outsider" welfare. We show how the political equilibrium can graphically be represented as being a weighted combination of these extreme scenarios, and discuss how the political equilibrium compares to the social optimum. A final section concludes the chapter.

9.2 The Model

9.2.1 Producers

As the examples cited in the introduction illustrate, the standards studied in this chapter can apply to a wide variety of agents, including professions (such as medical doctors or lawyers), artisans (as in the case of medieval guilds), or companies. For consistency with previous chapters, we will refer to these agents as "producers" throughout this chapter.

Since standards to include or exclude producers are often justified by referring to quality effects, our setup needs to account for intrinsic differences in their capacity to deliver a certain "quality." To this end, consider a continuum of producers indexed by i. All producers produce the same product but vary in the quality $\sigma(i)$ of their production, which we assume is exogenously given. Ranking the producers by decreasing levels of quality, we assume that their quality level can be represented by a continuous "quality function" $\sigma(i) > 0$ which is by construction decreasing in i ($\sigma_i < 0$).[3]

An important assumption in our analysis is that as the group of insiders expands, priority of entry is given to producers with higher quality levels. In other words, higher quality producers are admitted first. One example might be membership of a professional association that is granted only

---

[3]   As in previous chapters, subscripts denote partial derivatives.

to a limited number of applicants on the basis of test scores on an exam. A different example is that of a region with a geographical indication. In this setting, the index i could represent the distance from the center of the region, and the assumption then implies that the quality of a producer depends only on his location (i) and that producers located further away from the center of the region have lower quality. There could be objective aspects of the region, such as the soil, the microclimate, local traditions, or other factors that strongly influence the actual quality of the product, so that producers located further away from the center have objectively lower quality.[4]

In reality, standards that exclude certain producers do not always select the high-quality producers as insiders, even if this is ostensibly the purpose of the standard (Ogilvie, 2014). If so, the quality function $\sigma(i)$ does not necessarily decrease, which may imply that the standard that excludes producers may deprive consumers of higher quality production, contrary to the stated purpose of such standards. Under our assumption, this cannot be the case. The quality function $\sigma(i)$ is decreasing, implying a strict quality rationale behind such a standard.

Deciding on the size of the population of insiders implicitly determines output and average quality. To keep the model simple, we assume that producers have a fixed and identical productivity of one unit. Given this assumption, aggregate production is equal to the total population of insiders, and we use the symbol x to denote both. Average quality is then given by

$$s(x) = \frac{1}{x} \int_0^x \sigma(i) \, di \qquad (9.1)$$

Because quality $\sigma(i)$ is decreasing in i, the same is true for average quality as a function of total population of insiders: $s_x < 0$.

Following Moschini et al. (2008) and Langinier and Babcock (2010), we assume that the group of insiders incur costs of $F + cx$ where F represents fixed costs (e.g., marketing expenses) and c denotes variable costs (e.g., certification costs). Following Moschini et al. (2008), we assume that these costs are borne by the producers in proportion to their output: insiders pay a per-unit charge of $c + (F/x)$.

---

[4] Even if "terroir" is unimportant to intrinsic quality, if consumers attach importance to the degree to which a product is typical of a certain region, expanding the region covered by the GI may imply that the perceived quality for consumers decreases.

For simplicity, we assume that production itself is costless, and we normalize the income of outsiders to zero. Producer surplus is then given by $\Pi^i = p - c - (F/x)$ for an "insider" with rank i, and zero for an outsider. The aggregate surplus of insiders for a given group size x is given by $\Pi^I(x) = \int_0^x \Pi^i di$.

9.2.2 Consumers

We assume that consumers are unable to distinguish products from different producers. Consumers value quality as in previous chapters, but their perceived quality is now the average quality s of "insiders." Consumer utility is thus again given by $u(x,s)$ and the corresponding inverse demand is $p = u_x(x,s)$. Consumer surplus is $\Pi^C = u(x,s) - px$.

9.2.3 Impact of a Change in the Population of Insiders

How does an increase in the population of insiders (x) affect producer surplus? To answer this, we need to distinguish between the initial group of insiders, the "new" insiders, and the producers who remain excluded. The effect on the surplus of the initial insiders is

$$\frac{\partial \Pi^I}{\partial x} = x\left(p_x + p_s s_x\right) + \frac{F}{x} \qquad (9.2)$$

An increase in the population of insiders depresses the revenues of the original insiders (first term) while it leads to better cost sharing (second term). The first term, $x(p_x + p_s s_x)$, is negative as an increase leads to a higher quantity, which induces a lower price $(p_x < 0)$; in addition, the increase leads to a lower quality that is also associated with a lower price $(s_x < 0)$. Graphically, the first effect is the result of a downward movement along the demand curve while the second effect is the result of the downward shift of the demand curve. The second term, F/x, is positive and captures the fact that an expansion reduces the per-unit charge of initial insiders.

An expansion implies that some former "outsiders" become "insiders" who can now sell their product at a price p but have to pay the per-unit charge $c + (F/x)$. For an infinitesimal increase, the change in surplus for the marginal outsider who enters the group of insiders is given by $p - c - (F/x)$.

The surplus for all other outsiders remains zero. The effect of an increase in x on the aggregate surplus of initial outsiders is thus given by

$$\frac{\partial \Pi^O}{\partial x} = p - c - \frac{F}{x} \qquad (9.3)$$

Combining these effects, the effect of a change in the population on aggregate producer surplus is given by

$$\frac{\partial \Pi^P}{\partial x} = \frac{\partial \Pi^I}{\partial x} + \frac{\partial \Pi^O}{\partial x} = p - c + x\left(p_x + p_s s_x\right) \qquad (9.4)$$

The effect of a change in the population of insiders on consumer surplus is given by

$$\frac{\partial \Pi^C}{\partial x} = u_s s_x - x\left(p_x + p_s s_x\right) \qquad (9.5)$$

The first term, $u_s s_x$, represents the direct utility impact of the change in average quality as a result of the increase in population of insiders. This term is negative since an increase in the population of insiders decreases average quality. The second term, $x(p_x + p_s s_x)$, is the marginal change in consumer expenditures, which has a positive effect on consumer surplus since prices go down if the population increases.[5]

9.3 The Socially Optimal Population of Insiders

As a benchmark to compare the political equilibrium to, we first derive the socially optimal population of insiders. Social welfare is given by the sum of consumer surplus and aggregate producer surplus:

$$W = u\left(x,s\right) - cx - F \qquad (9.6)$$

Maximizing with respect to the population of insiders x, the first-order condition is

$$\frac{\partial W}{\partial x} = u_x + u_s s_x - c = 0 \qquad (9.7)$$

---

[5] The second term can be rewritten as $x(u_{xx} + u_{xs} s_x)$, which brings out the similarities between the analysis in this chapter and that introduced in Chapter 3. From this perspective, a key difference is that in earlier chapters the quality level itself was the decision variable, indirectly inducing a change in quantity, whereas in this chapter the size of the group of insiders (and hence output) is the decision variable, inducing a change in quality.

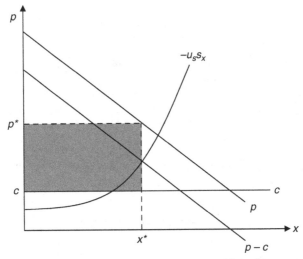

Figure 9.1. Socially optimal size of the group of insiders.

As in previous chapters, we thus see that the "rent transfer" $x\left(p_x + p_s s_x\right)$ cancels out. Equation (9.7) defines the optimal population of insiders x^*, assuming that the resulting social welfare is positive, that is, $u\left(x^*, s\right) - cx^* \geq F$.

An increase in the population of insiders x affects social welfare in three ways. First, it increases aggregate production x, which has a positive (but diminishing) effect on utility. Second, the increase in the population of insiders reduces the average quality ($s_x < 0$), which has a negative effect on utility. Third, the expansion of production means that extra variable costs c will be incurred. The optimal population of insiders balances these three effects.

Using the fact that $u_x = p$, equation (9.7) defines an interesting relationship between price and marginal cost:

$$p - c = -u_s s_x \tag{9.8}$$

Figure 9.1 shows this relationship, denoting the social optimum by x^*. The resulting consumer price p^* is above the marginal cost c of the common activities of the insiders.

Equation (9.8) can be rewritten as

$$\frac{p-c}{p} = -\frac{u_s s_x}{u_x} \tag{9.9}$$

That is, in the social welfare optimum, the markup of price over marginal cost should equal the relative effect on consumer utility of the change in quality ($u_s s_x$) and the change in quantity (u_x). Because $s_x < 0$ while all other terms are positive, the markup in the optimum will be positive, as shown in Figure 9.1. By contrast, if there is no quality effect ($s_x = 0$), the optimal markup is zero. In that case, the welfare optimum is to expand the group of insiders until price equals marginal cost.

Importantly, the markup does not arise because of the need to offer incentives to producers, as both quality and quantity are exogenously given. Rather, because quality effects of a further expansion would negatively affect consumer surplus, the optimal population of insiders will be smaller than what would be necessary to drive prices down to marginal cost. In short, if quality depends on the population of insiders, the socially optimal population size implies rents for insiders, shown in Figure 9.1 by the shaded area.

However, this result needs to be qualified in two ways. First, if insiders bear the fixed costs themselves, they will benefit only if the rents exceed the fixed cost $((p-c)x^* \geq F)$. By contrast, from a social welfare perspective, the existence of a group of insiders organizing common activities is beneficial as soon as the sum of consumer surplus and producer rents exceeds the fixed cost (i.e., $u(x^*,s) - cx^* \geq F$).[6]

The social planner would thus be willing to introduce insider groups with common activities even if producer rents are smaller than the fixed cost, as long as the difference is made up by consumer surplus. But in those cases, insiders would not be willing to organize these activities. The practical implementation would then necessitate government intervention, for example, by subsidizing the fixed costs of operating the group of insiders.[7]

A second qualification is that our result of rents accruing to the producers depends on our assumption of exogenously given quantities. By contrast, a typical assumption in the literature on geographical indications is that producers are perfectly competitive inside the GI region (e.g., Mérel and Sexton, 2012; Moschini et al., 2008), which implies that rents might be competed away. On the other hand, as land is the scarce factor of supply, there would still be some rents captured by the landowners (Moschini et al., 2008). Similarly, where licenses can be traded, the rents will tend to

---

[6] Since the curve labeled p in Figure 9.1 captures both the quality and quantity effect, it is not possible to interpret the triangle below p as consumer surplus (which is defined for a constant quality level).

[7] Similar results can be found regarding optimal product variety in the presence of fixed costs; see Spence (1976b).

be capitalized in the price of the license. As we see here, this result may be consistent with social welfare maximization.

9.4 The Political Equilibrium

Given the conflicting interests of consumers, "insider" producers, and "outsider" producers, the question is how the actual size of the group of insiders will be determined by the government. We study this question using the political economy approach of Chapter 4, where the government has to decide on the population of insiders x. We assume that insiders are politically organized, as are the "outsiders," but consumers are not organized.[8]

In previous chapters, we assumed fixed and exogenously given lobbying groups. By contrast, because of the nature of the present policy, interest groups change as the policy variable changes, that is, as the population expands or shrinks. As new producers are added to the group of insiders, their interest group thus increases in the process. The "insider" interest group uses a truthful contribution schedule of the form $C^I(x) = \max\{0, \Pi^I(x) - b^I\}$ defined over the different possible values x of the population of insiders of the GI region. In this formulation, b^I is a constant, representing a minimum level of profits the interest group does not wish to spend on lobbying.

Likewise, our definition of the lobbying group of the outsiders needs some care. In particular, increasing the size of the group of insiders from x_0 to x_1 only affects outsiders located in this interval, and has no effect on outsiders located beyond x_1. As a result producers beyond x_1 have no reason to lobby for an increase in the population of insiders to x_1. Taking this argument to its logical conclusion, every outsider is willing to make a personal contribution only to have the population of insiders expanded to include just himself. Given that joining the group of insiders leads to a profit increase of $[p - c - (F/x)]$ for an outsider, this will be the maximum an outsider is willing to pay. The marginal contribution of outsiders just outside the group of insiders x thus equals $[p - c - (F/x)]$. The lobby group of the outsiders can then be thought of as a continuum of producers, each willing to pay $[p - c - (F/x)]$ if the population of insiders is expanded to include himself. We therefore write the total contribution of the outsiders as $C^O(x) = \int_{x_0}^{x} [p - c - (F/x)] di$ starting from an initial population of insiders x_0.

---

8   This does not affect our results. As shown in the Appendix to Chapter 7, as the government maximizes a weighted sum, what matters are the relative weights.

The government's objective function $\Pi^G(x)$ is a weighted sum of the interest group contributions weighted by their relative lobbying strength (assumed exogenously given), and social welfare:[9]

$$\Pi^G(x) = \alpha^I C^I(x) + \alpha^O C^O(x) + \alpha^W W(x) \qquad (9.10)$$

The government chooses x to maximize its objective function (9.10). Each possible size of the group of insiders corresponds to a certain level of profits for insiders and outsiders, and hence also to a certain level of contributions. The government receives higher contributions from an interest group if the proposed level of x creates higher profits for that group. Therefore maximizing the contributions from one interest group is equivalent to maximizing their profits. The government's optimal population of insiders is thus defined by the following first-order condition:[10]

$$\frac{\partial \Pi^G(x)}{\partial x} = \alpha^I \frac{\partial \Pi^I(x)}{\partial x} + \alpha^O \left(p - c - \frac{F}{x} \right) + \alpha^W \frac{\partial W(x)}{\partial x} = 0 \qquad (9.11)$$

To understand the general political equilibrium, it is instructive to consider three special cases. The first case is where the government aims to maximize aggregate producer welfare, corresponding to a situation where $\alpha^I = \alpha^O > 0$ and $\alpha^W = 0$ in equation (9.11). The second case is where the government focuses only on maximizing insider producer welfare, which would be the case if $\alpha^I > 0$ while $\alpha^O = \alpha^W = 0$. Conversely, the third case is where the government maximizes the welfare only of outsider producers, corresponding to $\alpha^I = \alpha^W = 0$ and $\alpha^O > 0$. We discuss these three cases in turn, and then present the political equilibrium in the more general case.

9.4.1 Maximizing Aggregate Producer Welfare

If insiders and outsiders have equal lobbying weight, while the government is not concerned at all with social welfare, maximizing the government's

---

[9] In the traditional formulation, $\alpha^W = 1$. However, it aids our exposition if we explicitly attach a weight to social welfare. Because what matters are the *relative* weights, this does not influence the results (also see the Appendix to Chapter 7).

[10] If the lobbying strength of insiders and outsiders is zero ($\alpha^I = \alpha^O = 0$), this reduces to $\partial W(x)/\partial x = 0$ and the political equilibrium coincides with the social optimum.

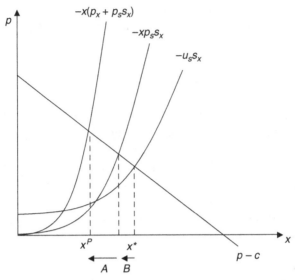

Figure 9.2. Size of the group of insiders that maximizes aggregate producer surplus.

objective function is equivalent to maximizing aggregate producer welfare. The first-order condition is

$$\frac{\partial \Pi^P}{\partial x} = p + x \left(p_x + p_s s_x \right) - c = 0 \tag{9.12}$$

The first term gives the positive impact on aggregate producer revenues of the extra production made possible by expanding the population of insiders. The second term denotes the negative impact on aggregate producer revenues caused by the expansion. The third term denotes the increase in variable costs. The optimal population of insiders from the point of view of aggregate producer welfare thus balances these effects. The situation is depicted in Figure 9.2, denoting the resulting population of insiders by x^P. As shown, compared to the social optimum, two effects play a role, which we call "rent-seeking through quantity" (denoted by A in Figure 9.2) and "rent-seeking through quality" (B).

To see both effects algebraically, we can rearrange the first-order condition to give

$$\frac{p-c}{p} = -\frac{u_s s_x}{u_x} - \frac{1}{\eta^D} - \left(\frac{x p_s s_x}{u_x} - \frac{u_s s_x}{u_x} \right) \tag{9.13}$$

The first term reflects the markup that would hold in the social optimum (see equation (9.9)). The other terms reflect how this optimal markup is distorted by aggregate producer welfare maximization. The second term, $-1/\eta^D$, is the traditional "inverse elasticity" rule, reflecting "rent-seeking through quantity." This term will always tend to increase the markup relative to the social optimum. Notice that if there was no quality effect ($s_x = 0$), the GI region would still be set to lead to a markup of $-1/\eta^D$ and hence rents for producers. The "rent-seeking through quantity" effect (A) will thus always tend to decrease the population of insiders, as a smaller population of insiders implies a restriction of production and thus a higher producer price, ceteris paribus.

The third term, $-\left[(xp_s s_x/u_x)-(u_s s_x/u_x)\right]$, captures the "rent-seeking through quality" effect (B) and could be positive or negative, depending on whether the price effect dominates the direct utility effect or not. Producers do not take into account the effect of lower quality on consumer utility ($u_s s_x$), but only its effect on price through consumers' marginal willingness to pay ($xp_s s_x$). Depending on how a change in quality affects demand, the impact on price may be larger or smaller than the impact on consumer utility. If a decrease in quality reduces prices strongly, producers will prefer a smaller region even if there is only a limited effect on consumer utility. The resulting population of insiders will be socially suboptimal. Conversely, if lower quality does not affect prices but strongly affects consumer utility, the preferred population of insiders of producers will be larger than what is socially optimal. Thus, the "rent-seeking through quality" effect can go in the direction of increasing or decreasing the population of insiders, depending on how changes in quality affect utility and prices.

9.4.2 Maximizing Insider Welfare

If insiders have positive lobbying weight ($\alpha^I > 0$) while outsiders have zero lobbying weight and the government is not concerned with social welfare ($\alpha^O = \alpha^W = 0$), the government would set the size of the group of insiders to maximize insider welfare. The corresponding first-order condition is

$$\frac{\partial \Pi^I}{\partial x} = x\left(p_x + p_s s_x\right) + \frac{F}{x} = 0 \tag{9.14}$$

The first term is the marginal effect on insider revenues. Because expansion leads to lower prices, while the output of insiders remains constant, this effect is always negative. The second term is the cost sharing effect.

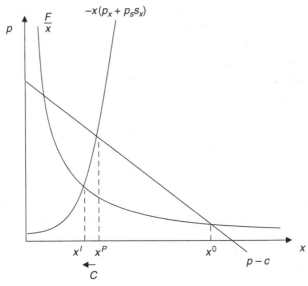

Figure 9.3. Optimal size of the group of insiders for insiders (x^1) and for outsiders (x^0).

If the cost sharing effect was absent, the effect of an expansion on insider surplus would always be negative. Insiders would have an incentive to try to get rid of the producers "at the periphery," as this would at the same time raise average quality and restrict quantity and thus increase the price for the remaining producers. Equation (9.14) would in that case imply a continuously shrinking population. External economies of scale in cost sharing prevent this.

Comparing equation (9.12) maximizing aggregate producer welfare with equation (9.14) maximizing insider welfare, we see that producers now equate $-x\left(p_x + p_s s_x\right)$ with F/x instead of with $p-c$. The situation is depicted in Figure 9.3. The population of insiders x^1, defined by equation (9.14), is smaller than the population of insiders x^P, an effect labeled C in the figure.[11]

[11] In theory, it is possible that x^1 lies to the right of x^P. However, in that case, the curve F/x would lie above $p-c$, which implies that $F > \left(p-c\right)x$ for both x^P and x^1. Because insiders would not be able to cover their fixed costs, they would not organize the common activities that necessitate the fixed costs. Hence, if the insider group organizes these activities, it must be the case that insiders prefer a smaller group size than that which would maximize aggregate producer surplus. As demonstrated in the Appendix, when outsiders can make side payments to the insiders, the insiders fully internalize the effects of an expansion on outsiders. As a result, maximizing insider welfare becomes equivalent with maximizing aggregate producer welfare and the resulting equilibria are the same.

9.4.3 Maximizing Outsider Welfare

The third special case of equation (9.11) is the situation where the government is only concerned with the outsiders. Maximizing the government's objective function then leads to

$$p - c = \frac{F}{x} \qquad (9.15)$$

That is, if the government maximizes outsider welfare, the result is an equilibrium where the rents $p - c$ are just sufficient to cover fixed costs. In Figure 9.3, the resulting equilibrium (denoted by x^O) corresponds to the right-most intersection of $p - c$ and F/x. Interestingly, if there is no quality effect ($s_x = 0$), the social optimum would be $p - c = 0$ and x^O would be too small from a social welfare perspective.[12] If there is a quality effect, x^O can either be too large or too small depending on whether $-u_s s_x$ intersects $p - c$ to the left or to the right of x^O. However, if the social optimum x^* is greater than x^O, producers cannot recover their fixed costs in the social optimum.

Given that outsiders are a heterogeneous group and hence probably less organized than the insiders, it may seem unrealistic to assume that the government would give consideration only to outsiders. However, this case is in fact equivalent to a situation where the government lets anyone join the group of insiders who wishes to do so (and who is willing to pay the per-unit charge $c + (F/x)$). The expansion would continue until at the margin, joining the group of insiders does not bring extra profits for producers. The case where outsider welfare is maximized can thus be interpreted as an "open access" equilibrium.

To summarize, the three special cases lead to a clear ranking: we find that $x^I < x^P < x^O$. However, with respect to the social welfare optimum x^* the conclusions are less clear cut. Because $-u_s s_x$ and $p - c$ may intersect anywhere, the social welfare optimum could be smaller than x^I, larger than x^O, or anywhere in between.

9.4.4 The Political Equilibrium

Having studied the three special cases, we now turn to the political equilibrium in general, that is, for arbitrary values of the lobbying weights α^I and

---

[12] This result follows from our assumption that the fixed cost F is financed using a per-unit charge, effectively transforming a fixed cost into a marginal cost, and thus restricting production. A similar result can be found in Moschini et al. (2008).

α^O and the weight attached to social welfare α^W. Substituting the appropriate expressions in equation (9.11), maximization of the government's objective function implies

$$\frac{\partial \Pi^G(x)}{\partial x} = \alpha^I \left(x(p_x + p_s s_x) + \frac{F}{x} \right) + \alpha^O \left(p - c - \frac{F}{x} \right) + \alpha^W (p - c + u_s s_x) = 0$$

(9.16)

We normalize the weight $\alpha^W = 1$, divide through by $(1 + \alpha^I)$ and rearrange:

$$\left(\frac{\alpha^I - \alpha^O}{1 + \alpha^I} \right) \left(\frac{F}{x} \right) + \left(\frac{1 + \alpha^O}{1 + \alpha^I} \right) (p - c) =$$
$$\left(\frac{\alpha^I}{1 + \alpha^I} \right) (-x(p_x + p_s s_x)) + \left(\frac{1}{1 + \alpha^I} \right) (-u_s s_x) \quad (9.17)$$

To interpret this expression, note that the left-hand side is a weighted sum of F/x and $p - c$. Likewise, the right-hand side is a weighted sum of $-x(p_x + p_s s_x)$ and $-u_s s_x$. These components all have a clear graphical interpretation, as discussed in earlier sections. If we assume that the lobbying strength of outsiders is smaller than that of insiders ($\alpha^I > \alpha^O$), the weights on both sides of the equation are between zero and one, and sum up to one. We can then interpret the political equilibrium x^* as the intersection of two curves, both of which are a "weighted average" of curves already encountered previously. Figure 9.4 shows this graphically.

The first panel of Figure 9.4 shows the right-hand side of equation (9.17) as a weighted average of $-x(p_x + p_s s_x)$ and $-u_s s_x$. If the lobbying power of insiders is zero ($\alpha^I = 0$), this curve coincides with $-u_s s_x$, the direct utility impact of a decrease in quality. By contrast, as the lobbying power of insiders grows, the curve moves closer to $-x(p_x + p_s s_x)$, the negative price impact of an increased population of insiders through expanded quantity and lower quality.

The second panel of Figure 9.4 shows how the left-hand side of equation (9.17) can be seen as a weighted combination of F/x and $p - c$. If outsiders and insiders have equal lobbying weights ($\alpha^I = \alpha^O$), the left-hand side coincides with $p - c$. If insiders have greater lobbying weight ($\alpha^I > \alpha^O$), the left-hand side would converge on F/x as α^I grows larger.

When outsiders have greater lobbying power than insiders, and α^O grows larger, the left-hand side of equation (9.17) would no longer lie between F/x and $p - c$. To see what happens if α^O grows large, multiply both sides by $(1 + \alpha^I)/(1 + \alpha^O)$. The right-hand side then converges to zero while the

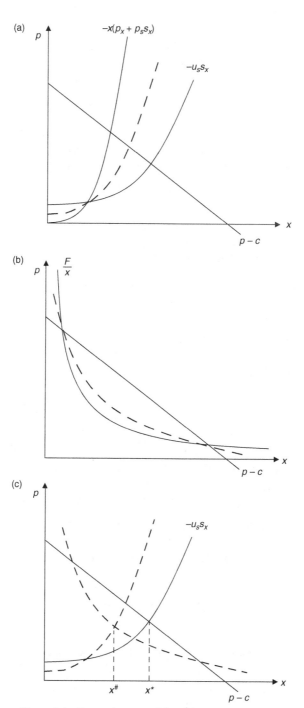

Figure 9.4. Determination of the political equilibrium.

left-hand side converges on $[p-c-(F/x)]$. Hence, this scenario results in the condition $p-c=F/x$, which defines the "open access" equilibrium x^O.

The third panel of Figure 9.4 shows how the combination of the two "weighted" curves determines the political equilibrium. Although the exact optimum depends on the specifics of the lobbying weights, it is clear that the special cases we considered earlier, as well as the social welfare optimum, are boundary solutions. Our political economy approach thus defines the political equilibrium x^* as lying somewhere in between four extreme cases, corresponding to the social welfare optimum x^*, the optimum for aggregate producer surplus x^P, the optimum for the insiders x^I and the "open access" outcome x^O.

9.4.5 Comparison of the Social Optimum and the Political Equilibrium

To see when the political equilibrium would be below or above the social optimum, we can evaluate the derivative of the government's objective function at the social optimum x^*:

$$\left. \frac{\partial \Pi^G(x)}{\partial x} \right|_{x^*} = \alpha^I \left. \frac{\partial \Pi^I(x)}{\partial x} \right|_{x^*} + \alpha^O \left(p - c - \frac{F}{x^*} \right) \tag{9.18}$$

If this expression is zero, then the political equilibrium would coincide with the social optimum; if positive, the political equilibrium would set a population greater than the social optimum, and if negative, the political equilibrium will be smaller than the social optimum.

Clearly, the expression will be zero if $\alpha^I = \alpha^O = 0$ (i.e., the government is not influenced by lobbying). To get more insight, we study the case where the government assigns equal weight to insiders and outsiders ($\alpha^I = \alpha^O > 0$). In this case the expression becomes $\partial \Pi^P(x)/\partial x \big|_{x^*} = p-c+x^*\left(p_x + p_s s_x\right)$. By definition, at the social optimum x^* we have $p-c=-u_s s_x$, and we get

$$\left. \frac{\partial \Pi^G(x)}{\partial x} \right|_{x^*} = -u_s s_x + x^*\left(p_x + p_s s_x\right) \tag{9.19}$$

If insiders and outsiders have equal lobbying weight, the derivative of the government's objective function is thus equal to minus the derivative of consumer surplus, $-\partial \Pi^C(x)/\partial x \big|_{x^*}$. The political equilibrium coincides with the social optimum only if it also coincides with the consumer's optimum. This result is due to the fact that at the social optimum, $\partial W(x)/\partial x\big|_{x^*} = \partial \Pi^C(x)/\partial x\big|_{x^*} + \partial \Pi^I(x)/\partial x\big|_{x^*} + \partial \Pi^O(x)/\partial x\big|_{x^*} = 0$. If $\partial \Pi^C(x)/\partial x\big|_{x^*} = 0$, the social optimum implies $\partial \Pi^I(x)/\partial x\big|_{x^*} = -\partial \Pi^O(x)/\partial x\big|_{x^*}$. If insiders and outsiders have equal lobbying weight, this in turn means that their lobbying efforts exactly offset each other, so that the social optimum is the political equilibrium. This is by no means true in general, and the political equilibrium may end up being greater or smaller than the social optimum.

A different way of looking at the case with $\alpha^I = \alpha^O$ is in terms of the "rent-seeking through quality" and "rent-seeking through quantity" effects introduced earlier. While the rent-seeking through quantity effect will always tend to restrict the population, the rent-seeking through quality effect might go both ways, depending on whether the direct utility impact of a change in quality $(u_s s_x)$ is greater or smaller than the price effect $(x p_s s_x)$. Clearly, this depends on the specifics of consumer demand, and no general statements are possible. However, if we take an "neutral" approach and assume that changes in quality lead to parallel shifts in demand, so that $x p_s s_x$ and $u_s s_x$ cancel out, the "rent-seeking through quality" effect would be zero. In this scenario, the "rent-seeking through quantity" effect implies that if $\alpha^I = \alpha^O > 0$, the political optimum will lead to a group of insiders which is inefficiently small, and the gap will increase to the extent that producers have greater lobbying power.

Compared to the neutral case, we see that if demand decreases clockwise with decreases in quality, the political equilibrium with $\alpha^I = \alpha^O > 0$ will definitely generate a group of insiders that is inefficiently small. A clockwise decrease in demand implies that a decrease in quality has a greater effect on prices than on consumer utility. On the other hand, if demand decreases counterclockwise, the "rent-seeking through quantity" effect is counteracted by the "rent-seeking through quality" effect. If the quality effect proves strong enough, the political equilibrium may lead to an inefficiently large group of insiders. This will be the case if a decrease in quality has only a small effect on price but a large effect on consumer utility.

9.5 Conclusion

In this chapter, we developed a theoretical model to study standards that are set by the government and explicitly include or exclude some producers. Our analysis derived both the socially optimal size of the group of "insiders" and the likely outcome if the population of insiders is decided by a government that is susceptible to lobbying. In our analysis, a larger group of "insiders" has three consequences. First, an expansion increases total production, which depresses the price of the product. Second, expansion allows the fixed costs of common activities undertaken by the group of insiders (e.g., marketing, training) to be spread over a larger production volume. Third, the expansion may have a negative effect on (actual or perceived) quality, which would reduce consumers' willingness to pay.

We showed that the social optimum is determined by a trade-off between the positive effect on consumer utility of extra production, the negative effect on consumer utility of lower quality, and the marginal cost of the common activities. The social optimum implies that prices will be greater than this marginal cost if there is a quality effect. However, the social optimum may also imply that this markup is not sufficient for insiders to recover their fixed costs.

Our analysis of the political equilibrium emphasizes the existence of two interest groups – insiders and outsiders. If the government aims to maximize aggregate producer surplus, the size of the group of insiders may be smaller or larger than the social optimum depending on two effects. The "rent seeking through quality" effect may induce either a smaller or a larger population of insiders than the social optimum, as producers take into account the effect of quality on prices and not on consumer utility. The "rent seeking through quantity" effect will always induce a smaller population of insiders. Whether the resulting population of insiders is larger or smaller thus depends on the sign of the "rent seeking through quality" effect and/or the relative magnitude of both effects. If the government aims to maximize insider welfare, the resulting population of insiders will be smaller than that which maximizes aggregate producer welfare. By contrast, if the government maximizes outsider welfare, the result is an "open access" equilibrium where rents are driven down to the point at which they just cover fixed costs.

Our analysis of the political equilibrium showed that in general the resulting population of insiders will be bounded by these four optima (for aggregate producer welfare, insider welfare, outsider welfare, and social welfare). The political equilibrium will generally not coincide with the social optimum. Compared to the aggregate producer optimum, the insider optimum and the outsider optimum, the social optimum may be smaller than all three, larger than all three, or somewhere in between, depending on how a change in quality affects prices and consumer utility.

9.6 Appendix: Side Payments from Outsiders to Insiders

Assume that outsiders can make side payments to the existing producers, in effect "buying" their entry into the group of insiders (or more precisely, buying the insiders' support for an expansion). In this case, potential entrants would be willing to pay up to their profits $p - c - (F/x)$. The first-order condition of the existing producers, deciding on an expansion, then becomes

$$\frac{\partial \Pi^I}{\partial x} = (p - c) + x(p_x + p_s s_x) = 0 \qquad (9.20)$$

This is exactly the same first-order condition as that which maximizes aggregate producer welfare (equation (9.12)). The result is intuitive: if potential entrants can make side payments, the existing producers will internalize the positive effect of increased revenues for these new producers. The possibility of side payments makes the group of insiders behave as if it maximized aggregate producer welfare instead of the welfare of the existing producers. This result is similar to our conclusion in Chapter 7, where we showed that side payments from the producers to the retailer induced the retailer to maximize their joint surplus.

10

Standards, Production Structure, and Inclusion in Value Chains

10.1 Introduction

In Part II of this book we analyzed and discussed the decisions to select and impose standards in value chains. In Part III we discuss and analyze the implications of these choices by governments and companies.

The early literature in this field posited that the rise of standards could have sharp negative influences on equity and poverty in developing countries because modern value chains would systematically exclude the poor. It was suggested that, unlike other waves of rising economic activity, the poor would suffer from this process (see Chapter 1). Studies on Latin America and Africa argued that small producers were being left behind in the supermarket-driven marketing and trade expansion (Dolan and Humphrey, 2000; Humphrey et al., 2004; Key and Runsten, 1999; Minot and Ngigi, 2004; Reardon et al., 2003; Weatherspoon et al., 2001). Modern value chains put intense pressure on smallholders. As a result of standards, exports were increasingly being cultivated on large industrial estates. Weatherspoon and Reardon (2003) argued that the rise of supermarkets in southern Africa failed to help small producers who were almost completely excluded from dynamic urban markets due to quality and safety requirements.

However, other research suggested a more nuanced picture of the effect on poverty and its overall development implications. Studies showed that in several cases small farmers did produce for modern value chains. For example, Huang et al. (2008) and Wang et al. (2009) showed that in China, where rising urban incomes and the emergence of a relatively wealthy middle class are associated with an enormous rise in the demand for fruits and vegetables and sharp shifts in the downstream segment of the food chain toward "modern retailing," almost all of the increased supply is being produced by small, relatively poor, farmers. Dries and Swinnen (2004) and

Dries et al. (2009) find that also in more developed regions, as in several Eastern European countries, small farmers are the dominant suppliers in modern value chains. In a review of several studies, Reardon et al. (2009) and Maertens et al. (2012) show that the involvement of small suppliers in high-standard production systems differs remarkably – even within similar commodity chains.

These conflicting empirical findings are puzzling. Why would one observe such different outcomes? To understand better why different outcomes may emerge, this chapter develops a formal theory of the process in which modern value chains and demand signals are directing suppliers to produce and sell high-standards goods. The theory allows analyzing whether this process could result in different outcomes when economies are characterized by different structural conditions. In particular, it is possible to study which suppliers are most likely to be included in these modern value chains, and how the inclusion process is affected by factors such as the productivity distribution of suppliers and the nature of the transaction costs involved.

Initial differences in income and capital and transaction costs are shown to affect the emergence and the size of the high-standards economy. There is an important interaction between standards and production structures: initial differences in the production structure influence the emergence of high-standards economic sectors and which suppliers are included in the high-standards economy and which not. Differences in transaction costs have similar effects.

The theory developed here analyzes the emergence and size of the "high-standards" economy. In this chapter, for the basic analysis, it is assumed that suppliers are not credit-constrained and that interactions between suppliers and processors are characterized by perfect competition without contract enforcement issues. In reality, however, these conditions are unlikely to be true: suppliers may suffer from credit constraints, contract enforcement may not be perfect, and processors may have market power over their suppliers. Subsequent chapters will analyze these issues (see Chapters 11 to 16).

The chapter is organized as follows. In Section 10.2, we present a formal model to analyze the endogenous process of the introduction of high-standards products in developing countries. We discuss the structural factors of the market equilibrium resulting from this model. Sections 10.3 and 10.4 analyze how the inclusivity of this process toward suppliers is influenced by respectively the production structure and the nature of transaction costs. Section 10.5 concludes the chapter.

10.2 The Model

Assume two open economies, indexed by superscript $v = D,F$, where D is the domestic, low-income country and F is the foreign, high-income country.

10.2.1 Demand

To model the demand side, in this chapter we draw on the vertical differentiation literature (as explained in Chapter 2). We consider the unit-demand version of the standard vertical product differentiation model whereby each consumer buys at most one unit of the good. The model is adjusted for a limited number of product types and relates income directly to the preferences for quality, following Tirole (1988).[1]

Assume that there are only two types of products with different standards in this market, a basic *low-standards* product with standard s_L and a *high-standards* product with standard $s_H > s_L$. When both varieties are available, consumers choose among three options:

$$U_i^v = \begin{cases} i^v s_H - p_H^v & \text{if the high standards good is bought} \\ i^v s_L - p_L^v & \text{if the low standards good is bought} \\ 0 & \text{otherwise} \end{cases} \quad (10.1)$$

where U is the consumer surplus derived from the consumption of the good, s_H and s_L are the standards and p_H^v and p_L^v are the unit consumer prices of respectively the high- and low-standards product in country v; the index $i^v \in [I^v - 1, I^v]$ represents consumer income. Consumers with higher incomes are assumed to have preferences for higher standards. The distribution of income $F(i^v)$ is uniform between $I^v - 1$ and I^v. We assume that the distribution of income does not change when income grows so that an increase of a country's aggregate income can be represented by an increase of I^v.

---

[1] Our approach implicitly assumes that the introduction of high-standards production reflects consumer preferences. Another reason why a company may want to introduce certain quality or process standards is to reduce transaction costs in sourcing and selling (Fulponi, 2007; Henson, 2006; McCluskey and Winfree, 2009). As the introduction of quality or process standards for these purposes would also require specific investments by suppliers (hence higher production costs) and (increased) transaction costs for the processors, most of such effects would be similar to the ones described in this chapter.

When both high-standards (HS) and low-standards (LS) products are bought by some consumers and other consumers buy nothing (i.e., the market is "uncovered"), country v's aggregate market demand functions Q_H^v and Q_L^v are

$$Q_H^v = M\left(I^v - \frac{p_H^v - p_L^v}{\Delta}\right); \tag{10.2}$$

$$Q_L^v = M\left(\frac{p_H^v - p_L^v}{\Delta} - \frac{p_L^v}{s_L}\right); \tag{10.3}$$

subject to $(p_L^v / s_L) + 1 > I^v > (p_H^v - p_L^v)/\Delta$, where M is the number of consumers (which we assume to be identical in both economies) and $\Delta \equiv s_H - s_L$ represents the difference in standards. If $I^v < (p_H^v - p_L^v)/\Delta$ there is no demand for HS products in country v (i.e., $Q_H^v = 0$).[2] Total demand for each product equals the sum of both countries' aggregate demand functions, that is, $Q_H = Q_H^D + Q_H^F$ for HS products and $Q_L = Q_L^D + Q_L^F$ for LS products.

10.2.2 Supply

On the supply side, we assume that both countries have a standard competitive industry populated by numerous suppliers who behave as price takers. In our model all suppliers are able to produce either the high-standards or the low-standards product. To start with, we assume that suppliers are identical. Later in the chapter we will relax this assumption and analyze how supplier differences affect their integration into the high-standards economy.

We assume further that suppliers have a production technology that requires a unit cost c_H^v and c_L^v, for the high- and low-standards product respectively, and that $c_H^v = c_L^v + k^v$, where k^v is the per unit additional capital costs for producing the high-standards product, which depends both on the amount of capital goods needed and on the cost of capital. Finally, for simplicity, we assume that the other costs remain the same and that suppliers can produce the same number of units of the commodity regardless of whether they produce low-standards or high-standards commodities.[3]

---

[2] See Gabszewicz and Thisse (1979) and Tirole (1988) for formal derivations of these conclusions.

[3] This assumption is consistent, for example, with a farmer who may produce 100 liters of noncooled, high-bacteria milk if operating in the low-standards market or, after an

10.2.3 Marketing and Trade

Once the products are produced in response to consumer demand, our model needs to account for the transfer of commodities from the supplier to the final consumer. For simplicity we assume that one unit of production is identical to one unit at retail (consumer) level for both high and low standards. We use different marketing assumptions for the LS products and the HS products. We assume that suppliers sell their LS commodity at price p_L^v under perfect competition. For the HS value chain, we assume that "processors" (which may represent any company involved in processing, marketing, or retailing) purchase the HS commodity from suppliers at price w_H^v and resell this commodity to consumers at price p_H^v. We consider that these companies incur a unit transaction cost τ^v in sourcing from suppliers. Under perfect competition and free entry and exit for processors, it follows that the consumer price of the commodity is the sum of the producer price and the transaction cost, such that $p_H^v = w_H^v + \tau^v$.[4]

We assume ad valorem international trade costs t between economies D and F. These trade costs include regulatory costs such as ad valorem tariffs as well as transportation costs.

10.2.4 Standards and the Market Equilibrium

The international allocation of production is determined by relative production costs and trade costs. For our analysis, we are particularly interested how export demand for the HS product affects production in the low-income country D. Export of HS will occur if $c_L^F + k^F + \tau^F > (1+t)(c_L^D + k^D + \tau^D)$.

We assume that $c_L^F > (1+t)c_L^D$. In this case (because of perfect competition and constant unit costs) all production is taking place in country D and country F imports both high-standards and low-standards products. Consumer prices in the foreign country F are then equal to $p_H^F = (1+t)p_H^D$ and $p_L^F = (1+t)p_L^D$. With all production in country D, we omit the unit

---

investment in a cooling tank is made, 100 liters of cooled, low-bacteria milk if operating in the high-standards market.

4 "Processing costs" are implicitly included in τ. We also considered an alternative model with a monopolistic market structure in processing. This vastly complicated the model without yielding substantial differences in the key results regarding the issues where this chapter focuses on. See Swinnen and Vandeplas (2010), as well as Chapter 12, for an analysis of the role and effects of competition in the emergence and growth of a high-standards economy.

production and transaction costs superscripts in the remainder of the analysis. With suppliers' supply of low and high-standards products determined by their respective marginal costs c_L and c_H and the sum of both countries' aggregate demand functions from (10.2) and (10.3), we can derive the market equilibrium level of LS products X_L^* and HS products X_H^* as follows:

$$X_L^* = M(2+t)\left(\frac{k+\tau}{\Delta} - \frac{c_L}{s_L}\right) \tag{10.4}$$

$$X_H^* = M\left(I^D + I^F - (2+t)\left(\frac{k+\tau}{\Delta}\right)\right) \tag{10.5}$$

Equilibrium equations (10.4) and (10.5) hold given that the marketing of LS products is allowed in both countries D and F. However, countries may impose public standards to prohibit the marketing of LS products. For example, in case the high-income country F imposes a public standard and bans LS products, its demand function for the HS product is

$$Q_H^F = M\left(I^F - \frac{p_H^F}{s_H}\right) \tag{10.6}$$

and the uncovered market conditions are $I^F > p_H^F / s_H > I^F - 1$. The market equilibrium equations are then

$$X_L^* = M\left(\frac{k+\tau}{\Delta} - \frac{c_L}{s_L}\right) \tag{10.7}$$

$$X_H^* = M\left(I^D + I^F - (1+t)\left(\frac{c_L + \kappa + \tau}{s_H}\right) - \frac{\kappa + \tau}{\Delta}\right). \tag{10.8}$$

In the rest of the analysis we use the more general case where both LS and HS products are available in both countries such that the set of equations (10.4) and (10.5) determines the market equilibrium. Our analysis can be applied to the other case (public standards) as well – the results remain qualitatively the same.

10.2.5 Impact of Structural Factors

Equations (10.4) and (10.5) incorporate the relationship between a series of structural variables and the relative importance of the high- and low-standards economies. For each of the key variables (I^v, k, τ, Δ) one can identify threshold levels (either minima or maxima) for the high-standards economy (HSE) to exist, that is, for $X_H^* > 0$. For positive levels of X_H^*, one can use comparative statics to show how the variables affect the size of the HSE.

Income (I^v). The size of the HSE is directly related to the level of income in the economies. A minimum level of income in either country D or F is required for a HSE to emerge. Formally, when $I^F > (1+t)\left((k+\tau)/\Delta\right)$, income in country F is sufficiently high such that HS production emerges in country D. Similarly, when $I^D > (k+\tau)/\Delta$, income in country D is sufficiently high to support the emergence of the HSE. Which of these is the actual driver of the emergence of the HSE depends on the relative sizes of I^D, I^F, and t. If $I^F > (1+t)\left((k+\tau)/\Delta\right)$ while $I^D < \left((k+\tau)/\Delta\right)$, the development of the HSE is export-driven. Oppositely, if $I^D > (k+\tau)/\Delta$ while $I^F < (1+t)\left((k+\tau)/\Delta\right)$, the emergence of the HSE is driven by domestic demand. Export-driven development of the HSE is consistent with the observation that HS production systems tend to emerge first in export sectors in developing countries. For example, in many African economies HS production is limited to value chains targeted to (high-income) foreign consumer markets while production for domestic markets is limited to LS production. Domestically driven development of the HSE is consistent with the observation that HS markets are more likely found in countries with higher incomes than in countries with lower incomes. In addition, once income in one of the countries is above its threshold, equation (10.5) shows that the HSE becomes larger when income increases, that is, $\partial X_H^* / \partial I^v = M > 0$.

Capital costs (k). As mentioned earlier, capital costs k consist of the amount of capital goods needed and the cost of capital. In many developing countries capital constraints are important and the real cost of capital is high. According to our model this is another reason that HS markets are less likely to emerge in poorer countries. If capital costs of producing HS are too high, that is, if $k > \Delta I^D - \tau$ and $k > \Delta I^F / (1+t) - \tau$, then no HSE will emerge. Moreover, given that a HSE exists, the size of the HSE will be smaller if capital costs are higher, as $\partial X_H^* / \partial k = -M(2+t)/\Delta < 0$ when HS products are consumed in both countries. If consumers in only one of these countries purchase HS products, $\partial X_H^* / \partial k$ is smaller in absolute value but also negative ($\partial X_H^* / \partial k = -M/\Delta$ for domestic consumption only and $\partial X_H^* / \partial k = -M(1+t)/\Delta$ for exports only).

Quality difference (Δ): An additional condition for the emergence of a HSE is that the high-standards level is sufficiently larger than the low-standards level, given the extra cost of that quality difference. Formally, the quality difference Δ must be such that $\Delta > (k + \tau)/I^D$ (for domestically driven development of the HSE) or $\Delta > (1 + t)(k + \tau)/I^F$ (for export-driven development of the HSE). Given that at least one of these conditions is fulfilled, the HSE will be larger for larger quality differences. If the HS product is consumed only domestically, then $\partial X_H^* / \partial \Delta = M(k + \tau)/\Delta^2 > 0$, and $\partial X_H^* / \partial \Delta = (1 + t)M(k + \tau)/\Delta^2 > 0$ for foreign consumption only. If the HS product is sold in both countries, then $\partial X_H^* / \partial \Delta = (2 + t)M(k + \tau)/\Delta^2 > 0$.

Trade costs (t): Export-driven development of the HSE can take place only when trade costs are not prohibitively high, that is, when $t < \Delta I^F / (k + \tau) - 1$. If so, the HSE will be larger for smaller trade costs because $\partial X_H^* / \partial t = -M(k + \tau)/\Delta < 0$. Not surprisingly, policy reforms which reduce t, such as reduction of export taxes in D or of import tariffs in F stimulate growth of the HSE in D.

As we will show in the next sections, these conclusions need to be nuanced when one allows explicitly for details on the production structure as well as on the nature of transaction costs.

10.3 Production Structure

In addition to being able to predict the factors that underlie the emergence of the HSE, our model can also be used to gain insights on what types of suppliers are most likely to join the HSE (when it emerges) and what types of suppliers will likely be left out. As discussed in the introduction, this issue has attracted much policy attention and academic debate. Some studies have argued that smallholders are excluded from HS production due to economies of scale and higher transaction costs; others have argued that this is not (necessarily) the case.

However, the impact of scale economies is not as trivial as often argued in the literature. Scale economies can differ strongly between activities (e.g., extensive grain farming compared to intensive vegetable or dairy production).[5]

---

[5] There is an extensive literature showing how farm productivity, and in particular the relationship between size and productivity, tends to differ importantly by commodity (e.g., Allen and Lueck, 1998; Pollak, 1985). For example, although large suppliers may have scale advantages in land-intensive commodities, such as wheat or corn, this is typically much less the case in labor-intensive commodities, such as fruits and vegetables. In fact, there are cases in which small-scale suppliers may have advantages over larger farmers.

Scale economies may also be influenced by local institutions and market constraints.

Although scale economies can be important, we focus on two other factors in our analysis: the initial production structure of the economy and the nature of the transaction costs. We will show that both factors have an important impact on the size of the HSE and on who is included in the HSE.

Initial conditions matter. One might expect different outcomes from the emergence of the HSE in rural settings that have highly unequal distributions of land resources (as in some nations in Latin America and parts of the former Soviet Union, which have some individuals holding massive estates and many smaller, relatively poor farmers) compared to rural societies characterized by more egalitarian distributions of cultivated land (e.g., China, Vietnam, and Poland). In the rest of the analysis we call this the *production structure* of the rural economy. In this section we formally show that the initial production structure indeed matters: the share of smallholders in the production system – and the existence of large holdings amongst the smallholders – affects both the size of the HSE and the integration of smallholders into the HSE. To analyze this we relax the assumption of a homogenous supplier structure such that k is not necessarily identical for all suppliers. Heterogeneity in k could be the result of different requirements in terms of the amounts of capital goods needed, or of differences in access to capital that affect the cost of capital, or of a combination of both factors. Hence, in line with our general model, we introduce supplier heterogeneity by varying the capital cost k.

We assume that capital cost k_j for supplier j is uniformly distributed across N suppliers with $k_j \in [k - \gamma_k, k + \gamma_k], \forall j = \{1, \ldots, N\}$ and $\gamma_k \in [0, k]$ with $k \geq 0$. For simplicity, we assume that individual suppliers only produce one unit of the HS product when they are involved in the HSE.[6] Suppliers with lower capital costs are more efficient.

We can now consider variation in the production structure by considering changes in γ_k. Specifically, the extreme case of homogeneous suppliers – which was the assumption in the first part of the chapter – is represented by

---

In the production of some HS commodities, small farmers may have an advantage over larger farmers because of the importance of labor governance and the quality of the labor input. This implies that the inclusion or exclusion of small farms is likely to depend importantly on the type of the commodity. This is consistent with findings from Wang et al. (2009) on China and Minten et al. (2009) on Madagascar showing that smallholders are extensively included in labor-intensive fruits and vegetable production.

6   Alternatively, one could fix the inputs and consider variation in output, or consider variations in input and/or output size. Our specification is closer to the basic model specification and allows us to derive the key results.

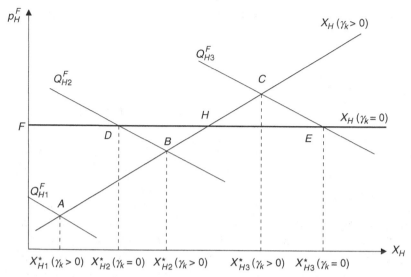

Figure 10.1. HS production under different production structures.

$\gamma_k = 0$. The efficiency distribution is increasingly unequal as γ_k increases. With any given distribution, the average efficiency is represented by capital cost k (as in the general model).

The supply curves for heterogeneous and homogeneous production structures are shown in Figure 10.1. In this graphical representation $X_H(\gamma_k = 0)$ represents the supply function for homogeneous suppliers. Likewise, $X_H(\gamma_k > 0)$ is the supply function for heterogeneous suppliers.[7]

When suppliers choose to produce the HS product, under the assumption that one supplier produces only one unit of output in the HSE, their profits are $w_H - c_L - k_j$, with $w_H = c_L + \tilde{k}$ where $\tilde{k}$ is the capital cost of the supplier who is indifferent between producing for the HSE and the low-standards economy (LSE). Using this, the aggregate supply of HS products is:[8]

$$X_H = \frac{N}{2\gamma_k} \int_{k-\gamma_k}^{\tilde{k}} dk_j = \frac{N}{2\gamma_k}\left(\tilde{k} + \gamma_k - k\right) \qquad (10.9)$$

---

[7] We use X_H to denote the supply function of the high-standards good, and X_H^* to denote the quantity in equilibrium.

[8] When $\gamma_k = 0$, the HS output X_H is completely determined by demand in equilibrium (perfectly elastic supply) and equation (10.9) is irrelevant.

This, in turn, leads to a new expression for the equilibrium quantity in the HS market:

$$X_H^* = M \left(I^D + I^F - \left(2+t\right)\left(\frac{k - \gamma_k + \tau}{\Delta}\right)\right)\left(\frac{\dfrac{N}{2\gamma_k}}{\dfrac{N}{2\gamma_k} + \left(2+t\right)M/\Delta}\right) \qquad (10.10)$$

Comparing equations (10.5) and (10.10) yields some important insights. The expression between the first brackets on the right-hand side of equation (10.10) shows that the HSE will emerge at lower income levels with a heterogeneous production structure than with a more homogeneous structure. Specifically, $I^D > (k - \gamma_k + \tau)/\Delta$ is the condition for domestically driven emergence of the HSE, and $I^F > \left(1+t\right)(k - \gamma_k + \tau)/\Delta$ for export-driven emergence of the HSE. With $\gamma_k > 0$ these required income levels are lower than when $\gamma_k = 0$. In addition, the required income level (for the emergence of a HSE) declines when the distribution is more unequal (that is, when γ_k is higher). The intuitive reason for this finding is that when an economy faces a more heterogeneous production structure, there are more efficient suppliers among the entire set of suppliers, ceteris paribus. As a result, these suppliers will be able to produce HS products when it is not possible when the economy is characterized by a homogeneous production structure.

However, the term between the second brackets on the right-hand side of equation (10.10) implies that the expansion of HS production – once it exists – proceeds more gradually when there is a heterogeneous distribution of suppliers. To see this, define $B = 2\left(2+t\right)M\gamma_k / N\Delta$. The third term then equals $1/\left(1+B\right)$, which is less than 1 with $B > 0$. Formally, $\partial X_H^* / \partial I^v = M/(1+B)$ given that both income thresholds are met. With $B = 0$ when $\gamma_k = 0$, and $\partial B / \partial \gamma_k > 0$, it follows that the growth in X_H^* with increasing income is more gradual for a more heterogeneous set of suppliers.

These results are illustrated in Figure 10.1. Our theoretical results hold in general, but to reduce the complexity of the graphical analyses, we assume in all figures that I^D is constant and smaller than $(k - \gamma_k + \tau)/\Delta$ such that in equilibrium only consumers in country F consume the HS product. Increasing demand is analyzed through increasing income of the foreign country, I^F, and because our graphical assumption implies that there is no domestic HS consumption in equilibrium, we only depict foreign demand

Q_H^F (and hence p_H^F) in the figures. Similar graphs can be drawn when only I^D is above its threshold level, or when both I^D and I^F are above their threshold values – the results are qualitatively the same.

In Figure 10.1 $X_H(\gamma_k = 0)$ represents the supply function for homogeneous suppliers and $X_H(\gamma_k > 0)$ the supply function for heterogeneous suppliers. As this graphical representation shows, the effect of heterogeneity is to rotate a perfectly elastic supply curve into an upward-sloping supply curve. For low income I^F, represented by demand function Q_{H1}^F for HS products, the equilibrium output in the HS market is zero with homogeneously distributed suppliers that is, $X_{H1}^*(\gamma_k = 0) = 0$. In contrast, under a heterogeneous supplier structure, the HSE does emerge and the equilibrium is at point *A*. HS output is equal to $X_{H1}^*(\gamma_k > 0)$. For increasing higher income levels, represented by demand curves Q_{H2}^F and Q_{H3}^F, the market equilibrium with the heterogeneous structure shifts to points *B* and *C*, respectively. For the homogeneous production structure, there is also positive HS output at Q_{H2}^F and Q_{H3}^F, represented by points *D* and *E*, respectively.

Figure 10.1 thus illustrates that HS production emerges at lower levels of income for a heterogeneous production structure (represented by point *A*). However, once the HS emerges in an economy characterized by a more homogeneous structure, the growth of HSE is more rapid as income grows. When examining Figure 10.1, note that the growth of production represented by the shift from point *D* to *E* is larger than for the shift from *B* to *C*.

These results are further illustrated in Figure 10.2. When income is too low, that is, $I^F < (1+t)(k + \tau - \gamma_k)/\Delta$, as illustrated by point *G*, there is no HSE under either the heterogeneous or homogeneous structure. As income increases, however, the HSE emerges first in the economy characterized by a heterogeneous production structure for $I^F > (1+t)(k + \tau - \gamma_k)/\Delta$, shown by point *A*. Under the assumption that a nation's production structure is homogeneous, the minimum income requirement for the emergence of a HSE is higher, that is, $I^F > (1+t)(k + \tau)/\Delta$. When income is low, that is, $(1+t)(k + \tau - \gamma_k)/\Delta < I^F < (1+t)(k + \tau)/\Delta$, an HSE exists under the heterogeneous structure (point *A*), but does not (yet) exist under the homogeneous structure (point *F*). At higher incomes, HS production is also positive for the homogeneous structure, but output remains higher for the heterogeneous production structure as long as income does not reach the level $I^F = (1+t)(k + \tau)/\Delta + (N/2M)$ (point *H*). At higher incomes, the homogeneous supplier structure produces higher output. Finally, when income is larger than $(1+t)(k + \tau)/\Delta + (N/M)$ but lower than

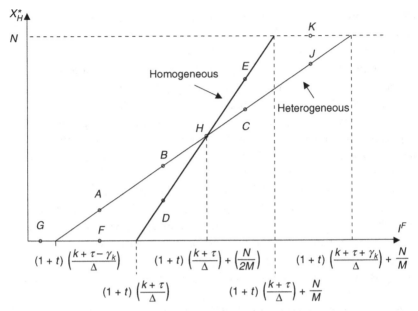

Figure 10.2. Size of the HSE under different production structures.

$(1+t)(k+\tau+\gamma_k)/\Delta+(N/M)$, the HSE includes all suppliers under the homogeneous structure but not under the heterogeneous structure, shown respectively by points K and J.

This approach also allows us to analyze *who is included in the HSE*. With a heterogeneous production structure, the most efficient suppliers will start producing HS at low income levels. However, given the same set of incomes and other factors, the less efficient suppliers will be excluded. When the production structure of an economy is more homogeneous, HS production will start only at higher income levels. Although beginning later in the development process, once started the process will be more inclusive. More suppliers will be included.

This insight can be seen graphically in Figure 10.3, which plots isoquants of HS production. The horizontal axis shows the heterogeneity parameter γ_k, while the vertical axis now represents income I^F. We show three isoquants. The first is the line showing the emergence of the HSE, that is, where the fraction of suppliers engaged in HS production first becomes greater than 0%. This line is characterized by $(1+t)(k+\tau-\gamma_k)/\Delta$, the minimum income level required for a HSE to emerge under given supplier heterogeneity γ_k. It illustrates again that when suppliers are more heterogeneous,

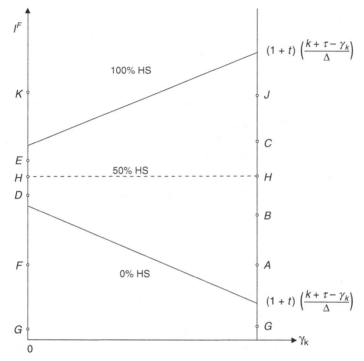

Figure 10.3. Combined impact of production structure and income on HSE.

a lower level of income is needed for the emergence of the HSE. The second isoquant shows all combinations of income and supplier heterogeneity which result in the HSE accounting for exactly half of production. As can be seen, there is only one income level at which this is the case, irrespective of γ_k. This corresponds to the observation that changes in γ_k lead to rotations around point H in Figure 10.2. The third isoquant is the exact mirror image of the first isoquant and shows all combinations of income and supplier heterogeneity for which 100% of the suppliers are part of the HSE. This income level is lower for lower heterogeneity. As this graphical illustration makes clear, for higher values of γ_k the HSE emerges at lower levels of income; but income growth leads to a slower growth of the HSE, and a higher income level is needed to achieve 100% HSE.

Figure 10.3 also illustrates that when income increases, a homogeneous supplier structure is more inclusive toward less efficient suppliers. For a given level of γ_k, as we move from low to high levels of income, it will be the suppliers with the lowest values of k_j who are first included in the HSE. Because we assume that every supplier produces one unit, and given the assumption that k_j is uniformly distributed, we can read the isoquants as quantiles of the distribution of k_j. Thus, a 10% isoquant would indicate the situation where 10% of total production consisted of HS product, or equivalently the point where the 10% most efficient suppliers were included in the HSE. Because a given increase in income leads to a stronger increase in total production if γ_k is lower, it thus follows that for low values of γ_k there is a more rapid inclusion of suppliers. Moreover, a situation of 100% HSE (including even the least efficient suppliers in the HSE) is reached at lower income levels with homogeneous structures. Of course, as the graph also makes clear, at sufficiently high income levels all suppliers will be included under any production structure.

10.4 Transaction Costs

The nature of transaction costs is another fundamental feature of an economy that may affect the HSE. First, transaction costs affect the overall size of HS production. Higher transaction costs constrain the size of the HSE. If both income thresholds are met, the formal effect is $\partial X_H^* / \partial \tau = -(2+t)(M / \Delta)$ < 0 (see equation (10.5)). It makes sourcing from suppliers more costly and therefore increases the relative cost of HS products.

Second, transaction costs will also affect *who is included*. In the literature, a standard argument is that there are fixed transaction costs per supplier for processors (Poulton et al., 2010; Raynolds, 2004). This implies that transaction costs per unit of output are lower for large producers and hence small suppliers will be excluded. However, such conclusion depends on the specific (often implicit) assumptions on the nature of the transaction costs. In reality there are different types of transaction costs that might be important when processors source HS commodities from suppliers.[9] For example, one common type of transaction costs might include costs of search (by company procurement agents that are looking for suppliers that are willing to supply to the HSE), supervision costs, quality and process control costs and the costs of enforcement of agreements. Some of these costs are fixed per supplier, while others depend on the amount of output or input. For conceptual purposes, one could thus distinguish three types of transaction costs: those that are fixed per supplier (e.g., contract negotiation costs), those that are fixed per unit of output (e.g., output control costs) and those

---

[9] We discuss different types of transaction costs in more detail in Chapter 16.

that are fixed per unit of production input (e.g., monitoring of plots and production activities).

To show that these different types of transaction costs have different effects on the emergence, size, and composition of the HSE, we compare two types of transaction costs. Specifically, we assume that τ_j is a supplier specific transaction cost. It is uniformly distributed over the interval $\left[\tau - \gamma_\tau, \tau + \gamma_\tau\right]$ with $\gamma_\tau \in \left[0, \tau\right]$ and $\tau \geq 0$. With transaction costs defined in this way, we first consider the case when transaction costs are fixed per supplier. This means that transaction costs are identical for all suppliers (or, $\gamma_\tau = 0$ and $\tau_j = \tau$). In the second case, we consider transaction costs which are fixed per unit of input. This implies that transaction costs are negatively related to supplier efficiency, that is, $(\partial \tau_j / \partial k_j) > 0$.

It is immediately clear that these different types of transaction costs will have fundamentally different implications for which suppliers are included in the HSE. In one case, the transaction costs will be "neutral" regarding productivity heterogeneity; in the other case, they will reinforce the productivity bias. Formally this can be seen from the new condition for the equilibrium output of HS products with supplier specific transaction costs:[10]

$$X_H^* = M\left[I^D + I^F - (2+t)\left(\frac{(k-\gamma_k)+(\tau-\gamma_\tau)}{\Delta}\right)\right]\left(\frac{\dfrac{N}{2(\gamma_k+\gamma_\tau)}}{\dfrac{N}{2(\gamma_k+\gamma_\tau)}+(2+t)\left(\dfrac{M}{\Delta}\right)}\right).$$

(10.11)

It follows from equation (10.11) that the structure with heterogeneous transaction costs, that is, γ_τ, will induce earlier emergence of HSE for increasing income levels. The HSE arises when $I^D > (\tau + k - \gamma_k - \gamma_\tau)/\Delta$ or when $I^F > (1+t)(\tau + k - \gamma_k - \gamma_\tau)/\Delta$, which are both less restrictive for higher γ_τ (more heterogeneity in transaction costs).

This effect is illustrated in Figure 10.4 (where, for ease of exposition, we now omit the demand curve Q_{H1}^F). The HS supply function with fixed transaction costs ($\gamma_\tau = 0$) per supplier is identical to that of Figure 10.1 with

[10] In this new equilibrium, the consumer price p_H equals $c_L + \tilde{k} + \tilde{\tau}$, where $\tilde{\tau}$ is the supplier-specific transaction cost of the supplier who is indifferent between producing for the HSE and the LSE. Because of perfect competition in the processing industry, the additional rents accrue to the suppliers who earn now profits equal to $\left(\tilde{k}-k_j\right)+\left(\tilde{\tau}-\tau_j\right)$.

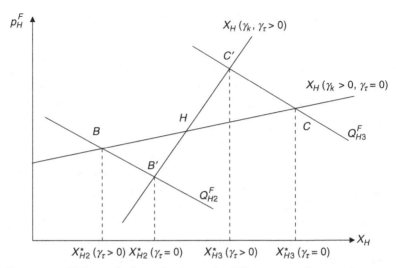

Figure 10.4. High-standards production under different types of transaction costs.

heterogeneous suppliers.[11] It follows from equation (10.11) that with heterogeneous transaction costs, the HS supply function pivots around point H. This implies more HS supply at lower levels of income but less supply at higher levels of income. As illustrated in Figure 10.4, the negative relation of transaction costs with productivity reinforces the productivity effect in the pivot of the supply function.

The impact on who gets included when considering the nature of transaction costs is also analogous to the discussion on the production structure of the economy. Low-productivity suppliers will be less likely included with transaction costs fixed per unit of input and vice versa. In this way, transaction costs reinforce the productivity effect, in the sense that they reduce the purchasing costs for processors from more productive suppliers. Suppliers with higher productivity will have even more cost advantages because the per unit transaction costs are lower. However, this result depends on the nature of "transaction costs." If transaction costs are fixed per supplier, this is not the case.

Notice that one should be careful in interpreting these findings. Our specific findings are conditional on our model specification, which

---

[11] Note that in case of homogeneous suppliers, there is no effect of the nature of the transaction costs on who gets included because all suppliers (and thus their transaction costs) are identical.

assumes there is a fixed output per supplier. However, our main result, that is, that the impact on the inclusion in the HSE depends on the nature of the transaction costs, holds in general. In reality, some transaction costs are fixed per supplier, such as those for bargaining and search. Other costs, however, such as product or process control costs, would at least have a component that is better modeled as per unit of output or input cost. To the extent that these variable transaction costs are more important, the cost advantage of large and more productive suppliers will change.

10.5 Conclusions

In this chapter we have developed a formal theory of the process of the endogenous introduction of high-standards production in developing countries. We used our theoretical model to analyze how different structural conditions of the economy and trade affect the emergence and size of the high-standards economy (HSE). Differences in income, trade barriers, capital costs, the extent and nature of transaction costs, and whether the production structure is homogeneous or heterogeneous are shown to affect the timing of the emergence and the size of the HSE.

We also examined which factors affect who is able to participate in the HSE as it is emerging. Not surprisingly, we find that the most efficient suppliers switch first to producing for the HS market. Importantly, our analysis shows how the nature of the initial production structure can affect both the size and distributional effects of the HSE. Ceteris paribus, in countries with a mixed production structure, combining, for example, large and medium size commercial farms with small-scale household farms, the growth of the HSE is likely to start earlier but lead to an initial exclusion of smallholders from the HSE. In contrast, in countries where the farm sector is more uniform and dominated by small farms, the emergence of the HSE will occur later but can be expected to be more inclusive.

The first conditions (mixed production structure) are those of several Latin American countries and parts of Eastern Europe and the former Soviet Union. A homogenous production structure dominated by small farms is that of countries such as China and Vietnam, India and parts of Africa, Eastern Europe, and Central Asia. However, to draw predictions (or explanations) for specific countries one should take into account all the structural variables together. For example, if in some countries the production structure is mixed but capital costs are high, they may face a "slow and exclusive" HSE process, and vice versa if in some countries small suppliers dominate but capital costs are relatively low, they may face an "early and inclusive" process.

Transaction costs also play an important role as they may or may not reinforce the disadvantaged position of less efficient suppliers – depending on the nature of the transaction costs. Reducing these transaction costs, for example, by investments in infrastructure, producer associations, third-party quality control and monitoring institutions, could also play a role in reducing the bias against small and less efficient suppliers and speed their integration into the HSE.

Although policies and institutions have not been explicitly modeled, they do affect the equilibrium indirectly through their effect on the various factors which we have discussed. For example, if foreign investment rules were liberalized, they could stimulate the HSE through their effect on the inflow of FDI and reduced capital costs for suppliers. Public investments in infrastructure and institutions that promote quality control and safety institutions could stimulate the HSE by reducing transaction costs in the HS market. Economic and institutional reforms could also have non-linear dynamic effects on the HSE if they initially increase the cost of capital because of disruptions (as they did during the early years of the transition in Eastern Europe). In the longer run, however, institutional reform reduces the cost of capital as the more efficient, post-liberalization economic system develops. More generally, policies that affect macroeconomic uncertainty and the security of property rights for investors are likely to affect the emergence and size of the HSE through their effects on the cost of capital for suppliers.

The model in this chapter is a basic one, with several simplifying assumptions to facilitate analyzing the introduction of HS products in developing countries. Interactions between the processors and the suppliers in the HSE were modeled under assumptions of perfect competition, the absence of credit constraints among suppliers, and perfect enforcement of contracts. In reality, processors may have some degree of market power over suppliers; suppliers may be credit constrained; and both processors and suppliers might have options to engage in contract breach. There is substantial empirical evidence that in response to these pressures the relationship between processor and supplier is often more complicated, taking the form of complex contracts or other forms of vertical integration. Moreover, to complete the analysis further one should also look at the interaction with labor markets. HS investments affect labor markets as the new investments create off-farm employment both inside the processing facility, as well as in the service sector (e.g., in the areas of extension, packaging, supervision, controlling, marketing and transport). Some – or most – of these jobs are low skilled and may be taken by the poorest of the poor. Empirical studies indicate that if HS production takes place through vertically integrated company-owned farms, this may have different effects on rural households than when they can start producing HS commodities themselves.[12] In the next chapters, we systematically address these points.

---

[12] See, e.g., Maertens and Swinnen (2009).

11

Standards, Market Imperfections, and Vertical Coordination in Value Chains

11.1 Introduction

In Chapter 10 we developed a formal theory of the endogenous process of the introduction of quality and safety standards. We showed that there is an important interaction between standards and production structures. Initial differences in the production structure are shown to influence the emergence of high-standards economic sectors and also which producers are included in the high-standards economy, and which are not. This theory provides an explanation for the remarkable heterogeneity in production structures in high-standards value chains.

The analysis of Chapter 10 assumed for simplicity that producers are not credit constrained and that there are no contract enforcement issues. In real-world settings, however, a crucial factor is the existence of market imperfections, in particular in credit and technology markets. Constrained access to necessary inputs implies major constraints to investments required for quality upgrading, especially for local producers who cannot source from international capital markets. In fact, the introduction of higher quality requirements has coincided with the growth of contracting and technology transfer between buyers and suppliers. Contracts for quality production with local suppliers in developing countries not only specify conditions for delivery and production processes but also include the provision of inputs, credit, technology, and/or management advice (Minten et al., 2009; World Bank, 2005). Empirical evidence shows indeed that vertical coordination, under the form of interlinked contracting,[1] plays an important role in the integration of small producers in high-standards

---

[1] Interlinked contracting refers to contracts which come as a "package deal," with the terms of one transaction (e.g., product sales) depending on the terms of another transaction (e.g., credit or input provision) (Bardhan and Udry, 1999: 110).

value chains, by improving access to credit, technology and quality inputs in Eastern Europe, Asia, and Africa (Dries et al., 2009; Swinnen, 2006, 2007; World Bank, 2005).

However, the enforcement of contracts for quality production is difficult in developing countries, which are often characterized by poorly functioning enforcement institutions – another crucial factor. These enforcement problems can add significantly to the cost of contracting and may prevent actual contracting from taking place.[2]

In this chapter we formally analyze how vertical coordination can play a role in the presence of factor market imperfections and weak contract enforcement.[3] We analyze how these factors affect surplus creation and rent distribution and how the process of development affects both. Our model starts from the assumption that vertical coordination can emerge as a spontaneous response to, on the one hand, the demand for high-standards products and on the other hand suppliers' credit constraints. However, this vertical coordination is vulnerable to both supplier and buyer holdup, which affects the feasibility of the contract as well as the distribution of the gains.

Our analysis leads to a number of insights. First, we show that local suppliers in developing countries can benefit importantly from integration in high-standards value chains.

Second, even if a contract is mutually beneficial, the feasibility of contracting is not guaranteed. We show that the extent of such "inefficient separation" (defined as the absence of socially efficient contracting) is a decreasing function of the "value" in the value chain, and increasing in the payoff the supplier would achieve under a holdup and in the cost of external contract enforcement.

Third, also the distribution of the gains from contracting depends on the cost of third-party enforcement and on the payoffs under supplier and/ or buyer holdup. If third-party enforcement (formal or informal) is very

---

[2] There is an extensive literature on the role of formal and informal enforcement institutions in development, e.g., Dhillon and Rigolini (2006), Fafchamps (2004), Greif (2006), North (1990), Platteau (2000), and so forth.

[3] The analysis in this chapter is related to other research fields, in particular to research on foreign direct investment spillovers, which suggests that foreign companies are more likely to engage in vertical integration and vertical coordination (Aghion et al., 2006), and on the distribution of rents within companies, domestically (Blanchflower et al., 1996) and internationally (Borjas and Ramey, 1995; Budd et al., 2005). The analysis also relates to a large body of research on interlinked markets (Bardhan, 1989; Bell, 1988); on enforcement in contracts and credit markets (Genicot and Ray, 2006; Gow and Swinnen, 2001; Kranton and Swamy, 2008; Mookherjee and Ray, 2002).

costly, buyers may prefer to make the contract self-enforcing by means of an "efficiency premium" paid to the supplier to ensure contract compliance. Because of this efficiency premium, lack of external enforcement may increase the supplier's income. Conversely, suppliers may prefer to use an "efficiency discount" to avoid ex post contract renegotiation by the buyer.

Fourth, access to cheaper third-party enforcement improves contract feasibility. However, as it reduces the need for an efficiency premium, it may have an adverse impact on supplier income.

Fifth, we find that "development," modeled as an exogenous improvement of output markets, factor markets and enforcement institutions, may have some nonintuitive effects on equity and efficiency, and may hurt some of the contracting parties depending on the circumstances.

This chapter is organized as follows. The next section sets up the basic model and discusses the benchmark case of perfect enforcement, as well as the more realistic case of imperfect enforcement. Sections 11.3 to 11.5 explore how contracts can be made self-enforcing under different holdup conditions, and Section 11.6 discusses the possibility of third-party enforcement of contracts. In Section 11.7 we discuss the impact of development on efficiency and equity within the contract. Section 11.8 concludes the chapter and introduces a set of extensions and applications of this model that will be reviewed in more detail in the next chapters.

11.2 The Model

11.2.1 Setup

We consider a general setting where a local household or company in a developing country – which we refer to as "the supplier" – can sell high-standards products to a trader or a retailing or processing company – which we refer to as "the buyer." This buyer can sell the product (possibly after processing) to consumers – either domestically or internationally – at a unit price p_H.[4]

To produce one unit of the high-standards product, the supplier needs to invest an amount of labor that has an opportunity cost of l. For instance, if the supplier's best alternative is to produce one unit of a low-standards product for the local market, his opportunity cost equals the price of the

---

[4] We assume here that p_H is net of any possible marketing and/or processing costs. This means that an improvement in technical efficiency in the value chain will be reflected in an increase in p_H.

low-quality product ($l = p_{\text{L}}$). As the supplier earns l in the absence of a contract, we refer to this l as the supplier's "disagreement payoff."

The production of high-standards commodities also requires an extra capital investment to buy specific inputs (e.g., fertilizers, credit, seeds, technology). We assume that the supplier does not have access to capital by himself because of credit market imperfections. This is a realistic assumption as in many developing countries local producers and households face important factor market constraints (e.g., Dercon and Christiaensen, 2007). These constraints hurt both suppliers and buyers: they prevent the supplier from producing high-standards products and constrain the buyer's access to high-quality raw materials.

If the buyer has access to the required capital, he can offer a contract to the supplier, which includes the provision of inputs on credit and the conditions (time, amount and price) for purchasing the supplier's product. This, again, is a realistic case because the buyer may have better collateral or more cash flow or face lower transport or transaction costs in accessing the inputs. We refer to the buyer's opportunity cost of capital as k. The opportunity cost of capital for high-standards production will depend on the capital intensity of the crop as well as on the buyer's potential return to alternative investments. In the absence of a contract, the buyer's payoff is k. We refer to this payoff as the buyer's "disagreement payoff."

For simplicity, we assume that labor and capital are used in fixed proportions. Under this assumption, producing one unit of the high-standards product will cost $l + k$. As the high-standards good is sold at a price p_{H}, the net surplus of the collaboration between the supplier and the buyer is $S = p_{\text{H}} - l - k$. We will use S as an indicator of the "value" in the value chain.

A central question is how this surplus (value) will be divided among the supplier and the buyer. In what follows, we denote the supplier's payoff by Y and the buyer's payoff by Π.

11.2.2 Perfect and Costless Enforcement

As a baseline for comparison, we first study a situation of perfect and costless contract enforcement. The division of the contract surplus can be modeled as a Nash bargaining problem, where each party receives his or her disagreement payoff and a share of the contract surplus. We denote the share that accrues to the supplier as β with $0 \leq \beta \leq 1$.[5] Given the

---

[5] We assume the sharing rule is exogenously determined; we return to this issue in more detail in the next chapter.

disagreement payoffs of both parties, the contract payoffs in case of perfect enforcement are

$$Y^* = l + \beta S = l + \beta \left(p_{\mathrm{H}} - l - k \right) \tag{11.1}$$

$$\Pi^* = k + (1-\beta) S = k + (1-\beta)\left(p_{\mathrm{H}} - l - k \right) \tag{11.2}$$

Here we use an asterisk to denote the "perfect enforcement" outcome. Under perfect enforcement, high-standards production always gives the supplier and the buyer at least as much as their disagreement payoff. As a result, whenever high-standards production is socially efficient (i.e., whenever $S \geq 0$), contracting will occur.

Figure 11.1 illustrates how the "value" in the value chain is distributed between the supplier and the buyer when contract enforcement is perfect. The horizontal axis shows the payoff to the buyer (Π), while the vertical axis shows the payoff to the supplier (Y). The value of the disagreement payoff – which determines the participation constraint – is indicated for both the buyer ($\Pi \geq k$) and the supplier ($Y \geq l$). All points to the northeast of the point (k, l) constitute a (weak) Pareto improvement compared to a situation where no contracting takes place.

The downward-sloping line indicates all possible ways of distributing the gross revenue p_{H} of selling the high-standards good. Under perfect enforcement, the Nash bargaining solution implies that both parties will receive their disagreement payoff and a share of the surplus determined by an exogenously set sharing rule β. The upward-sloping line in Figure 11.1, with slope $\beta / (1-\beta)$, represents the relative share of the surplus that accrues to the supplier. The intersection of this line with the p_{H}-line gives the perfect enforcement outcome (Π^*, Y^*), where $Y^* = l + \beta S$ and $\Pi^* = k + (1-\beta) S$.

11.2.3 Imperfect Enforcement

In many developing and transition countries, the enforcement of contracts is not perfect and costless. In practice, contracts such as the ones described here are often merely informal or oral agreements, making legal enforcement practically impossible. Opportunistic behavior may then lead to "holdups" if one of the agents has an attractive alternative to contract compliance (Williamson, 1981).

In the setting considered here, we can distinguish three possibilities for holdup.[6] First, after the buyer has provided the supplier with the necessary

---

[6] Note that we maintain the assumption of perfect information throughout our modeling framework. This means that both agents are perfectly aware of each other's holdup

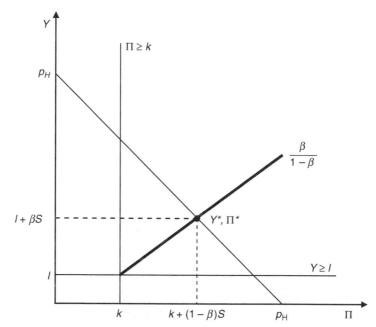

Figure 11.1. Rent distribution under perfect enforcement.

inputs for high-standards production, the supplier could decide to divert these inputs by selling them or applying them to other production activities (e.g., subsistence crops). We assume that when the supplier diverts the inputs, he obtains a value of k, equal to the value of the inputs to the buyer.[7] In addition, the supplier can use his labor to realize his opportunity cost of labor l. However, by violating his contract with the buyer, we assume he suffers a reputation cost ϕ.[8] Hence, with input diversion, the payoffs are[9]

---

options, and they expect each other to violate the contract as soon as they have a profitable opportunity to do so. It is important to be aware of this assumption, as it is frequently not fulfilled in actual situations. However, this assumption allows us to uncover important basic mechanisms. Extending our theory framework to a setting with uncertainty is a fruitful venue for future research.

[7] We relax this assumption in Chapter 16.

[8] This reputation cost can be interpreted in different ways. First, the supplier could suffer a moral cost of breaking his word. Second, he could suffer a loss of social standing. Third, he could lose future trade opportunities with others (cfr. Klein, 1992; McLeod, 2006). Yet another way of interpreting this cost parameter is by analogy to the role of the discount rate of a player in a repeated game. For a patient player, the loss of future revenues outweighs the potential benefits of contract breach in the present. This would be equivalent to a high reputation cost ϕ in our model.

[9] Note that we model k and l as "sunk" costs, which is why they do not directly show up in the buyer and supplier's payoffs. These costs will be reflected in the buyer and supplier's respective participation constraints in Section 11.3.

$$Y_d = l + k - \phi \qquad (11.3)$$

$$\Pi_d = 0 \qquad (11.4)$$

A second possibility to hold up the buyer is when the supplier applies the inputs to the crops, as agreed in the contract, but then sells the high-standards output to an alternative buyer. Such "side selling" can be profitable as the alternative buyer does not need to account for the cost of the provided inputs. On the other hand, the competing buyer may not value the product as much as the contract buyer who outlined the production process from the start according to his specific needs.

To capture these different possibilities, we denote by p_s the "spot market" price at which the supplier can engage in side selling. If the high-standards product is tailored to very specific needs, so that the value of the product to alternative buyers is low, p_s will be low. One possibility is that alternative buyers do not value the higher quality at all, in which case $p_s = p_L$, that is, the high-standards good gets sold as a low-standards product.[10] On the other hand, if the high-standards product is homogeneous and can easily be sold, p_s may be as high as p_H. The payoffs in case of side selling are thus given by[11]

$$Y_s = p_s - \phi \qquad (11.5)$$

$$\Pi_s = 0 \qquad (11.6)$$

Finally, a third possibility for holdup occurs if the buyer reneges on the contract when the supplier delivers the high-standards product. Instead of paying the agreed contract price, the buyer can pay the supplier p_s, the value of his best alternative at that point. We assume that the buyer in this case suffers a reputation cost ψ. The payoffs in case of reneging by the buyer are[12]

---

[10] In some cases, p_s is even lower than p_L, for example, if there is no local market (yet) for the high-quality product. An example is the case of broccoli and cauliflower, which were locally produced for exports, but not locally consumed in Guatemala, as discussed by Glover and Kusterer (1990).

[11] We henceforth refer to expressions (11.3) and (11.5) as the supplier's holdup payoffs from input diversion or side selling. These determine the supplier's incentive compatibility constraints (see later).

[12] In what follows, expression (11.8) will be referred to as the buyer's holdup payoff from contract renegotiation. As we note later, it determines the buyer's incentive compatibility constraint.

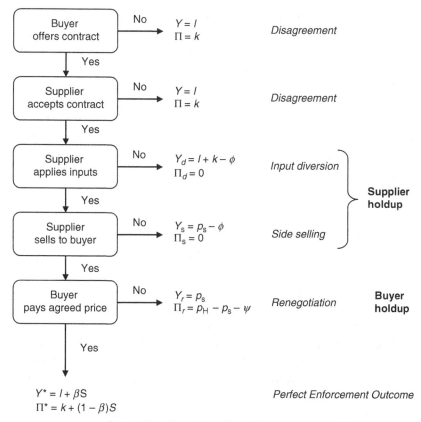

Figure 11.2. Overview of possible outcomes.

$$Y_r = p_s \tag{11.7}$$

$$\Pi_r = p_H - p_s - \psi \tag{11.8}$$

Figure 11.2 summarizes the different possibilities. For pedagogical purposes, in the next sections we first introduce the effects of supplier holdup (input diversion and side selling) and buyer holdup (reneging) separately.

11.3 Self-Enforcing Contracts with Supplier Holdup

When supplier holdup is possible, any contract offered by the buyer must offer the supplier at least as much as his holdup payoffs. That is, the supplier's payoff under the contract must not only cover his disagreement payoff l

but also his potential holdup payoff from input diversion ($Y_d = l + k - \phi$) and side selling ($Y_s = p_s - \phi$). In other words, three conditions must now be satisfied for a contract to be feasible and abided by: the supplier's participation constraint ($Y \geq l$) and his incentive compatibility constraints ($Y \geq l + k - \phi$ and $Y \geq p_s - \phi$). The perfect enforcement outcome will be applied in this scenario only if it satisfies these three conditions. The resulting contract will thus give the supplier his "perfect enforcement" payoff Y^* as long as his incentive compatibility constraints are not binding. If any of the constraints is binding, the contract will give the supplier as much as his holdup payoff from input diversion or side selling respectively. As a result, the contract is defined by

$$Y^{\#} = \max\left\{l + \beta S; \, l + k - \phi; \, p_s - \phi\right\} \tag{11.9}$$

$$\Pi^{\#} = p_H - Y^{\#} \tag{11.10}$$

where we use the # symbol to denote the self-enforcing contract with supplier holdup.

The situation is illustrated in Figure 11.3 for the case of input diversion (a similar analysis applies to the case of side selling). With input diversion, the supplier can obtain an income $Y_d = l + k - \phi$. If this income is higher than the perfect enforcement income Y^*, a self-enforcing contract will lead to an allocation ($\Pi^{\#}, Y^{\#}$), where $Y^{\#} = l + k - \phi$ and $\Pi^{\#} = p_H - Y^{\#}$. The threat of supplier holdup thus leads to a higher payoff for the supplier.

11.3.1 Efficiency Premiums in Self-enforcing Contracts

In the adjusted contract, the buyer pays the supplier a premium on top of the perfect enforcement outcome to prevent violation of the contract after the inputs are delivered. This is equivalent to the concept of "efficiency wages" (Salop, 1979), where the employer pays a higher wage to his employees to minimize their incentive to quit and seek a job elsewhere, after having trained them. We therefore refer to the difference between the supplier's payoff under the self-enforcing contract ($Y^{\#}$) and under perfect enforcement (Y^*) as an "efficiency premium" ε, defined as

$$\varepsilon \equiv Y^{\#} - Y^* = \max\left\{0; \, k - \phi - \beta S; \, p_s - \phi - l - \beta S\right\}. \tag{11.11}$$

Making the contract "self-enforcing" by paying an efficiency premium is a rational strategy for the buyer, as it can earn him a better payoff than when

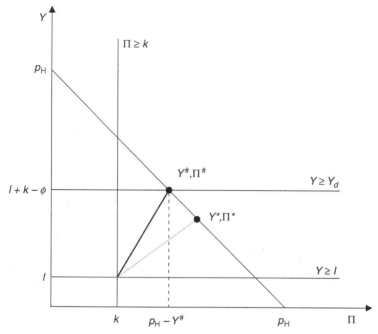

Figure 11.3. Rent distribution under supplier holdup through input diversion.

being held up, or on contract breakdown. There is substantial evidence that processors and retailers offer their suppliers an "efficiency premium" in environments with weak contract enforcement to induce them to produce and deliver according to the contract terms, for example, by paying prices above usual market prices (Birthal et al., 2005; Gulati et al., 2007) or by offering suppliers additional inputs as fertilizers and pesticides for their own food crops to avoid input diversion (Govereh et al., 1999).

The efficiency premium ε is increasing in the value of capital inputs k and in the price at which the supplier can engage in side selling, p_s. As both would increase the supplier's holdup payoff, a higher efficiency premium is needed to make the contract self-enforcing. The efficiency premium is decreasing in ϕ: a larger reputation cost implies that a lower efficiency premium is needed to prevent cheating.[13] Moreover, the efficiency premium is decreasing in $\beta S = \beta(p_H - k - l)$. If the supplier receives a higher share (β)

[13] This result corresponds to the findings of Bardhan and Udry (1999:218) in the context of mercantile contracts. If monitoring is not possible, a long-distance trading agent has to be paid an efficiency wage by the merchant to keep him honest. However, in more "collectivist" forms of enforcement (in which, e.g., the whole community is jointly liable if one of

of the surplus under the contract, or if the surplus is higher, contract breach becomes relatively less attractive. To summarize, if the contract is made self-enforcing, the supplier's income will be increasing in his disagreement payoff as well as his holdup payoffs.

11.3.2 Value and Feasibility

However, this contract is feasible only if it also satisfies the buyer's participation constraint $\Pi^* \geq k$, which imposes a lower bound on p_H. If p_H is sufficiently high, it is possible to adjust the contract terms to satisfy the supplier's incentive compatibility constraints without violating the buyer's participation constraint. For low p_H, however, the total value created by engaging in high-standards production may not be sufficient to prevent the supplier from cheating while giving the buyer at least his opportunity cost k. As a result, contracts will be feasible only for a certain range of parameter values. The conditions for contract feasibility are summarized in the following restriction on p_H:

$$p_H \geq p_H^{\min} = \max\left\{l+k;\ l+2k-\phi;\ p_s+k-\phi\right\} \qquad (11.12)$$

This condition captures the possible reasons for contract failure. If $p_H < l+k$ the net surplus S of the transaction will be negative, and there is no incentive for contract formation. We refer to this situation as "efficient separation." If $p_H > l+k$ but smaller than $l+2k-\phi$ or $p_s+k-\phi$, there is no payoff the buyer can offer to the supplier to make him comply with the contract without operating at a loss himself. Under these conditions, the contract will not be realized, even if it would be socially efficient to do so. We refer to this outcome as "inefficient separation." Hence, contracting is more likely to break down if the "value" in the value chain (p_H relative to the opportunity cost of capital k and labor l) is low, if there are good opportunities for side selling (i.e., p_s is high), and if the supplier's reputation costs ϕ are low.

Figure 11.4 illustrates these separation effects for the case where input diversion is more attractive than side selling. The figure shows the gains in the supplier's income ($\Delta Y = Y - l$) and in the buyer's profits ($\Delta \Pi = \Pi - k$) as a function of the price of the high-standards product, p_H. The line S represents the net surplus that can be created, while βS shows the supplier's payoffs under perfect enforcement. The vertical distance between S and

---

its members cheats), this wage need not be as high, as the penalty for cheating is higher or else peer monitoring makes cheating more difficult.

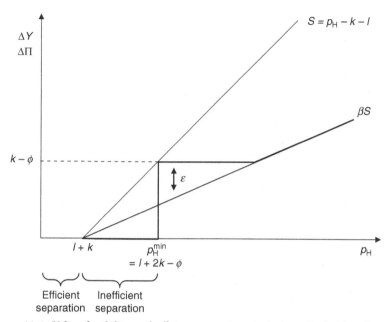

Figure 11.4. Value, feasibility, and efficiency premium under supplier holdup through input diversion.

βS then gives the buyer's payoffs under perfect enforcement. If $p_H < k + l$, there is no net surplus, and no contracting takes place (efficient separation). However, contracting is only feasible when $p_H > l + 2k - \phi$. At that point, the supplier receives an efficiency premium ε above his perfect enforcement payoff. Only when p_H is sufficiently high does the perfect enforcement payoff "catch up" with the supplier's payoff from a self-enforcing contract.

11.4 Self-Enforcing Contracts with Buyer Holdup

Until now, we have assumed that the buyer can commit to the agreed price. This is equivalent to assuming that reneging on the contract would lead to a reputation loss of ψ, which is prohibitively high. We now relax this assumption. For simplicity, we first study buyer holdup separately and then discuss the case where both supplier and buyer holdup are possible.

For low values of his reputation cost ψ, the buyer may be tempted to renegotiate the price upon receipt of the goods by offering the supplier his best alternative at that moment, that is, p_s. The payoff to the buyer is then $\Pi_r = p_H - p_s - \psi$, and the payoff to the supplier is $Y_r = p_s$. To avoid this outcome, the supplier will agree to a contract that satisfies the buyer's incentive

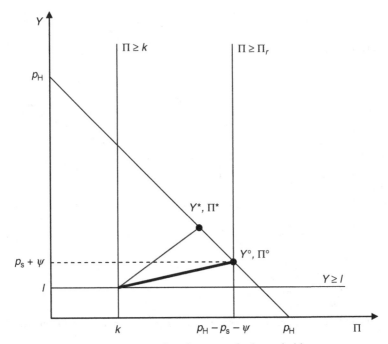

Figure 11.5. Rent distribution under buyer holdup.

compatibility constraint, with a view to making it self-enforcing. In particular, this contract will be

$$Y° = p_H - \Pi° \tag{11.13}$$

$$\Pi° = \max\left\{k + (1 - \beta)S;\ p_H - p_s - \psi\right\} \tag{11.14}$$

Here we denote by ° the adjusted contract that prevents buyer holdup. The situation is demonstrated in Figure 11.5.

In the self-enforcing contract, the supplier is willing to accept a lower price in order to guarantee the buyer's compliance with the contract. Hence, in analogy with the supplier holdup case, we can define a "reverse" efficiency premium, which we refer to as the *efficiency discount* δ:

$$\delta \equiv \Pi° - \Pi^* = \max\left\{0;\ p_H - p_s - \psi - k - (1 - \beta)S\right\} \tag{11.15}$$

The supplier needs to grant a larger efficiency discount the more attractive renegotiation is to the buyer. Hence, the efficiency discount is increasing in p_H but decreasing in ψ, p_s, and k.

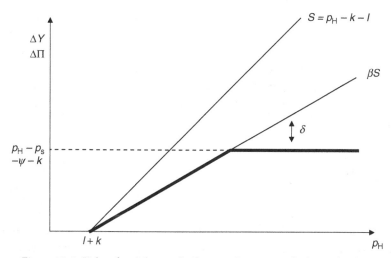

Figure 11.6. Value, feasibility, and efficiency discount under buyer holdup.

The possibility of buyer holdup sets an upper limit to the gains the supplier can derive from the contract. This is illustrated in Figure 11.6, which again shows the gains for the supplier and the buyer as a function of the price p_H. As long as the price is relatively low, so that $p_H - p_s - \psi < (1-\beta)S$, the buyer prefers the unconstrained bargaining outcome. However, if p_H rises and reneging becomes attractive, the supplier will agree to an efficiency discount δ, which effectively limits the supplier's payoff to $p_s + \psi$.

Which conditions determine the feasibility of such a contract? The supplier will agree to $Y°$ as long as his participation constraint is satisfied, that is, $p_s + \psi \geq l$. This implies

$$p_s \geq p_s^{\min} = l - \psi \tag{11.16}$$

Hence, if the spot market price p_s is smaller than $l - \psi$, the contract would not be acceptable to the supplier. Changing the terms of contract to offer a better price to the supplier would, however, not be credible, as the buyer would have an incentive to renege on the contract. Thus, there is a lower bound on p_s. Since the buyer's reputation cost ψ is non-negative, a sufficient condition for contract feasibility is that $p_s = l$. This would be the case, for instance, if the spot-market price equals the price p_L of a low-quality product that the supplier could produce with his labor.

From the perspective of the buyer, the contract is attractive as long as $p_H - p_s - \psi \geq k$. However, the buyer always has the choice of agreeing to the perfect enforcement payoff, which satisfies his participation constraint by construction. If the possibility of reneging on the contract is more attractive than the perfect enforcement payoff, it must therefore satisfy his participation constraint automatically.

Adding up the two participation constraints, we find that $p_H \geq k + l$; that is, feasibility under buyer holdup does not impose extra requirements on p_H, in contrast with supplier holdup.

11.5 Self-Enforcing Contracts with Two-Sided Holdup

We can now extend the previous analysis to the case of two-sided holdups, that is, the situation where both supplier holdup and buyer holdup are possible. The supplier's income will then be as in equation (11.9), unless the buyer's payoff from holdup binds. In the latter case, the supplier's contract payoff is $p_s + \psi$, as was discussed previously. Conversely, the buyer's income under the contract will be as in equation (11.10), unless his payoff from holdup binds: then, his contract payoff is $p_H - p_s - \psi$. Hence, the self-enforcing contract with two-sided holdup opportunities can formally be written as

$$Y^\$ = \min\left[\max\left\{l + \beta S; \, l + k - \phi; \, p_s - \phi\right\}; p_s + \psi\right] \qquad (11.17)$$

$$\Pi^\$ = \max\left[\min\left\{k + (1 - \beta) S; \, p_H - k - l + \phi; p_H - p_s + \phi\right\}; p_H - p_s - \psi\right] \qquad (11.18)$$

If buyer holdup occurs only at relatively high prices p_H while supplier holdup is binding only for relatively low prices p_H, the situation is as in Figure 11.7. As we move from a low price p_H to higher values, we first pass through a region where supplier holdup is binding, and an efficiency premium ε is paid by the buyer. Next, there is a region where neither supplier holdup nor buyer holdup are binding, so that the perfect enforcement outcome prevails. However, for higher prices, the possibility of buyer holdup is binding and the supplier has to agree to an efficiency discount for the buyer. The analysis in this case simply corresponds to that of supplier holdup and buyer holdup for the relevant values of p_H.

However, the situation shown in Figure 11.7 assumes that the contract remains feasible, which is not necessarily the case. Starting with the case in which only input diversion is binding, note that the sum of the supplier's

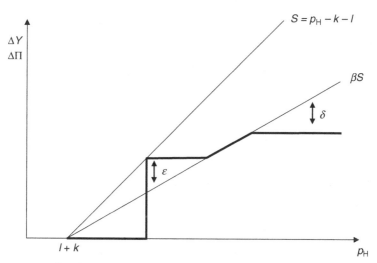

Figure 11.7. Value, feasibility, and efficiency premiums under two-sided holdup.

income Y and the buyer's profits Π must always add up to gross revenues p_H for a contract to be feasible. However, when both the input diversion and the buyer holdup constraint are binding, the supplier's income must be at least $Y_d = l + k - \phi$ and the buyer's profits must be at least $\Pi_r = p_H - p_s - \psi$ for a contract to be self-enforcing. Combining these, the condition for contract feasibility is $Y_d + \Pi_r = l + k + p_H - (\phi + p_s + \psi) \le p_H$, which is equivalent to $p_s \ge k + l - \phi - \psi$. Contract feasibility thus sets a lower bound on the spot market price p_s. If the spot market price p_s is low, if the opportunity costs of capital and labor are high, or if reputation costs are low, it is possible that there is no feasible contract. This is demonstrated in Figure 11.8, where there are no possibilities to share the surplus so that both $Y \ge Y_d$ and $\Pi \ge \Pi_r$ are satisfied. Note in particular that the combination of buyer holdup with input diversion in this case leads to a situation where no feasible contract exists, even though by itself the input diversion possibility would not be binding (since $Y^* > Y_d$), and buyer holdup would not threaten feasibility (as the resulting payoff for the supplier would not violate the supplier's participation constraint, i.e., $Y^\circ > l$).

By contrast, in case side selling is the binding constraint on the suppliers' side, $Y_s = p_s - \phi$ and the condition for contract feasibility becomes $Y_s + \Pi_r \le p_H$ or $p_s - \phi + p_H - p_s - \psi \le p_H$, which can be rearranged to give $p_H - \phi - \psi \le p_H$. As both reputation costs are (weakly) positive, this condition will always be satisfied. So, interestingly, if side selling is more attractive

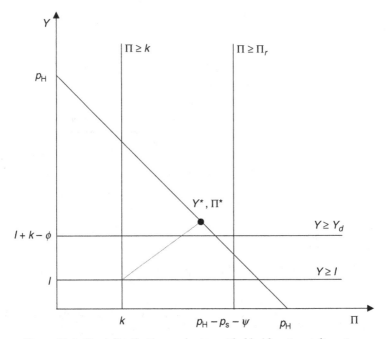

Figure 11.8. Rent distribution under two-sided holdup: input diversion.

than input diversion to the supplier, the threat of buyer holdup does not impose extra requirements for feasibility. While a high spot-market price p_s makes it more interesting for the supplier to engage in side selling, it makes reneging on the contract less attractive to the buyer – and vice versa. Given (weakly) positive reputation costs, both constraints cannot be binding at the same time. The situation is shown in Figure 11.9.[14] The vertical dotted line at $p_H - p_s$ and the horizontal dotted line at p_s would constitute the binding incentive compatibility constraints in the "worst case scenario" where neither the supplier nor the buyer faced any reputation costs ($\phi = \psi = 0$). Even in this case, a contract would remain feasible, as the intersection of these lines must coincide with the p_H-line. To the extent that reputation costs are positive, the actual incentive compatibility constraints are less binding, as drawn. The combination of buyer holdup and side selling thus does not create an extra threat to feasibility, in contrast with the input diversion case.

---

[14] For ease of exposition, this figure suppresses the lines corresponding to the participation constraints, as well as the perfect enforcement outcome.

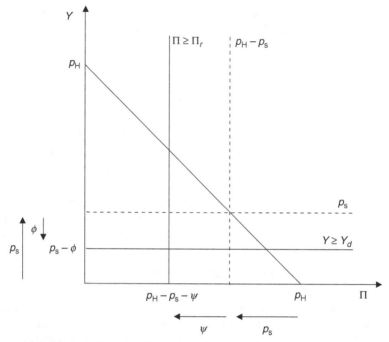

Figure 11.9. Rent distribution under two-sided holdup: side selling.

The preceding analysis looks only at the effects of the holdup opportunities on contract feasibility. In addition to the incentive compatibility constraints, however, also the participation constraints of the buyer and the supplier need to be satisfied. In this regard, we note that an agent's participation constraint and incentive compatibility constraint cannot both be binding at the same time. For instance, for the supplier, the relevant constraint will either be the participation constraint ($Y \geq l$) or the incentive compatibility constraint ($Y \geq l + k - \phi$ in case of input diversion; $p_s - \phi$ in case of side selling), whichever is higher. If the participation constraint is more demanding, supplier holdup plays no role and the two-sided holdup scenario reduces to the buyer holdup scenario analyzed earlier. Likewise, for the buyer, the relevant constraint is either the participation constraint $\Pi \geq k$ or the incentive compatibility constraint $\Pi \geq p_H - p_s - \psi$, whichever is higher. If the participation constraint is more demanding, the two-sided case reduces to the case of supplier holdup analyzed earlier.

As a result, the necessary conditions for contract feasibility that we identified in the case of supplier holdup and in the case of buyer holdup also hold in the case of two-sided holdup. The full set of conditions for feasibility of a contract in case of two-sided holdup is therefore

$$p_{\mathrm{H}} \geq p_{\mathrm{H}}^{\min} = \max\left\{l+k;\, l+2k-\phi;\, p_{\mathrm{s}}+k-\phi\right\} \qquad (11.19)$$

$$p_{\mathrm{s}} \geq p_{\mathrm{s}}^{\min} = \max\left\{l-\psi;\, k+l-\phi-\psi\right\} \qquad (11.20)$$

In equation (11.19), the first term denotes the efficiency condition $p_{\mathrm{H}} \geq l+k$. The second and third terms refer to the situation where the buyer's participation constraint is more demanding than his incentive compatibility constraints, so that buyer holdup is irrelevant. The relevant conditions are then the same as in the case of supplier holdup: the second term is the lower bound when input diversion is more attractive to the supplier than side selling; the third term is the relevant lower bound when side selling is the more attractive option.

Likewise, in equation (11.20) the first term refers to the case in which the supplier's participation constraint dominates his incentive compatibility constraints, so that only buyer holdup is an issue. The relevant condition then is the same as in case of buyer holdup. The second term applies in case the incentive compatibility constraints dominate the participation constraints for both the supplier and the buyer. In particular, this second term refers to the case where input diversion dominates for the supplier. As noted before, in case side selling is the more attractive option for the supplier, no extra condition is required for feasibility.

11.6 Endogenous Third-Party Enforcement

Another way to enforce contracts is by investing in supervision, or by engaging third-party enforcement, if it is not prohibitively costly. Less inefficient separation will then occur, but the total contract surplus will be reduced. Minten et al. (2009) document investments in extensive supervision and monitoring systems in African horticultural exports value chains where quality characteristics are unobservable. But also in the case quality characteristics are observable, monitoring can be used to ensure contract compliance and avoid input diversion or side sales of the crop (e.g., Conning, 2000).

To illustrate the effects of third-party enforcement, we first study the case of supplier holdup when the buyer can precommit to buying third-party enforcement. Next, we discuss the more general case of two-sided holdup.

11.6.1 Third-Party Enforcement with Supplier Holdup

We introduce the possibility for the buyer to pay an amount E for guaranteed enforcement through supervision or third-party enforcement. Moreover, we assume that E is paid ex ante by the buyer as in Dye (1985) and Bajari and Tadelis (2001). E could be the cost of hiring lawyers or paying the local mafia to enforce the contract, or wages of local staff to monitor contract compliance. The surplus is then reduced to $S - E = p_H - k - l - E$.[15] As third-party enforcement prevents contract breach, the payoffs in this case are given by

$$Y_E = l + \beta(S - E) \qquad (11.21)$$

$$\Pi_E = k + (1 - \beta)(S - E) \qquad (11.22)$$

It is in the buyer's interest to invest in supervision if $\Pi_E > \Pi^*$, that is, if his profits with third-party enforcement are higher than his profits under a self-enforcing contract. This condition is equivalent to $\Pi^* - (1 - \beta)E > \Pi^* - \varepsilon$. As this formulation makes clear, the buyer will prefer third-party enforcement whenever $E < \varepsilon/(1 - \beta)$. This means third-party enforcement is more attractive when ε is higher, that is, when k or p_s is higher or when ϕ is lower.

The opportunity for supervision or third-party enforcement will impose an upper limit to the supplier's payoff from the contract. The modified contract can then be written as

$$Y_E^\# = \begin{cases} l + \beta S + \varepsilon & \text{if } E \geq \varepsilon/(1 - \beta) \\ l + \beta(S - E) & \text{if } E < \varepsilon/(1 - \beta) \end{cases} \qquad (11.23)$$

$$\Pi_E^\# = \begin{cases} k + (1 - \beta)S - \varepsilon & \text{if } E \geq \varepsilon/(1 - \beta) \\ k + (1 - \beta)(S - E) & \text{if } E < \varepsilon/(1 - \beta) \end{cases} \qquad (11.24)$$

---

[15] Note that in this chapter, we consider the social gains of the contract as the sum of the gains of the supplier and the buyer. As such, E is a cost to society. One could argue that payments to third parties, be it lawyers, or local people hired to supervise, also benefit society and should be included in the gains, rather than the costs.

Here we add the subscript E to the notation for supplier and buyer payoffs to indicate that this is the adjusted contract if third-party enforcement is possible in a context of supplier holdup.

The condition for contract feasibility becomes

$$p_H \geq p_H^{\min} = \min\left\{\max\left\{l+k;\ l+2k-\phi;\ p_s+k-\phi\right\};\ l+k+E\right\} \qquad (11.25)$$

The possibility of third-party enforcement has effects on both efficiency and equity. Third-party enforcement may enable contracting that was previously not feasible, thus increasing efficiency. In this scenario, both the supplier and the buyer gain. However, third-party enforcement may also substitute for the efficiency premium in the range where contracting was feasible before. In that case, enforcement reduces the total surplus by an amount E and reduces the payoff to the supplier, who no longer receives an efficiency premium. All gains then go to the buyer, who now has a cheaper solution to enforce the contract. Hence, third-party enforcement has ambiguous effects on efficiency and equity.

The effects of third-party enforcement are illustrated in Figure 11.10. The dotted line represents the outcome in case third-party enforcement is not available, while the full line shows the outcome if the buyer can make use of third-party enforcement. The top panel shows that enforcement reduces the available surplus to $S - E$. As a result of third-party enforcement, contracting is now feasible for lower prices p_H, which implies an improvement in income for suppliers.[16] However, the shift away from using an efficiency premium to using enforcement leads to a reduction in income for suppliers in an intermediate range of p_H. For high values of p_H, the introduction of third-party enforcement does not change the outcomes.

The bottom panel shows the payoff of the buyer. As this panel shows, the introduction of third-party enforcement has a (weakly) positive effect on buyer profits. If $E < \varepsilon/(1-\beta)$, the buyer uses third-party enforcement and profits increase. If $E > \varepsilon/(1-\beta)$, enforcement is not used and the payoffs are as before.

11.6.2 Third-Party Enforcement with Two-Sided Holdup

In case of two-sided holdup, the possibility arises that not only the buyer wants to invest in third-party enforcement (to avoid supplier holdups), but

---

[16] Incidentally, this implies that suppliers would be willing to invest in third-party enforcement themselves over this range. We return to this point in Section 11.6.2.

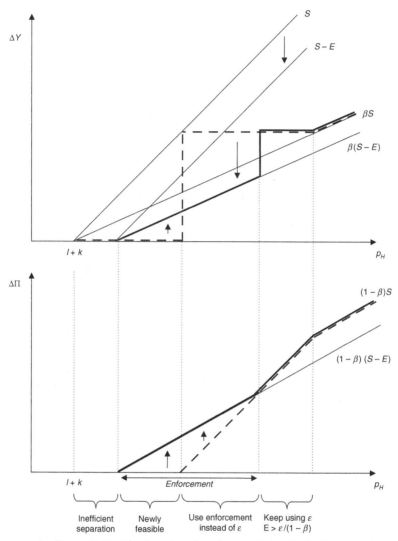

Figure 11.10. Third-party enforcement with supplier holdup.

that also the supplier has an incentive to invest in third-party enforcement to prevent the buyer from reneging on the contract. Using third-party enforcement reduces the surplus to $S - E$ and leads to a payoff of $Y_E = l + \beta(S - E)$ for the supplier. Over the relevant price range where buyer holdup is possible, a self-enforcing contract requires an efficiency discount δ to be paid to the buyer, so that the payoff to the supplier in this case

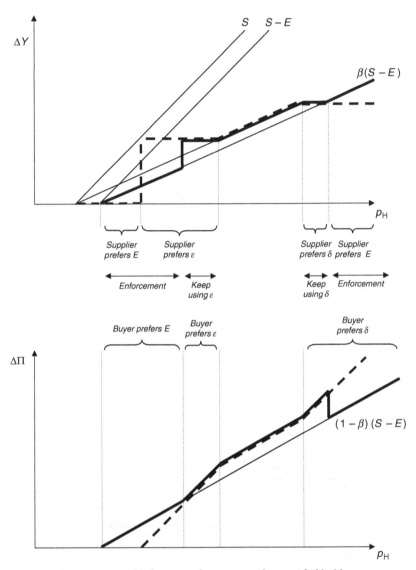

Figure 11.11. Third-party enforcement with two-sided holdup.

is $Y^\circ = Y^* - \delta$. Since $Y_E = Y^* - \beta E$, the supplier prefers using third-party enforcement if $E < \delta / \beta$.

The logic of the previous case extends to this situation, and is depicted in Figure 11.11. The dotted line again represents the situation without third-party enforcement, while the full line shows the outcome when the supplier or the buyer can invest in third-party enforcement. As demonstrated in the top panel, the supplier will prefer enforcement to prevent buyer holdup for large values of p_H, although there exists an interval where the benefits of enforcement do not outweigh the costs, and the supplier prefers paying the efficiency discount δ to the buyer.

The bottom panel shows the situation for the buyer. For low and intermediate values of p_H, the situation is identical to that in Figure 11.10. However, as soon as $p_H - p_s - \psi > (1 - \beta) S$, the supplier pays an efficiency discount δ to the buyer to prevent him from reneging. Once $\delta / \beta > E$ it becomes optimal for the supplier to invest in third-party enforcement – and in this case the buyer's payoff falls discontinuously to $(1 - \beta)(S - E)$. With buyer holdup and third-party enforcement, an increase in the price p_H may thus *reduce* the payoff to the buyer.

Figure 11.11 also identifies when the supplier or the buyer prefer using third-party enforcement or a self-enforcing contract. Assuming that one party can unilaterally decide to use third-party enforcement, we also denote when enforcement, an efficiency premium ε or an efficiency discount δ will be used. As shown, there is a range of low prices p_H where both the supplier and the buyer prefer using third-party enforcement. This occurs where $S - E > 0$ but $p_H \leq l + 2k - \phi$. In this region, the possibility of supplier holdup prevents contracting. Interestingly, we thus see that the supplier would be willing to "tie his own hands" by agreeing to third-party enforcement to enable contracting.

In the range where $E < \varepsilon / (1 - \beta)$, the buyer prefers using third-party enforcement whereas the supplier would prefer receiving the efficiency premium ε. As soon as $E > \varepsilon / (1 - \beta)$, both the supplier and the buyer prefer bargaining (using either a constrained contract or the unconstrained bargaining solution) until the point where $E < \delta / \beta$, at which point the supplier would prefer third-party enforcement but the buyer would prefer receiving the efficiency discount δ. Thus, Figure 11.11 identifies certain zones where the buyer and the supplier agree on the preferred enforcement mechanism, and certain zones where their preferences conflict.

11.7 The Impact of Development

Economic development, in the sense of an increase in average local income I, may affect interlinked contracts in different ways. In the context of our model, we focus on three channels: increases in average income may improve the enforcement of contracts and they may improve the functioning of output and factor markets. First, if enforcement becomes less costly with the emergence and better functioning of formal institutions, this will affect the emergence and distributional effects of interlinked contracts. Second, output market development may stimulate local demand for high-standards products and have important effects on equity and efficiency of contracting as well. Finally, if factor markets develop, suppliers' access to specific inputs will become less constrained, and this will affect contractual arrangements.[17] To precisely identify the mechanisms through which these effects come about, we analyze them separately and then study their joint effect. To keep the analysis tractable, we focus on the case of supplier holdup.[18]

11.7.1 Improvement of Contract Enforcement Institutions

It is generally observed that formal enforcement institutions become more effective with development (Djankov et al., 2003; North, 1990). In our model, we can represent this effect by assuming that third-party enforcement becomes less costly ($\partial E / \partial I < 0$).[19] An obvious implication is that third-party enforcement will now be preferred to efficiency premiums for a larger range of p_H. This will have implications for both efficiency as well as equity.

First, a reduced enforcement cost E can extend the range where contracts are enforceable. Indeed, as E decreases, there is a wider interval for which $S - E \geq 0$.

Second, when third-party enforcement was already the cheapest option for contract enforcement with a higher E, third-party enforcement now becomes cheaper. This increases the contract surplus, with a positive effect on efficiency.

---

[17] Additional impacts of development may come through its effect on k. Assessing the direction of this effect based on the literature is, however, not straightforward, and beyond the scope of this chapter.

[18] The analysis of buyer holdup and two-sided holdup would proceed along similar lines.

[19] An increase in average income can lower E in different ways. First, as public contract enforcement improves, corruption and red tape may be reduced, which lowers the cost of using public institutions. This lowers E directly if we interpret this parameter to be the cost of using public enforcement. Second, economic development may lower the cost of monitoring, for example, by introducing new technology which makes it easier to monitor compliance. Relevant examples include the introduction of an ID system or of computerized land property records to identify contract violators. Conceivably, development may also increase the cost of enforcement as higher salaries need to be paid. However, it seems plausible that the net effect of development is to lower the cost of enforcement.

However, a third effect is that as the cost of third-party enforcement decreases, it will substitute for efficiency premium payment at certain values of p_H. As discussed earlier, the use of third-party enforcement then reduces efficiency (as the contract surplus is reduced to $S - E$) and shifts a share of the contract surplus back from the supplier to the buyer, leaving the supplier worse off as compared to the self-enforcing contract.

These effects can be seen in Figure 11.10 by assuming that the cost of enforcement E is reduced all the way to zero, in which case the solution coincides with the perfect enforcement outcome. Clearly, the zone of inefficient separation between $k + l$ and $2k + l - \phi$ disappears, which improves efficiency and which improves the payoffs for both the supplier and the buyer. Moreover, in the zone where third-party enforcement was already being used, the supplier now receives βS instead of $\beta(S - E)$, and the buyer receives $(1 - \beta)S$ instead of $(1 - \beta)(S - E)$, so both parties gain. However, between the point where $p_H = l + 2k - \phi$ and the point where $E = \varepsilon / 1 - \beta$, there is a substitution from using the efficiency premium to using third-party enforcement; the buyer gains while the supplier loses.

To summarize, improved enforcement institutions do not always benefit both contracting parties. The buyer will gain and the supplier will lose when cheaper third-party enforcement deprives the latter of his efficiency premium.[20] This is consistent with other literature (e.g., Anderson and Young, 2002) demonstrating that better enforcement does not necessarily benefit all contracting agents.

11.7.2 Output Market Development

Also the output market may develop with increased average incomes. In particular, if local consumers become richer, they may acquire stronger preferences for high-standards food products, as discussed in Chapters 10 and 17. However, this does not necessarily imply that p_H will be affected. If the high-standards value chain is an export industry, p_H will be determined by international market conditions and may not be affected by local development. In Chapter 12, we discuss how competition can impact p_H; here, we assume that development does not affect p_H. Rather, with more options to sell high-standards products, it may become easier for suppliers to engage in side selling and p_s may increase $(\partial p_s / \partial I > 0)$. As long as paying

---

[20] Conversely, in the case of buyer holdup, the buyer will lose and the supplier will gain when third-party enforcement removes the need to apply an efficiency discount.

an efficiency premium is cheaper than using third-party enforcement, this will increase the supplier's income from the contract.

11.7.3 Factor Market Development

Finally, the development of factor markets is expected to relax credit constraints and to improve access to input markets. As a result, suppliers may obtain better access to profitable market opportunities even before starting to negotiate a contract. This would imply an increase in the supplier's disagreement payoff, that is, his opportunity cost of labor l ($\partial l / \partial I > 0$). As long as the contract remains feasible, the payoff to the supplier will improve because of the increasing disagreement payoff. However, because the contract surplus decreases, it is possible that the contract is no longer feasible.

On the input side, development can change the organization of agricultural production even more dramatically by giving suppliers direct access to inputs. If credit constraints are relaxed, or input markets develop, buyers do no longer need to give inputs on credit. Pure output contracts become feasible. With pure output contracts, the setup of the model will change into a standard specific investment setting à la Klein et al. (1978). Buyers no longer need to give efficiency premiums to make suppliers comply with the contract. This will reduce the suppliers' income from the contract, but it will increase contract feasibility by reducing inefficient separation. However, the possibility of buyer holdup remains.[21]

Thus, improving factor markets again does not necessarily benefit the supplier. An increase in his opportunity cost l reduces the set of feasible contracts. Moreover, better access to inputs expands the set of feasible contracts, but they reduce the need for an efficiency premium, thus reducing the supplier's payoff.[22]

---

[21] To analyze the case of pure output contracts with specific investments in greater detail, a different model setup may be required. If suppliers are investing by themselves in very specific products for which local markets are not well developed, they may be prone to buyer holdup. Gow et al. (2000) provide an interesting discussion of a case in which suppliers need to make specific investments, and buyers choose to do part of the upfront investment as a precommitment device to ensure contract feasibility.

[22] A similar result is found by Marcoul and Veyssiere (2010), who show that poor suppliers who require incentive payments to comply with the contract will receive a better price than rich suppliers who do not (as the latter do not require credit provision).

11.7.4 Aggregate Effect of Development

If we maintain the model setup where inputs are fully provided by the buyer, the impact of development on the payoff of the supplier can be decomposed as follows:

$$\frac{\partial Y_E^\#}{\partial I} = \frac{\partial Y_E^\#}{\partial E} \cdot \frac{\partial E}{\partial I} + \frac{\partial Y_E^\#}{\partial l} \cdot \frac{\partial l}{\partial I} + \frac{\partial Y_E^\#}{\partial p_s} \cdot \frac{\partial p_s}{\partial I} \qquad (11.26)$$

If third-party enforcement is more expensive for the buyer than using an efficiency premium ($E \geq \varepsilon / (1 - \beta)$) we have $\partial Y_E^\# / \partial E = 0$, $\partial Y_E^\# / \partial l > 0$, and $\partial Y_E^\# / \partial p_s > 0$. Hence, as long as the buyer prefers using an efficiency premium and contracts remain feasible, development will have a (weakly) positive effect on $Y_E^\#$, because the supplier's opportunity cost of labor (l) and his payoff from side selling (p_s) are improving.

In case third-party enforcement is the buyer's preferred option ($E < \varepsilon / (1 - \beta)$), we have $\partial Y_E^\# / \partial E < 0$, $\partial Y_E^\# / \partial l > 0$, and $\partial Y_E^\# / \partial p_s = 0$. In this case, development will have a positive effect by reducing the costs of enforcement (thus increasing the surplus) and through an increased opportunity cost of labor, while side selling by the supplier is ruled out.

However, as can be seen from Figure 11.10, $Y_E^\#$ changes discontinuously at the point where third-party enforcement becomes binding, that is, at the point $E = \varepsilon / (1 - \beta)$ where the buyer is indifferent between using a self-enforcing contract or third-party enforcement. We can look at the "gap" between E and $\varepsilon / 1 - \beta$ to study whether third-party enforcement becomes relatively more or less attractive. Assuming that development does not affect the sharing rule β or the supplier's reputation cost ϕ, the effect of development on this "gap" is:

$$\frac{\partial}{\partial I}\left(E - \frac{\varepsilon}{1 - \beta} \right) = \frac{\partial E}{\partial I} - \left(\frac{1}{1-\beta} \right) \cdot \frac{\partial \varepsilon}{\partial l} \cdot \frac{\partial l}{\partial I} - \left(\frac{1}{1-\beta} \right) \cdot \frac{\partial \varepsilon}{\partial p_s} \cdot \frac{\partial p_s}{\partial I} \qquad (11.27)$$

with $\partial \varepsilon / \partial p_s \geq 0$. The sign of $\partial \varepsilon / \partial l$ depends on which of the supplier's incentive compatibility constraints is binding. If input diversion binds, $\partial \varepsilon / \partial l = \beta > 0$. Conversely, if side selling binds, $\partial \varepsilon / \partial l = \beta - 1 \leq 0$.[23] Hence, the impact of development on the use of third-party development is

---

[23] Recall that with input diversion, the supplier chooses between $Y_d = l + k - \phi$ and $Y^* = l + \beta S$. A higher opportunity cost of labor decreases $\beta S = \beta(p_H - k - l)$ and hence makes input

ambiguous. While the first and third term are negative or zero, the sign of the second term may be positive or negative.

If input diversion binds, the second term is negative while the third term is zero. This means that the gap presented in expression (11.27) declines with development, in other words, that development leads to a higher incidence of third-party enforcement, which may depress supplier income.

If side selling is binding, the first and the third term are negative and the second term is positive: the increased opportunity cost of labor makes abiding with the contract more attractive to the supplier and reduces the need for an efficiency premium. At the same time, however, the increase in p_s increases the required efficiency premium. If the "labor" effect dominates the "spot market" effect, development makes contract self-enforcement cheaper and reduces the need for third-party enforcement, while improving the supplier's payoff. If the "spot market" effect dominates, development increases the cost of self-enforcement and again leads to a higher incidence of third-party enforcement, with potentially worse outcomes for the supplier.

We can use a similar derivation to study the effect of development on contract feasibility. For this, we can analyze the "gap" between p_H and the minimum price needed to make contracts feasible $\left(p_H^{\min} = \min\left\{\max\left\{l+k;\ l+2k-\phi;\ p_s+k-\phi\right\};\ l+k+E\right\}\right)$. If development increases this gap $p_H - p_H^{\min}$, the effect on feasibility is positive.

$$\frac{\partial\left(p_H - p_H^{\min}\right)}{\partial I} = \frac{\partial p_H}{\partial I} - \frac{\partial p_H^{\min}}{\partial E}\cdot\frac{\partial E}{\partial I} - \frac{\partial p_H^{\min}}{\partial l}\cdot\frac{\partial l}{\partial I} - \frac{\partial p_H^{\min}}{\partial p_s}\cdot\frac{\partial p_s}{\partial I} \qquad (11.28)$$

Note that we have earlier assumed away any impacts of I through p_H (cfr. footnote 15), which implies $\partial p_H / \partial I = 0$. As for the other terms in equation (11.28), we have $\partial p_H^{\min} / \partial E \geq 0, \partial E / \partial I < 0,\ \partial p_H^{\min} / \partial l \geq 0,\ \partial l / \partial I > 0,$ $\partial p_H^{\min} / \partial p_s \geq 0$ and $\partial p_s / \partial I > 0$. Hence, the outcome is ambiguous. Development will increase contract feasibility if the feasibility-enhancing effect of cheaper third-party enforcement dominates the feasibility-reducing effect of an increased l and p_s.[24]

---

diversion more attractive. This, in turn, raises the efficiency premium. With side selling, however, the supplier chooses between $Y_s = p_s - \phi$ and $Y^* = l + \beta S$. An increase in the cost of labor thus raises Y^* by $(1-\beta)$ times that increase, reducing the efficiency premium by the same amount.

[24] As mentioned earlier, if development gives suppliers direct access to inputs, the possibility of supplier holdup disappears and contract feasibility improves (abstracting from the possibility of buyer holdup).

As this analysis shows, the effect of development on efficiency and equity is ambiguous. While cheaper third-party enforcement potentially improves the feasibility of contracts, this effect can be counteracted by a reduction in the contract surplus and an increase in the supplier's holdup payoff.

11.8 Conclusion

In this chapter we presented a basic model for analyzing efficiency and equity effects of modern value chains characterized by high-quality requirements, the need for specific inputs, and suppliers facing factor market constraints. Processors or traders then have an incentive to engage in interlinked contracts with suppliers, providing them with the necessary inputs (seeds, fertilizer, credit, and so on) to enable the production of the high-standards product. However, in weakly institutionalized contexts (characteristic of many developing and transition countries) various holdup opportunities threaten the viability of such schemes. Suppliers could divert the inputs to other uses, or they could sell the resulting high-standards product to other buyers. The buyer, in turn, could renege on the contract by offering a lower price than initially agreed on. To guarantee the enforcement of the contract, the supplier and the buyer could choose a self-enforcing contract with an efficiency premium or discount to ensure mutual compliance; or they could decide to pay for third-party enforcement of the contract.

Our analysis leads to several interesting conclusions. First, some contracts that would be socially efficient are not feasible. The extent of inefficient separation (defined as the absence of socially efficient contracting) is decreasing in the value in the chain, and increasing in the payoff the supplier would achieve under a holdup and in the cost of external contract enforcement.

Second, holdup opportunities lead to efficiency premiums. To prevent supplier holdup (such as input diversion or side selling), the buyer will offer a higher price than what would be offered under perfect enforcement. Poor suppliers can thus benefit from the introduction of quality standards in this context. However, a similar argument can be made for buyer holdup. In this case, the supplier will be willing to accept a lower price to prevent opportunistic behavior by the buyer. Opportunistic behavior thus appears to be an important determinant of the terms of contract if enforcement institutions are weak.

Third, we find that third-party enforcement may improve the feasibility of contracts. However, since it reduces the need for an efficiency premium (resp. discount), better institutions or cheaper enforcement possibilities may end up reducing the income of suppliers (resp. buyers).

Fourth, development – interpreted as an improvement in output markets, factor markets and enforcement institutions – has ambiguous effects on the feasibility of contracts and on the income of the supplier. Cheaper third-party enforcement may improve feasibility, but reduces supplier income by taking away the efficiency premium. On the other hand, improved output and factor markets increase the supplier's holdup payoff as well as his opportunity cost of labor. As long as an efficiency premium is used and contracting remains feasible, this will improve the supplier's income; but these changes may induce a shift to third-party enforcement or may render the contract infeasible.

The model presented in this chapter is a simple yet powerful tool for analyzing modern value chains. In the next chapters, we develop a series of extensions and applications of the model.

Chapter 12 provides a more in-depth discussion of the role of market power in modern value chains. Chapter 13 discusses the implications of our model for the transmission of consumer prices to producer prices. Chapter 14 uses the model to show how differences in the characteristics of commodities influence the organization of the value chain, paying particular attention to the "value" in the value chain, the opportunities for side selling and the institutional context. Chapter 15 shows how our model of value chains can shed light on the diverging results of liberalization in China, Eastern Europe and Sub-Saharan Africa. Finally, Chapter 16 explicitly takes into account the degree of relationship specificity of buyer investments as well as the cost advantage to the buyer of repeated interaction with the same supplier. We derive a typology of costs and trace the effects of these different types of costs on efficiency and equity in the value chain.

12

Market Power and Vertical Coordination in Value Chains

12.1 Introduction

Market power and competition in value chains are important items on the policy agenda around the world. In many value chains there are stages where a few firms dominate the market. The exercise of market power may lead to higher consumer prices and lower supplier prices, and therefore economic distortions and reduced consumer and/or supplier welfare. Claims that large, often multinational companies such as global retailers and food companies are driving up consumer prices and/or depressing local supplier prices have been made in many countries. For example, in 2006, demonstrators outside the Walmart shareholders' meeting in Mexico City protested against "the low wages Wal-Mart pays its employees, the low prices it pays to its suppliers" (Globalexchange.org, November 14, 2006). Also Monsanto, the world's largest seed company, has been frequently accused in the press of "using monopoly powers to drive up [seed] prices and stymie competition" (e.g., Reuters, January 8, 2010).

However, the effects of market concentration on the exercise of market power and the associated welfare effects are less straightforward than often claimed. For instance, increased concentration could lead to economies of scale, resulting in efficiency gains for society. Moreover, increased concentration among retailers may lead to "countervailing power" in their bargaining with large processing companies; these lower prices could in turn be passed on to consumers. Mirroring these ambiguous theoretical predictions, the empirical literature shows little consensus on the welfare effects associated with market concentration.

The issue of market concentration is also important in relation to standards. Large multinational companies with dominant market positions have introduced their own private standards which, because of their size, have become de facto mandatory for many suppliers (Henson, 2006; Smith, 2009). Moreover, suppliers have often been confronted with a limited number of buyers willing (or able) to reward high standards, for example, because standards (and the associated quality premiums) are company-specific. Finally, high-standards product perishability may reduce supply elasticity and therefore reduce supplier bargaining power (Sexton and Zhang, 1996).

In this chapter we analyze the impact of market concentration and, conversely, competition in value chains when there are factor market imperfections and vertical coordination. We first briefly review some of the literature on the effects of increased concentration on both consumers and suppliers. Because there is a huge literature on this topic, we focus on concentration in retailing, an issue that has attracted much attention recently. Although this literature yields interesting insights, a major shortcoming is that models typically focus on the trade-off between market power and scale economies, and mostly assume that factor markets work well and that contracts are enforced – aspects that are not realistic in many countries, in particular poorer ones. Therefore, we subsequently use the theoretical model developed in Chapter 11 to study the effect of market concentration and competition on suppliers.

This chapter is organized as follows. Section 12.2 reviews the literature on the effects of market concentration, with special attention for the food retail sector. Section 12.3 shows how rents are distributed in the basic setup of our theory model; and Section 12.4 shows what the effects of buyer competition are in this framework. Section 12.5 explores whether the existing literature provides empirical support for our theoretical findings; and Section 12.6 concludes the chapter.

12.2 Effects of Market Concentration: A Brief Literature Review

In this section, we review the literature on the effects of market concentration on other stages of the value chain. We first discuss different mechanisms through which market concentration may affect consumer and supplier welfare. Next, we discuss empirical evidence on the effects of concentration in retailing on welfare of consumers and suppliers, respectively.

12.2.1 Theory

Basic economic principles suggest that high concentration will lead to the exercise of market power. A monopolist will set a markup over marginal cost, which leads to consumer prices above the competitive equilibrium. Similarly, a monopsonist will set a supplier price below the competitive level. In both cases, the exercise of market power is associated with a lower output level, and hence Pareto-inefficiencies. When the number of players in a market increases, output levels may still be Pareto-inefficient, as for instance when oligopolists engage in Cournot competition. However, as the number of firms increases, each firm's market power decreases, which results in increased output and efficiency gains. This is the basic argument linking market concentration to market power and welfare losses.

Several scholars have argued, however, that although buyer concentration is a useful first indicator of possible market power, higher concentration does not necessarily translate into the exercise of market power (Clarke et al., 2002; Peltzmann, 1977). In fact, concentration may be welfare improving for more than one reason.

First, it may lead to important gains in efficiency if there are scale economies in the industry (e.g., Demsetz, 1973; Guy et al., 2004). There is some evidence that this applies to the food industry. A 2006 USDA-ERS report examined mergers and acquisitions in the meat, poultry, dairy, and grain processing industry in the United States in the period 1972–1992. After the merger, labor productivity in the acquired plants increased substantially, up to twice the initial level. Second, efficiency will also increase if transaction costs caused by high asset specificity and/or uncertainty are substantially lower as a result of high market concentration (Shervani et al., 2007).

Third, investments in research, development and innovation may require a certain degree of market concentration, so as to ensure that companies that invest can reap the benefits from the innovation. In a fully competitive market, certain efficiency improving innovations may not emerge (e.g., Pray et al., 2005; Sanyal and Ghosh, 2013).[1]

Fourth, the efficiency and price effects of concentration depend on the architecture of the other stages of the value chain. For example, retailer concentration may lead to higher bargaining power vis-à-vis major suppliers with market power, which may feed through to lower consumer prices eventually (e.g., Chen, 2003; Dobson and Waterson, 1997). In fact, before the consolidation wave in the retail sector during the 1990s, most studies about market structure in retailing focused on the strong bargaining power

---

[1] This is a controversial issue in the literature, however, as other authors claim exactly the opposite (see, e.g., Boldrin and Levine, 2004, 2008), for example, because competition would reduce the cost of innovation. Aghion et al. (2005) find an inverted-U relationship between competition and innovation.

of suppliers with respect to retailers, whereas retailers were usually considered to be price-takers (e.g., Lustgarten, 1975). Increasing consolidation of retailers was perceived as potentially improving social welfare, as it would allow them to exert "countervailing power" vis-à-vis their main suppliers.[2] As such, the exercise of upstream market power by supermarkets is a relatively recent phenomenon and tends to be more of a concern in relations between retailers and (small) farmers, than between retailers and large suppliers such as Unilever, Nestle, Philip Morris, and Danone. In the latter case the market power issue of concern is between (small) farmers and food processors.[3]

The reverse argument can also be made. A retailer that is able to extract monopoly rents from consumers may have an incentive to share these rents with suppliers. This argument has been made (and investigated empirically) in the labor economics literature (see, e.g., Blanchflower et al., 1996; Nickell, 1999). In buyer–supplier relations, this argument has received less attention; but a recent paper by Ngeleza and Robinson (2013) finds that fresh tomato spot market traders do engage in rent-sharing with their suppliers in Ghana.

Finally, another reason why concentration may not result in higher consumer prices and/or lower supplier prices, and why intense price competition may be observed in relatively concentrated markets relates to firm heterogeneity. If an industry is highly concentrated but firm sizes are very unequal, the costs of collusion will be higher. The result is a lower likelihood of collusion in an "asymmetric" market environment where a dominant firm coexists with a competitive fringe (e.g., Compte et al., 2002; Kühn, 2002, 2004).

12.2.2 Retail Concentration and Consumer Welfare

While the theoretical arguments apply both to the exercise of monopsony and monopoly power, and consider the welfare effects for both suppliers and consumers, the empirical studies and policy debates typically focus on

---

[2] Countervailing power was a term coined by Galbraith (1952) to describe the ability of large buyers in concentrated downstream markets to extract price concessions from suppliers (Snyder, 2008).

[3] There is anecdotal evidence of intensive bargaining between the "successive oligopolies" in the food chain. For example, Dobson et al. (2001) mention that Nestle's strong position in the United Kingdom enabled it to resist downward pressure on prices by supermarket chains. Another recent example is from 2009 in Belgium, where retail chain Delhaize refused to give in to a unilateral price increase by Unilever, one of their main suppliers.

one of these groups only.[4] Until recently, most empirical studies focused on consumer effects.

The empirical studies which relate consumer prices to local concentration of retailers arrive at diverging conclusions. On the one hand, Hall et al. (1979), Lamm (1981), Marion et al. (1993), and various studies by Cotterill (Cotterill 1986; 1999; Cotterill and Harper, 1995) and Yu and Connor (2002) find that there is a positive correlation between retailer concentration and food prices. On the other hand, Binkley and Connor (1998), Kaufman and Handy (1989), and Newmark (1990) find a negative or insignificant correlation between concentration and food prices. Interestingly, Newmark (1990) argues that successful firms may compete on other levels than price, for example, by offering higher quality or better services, which may be reflected in higher prices and means that these should not be interpreted as the exercise of market power. Likewise, Binkley et al. (2002) find "little compelling evidence that consolidated markets engage in non-competitive pricing behaviour." The U.K. Competition Commission found that in U.K. supermarkets, prices did not vary with the number of local competitors, although they were often lower in the proximity of discounters, as supermarkets tend to benchmark the prices of certain key products with the prices of their main competitors (Cooper, 2003).

Many, but not all, studies on developing and emerging countries find that the arrival of large modern retailers leads to lower consumer prices. For example, Hausman and Leibtag (2007) discuss how Walmart's increasing market share has led to strong consumer benefits driven by declines in retail prices, especially for product varieties purchased by low-income consumers. Reardon and Hopkins (2006) argue that modern supermarkets in Chile reduced the cost of the food consumption basket of lower and middle income consumers, by charging lower prices than traditional markets. This may be due to their capacity to reduce value chain inefficiencies (Tandon et al., 2011). Similar observations are reported by D'Haese and Van Huylenbroeck (2005) for South Africa, and by Neven et al. (2006) for Kenya (especially for processed foods and nonfood items). Schipmann and Qaim (2011) argue that the first wave of modern retailers supply higher quality at higher prices in Thailand. However, Minten (2008) finds that food prices in modern retail chains in Madagascar are 40% to 90% higher than in traditional retail markets, even after controlling for quality.

---

[4]   An exception can be found in the studies by Richards and Patterson (2003) and by Sexton et al. (2005), who study retailer pricing behavior relative to both consumers and suppliers in U.S. markets for fresh produce.

Studies that have focused on the relation between increased retail concentration and profitability have also found little conclusive evidence that consolidation has led to increased profits for retailers. For example, Farris and Ailawadi (1992) and Messinger and Narasimhan (1995) find little change in retailer profitability as a result of increased consolidation. Barla (2000) provides empirical evidence that the strong competition in the presence of apparent concentration in the industry may be due to the difficulties of collusion between heterogeneous firms. Another reason may be the presence of discounters. For example, although retail concentration in Germany is quite high, there is strong competition on the selling side, with as main engine the "hard discounters" such as Aldi and Lidl (Dobson et al., 2001).

12.2.3 Retail Concentration and Supplier Welfare

Likewise, there is relatively little compelling evidence about abuse of market power vis-à-vis suppliers. A classic case of suspected abuse of upstream market power, which attracted a great deal of policy attention and resulted in important new anti-trust regulations, can be found in the U.S. meat-packing industry.[5] Azzam and Pagoulatos (1990) have been able to empirically establish the presence of uncompetitive behavior in this industry. Lloyd et al. (2009) test retailer market power and show that the hypothesis of perfect competition can be rejected in seven of the nine food products under consideration. However, studies by Sexton et al. (2005) and by Richards and Patterson (2003) on the U.S. retail markets for fresh produce arrive at diverging conclusions. For example, although they find that retailers influence supplier prices for iceberg lettuce, apples, and grapefruit, they do not find significant deviations from the competitive equilibrium in Florida or California tomatoes or in California grapes.

Apart from some weak anecdotal evidence, also Dobson et al. (2001) fail to find clear evidence of abuse of market power vis-à-vis farmers. They review a case in which a farmers' organization in the United Kingdom alleged "that supermarket chains pay very low prices for farm products, but fail to pass low prices on to consumers." After an investigation, however, the Competition Commission (2000) argued that the low producer prices were mainly a result of excess supply, and had been passed on to consumers, or were compensated by other cost increases.

---

[5] For a historical review of the issues, see Yeager (1981) or Ward (2010).

It must be said, however, that the measurement of retailer's market power is a contentious issue, as prices paid by retailers to their suppliers are "typically not revealed" (Sexton et al., 2005). An additional complicating factor is that, apart from the prices paid to suppliers, there may be other factors affecting supplier welfare, such as the application of volume discounts, the charge of "slotting fees" for shelf space, or the requirement of other costly services, which makes the measurement of supplier welfare effects even more complex (Dimitri et al., 2003; Wilkie et al., 2002).

In a developing country setting, Michelson et al. (2012) find that local suppliers receive lower prices from Walmart as compared to domestic retail chains. They argue that this may reflect a "risk premium" charged to suppliers in return for lower price volatility. However, it is hard to establish whether this risk is correctly priced: in their view, suppliers may be overcharged.

Despite the inconclusive evidence on the impact of concentration in food retail, one may still wonder whether there are reasons why farmers and consumers may be differently affected despite the fact that both are small atomistic agents and often weakly organized. One possible argument why consumers may be less vulnerable to retail and food industry concentration is that consumers may have more choice than suppliers do. Dobson et al. (2001) argue that if retail concentration is high, the concentration of buyer groups may be even higher. If retailers are organized in buyer groups, which collectively bargain for supplies, but compete against each other in the sellers' market, customers may face a lower concentration ratio than suppliers do. Along similar lines, Sexton and Zhang (2001) argue that the relevant geographic and product markets for the purchase of raw agricultural commodities are usually narrower, and concentration thus higher, than in the relevant markets for the associated finished products. Geographic markets are narrower because farm products are often bulky and/or perishable, causing shipping costs to be high, restricting the products' geographic mobility, and limiting farmers' access to only those buyers located close to the production site.

That said, in many developing and emerging countries the arrival of modern food and retail companies is likely to reduce trading restrictions, and to enhance, rather than reduce, competition for farmers' products – and hence to offer benefits for them. Furthermore, once one accounts for the specificities of production processes and the institutional environment, the so-called weak bargaining position of local suppliers vis-à-vis larger companies should be qualified. We explain this in detail in the next section.

12.3   Market Concentration and Rent Distribution in Value Chains

As discussed in Chapter 11, two key characteristics of rural areas in developing and emerging countries are factor market constraints and weak institutions for formal contract enforcement. These conditions have important implications for the distribution of rents in high-standards value chains and the impact of market power and competition. We start off by discussing how rents are distributed in the basic setup of our theory model. In the next section, we then analyze how increased competition between buyers affects the outcomes. As earlier, we begin our analysis by looking at the perfect enforcement scenario, and then expand our analysis by taking into account the possibility of supplier and buyer holdup.

12.3.1   Rent Distribution with Perfect Enforcement

In our value chain model discussed in Chapter 11, rent distribution is determined by the factor β, the sharing rule, if contract enforcement is perfect and costless. As is clear from Figure 11.1, an increase in β will improve the payoff of the supplier under perfect enforcement. In particular, as β increases, the line with slope $\beta/1-\beta$ will rotate upward. If $\beta=1$, the supplier receives the entire surplus, and the buyer merely receives his opportunity cost k. Conversely, if $\beta=0$, the buyer extracts all surplus and the supplier is driven down to his participation constraint. In this case, $Y^{*}=l$. Hence, β is a good indicator of rent distribution in the value chain in the case of perfect contract enforcement.

The determination of β is a question that has received a great deal of attention in the literature but, as yet, has not been fully resolved (see, e.g., Doyle and Inderst, 2007). One strand of the (predominantly theoretical) literature argues that β should be 0.5 in the case of perfect rationality in a perfect information setting (e.g., Nash, 1953), while another part of the literature argues that bargaining need not be symmetric and that in the real world β may reduce to 0 in a context of extremely unequal bargaining positions (e.g., Svejnar, 1986). As entering into this debate is beyond the scope of this book, we consider β as an exogenous parameter in this and other chapters.

12.3.2   Rent Distribution with Two-Sided Holdup

When contract enforcement is not perfect, β is no longer a good indicator for rent distribution. In this case the opportunities for contract breach will affect surplus distribution. This was illustrated in Figure 11.3 (for supplier holdup) and Figure 11.5 (for buyer holdup). If enforcement is costly, the surplus is not necessarily distributed according to the sharing rule. Additional factors come into play that affect this distribution, and β may then no longer be a relevant indicator of how the surplus is shared. A more appropriate indicator of market power is the "ex post sharing rule," defined by $\beta = (Y - l) / S = 1 - (\Pi - k) / S$. In the case of perfect contract enforcement, $\tilde{\beta} = \beta$; with imperfect enforcement the ex post sharing rule will typically be different. For instance, when the supplier has the possibility to hold up the buyer through input diversion, the ex post sharing rule is given by

$$\tilde{\beta} = \frac{Y - l}{S} = \max\left(\beta, \frac{k - \phi}{p_H - l - k} \right) \qquad (12.1)$$

If input diversion is binding, equation (12.1) implies that $\tilde{\beta} > \beta$.

The ex post sharing rule $\tilde{\beta}$ is illustrated graphically in Figure 11.3 and Figure 11.5. The slope of the line connecting the point (k, l) with the point $(Y^{\#}, \Pi^{\#})$ (in the case of supplier holdup, as in Figure 11.3) or (Y°, Π°) (in the case of two-sided holdup, as in Figure 11.5) equals $\tilde{\beta} / (1 - \tilde{\beta})$. If supplier holdup is binding, $\tilde{\beta} > \beta$, and conversely, if buyer holdup is binding, $\tilde{\beta} < \beta$. Importantly, the possibility of supplier holdup thus implies that even in a context where $\beta = 0$, suppliers may still be able to capture a positive share of the surplus (with $\tilde{\beta} > 0$).

12.4 The Effects of Increased Buyer Competition

In a traditional economic analysis, an increase in competition on one side of the market is beneficial for agents on the other side of the market.[6] For instance, the Cournot–Nash equilibrium in a simple oligopoly model converges on the perfect competition outcome as the number of players grows larger. However, this logic does not necessarily carry over to a situation in which contract enforcement is imperfect, as we show in this section. We again first discuss the effect of competition in our model if contract enforcement is perfect, and then discuss the effects with supplier and buyer holdup respectively.

---

[6] Credit markets are a well-known exception to this rule (e.g., Petersen and Rajan, 1995).

12.4.1 Competition and Rent Distribution
with Perfect Enforcement

In the perfect enforcement case, $Y^* = l + \beta S$ and $\Pi^* = k + (1-\beta)S$. An increase in the number of buyers may then affect the supplier's outside option l and the output price p_{H}.[7] If we denote the degree of competition between buyers with Ψ, so that $\Psi = 0$ corresponds to monopsony and $\Psi = 1$ corresponds to perfect competition among buyers, we can decompose the effect of competition on the supplier's payoff in this case as

$$\frac{\partial Y^*}{\partial \Psi} = (1-\beta)\frac{\partial l}{\partial \Psi} + \beta \frac{\partial p_{\mathrm{H}}}{\partial \Psi} \qquad (12.2)$$

The first term captures the effect of increased buyer competition on the supplier's disagreement payoff (l). It reflects the traditional argument that an increased number of buyers has a positive impact on supplier income by expanding demand for the supplier's labor, possibly under alternative contractual setups – although it could as well happen through the increased demand for low-standards products, or the availability of alternative salaried jobs. In our model, this implies an increase in the supplier's opportunity cost of labor, so that $\partial l / \partial \Psi > 0$.[8]

The second term captures the effect of competition on the output price p_{H}. Ex ante, it is not clear whether this effect will be negative or positive. An increase in the number of buyers may increase the supply of high-standards products, thus leading to a decrease in p_{H}. If this effect dominates, $\partial p_{\mathrm{H}} / \partial \Psi < 0$. However, to the extent that buyers sell the high-standards product on the international market, an increase in local buyer competition will not have much effect on p_{H}.

On the other hand, one might argue that competition will increase the price p_{H} which has been defined in Chapter 11 as being net of any processing

[7] For simplicity, we abstract away from the effects of competition on k, the opportunity cost of the inputs provided by the buyer. At any rate, it is not clear ex ante whether this effect would be positive or negative.

[8] As mentioned earlier, there is no unanimity in the literature regarding the correct interpretation of β. If one takes the position that this parameter is always fixed, the increased opportunities for the supplier will be translated into an increase in his outside options l. On the other hand, if one interprets increased competition as strengthening β directly, it is not clear whether a separate effect on l should be taken into account. For simplicity, we assume that β is fixed and the effect of competition operates through l, although both approaches lead to similar conclusions.

and marketing costs and overhead on the side of the buyer. One argument that has been made in the literature is that a company manager's incentives for cost reduction and innovation will be stronger in a competitive environment (see, e.g., arguments by Konings and Walsh, 1999; Nickell, 1999; Roland, 2000; or the "quiet life of the monopolist" hypothesis by Hicks, 1935). Simply put, this literature argues that profit maximization requires effort; if the marginal return to effort (in terms of extra profits) is decreasing, profit maximization does not coincide with utility maximization. A monopolist may maximize utility instead of profits. Competitive pressure may then increase the incentive to reduce inefficiencies, with higher profits as a result. Another argument is that competitive pressure may generate incentives to "escape competition" through quality differentiation (Shaked and Sutton, 1982). In other words, a firm may start to target high-end markets by increasing the quality of its products. To the extent that this effect dominates, we would have $\partial p_H / \partial \Psi > 0$.[9]

Thus, under perfect enforcement, it is not clear ex ante what the effect of competition is on the payoff to the supplier. The net effect on the supplier's income is a weighted average of the increase in l and the change in p_H, with the weights determined by β. In the extreme case where $\beta = 0$, competition has an unambiguously positive impact on supplier income through its effect on l. If $\beta = 1$, competition will have an impact only through p_H. This means that competition increases his income if it increases buyer efficiency; all benefits are then extracted by the supplier. However, it reduces supplier income if competition reduces the price p_H at which the buyer can sell high-standards products. For the more realistic case where β takes on an intermediate value, the net effect is a weighted average of these effects. Note that even if increased competition leads to a reduction in the output price p_H the supplier may still gain if the effect through l dominates, as long as contracting remains socially efficient ($p_H > k + l$).

12.4.2 Competition and Rent Distribution with Supplier Holdup

If contract enforcement is imperfect, the effect of buyer competition on the distribution of rents and on the income of the supplier is more complex.

---

[9] If product quality is improved by using more expensive inputs, this would imply a concomitant rise in k. We assume that the increase in k is not high enough, however, to offset the increase in p_H. In other words, if quality improves, we assume that value added in the chain improves as well. This is not a very strong assumption.

An increase in the number of competing buyers can affect both rent creation (efficiency) and rent distribution (equity) in the value chain. We first analyze rent distribution, assuming the contract remains feasible, and then study under what conditions an increase in competition may threaten feasibility. We first study the case of supplier holdup, and then turn to the case of two-sided holdup.

As in the previous section, we expect buyer competition to have an impact on l (with $\partial l / \partial \Psi > 0$) and on p_H (with $\partial p_H / \partial \Psi \lessgtr 0$). An increase in the number of buyers may as well increase the opportunities to engage in side selling, which raises p_s. Hence, $\partial p_s / \partial \Psi > 0$. Lastly, competition may affect the supplier's reputation cost of violating the contract. With more buyer competition, this penalty for opportunistic behavior becomes lighter, because the threat of cutoff from future contract arrangements is less stringent, as there are other contract partners available (Hoff and Stiglitz, 1998). This argument is in line with Eswaran and Kotwal's (1985) argument that reputation is an effective weapon against moral hazard only for suppliers of factors that are in excess supply. Another reason why ϕ is lower, is that buyers are less likely to coordinate and share information on suppliers (see, e.g., Zanardi, 2004) in a competitive market. Local information networks work less well when the number of agents expands, as it costs more in terms of effort, money, and/or time to let information spread among a larger group of agents. For these reasons, competition will reduce ϕ, and hence $\partial \phi / \partial \Psi < 0$.

As discussed in Chapter 11, the payoff to the supplier under supplier holdup is given by $Y^{\#} = \max \left\{ l + \beta S; \, l + k - \phi; \, p_s - \phi \right\}$. The resulting impact of competition on supplier income can be summarized as follows:

$$\frac{\partial Y^{\#}}{\partial \Psi} = \frac{\partial Y^{\#}}{\partial l} \frac{\partial l}{\partial \Psi} + \frac{\partial Y^{\#}}{\partial p_H} \frac{\partial p_H}{\partial \Psi} + \frac{\partial Y^{\#}}{\partial p_s} \frac{\partial p_s}{\partial \Psi} + \frac{\partial Y^{\#}}{\partial \phi} \frac{\partial \phi}{\partial \Psi} \qquad (12.3)$$

The first, third, and fourth terms of equation (12.3) are unambiguously non-negative. The second term is negative only if local competition reduces p_H. Otherwise, all terms are positive and competition has a positive impact on the supplier's contract income. For the supplier to be worse off under the contract with increased competition, the impact of the reduction in p_H must dominate all other effects. This can happen only if none of the supplier's holdup options is binding in the first place. These conditions are very restrictive and rather unlikely to occur. Hence, we expect increased competition to increase the supplier's payoff, as long as the self-enforcing contract is still feasible.

To study the feasibility of contracts when competition increases, we use the minimum feasible price $p_{\mathrm{H}}^{\min} = \max\left\{l + k; l + 2k - \phi; p_s + k - \phi\right\}$ as defined by equation (11.12) in Chapter 11. If we measure feasibility as the "gap" between p_{H} and $p_{\mathrm{H}}^{\min}$, or $p_{\mathrm{H}} - p_{\mathrm{H}}^{\min}$, we can decompose the effect of competition as

$$\frac{\partial\left[p_{\mathrm{H}} - p_{\mathrm{H}}^{\min}\right]}{\partial\Psi} = \frac{\partial p_{\mathrm{H}}}{\partial\Psi} - \frac{\partial p_{\mathrm{H}}^{\min}}{\partial l}\frac{\partial l}{\partial\Psi} - \frac{\partial p_{\mathrm{H}}^{\min}}{\partial p_s}\frac{\partial p_s}{\partial\Psi} - \frac{\partial p_{\mathrm{H}}^{\min}}{\partial\phi}\frac{\partial\phi}{\partial\Psi} \quad (12.4)$$

As before, the sign of $\partial p_{\mathrm{H}} / \partial\Psi$ can be positive or negative. The second and the third term are both negative or zero, since $(\partial p_{\mathrm{H}}^{\min} / \partial l)$ $(\partial l / \partial\Psi)$ and $(\partial p_{\mathrm{H}}^{\min} / \partial p_s)$ $(\partial p_s / \partial\Psi)$ are positive. Finally, the fourth term is negative as well, since both $\partial p_{\mathrm{H}}^{\min} / \partial\phi$ and $\partial\phi / \partial\Psi$ are negative. Hence, unless $\partial p_{\mathrm{H}} / \partial\Psi$ is positive and sufficiently large to counteract all three remaining negative impacts, we expect competition to have a negative impact on contract feasibility. This means competition would make it less likely that a self-enforcing contract can arise.

In summary, with supplier holdup competition is expected to increase the supplier's payoff as long as the contract remains feasible. However, the same forces which improve the supplier's payoff also threaten the feasibility of the contract and make it less likely that contracts are concluded.

12.4.3 Competition and Rent Distribution with Two-Sided Holdup

If there is a relevant opportunity for buyer holdup, the supplier's payoff changes to $Y^{\$} = \min\left[\max\left\{l + \beta S; l + k - \phi; p_s - \phi\right\}; p_s + \psi\right]$ (cfr. equation (11.17)). In addition to the effects listed in the previous section, buyer competition may now as well have an impact through ψ, the reputation cost suffered by the buyer in case he renegotiates the contract. If there is little or no competition between buyers, this reputation cost will be minor, as the supplier has limited alternatives to dealing with the buyer. As competition increases, the effects of a loss of reputation will be more severe for the buyer. Hence, $\partial\phi / \partial\psi > 0$. The effect of competition is now

$$\frac{\partial Y^{\$}}{\partial\Psi} = \frac{\partial Y^{\$}}{\partial l}\frac{\partial l}{\partial\Psi} + \frac{\partial Y^{\$}}{\partial p_{\mathrm{H}}}\frac{\partial p_{\mathrm{H}}}{\partial\Psi} + \frac{\partial Y^{\$}}{\partial p_s}\frac{\partial p_s}{\partial\Psi} + \frac{\partial Y^{\$}}{\partial\phi}\frac{\partial\phi}{\partial\Psi} + \frac{\partial Y^{\$}}{\partial\psi}\frac{\partial\psi}{\partial\Psi} \quad (12.5)$$

The addition of the last term reinforces the positive impact of competition on supplier income. Hence, even if buyer holdup is binding, increased competition benefits the supplier as long as the contract remains feasible.

As discussed in Section 11.5, feasibility in the case of two-sided holdup not only requires that $p_H \geq p_H^{min}$ but also that $p_s \geq p_s^{min}$. The effects on p_H^{min} are the same as in the previous case with only supplier holdup, which implies that buyer competition reduces contract feasibility also in the case of two-sided holdup. In addition, however, we have the condition that $p_s \geq p_s^{min} = \max\{l - \psi; k + l - \phi - \psi\}$. Competition increases p_s and ψ, which tends to improve feasibility. However, competition also increases ℓ and reduces ϕ, both of which reduce feasibility. Buyer competition thus has an ambiguous effect on feasibility with two-sided holdup.

12.5 Empirical Evidence

Empirical studies indeed suggest such mixed and conditional effects of competition in value chains. Studies show that competition can increase suppliers' contract income, by forcing buyers to provide better contract terms or by inducing supplier assistance programs.

Especially if suppliers are scarce, buyers may use credit or input provision as an instrument to attract suppliers, and/or keep them loyal. For example, Larsen (2002) describes how ginners compete on services provided to cotton farmers in Zimbabwe. In Eastern Europe, competition among dairy and sugar processors is said to have contributed to the spreading of farm assistance programs (Gow et al., 2000; World Bank, 2005). Smith et al. (1999) and Stockbridge et al. (1998) show how extending credit to farmers may be the only way to ensure availability of supply in Pakistani cotton and wheat markets; Minten et al. (2011) make a similar observation on traditional horticultural markets in India.

A comparative analysis of contracting and interlinking in the cotton sector in Central Asia confirms the importance of competition as an important factor to protect small farms against rent extraction by large processors (Swinnen et al., 2007). In Uzbekistan, Tajikistan, and Turkmenistan, where cotton sectors are dominated by monopsony buyers, cotton producers have been reported to suffer from low producer prices. In contrast, in Kazakhstan and Kyrgyzstan, the cotton chain is characterized by strong competition among private gins buying cotton seeds from small farms for processing, with much better conditions for farmers. Competition plays a very important role in the cotton value chains by inducing both beneficial equity and efficiency effects.

However, the empirical literature also shows that increased competition may lead to the collapse of input programs and vertical coordination. For example, Poulton et al. (2004) find that strong competition has led to contract breakdowns in several African cotton chains. Delpeuch and Vandeplas (2013) relate the different effects in African cotton value chains to different liberalization policies, using a theoretical framework similar to the one used in this chapter.

12.6 Concluding Comments

The rise of modern value chains, dominated by large processors and retailers, has led to concerns over the effects of market concentration on consumers and suppliers. However, as shown in this chapter, the welfare effects of concentration are more complex than is often assumed. A number of mechanisms could lead to positive welfare effects from increased concentration, for instance if this leads to economies of scale or to "countervailing power" in the value chain. The empirical literature provides mixed evidence on the effects of increased retail concentration on consumers or suppliers.

As our own theoretical analysis shows, in a context of factor market imperfections and costly contract enforcement, the buyer's capacity to extract rents can be constrained by the possibility of supplier holdup. If this is the case, the supplier can achieve a higher "ex post" share of the contract surplus than what would be possible under perfect and costless contract enforcement. On the other hand, the possibility of buyer holdup can be an extra source of rent extraction by the buyer.

As a result of these mechanisms, increased buyer competition is not unambiguously positive for suppliers. As long as contracts remain feasible, more competition leads to a higher payoff for suppliers; but it is possible that contracts are no longer feasible, leaving suppliers worse off. Increased competition may improve or worsen the outcomes for suppliers, depending on the circumstances: which of the indicated effects dominates is ultimately an empirical issue.

13

Price Transmission in Value Chains

13.1 Introduction

Dramatic price swings in global energy and food markets have caused much concern around the world about price policies. These price swings have resuscitated interest among policymakers on the issue of price transmission, and the implications for producer and consumer welfare.[1] The debate was strongest for developing countries as some argued that consumers in developing countries were hurt by increasing food prices while producers were not benefiting from higher prices for their products, increasing hunger and poverty.[2] However, also in richer countries the policy discussion on price transmission was reinvigorated.[3]

---

[1] There is an intriguing difference in the policy reactions to high and low prices before and after 2007, as documented by Swinnen (2011) and Swinnen and Squicciarini (2012).

[2] Empirical evidence shows a mixed picture. FAO (2009) argues that in African countries such as Kenya and Mozambique, consumer prices rose significantly, while farm gate prices remained flat (FAO 2009). A review of cereal markets in 52 countries over the period 2007–2011 finds that transmission of price shocks from the world market to domestic markets varied from 50% to 100% (Sharma, 2011). Based on an analysis of price volatility of agricultural and food commodities in Africa, Minot (2012) finds that only seven out of seventeen prices have been more volatile since 2007, while seventeen show significantly less volatility. Jacoby (2013) argues that the price hikes benefited poor rural households in India through positive wage effects. Headey (2011) and Verpoorten et al. (2013) find that, on average, self-reported food security improved in net food-producing countries and in rural areas over the same period.

[3] For example, in the European Union, it was argued that when agricultural commodity prices were on the rise in 2007/2008, these increases were passed on to consumers but, when prices declined again in 2008/2009, these price declines were less than fully transmitted to consumers (Swinnen et al., 2013), hindering demand recovery and exacerbating the negative effect of declining producer prices on suppliers (European Commission, 2009). The European Commission (2009) argued that the observed discrepancies between producer and consumer price developments reflect "structural weaknesses in the system, such as the number of intermediaries operating along the chain and the competitive

The extensive literature on the transmission of price shocks discerns different types of price transmission. Transmission of price shocks at the consumer level (e.g., triggered by a demand shock) to producers in domestic markets – and vice versa – is referred to as *vertical* price transmission. Transmission of price shocks in the world market to domestic markets – and vice versa – is referred to as *spatial* price transmission. Imperfections in spatial price transmission have been attributed to factors including government intervention in markets (such as import tariffs and price stabilization measures), transport and marketing costs, the degree of processing, market structure, and consumer preferences (e.g., if imported products are imperfect substitutes for domestic products) (e.g., Rapsomanikis, 2011).

Imperfect vertical price transmission, on the other hand, has most often been interpreted as providing evidence of market failure, such as the exercise of market power by processing companies and/or retailers, enabling them to capture value chain rents and reduce social welfare (Meyer and von Cramon-Taubadel, 2004; Wohlgenant, 2001). The existing literature focuses mostly on the effects for consumer welfare, and generally assumes a positive correlation between the degree of downstream vertical price transmission and consumer welfare – as a lower degree of price transmission would attest to a greater share of the rents being captured by powerful intermediaries in the chain.

However, this is not a consensus argument. There is also a set of studies contesting the direct link between the degree of price transmission and market power, arguing that one should account for the incidence of vertical coordination in value chains, the existence of increasing returns to scale, risk mitigating behavior by intermediaries, and the degree of processing (McCorriston et al., 2001; Wang et al., 2006; Weldegebriel, 2004; Wohlgenant, 2001). For example, Wang et al. (2006) show that in the presence of market power, price transmission can be weaker, identical, or even stronger than in the competitive markets case.

Most of the studies of price transmission focus on the transmission of (global and domestic) producer prices to consumer prices (Bonnet and Requillart, 2012; Chang and Griffith, 1998; Davidson et al., 2012; Goodwin and Holt, 1999; Holm et al., 2012; von Cramon-Taubadel, 1998). Less attention has been paid to studying upstream vertical price transmission, that is, the effects of price shocks originating in consumer markets on producer prices (Wohlgenant, 2001). However, as globalization and income growth

structure," and "pervasive inequalities in bargaining power between contracting parties" and established in 2012 a "Task Force Food" within DG Competition to oversee competition in the food sector.

have brought about important shifts in consumer demand, transforming value chains all over the world, such upstream vertical price transmission is likely to have important effects on local producers.[4]

In this chapter, we examine how exogenous consumer price shocks (triggered for instance by income changes, global shocks, or by changes in consumer preferences) are transmitted to producer prices, taking into account the particular nature and institutional characteristics of modern value chains, as first discussed in Chapter 11. In this chapter we apply the model developed in Chapter 11 to show that price transmission depends on the nature of vertical coordination in the value chain. Our analysis shows that price transmission is likely nonlinear in the presence of vertical coordination in the value chain. We also show that, contrary to what is often assumed in empirical research, weaker price transmission from consumer to producer prices does not necessarily imply a lower welfare for suppliers.

The remainder of this chapter is structured as follows. The next section outlines our theoretical model and shows how the degree of price transmission can be derived under different conditions (perfect contract enforcement, supplier holdup, and two-sided holdup). The last section concludes the chapter.

13.2 A Model of Price Transmission in Modern Value Chains

As in previous chapters, we consider the case where a supplier (e.g., a farmer) can sell products to a buyer (e.g., a trader or a retailing or processing company). The setup of our model is similar to that in Chapter 11. To produce 1 unit of a high-standards product, the supplier needs to invest own resources with an opportunity cost of l. In addition to the supplier's resources, the buyer provides inputs with opportunity cost k. The resulting high-standards product can be sold at a unit price p_H. The surplus or "value" in the high-standards value chain is $S = p_H - k - l$.

The distribution of this surplus between the supplier and the buyer, and the resulting price transmission pattern, will depend on the sharing rule under perfect enforcement, and on the conditions for enforcement of the contract. As in Chapter 11, we first analyze price transmission for the benchmark case of perfect and costless enforcement. Then we study

---

[4] In addition, most of the existing literature on price transmission is empirical in nature and builds on theoretical work by McCorriston and Sheldon (1996) and McCorriston et al. (1998, 2001). Relatively little attention has gone out to refining the theoretical assumptions underlying these empirical analyses (Meyer and von Cramon-Taubadel, 2004), such as the changing architecture of markets.

the case where the supplier and/or the buyer may face attractive holdup options, and external enforcement is costly such that contracts need to be made self-enforcing.

13.2.1 Price Transmission with Perfect Contract Enforcement

If formal contract enforcement institutions work well and are costless (or if a supplier does not have an attractive opportunity for contract violation once a contract is agreed upon), the "perfect enforcement" outcome results. Following the reasoning in Chapter 11, the resulting contract then implies the following payoffs:

$$\begin{cases} Y^* &= l + \beta\big(p_{\mathrm{H}} - k - l\big) \\ \Pi^* &= k + \big(1 - \beta\big)\big(p_{\mathrm{H}} - k - l\big) \end{cases} \tag{13.1}$$

As the supplier only produces 1 unit of output, his payoff is in fact the unit price for the product he sells. Hence the producer price p^* is given by

$$p^* = l + \beta\big(p_{\mathrm{H}} - k - l\big) \tag{13.2}$$

If we assume that the supplier's disagreement payoff is the payoff from producing one unit of low-standards goods ($l = p_L$), then equation (13.2) reduces to

$$p^* = p_L + \beta\big[(p_{\mathrm{H}} - p_L) - k\big] \tag{13.3}$$

The second part of the right-hand side term in equation (13.3) shows how the producer price is a function of the quality premium for high-standards products ($p_{\mathrm{H}} - p_L$), investments by the buyer (k) and the sharing rule (β). The producer price is positively (and linearly) related to the consumer price for high-standards products p_{H} and to the sharing rule β. The higher p_{H} and the higher β, the higher p^*.

We now look at how shocks in consumer prices are transmitted to prices at the supplier-level. Price transmission can be defined as $\tau = \partial p / \partial p_{\mathrm{H}}$ and is illustrated in Figure 13.1. The top panel shows the relation between producer and consumer prices, while the bottom panel plots the degree of price transmission τ. In region A, where $p_{\mathrm{H}} \leq p_L + k$, we have $p^* = p_L$. In this region, $S \leq 0$; there is no contracting and the supplier produces a low-standards good. It is obvious that in this price region, price transmission from high-standards consumer markets to low-standards producing

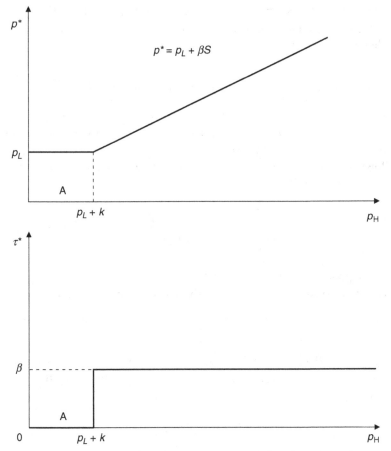

Figure 13.1. Producer price (p^*) and price transmission (τ^*) with perfect enforcement.

suppliers is zero. In other words, by producing low-standards goods, the supplier is shielded against shocks in the high-standards market (although he may be prone to shocks in the low-standards market).

If $p_H > p_L + k$, $S \geq 0$; contracts are feasible, and the supplier participates in high-standards production. Our bargaining model predicts that the producer price varies with changes in the consumer price for high-standards goods (p_H). More specifically, price transmission $\tau = \partial p/\partial p_H = \beta$. As the producer price is determined through a bargaining process, an exogenous price shock in the consumer price will be transmitted to the producer only partially. The degree of price transmission equals the share of the surplus that accrues to the supplier. This, of course, is not surprising as a change in the consumer price affects the surplus, and the change in the surplus is distributed in the same way as the initial surplus.

The process of bargaining for price determination partially isolates the farmer from the market. The lower β, the stronger he is shielded from price shocks – both when prices go up and when they go down. This reduces the negative effect when prices fall, but it also reduces his gains when prices rise. In the extreme case where the surplus share of the supplier is zero ($\beta = 0$), the supplier is pushed back to his opportunity cost, and the buyer is the residual claimant of the full surplus. In this case, there will be no price transmission at all to the supplier level. Every change in the surplus (either an increase or a decrease) is absorbed by the buyer.

In summary, with perfect contract enforcement, a higher β implies a larger surplus share appropriated by the supplier and a stronger degree of price transmission. Within this scenario the traditional logic holds, that a stronger degree of price transmission indicates stronger benefits for suppliers, as there is a positive correlation between β and p^* (or equivalently Y^*). Note, however, that this also implies that suppliers are more exposed to price volatility, and hence that they will lose more when prices decline.

13.2.2 Price Transmission with Supplier Holdup

If contracts are not perfectly enforceable, the outcome may be different. Opportunistic behavior may lead to holdups if one of the agents has an attractive alternative to contract compliance. We now study price transmission in a context where contracts need to be made self-enforcing to avoid these holdups. For pedagogical purposes, we first consider the effects of supplier holdup, and later add the possibility of buyer holdup.

As in Chapter 11, the supplier has two holdup options: on the one hand he can divert the inputs and earn $Y_d = l + k - \phi$; on the other hand he can side sell high-standards produce and earn $Y_s = p_s - \phi$. To make the contract self-enforcing, the buyer must ensure that the supplier's contract income covers at least his potential income from input diversion or side selling, which implies the following supplier price p^*:

$$p^* = \max\left\{l + \beta\left(p_H - l - k\right);\ l + k - \phi;\ p_s - \phi\right\} \tag{13.4}$$

The first term in equation (13.4) is the supplier price under perfect enforcement (see equation (13.2)). This constitutes the lower bound to the supplier price under imperfect enforcement. The supplier price may be higher, however, if the supplier has attractive options outside of the contract once the buyer has made the required investment.

If we assume that the supplier's best alternative option is to produce a low-standards product (so that $l = p_L$), equation (13.4) can be rewritten as

$$p^\# = \max\left\{p_L + \beta(p_H - p_L - k); \; p_L + k - \phi; \; p_s - \phi\right\} \qquad (13.5)$$

As can be seen from equation (13.5), the producer price under imperfect enforcement will be at least as high as under perfect enforcement, conditional upon the contract being feasible. Contracts will be feasible only if p_H is sufficiently high to set the contract terms such that both agents' participation constraints ($\Pi \geq k$ and $Y \geq l$) as well as the supplier's incentive compatibility constraints are simultaneously satisfied. The specific conditions for contract feasibility are summarized in the following restriction on p_H:

$$p_H \geq p_H^{\min} = \max\left\{p_L + k; \; p_L + 2k - \phi; \; p_s + k - \phi\right\} \qquad (13.6)$$

This condition captures two major reasons for potential contract failure. First, if $p_H < p_L + k$, the net surplus of the transaction will be negative, and there is no incentive for contract formation. Second, and more importantly, if $p_H \geq p_L + k$ but smaller than $p_L + 2k - \phi$ or than $p_s + k - \phi$ the contract surplus is positive, but the surplus is too small to allow the buyer to offer a price to the supplier which makes him comply with the contract. Under these conditions, the contract will not be realized, despite its potential positive contribution to social welfare. These conditions are represented by price regions A and B in the top panel of Figure 13.2.[5] When the potential surplus is negative (region A) or when the potential surplus is too low for the buyer to pay a sufficiently high price to the supplier (region B) there will be no contract and the income for the supplier will be his disagreement payoff p_L.

Once consumer prices for high-standards products are high enough such that $p_H \geq p_L + 2k - \phi$ and $p_H \geq p_s + k - \phi$, contracting will occur and producer prices will increase. As we discussed earlier, with imperfect contract enforcement, the buyer may need to pay his supplier an "efficiency premium" which equals the difference between the supplier's price under costly enforcement ($p^\#$) and under perfect (costless) enforcement (p^*):

$$\varepsilon \equiv p^\# - p^* = \max\left\{0; k - \phi - \beta S; p_s - p_L - \phi - \beta S\right\} \qquad (13.7)$$

---

[5] For ease of exposition, we here assume that input diversion is more attractive to the supplier than side selling; the analysis for the case where side selling is more attractive, is similar.

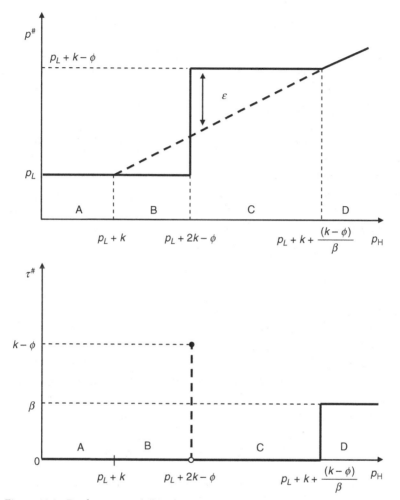

Figure 13.2. Producer price ($p^\#$) and price transmission ($\tau^\#$) with supplier holdup.

In Figure 13.2, this efficiency premium ε is represented by the difference between the full line and the dashed line. Notice that over price region C the producer price remains fixed at $p^\# = p_L + k - \phi$. This means that price transmission is zero in this region, as shown in the bottom panel of Figure 13.2. In region C, producer prices are higher than they would be with perfect enforcement, represented by the dashed line in the top panel of Figure 13.2. In region B however, producer income with perfect enforcement is higher than with imperfect enforcement, as in the latter case the supplier reverts back to low-standards production (and zero price transmission). All this implies that there is no direct relationship between price transmission and producer incomes.

Once consumer prices increase further to where $p_H \geq p_L + k + [(k - \phi) / \beta]$ (region D), producer prices will again start following the increase in consumer prices. Producer prices under imperfect enforcement are then $p^{\#} = p_L + \beta(p_H - p_L - k) = p^*$, the price with perfect enforcement. In this case price transmission is β.

The bottom panel of Figure 13.2 summarizes the variation in price transmission over the range of the consumer price p_H. Price transmission (τ) is zero for price changes within regions A, B, and C. If the consumer price changes between region B and C there is a large, discontinuous price effect for producers. Similarly, if the consumer price shifts between regions C and D there is a discontinuous effect. In region D, where the threat of supplier holdup is no longer binding, price transmission is again β as under perfect enforcement.

13.2.3 Price Transmission with Buyer Holdup

We now turn to the case where buyer holdup is possible as well. For simplicity, we first discuss the case of buyer holdup, and then discuss the implications if both supplier and buyer holdup may occur.

As shown in Chapter 11, if the buyer reneges on the contract and offers the supplier the spot-market price p_s for his produce rather than the price agreed in the contract, the payoff to the buyer is $\Pi_r = p_H - p_s - \psi$, and the payoff to the supplier is $Y_r = p_s$. Assuming $l = p_L$, the supplier price p° in this contract is

$$p^\circ = \min\left[p_L + \beta(p_H - p_L - k); p_s + \psi \right] \qquad (13.8)$$

We can again define an efficiency discount δ as the difference between the price under perfect enforcement p^* and the price p° which prevents buyer holdup:[6]

$$\delta \equiv p^* - p^\circ = \max\{0; p_L + \beta(p_H - p_L - k) - p_s - \psi\} \qquad (13.9)$$

In the top panel of Figure 13.3, this efficiency discount δ is represented by the difference between the full line and the dashed line. The producer price equals the price under perfect enforcement as long as $p_H \leq p_L + k + (1 / \beta)(p_s - p_L + \psi)$.

---

[6]   In equation (11.15), the efficiency premium was derived as $\delta = \max \{0; p_H - p_s - \psi - k - (1 - \beta)S\}$. Expression (13.9) can be derived by noting that $p_H - k - (1 - \beta)S = l + \beta S$ and setting $l = p_L$.

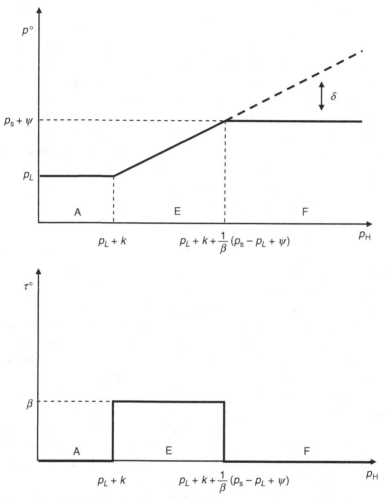

Figure 13.3. Producer price ($p°$) and price transmission ($\tau°$) with buyer holdup. *Note*: This figure depicts the situation where $p_L + k \geq p_s$.

At that point, the possibility of reneging by the buyer becomes binding, and the producer price will be fixed at $p° = p_s + \psi$. As with the case of supplier holdup, this implies that price transmission is zero in this region, as indicated in the bottom panel of Figure 13.3. However, in contrast with the case of supplier holdup, the case of buyer holdup implies that the producer price is lower than what it would be under perfect enforcement.

The bottom panel of Figure 13.3 illustrates the variation in price transmission over the consumer price region. Price transmission (τ) is equal to β

in region E, that is, as long as $p_L + k < p_H \leq p_L + k + (1/\beta)(p_s - p_L + \psi)$; for all other prices, price transmission becomes zero. Hence, with buyer holdup, price transmission follows an opposite pattern compared to supplier holdup. With supplier holdup, price transmission was zero for low values of p_H, and determined by the sharing rule β for higher prices. With buyer holdup, the opposite is true. For low prices, price transmission depends on β. For higher prices, however, the possibility of buyer holdup implies that there is no price transmission above a certain threshold value. Moreover, the effects on the supplier's welfare are also different. In the case of supplier holdup, the zone with no price transmission implies an efficiency premium for the supplier; with buyer holdup, the zone with no price transmission implies an efficiency discount given by the supplier to the buyer.[7]

13.2.4 Price Transmission with Two-Sided Holdup

In the case of two-sided holdup, the nonlinearity of price transmission is reinforced. First, at low levels of p_H, contracts are not feasible. The supplier produces low-standards products, and price transmission is zero. With rising p_H, contracts become feasible; but price transmission remains zero as long as an efficiency premium needs to be paid to the supplier to avoid supplier holdup. At higher levels of p_H, abiding by the contract becomes more attractive to the supplier than his holdup options, and price transmission is determined by the sharing rule. However, if p_H becomes very high, the buyer may demand an efficiency discount. From that point onwards, price transmission is zero again. Hence, as this analysis shows, the nature of vertical coordination in value chains plays an important role for the analysis of price transmission; data on price transmission alone is not sufficient to draw conclusions about welfare implications in value chains unless information is available on whether buyer or supplier holdup is the binding constraint.

13.3 Concluding Remarks

The empirical literature on price transmission usually assumes that perfect competition among buyers makes farmers best off; and that perfect competition will result in perfect transmission of price shocks along the

---

[7]   It is nevertheless important to remember that in our model setup with perfect information, neither the efficiency premium nor the efficiency discount will ever lead to the supplier or the buyer being worse off with the contract than without the contract. With perfect foresight, they know exactly which payoff to expect. If it does not satisfy their participation constraint, the contract will not be concluded.

value chain, as buyers operate at a zero profit margin. A shortcoming of such models is the assumption that factor markets work well and that contracts are enforced. Moreover, such models often ignore vertical coordination and the possibility of holdups. In reality, however, factor markets work imperfectly in many less developed regions, while vertical coordination is ubiquitous in modern food chains, as is the possibility of holdups. These conditions not only have major implications for the distribution of rents in food value chains (as demonstrated in earlier chapters), but they also have an important impact on price transmission.

The specific architecture of modern value chains implies that the traditional logic, which equates weaker price transmission with lower supplier welfare, is no longer universally applicable. First, when holdups are possible, price transmission will be nonlinear. Second, if supplier holdups dominate in vertically coordinated value chains, suppliers may be better off in a context where price transmission is weaker. Third, when buyer holdup binds, high prices for the high-standards product will not be transmitted to the supplier beyond a certain level, and in this case weak price transmission indeed happens alongside a welfare loss for suppliers.

One implication of our analysis is that it is necessary to study the characteristics of value chains in more detail before making any definite judgments on the link between price transmission and supplier welfare.

Finally, it is important to note that our discussion of the impact of consumer price shocks on suppliers involved in vertical contracts has focused on price shocks originating in the high-standards market. Welfare of suppliers involved in high-standards value chains may as well be affected by price shocks originating in the low-standards market. More generally, the structural processes affecting the price of the high-standards product p_H may well affect p_L and/or p_s. It is straightforward to incorporate such effects in the model.

14

Commodity Characteristics and Value Chain Governance

14.1 Introduction

In the previous chapters we discussed the emergence of high-standards value chains and the distribution of rents. The rise of these high-standards value chains is important for emerging and developing countries. The 2008 World Development Report showed that high-value export products accounted for 40% of the export value for developing countries and that domestic demand for high-standards products in developing countries was growing at a speed of 6% to 7% per year (World Bank, 2007).

However, it remains unclear whether the economic potential of these high-value chains in poor countries is sufficiently large to become a poverty reduction mechanism for (a substantial part of) the rural population. Despite their robust growth in the poorest countries, and especially in Sub-Saharan Africa (SSA), the relative contribution of high value chains to output and employment remains limited (Humphrey, 2006; Minten, 2008; Tschirley et al., 2009a). Hence, an important question is to what extent the success factors of high-standards value chains can be translated into value chains of other commodity types such as traditional export crops and staple food crops, to leverage growth and achieve broad-based poverty reduction.[1]

As is well known from work by Oliver Williamson (2002) and others, governance of exchanges along the value chain is determined by economic conditions such as the frequency of market transactions, and commodity

---

[1] Recent policy discussions have reemphasized the importance of focusing on the staple food crop sector in SSA to alleviate poverty (see, e.g., the African Union Summit on Food Security in Africa in Abuja, Nigeria in December 2006). A central issue of debate is how the staple food sector can generate sufficient surplus for widespread poverty reduction, as stagnating cereal yields in SSA and the widening yield gap with the rest of the developing world have induced calls for policy action (World Bank, 2007).

characteristics such as asset specificity. Earlier research has identified a range of commodity characteristics affecting governance of value chains, such as perishability and input requirements (see, e.g., Benfica et al., 2002; Binswanger and Rosenzweig, 1986; Delgado, 1999; Jaffee, 1994).

In this chapter we apply the model of Chapter 11 to analyze how commodity market characteristics affect vertical coordination, explicitly accounting for two important aspects of the developing country institutional environment: market imperfections and weak enforcement mechanisms. Our analysis helps to identify the conditions under which vertical coordination could work for different commodity types.

The structure of this chapter is as follows. The next section summarizes the key differences in observed value chain governance systems for different types of commodities. Then, Section 14.3 uses the model developed in Chapter 11 to analyze how the "value" in the chain, as well as other commodity characteristics, affect the nature of value chain governance. Section 14.4 compares the theoretical outcomes of the model with observed patterns of governance in different types of commodity chains in Africa. The last section concludes the chapter.

14.2 A Comparative Perspective on Commodity Chain Governance

Governance systems of value chains vary across commodity types (and countries). Within agri-food value chains, we follow the commodity classification identified by Poulton et al. (2006) and focus on three types of agricultural markets: *staple food crops* (such as grains, tubers), *traditional export commodities* (such as coffee, cocoa, tea, cotton), and *nontraditional export crops* (such as fresh fruits and vegetables, fish, and seafood products). In this section, we discuss the basic characteristics of value chain governance for these three commodity groups. To minimize additional factors of variation, the empirical evidence presented here is focused on SSA.

14.2.1 Staple Food Crops

Staple food value chains in SSA are characterized by a mixture of private market-based governance systems involving a large number of small private traders and the remainders of state governance.

Liberalization of staple food markets has prompted large numbers of small informal traders to enter into grain trade and in most countries these small private traders account for the majority of traded produce. For example, government agencies accounted for less than 3% of the traded volume of cereals in Ethiopia in the 2000s (Rashid and Negassa, 2011) and only 0.15% of the traded volume of maize in Benin (Gabre-Madhin et al., 2001).

In some countries, such as Kenya, Malawi, Zambia, and Zimbabwe, marketing boards continue to be main players in the grain markets. For example, government agencies retained a market share of respectively 24%, 14%, and 34% in the Kenya, Malawi, and Zambia maize market in 2003 – and their full impact on domestic markets was even stronger as a result of their control over international maize trade (Jayne et al., 2010).[2] In Zimbabwe, the Grain Marketing Board (GMB) continues to play an important role in maize markets (Esterhuizen, 2010).

Private traders in the staple food sector generally have limited capacity to innovate, poor access to credit and other resources, and limited storage capacity (Coulter and Poulton, 2001) and tend to rely on simple spot market transactions and social and ethnic-based networks (Fafchamps and Minten, 2001). Specialization, vertical coordination, and investments are low or absent. The use of capital inputs, especially chemical fertilizers and improved seeds, stagnated or declined in many countries after the end of state governance. For example, in the smallholder grain sector in Zimbabwe fertilizer use dropped from 120 thousand tons in the mid-1980s to 86 thousand tons in the mid-1990s (Jayne and Jones, 1997). Only in some countries fertilizer use in grain production increased substantially, for example, in Kenya and Ethiopia (Kherralah et al., 2002).

In countries where marketing boards remain important, the government is still an important source of input, credit, and extension provision. For example, in 2006/2007, parastatal agencies were responsible for 42% of the fertilizer sales in Malawi, and 60% of total fertilizer sales were subsidized (Dorward et al., 2008).

14.2.2 Traditional Export Crops

In the past fifteen years, there has been a remarkable shift from state governance in the value chains of traditional export commodities toward private

[2] Interestingly, in spite of heavy government involvement, these countries have achieved disappointing growth in cereal production – in fact, according to Jayne et al. (2010), Kenya, Malawi, and Zambia are "barely achieving cereal production levels of the 1980s." In contrast, Mali, Mozambique, and Uganda, countries where the government has taken a strong noninterventionist stand, have all experienced at least a 90% or more increase in cereal production since the 1990s.

governance systems by trading and processing companies. In most SSA countries, the coffee, cocoa, and sugar sectors have been liberalized with the removal of state export and purchasing monopolies and the removal of government price controls (Akiyama et al., 2003; World Bank, 1994). Notable exceptions are the cotton value chains in West and Central Africa, where state governance remains dominant: cotton farmers still receive intensive input packages on credit through monopolistic parastatal cotton marketing agencies (Tschirley et al., 2009b). In some sectors state-governed and private governed value chains coexist, but they usually operate in different regions of a country, giving rise to regional monopsonies. An example can be found in the cotton sector in Côte d'Ivoire (Gergely, 2010) and Burkina Faso (Tschirley et al., 2009b).

The removal of the monopoly status of (para)-statal processing companies and government marketing boards has resulted in an inflow of private capital into processing and marketing. For example, in Tanzania and Uganda, a large number of private buyers and ginners entered the cotton sector after liberalization (Tschirley et al., 2009b: 41). Value chains developed around private companies, often involving supplier contracting and interlinked market transactions, with mixed success.

Market liberalization and the shift in governance system have improved the availability and access to inputs and credit in those traditional export sectors where private contracting was financially sustainable (Kherallah et al., 2002). Increased competition in the Ghana cotton sector has induced private companies to improve their services to farmers, including timely plowing services, reliable fertilizer and pesticide supplies, prompt payment after harvest, and even plowing for farmers' food crops. The same goes for the Tanzanian cashew sector (Poulton, 1998).

However, in those sectors where private contracts proved hard to enforce, provision of inputs turned out to be problematic. This has been the case, for example, in the cotton sector in Tanzania and Uganda following reform (Poulton et al., 2004).

14.2.3 Nontraditional Export Crops

Since the 1980s the structure of SSA agricultural exports has changed significantly, with nontraditional high-value export crops such as fruits and vegetables, fish, meat, and dairy products gaining importance. Their share in total SSA agricultural exports increased from 14% in 1985 to 30% in 2005.

The value chains of high-standards exports developed during the 1980s and 1990s and have not been subject to much state intervention (Poulton et al., 2010). They are completely governed by private traders, including large multinational holdings such as international food companies and supermarkets. The production of high-standards crops is partially organized on large-scale plantations, often vertically integrated within export companies, and partially via outgrower schemes in which contracted smallholder production dominates (see examples in Chapter 10). These value chains are characterized by high degrees of vertical coordination and widespread occurrence of interlinking. Extensive forms of contracting and market interlinking provide producers with inputs, credit, and extension and management services in return for timely and high quality supplies of fresh products. There has been strong growth in these sectors and, through vertical coordination mechanisms, they have reduced local production constraints, increasing productivity and ultimately increasing farm income (Maertens et al., 2012).

14.2.4 Summary

Supply systems for staple food crops are governed through simple market-based governance and remainders of state-controlled governance. In traditional export sectors there has been a shift from state governance to private contract-based governance, with the occurrence of market interlinking, with mixed success. High-standards nontraditional export chains are primarily based on private governance systems with high degrees of vertical coordination and widespread interlinking.

In the next sections we show that these differences in value chain governance across commodity types can be explained by differences in product value, the degree of competition in the market, and other product characteristics such as the perishability of the product, and that these differences in governance systems are crucial in determining the creation and distribution of surplus along the value chain.

14.3 Impact of Commodity Characteristics

We can use the theoretical analysis of Chapter 11 to explain the observed differences in value chain governance across commodity types, in particular the (lack of) emergence of interlinking and the distribution of the created surplus along the value chain. To do so, we first introduce an extended version of the conceptual model to take into account the possibility that specific investments by the buyer may increase the yield of the supplier, but not necessarily the output price. To avoid overly complicating our modeling exercise, we will as of now assume that the buyer's reputation cost is sufficiently high to rule out buyer holdup.[3] Next, we analyze how different commodity characteristics affect contract feasibility. We then discuss the effects of competition between buyers and of other commodity characteristics.

14.3.1 Integrating Yield Effects with Perfect Enforcement

As in Chapter 11, we consider the situation where a supplier such as a local household or company can sell products to a trader or a company. This buyer then sells the product to consumers (either domestically or internationally) at a unit price p_H. The required inputs for high-standards production are labor, on the one hand, and capital, on the other hand.

However, in contrast with the basic model, we now incorporate crop yield into our model. To produce the products demanded by the buyer, the supplier needs to invest his own labor at an opportunity cost l. As before, the buyer provides inputs with an opportunity cost of k. The use of these specific inputs may on the one hand give rise to a product of higher quality, but on the other hand also to a higher yield, and hence a higher quantity of produce. We denote total quantity of production by q.

The net surplus in the value chain is then given by $S = p_H q - l - k$. As before, with perfect contract enforcement the supplier receives $Y^* = l + \beta S$ and the buyer receives $\Pi^* = k + (1 - \beta)S$.

An increase in surplus can be brought about either by an increase in p_H or by an increase in q. In some commodities, such as cotton, the use of buyer-provided inputs is more likely to lead to an increase in q than in p_H. We will go more in depth on this issue in Section 14.3.3. The benefits of increased yields will be distributed between the supplier and the buyer according to sharing rule β.[4]

14.3.2 Integrating Yield Effects with Imperfect Enforcement

If contracts are not legally enforceable, opportunistic behavior may emerge. First, the farmer may divert the received inputs and receive a payoff of $Y_d = l +$

---

[3] Extensions of our model with buyer holdup are straightforward. The implication of this simplifying assumption is that by ignoring buyer holdup, we may overestimate supplier holdup; and underestimate contract feasibility under some conditions. However, the main results should not be affected.

[4] Note that this means that if $\beta = 0$, all rents generated by the yield increase will accrue to the buyer.

$k - \phi$. Alternatively, the farmer may apply the inputs but side sell the high-standards output to an alternative buyer at a price p_s, resulting in a payoff $Y_s = p_s q - \phi$. A self-enforcing contract will thus need to offer the following payoffs:

$$Y^* = \max\{l + \beta S; \ l + k - \phi; \ p_s q - \phi\} \qquad (14.1)$$

$$\Pi^* = p_H q - Y^* \qquad (14.2)$$

The participation constraint of the buyer is $\Pi \geq k$. The resulting condition for contract feasibility is then $p_H q \geq p_H^{\min} q = \max\{l + k; \ l + 2k - \phi; \ p_s q + k - \phi\}$, or

$$p_H \geq p_H^{\min} = \max\left\{\frac{l+k}{q}; \ \frac{l+2k-\phi}{q}; \ p_s + \frac{k-\phi}{q}\right\} \qquad (14.3)$$

Equation (14.3) captures the relevant commodity characteristics that determine contract feasibility (and hence the emergence of modern value chains).

Ceteris paribus, a higher output price p_H (on the left-hand side) makes it more likely that contracts can be sustained. Hence, all else equal, it should be easier for modern value chains to emerge for goods with a high value added compared to undifferentiated commodities with a relatively low value added.[5]

Second, lower opportunity costs l and k (all else equal) make it more likely that contracts will be feasible. This is the case since lower opportunity costs increase the net surplus S of the contract (and hence the "value" in the value chain).

Note that if $k = 0$, so that no specific inputs are required, suppliers are able to produce independently, and no vertical coordination is needed. This case is equivalent to a situation where factor markets work efficiently. For commodities where little or no specific inputs are needed, or for regions where factor markets work well, we do not expect to see much vertical coordination, as production can come about without it.[6]

---

[5] Note that in reality, value added tends to be positively correlated with gross value in the chain – which means that high-standards crops, even if input requirements tend to be higher, usually also have higher added value (gross value – input requirements). In other words, even if costs tend to be higher as well, profit margins are usually higher in high-standards crops. One reason is that the price elasticity of demand for these crops is usually lower, as they are mostly consumed by better-off consumers.

[6] See also our discussion in Section 11.7.3.

A third factor are the possibilities for side selling, captured by p_s. A lower price at which suppliers can side sell will improve the feasibility of contracts. The price p_s will be lower if there are fewer alternative buyers, if the commodity is highly specific, or if other characteristics of the commodity make it difficult for the supplier to side sell. For instance, high perishability of the commodity limits the supplier's options in finding and negotiating with alternative buyers. A low value per volume might likewise make it harder (or less profitable) for the supplier to transport the commodity to a market or to an alternative buyer.

Finally, potential yield improvements have an impact on contract feasibility as well. As can be seen from equation (14.3), if $k > \phi$, $p_H^{\min}$ is strictly decreasing in q, with p_s as the lower bound. This means that contract feasibility will improve with rising q, but $p_H \geq p_s$ remains a necessary condition.

Yield improvements also have some interesting effects on the distribution of the surplus under imperfect enforcement. Notably, yield improvements are likely to enhance the supplier's payoff through the option of side selling since $\partial Y_s / \partial q = p_s$. If side selling binds and if $p_s > \beta p_H$, yield improvements will lead to a greater improvement in the supplier's income under imperfect enforcement than under perfect enforcement.

14.3.3 Yield Improvements for Undifferentiated Commodities

An interesting application is the case where the use of specific inputs only results in an increased yield q, rather than an increased quality and therefore a higher unit value p_H. This is, for example, often the case for the cultivation of cotton in developing countries, where the value of raw cotton is similar for all possible buyers, whether or not they were the ones who initially provided the inputs on credit to the cotton producers (see, e.g., Tschirley et al., 2009b). This seriously constrains buyers' incentives to provide inputs; but without specific inputs, cotton yields would substantially decline.

If the use of specific inputs only results in a yield increase without any price differentiation, in terms of our model this would mean that $p_s = p_H$, with equations (11.9) and (11.10) reducing to

$$Y^* = \max\left\{l + \beta\left(p_H q - k - l\right); \; p_H q - \phi\right\} \tag{14.4}$$

$$\Pi^* = p_H q - Y^* \tag{14.5}$$

Note that the input diversion option has disappeared, as this option will now always be dominated by side selling. A necessary condition for a contract to emerge is that $p_H q - k - l \geq 0$, which implies that $p_H q - \phi \geq k + l - \phi$, that is, if the value in the value chain is positive, side selling always dominates input diversion. The corresponding condition for contract feasibility becomes

$$p_H \geq p_H^{min} = \max \left\{ \frac{l+k}{q}; \; p_H + \frac{k - \phi}{q} \right\} \qquad (14.6)$$

However, it is clear that $p_H \geq p_H + (k - \phi / q)$ is possible only if $\phi \geq k$. Interestingly, this condition itself does not depend on the magnitude of the yield improvement q. If the reputation cost to the supplier of breaking the contract is smaller than the value of the specific inputs, no contracting is possible. On the other hand, if $\phi \geq k$, the condition for contract feasibility is simply the condition for socially efficient contracts: $p_H q \geq l + k$. An increase in yields will then make it more likely that this condition is met; in fact, yield increases would have the same effect as increases in p_H.

Our results show that in the absence of quality differentiation (implying that $p_H = p_s$), the extent of inefficient contract breakdown is completely determined by the reputation cost. If the reputation cost is sufficiently high (i.e., $\phi \geq k$), there will be no inefficient contract breakdown. If, conversely, the reputation cost is too low (i.e. $\phi < k$), contracts will break down at any level of p_H. Interestingly, the level of inefficient contract breakdown is thus entirely independent of the size of the yield improvement q which can be brought about by using specific inputs.

14.3.4 Buyer Competition

As discussed in Chapter 12, the impact of buyer competition Ψ on the feasibility of contracts can be decomposed as follows:

$$\frac{\partial \left[p_H - p_H^{min} \right]}{\partial \Psi} = \frac{\partial p_H}{\partial \Psi} - \frac{\partial p_H^{min}}{\partial l} \frac{\partial l}{\partial \Psi} - \frac{\partial p_H^{min}}{\partial p_s} \frac{\partial p_s}{\partial \Psi} - \frac{\partial p_H^{min}}{\partial \phi} \frac{\partial \phi}{\partial \Psi} \qquad (14.7)$$

and the effect of competition on p_H will depend on the characteristics of the value chain. If the value chain is export-oriented, the actual output price will be determined by the world market and will not be influenced much by local competition. The net effect of local competition might be to improve the efficiency of the buyer's operations or provide incentives to differentiate quality and target higher-end markets, which would raise the net price p_H, that is, $\partial p_H / \partial \Psi > 0$. On the other hand, if the value chain mainly deals with commodities for a small local market, an increase in competition drives down the output price, that is, $\partial p_H / \partial \Psi < 0$. For the other terms in equation (14.7), the interpretation is the same as in Chapter 12: an increase in competition will tend to drive up the suppliers' opportunity cost of labor ($\partial l / \partial \Psi > 0$), the price at which they can side sell ($\partial p_s / \partial \Psi > 0$), and reduce their reputation cost of doing so ($\partial \phi / \partial \Psi < 0$).

14.3.5 Other Commodity Characteristics

In addition to the elements mentioned earlier, other commodity characteristics may also influence the occurrence of interlinking. For example, Jaffee (1994) emphasizes the importance of characteristics such as perishability, degree of heterogeneity and quality differentiation, crop gestation period,[7] labor intensity (leading to diseconomies of scale), and value per weight: these factors would favor the use of vertical coordination (relative to spot market governance). As noted earlier, some of these characteristics can in fact be interpreted as leading to a higher price p_H, a higher k or a lower price for side selling p_s. Binswanger and Rosenzweig (1986) argue that a long crop gestation period, economies of scale, and coordination problems between harvest and processing are conducive to vertical coordination. Delgado (1999) and Mason et al. (2009) present an even more comprehensive list of relevant crop characteristics, as well as institutional (economic and political) characteristics of the market environment, which play a role in determining which organizational form is most suited to the value chain under consideration.

14.4 Implications for Commodity Chain Governance

These theoretical results can provide insights why, after liberalizations, interlinked private contracting has appeared in certain sectors but not in others. As explained in Section 14.2 there is a large variation in governance systems in agricultural markets. Typically, the staple food crop sector is characterized by remainders of state-controlled governance and/or simple (noninterlinked) private spot market transactions; the traditional export crop sector is governed by state-controlled and/or private interlinked contracts; and the nontraditional export sector is primarily based on private interlinked transactions.

---

[7] A long crop gestation period means a relatively high capital investment and high asset specificity, as the time between investment and harvest is long. This can be reflected in a high k.

Table 14.1. *Commodity characteristics and value chain governance*

	Examples	Value	Degree of competition	Perishability (in general)	Value Chain Governance
Staple food crops	Grains, roots, tubers	Low	High	Less perishable	Spot markets and state interlinking
Traditional export crops	Coffee, cocoa, cotton	Medium	Low	Less perishable	State and private interlinking
Nontraditional export crops	Vegetables, fruits, fish, meat	High	Low	More perishable	Private interlinking

In line with the results derived from our model, these differences in value chain governance can be explained by (1) differences in potential surplus creation across commodity types, (2) the ease of side selling commodities, and (3) differences in the degree of buyer competition. Based on our model, we expect to find more extensive private market interlinking when potential value is higher, when products are more perishable, and when there is less buyer competition (Table 14.1).

14.4.1 Staple Food Crops

In the staple food crop sector, separation (whether efficient or inefficient) is likely to occur because of a low degree of quality differentiation leading to a low price p_H compared to the opportunity costs of production. The potential contract surplus (relative to alternative employment or cultivation options) is low because of a low potential for quality upgrading in production or processing. Staple food crops are mostly consumed in the home markets of SSA countries (rather than being exported) where quality standards are typically lacking and where staples are often acquired by consumers in unprocessed form to be processed at home or by small-scale hammer mills for a fee.[8]

---

[8] For example, Traub and Jayne (2006) report that in South Africa, 38% of consumers reported to have bought maize grain (rather than meal) or used services of small-scale mills in 2003/2004. Similarly, in Mozambique, about 70% of the consumers in the surveyed second-tier cities reported to pound their own maize grain, or take it to small-scale hammer mills. In Maputo, in contrast, only 30% consumers reported to buy unprocessed maize (Tschirley et al., 2005).

In addition, there are typically a high number of potential buyers in staple food markets (as long as the region is not geographically isolated from the market or the state is not ruling out alternative marketing channels). Many farm households buy staple foods directly, in addition to many, often very small, traders (Govereh et al., 1999). This puts upward pressure on the spot market price p_s and weakens reputation mechanisms (through ϕ). Furthermore, staple foods such as grains are relatively easily to store and transport with minimal investments, and not highly perishable; which further facilitates side selling. In combination, these factors impede private interlinking and make vertical coordination and technology transfer difficult in staple food chains.

These findings are in line with earlier literature. For example, Binswanger and Rosenzweig (1986) argue that contract farming with smallholders is unlikely to arise in wheat and other food grains. Delgado (1999) concludes that contract farming in coarse grains and root crops is not feasible, while making an exception for rice production, where labor intensity is higher and there is more scope for quality differentiation. Coulter and Poulton (2001: 197) argue that interlinked schemes "rarely work with cereal crops" as the cereal market structure facilitates contract violation. Benfica et al. (2002) study the maize subsector in rural Mozambique and find that the product characteristics of maize favor production by independent producers rather than in vertically coordinated production systems. Demont and Rizotto (2012) describe the challenges of quality differentiation and creating surplus in rice value chains in Senegal.

There are a few examples where private contracting – with input provision on credit – has been taken up in staple crops. These contracts mostly concern staple crop chains in which quality differentiation was important. Several studies show the importance of interlinked contracting for malting barley production in various emerging and developing countries, but not without problems. This was the case in the 1990s in Central and Eastern Europe, where international brewing companies initially were unable to source high-standards barley from local independent producers. As a result, they started up interlinked contracts with local farmers (Van Herck et al., 2012). Barley contract production by Jos International Breweries in Nigeria faced many problems related to opportunistic behavior in the initial phase (Porter and Phillips-Howard, 1994). SABMiller started up similar programs for malting barley on different locations in India (Arora et al., 2011), and for barley, sorghum, and cassava with smallholders in various countries in Africa (SABMiller, 2011). Likewise, Guinness is sourcing specific sorghum varieties through contracts with small farms in Ghana and Burkina Faso (Muller et al., 2006).[9]

Other examples include basmati rice contracting in India (Singh, 2005) or organic rice contract farming in Thailand (Setboonsarng et al., 2006). There could be more scope for similar schemes in producing aflatoxin-free maize or micronutrient enriched cereal varieties and/or the production and multiplication of improved cereal seeds. However, what is clear is that although in principle these cases concern staple foods (e.g., barley, rice, sorghum), the specific contracts are for high-standards versions of these cereals, and the commodity as such no longer qualifies as a low-standards staple.

14.4.2 Traditional Export Crops

Traditional export commodities such as coffee, tea, cotton, and cocoa have an intermediate added value. Moreover, these export commodities are often processed industrially, which means that in contrast with staples, they are usually not sold to households directly, which reduces the number of buyers in the market. Still, a relatively large number of processing companies may exist that compete for primary produce such as green coffee and cocoa beans. Farmers might therefore still have opportunities to find alternative buyers, leading to side selling and holdups (Baumann, 2000).

As a result, after the removal of state governance, private interlinking schemes have experienced many challenges. For example in the cotton sector, where the cost of inputs is quite high relative to the producer price for cotton (up to 40% according to some sources), interlinking has often been considered to be crucial for production, but difficult to sustain (e.g., Tshirley et al., 2009). This is one of the reasons why in West and Central Africa, governments have retained a strong hold on their cotton sectors – especially given the fact that cotton export revenues are major contributors to public budgets (Delpeuch and Vandeplas, 2013). A major problem in private cotton interlinked schemes is the difficulty of quality differentiation. As we discussed in Section 14.3.3, in absence of quality differentiation, interlinked schemes can only be sustained if reputation costs associated with

---

[9]   In some cases, cooperatives have played a role in contract enforcement. For example in Tanzania, Breweries Ltd. at first experienced strong opportunistic behavior from its contract suppliers of malting barley – as suppliers found it more profitable to sell their barley to other buyers. Later, the brewery collaborated with producer cooperatives, who receive credit from the brewery and supply inputs to their members. This improved the viability of the schemes (Wangwe and Lwakatare, 2004).

contract breach are sufficiently high. However, in countries with unclear property rights and a lack of individual identification systems, most reputation mechanisms seem to fail (Giné et al., 2012; Poulton, pers. comm.,).

In the coffee and cocoa sectors, where the bulk of the investment is done at the time of planting trees, and should be considered a "fixed" rather than a "variable" cost, state-governed interlinked schemes have generally not been replaced by private interlinked schemes after liberalization. The coffee and cocoa sectors are mostly governed through spot market exchanges. In some cases, processors buy directly from farmers through village-level collection centers, but mostly without providing inputs on credit. For example, Nestlé has adopted this strategy to avoid intermediation by small traders (Kaplinsky, 2004; Kolk, 2005). Sugar cane, tea, and rubber are more perishable, which means side selling is more difficult and contract farming schemes somewhat easier to sustain (Binswanger and Rosenzweig, 1986).

Sustainable contracts have been observed in "niche markets" where quality differentiation has proved viable. Examples include organic coffee (Bolwig et al., 2008), biodiversity-conserving shade-grown coffee (Larson, 2003), or fair-trade products (see, e.g., Bacon, 2005). However, again, although these cases in principle concern traditional export crops (e.g. coffee), the specific contracts are for high-standards versions of these commodities.

14.4.3 Nontraditional Export Crops

In the case of nontraditional export crops such as fruits and vegetables, high standards are imposed by overseas markets where consumers are willing to pay for quality. Yet, input requirements are typically high for reaching high standards. The high potential surplus, the possibility for quality differentiation, and the need for specific inputs increase the likelihood of interlinking in the nontraditional export sector.

In addition, contract enforcement is easier as the number of buyers is limited. Nontraditional export sectors generally include only a limited number of buyers as these sectors are relatively new with less developed marketing channels and often dominated by large multinational food companies. Local consumers do not compete for these types of high-standards products as they are generally not prepared to pay high prices for quality. As a result, there is usually only modest competition for these high-standards commodities.

Finally, contract enforcement is also facilitated by the perishable nature of the products. Products usually require carefully designed cold chains for transport to avoid post-harvest damage and losses, and the time between harvesting and marketing is restricted. In such circumstances, farmers do not have enough time to look out for more profitable opportunities.[10]

14.5 Conclusion

The rise of high-value chains in developing and emerging economies has prompted the question of whether this mode of governance could also be applied to other commodities with lower value. In this chapter, we applied the theoretical tools developed in the previous chapters to shed some light on this issue. Our analysis emphasizes that the characteristics of commodities and the market conditions play an important role in enabling the emergence of vertical coordination. If the "value" in the value chain is too low to cover opportunity costs and (importantly) to offer the supplier a contract which is at least as attractive as his opportunities for input diversion or side selling, no vertical coordination will emerge. This, in turn, will likely be the case for low-value commodities, for commodities which require the use of specific inputs with a relatively high resale value, and commodities with good opportunities for side selling. Commodity characteristics such as low perishability and market conditions such as high competition make it likely that suppliers will have good opportunities for contract breach, making vertical coordination less likely. Observations on commodity chains in Sub-Saharan Africa confirm these predictions.

While the present chapter applies a "static" analysis of failure of governance in value chains, the next chapter goes a step further by applying the model to explain the diverging effects of liberalization on agricultural output in China, in the former communist countries of Eastern Europe, and in Sub-Saharan Africa.

---

[10] Obviously, there are examples of opportunistic behavior in nontraditional export schemes as well – especially in initial stages – see, e.g., Ruotsi (2003) for empirical evidence on side selling in French bean production in Kenya and bell pepper production in Zambia.

15

Economic Liberalization, Value Chains, and Development

15.1 Introduction

Thirty years ago, value chains in many poor and middle income countries were heavily state controlled. This was most extreme in the Communist world, spreading from Central Europe to East Asia, but also in many African, Latin-American, and South Asian countries the state played a very important role in value chain governance.

The first major liberalization started in Indonesia in 1968. Other Asian countries such as Sri Lanka, China, and Vietnam followed. Countries in Sub-Saharan Africa (SSA), in Eastern Europe, and in the former Soviet Union pursued reforms in the 1980s and 1990s. The liberalization of trade, prices, and exchange rates, and the removal of state control over commodity chains were to improve incentives to suppliers and to yield growth, thereby raising incomes and reducing poverty (Commander, 1989; Krueger et al., 1988; Timmer, 1986).

The impact has been dramatic. The reforms in China and Vietnam lifted hundreds of millions of people out of poverty. The effects of the reforms in other regions were however very different than in China (see Figure 15.1). In Russia and other Eastern European countries, the reforms caused a dramatic decline in output and incomes and it took several years before recovery took off (Rozelle and Swinnen, 2004). In Africa, the effects of the liberalizations – often embedded in structural adjustment programs – were also disappointing. Although there is some progress, the general consensus is that market reforms did not meet expectations in SSA in the 1990s (Kherallah et al., 2002).

What explains these diverging experiences with economic liberalization? In this chapter we argue that the effects of liberalization are best understood in terms of their effects on value chains in the countries involved. Using the

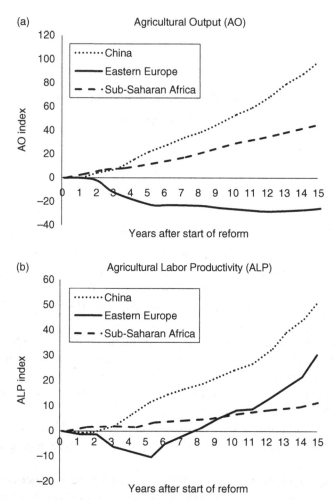

Figure 15.1. Post-reform performance of agriculture.
Source: Based on Swinnen and Rozelle (2006), Swinnen et al. (2010), and FAO data.

theoretical model developed earlier, together with information on key institutional and structural characteristics of developing and transition countries, we will analyze the effects of liberalization and show how our models can be useful to understand the observed patterns.

The structure of this chapter is as follows. In the next section, we discuss the institutional characteristics of the countries where liberalization took place, paying attention both to initial conditions and to the characteristics of reform. Section 15.3 presents a variation on the model of Chapter 11 to study how liberalization affects agricultural output. In Section 15.4 we use these insights to provide an explanation for the diverging effects of liberalization in Eastern Europe, China, and SSA. To further demonstrate the usefulness of our value chain model, Section 15.5 uses the model to offer hypotheses on the variations in commodity sector performance in Africa. The last section concludes the chapter.

15.2 Institutional Characteristics

15.2.1 The Pre-liberalization Economy

To illustrate the different patterns, we focus on (averages of) Eastern Europe, China, and SSA. For more country-level detail and specifics, we refer to Swinnen and Rozelle (2006), Swinnen et al. (2010), and Macours and Swinnen (2000a, 2000b, 2002). Although there are important differences across regions in certain attributes of the pre-reform economy, countries in Eastern Europe, China, and SSA had several characteristics in common – especially with respect to governance of value chains.[1]

First, government institutions were monopoly buyers of many agricultural products. This was most extreme in the Communist world where the entire agricultural production system was under strict state control. However, also in most SSA countries, in the decades after independence from colonial power, governments regulated agricultural production, marketing and processing through marketing boards, government-controlled cooperatives and parastatal companies.

Second, interlinked contracting was widespread: contracts were often offered as a "package deal," with the buyer of the output acting as the provider of (some of) the inputs required for production (see Chapter 11). Again this was most extreme in the Communist system where agricultural value chains were fully integrated and completely state-controlled. Production, processing, marketing, the provision of inputs and credit, and retailing were all government controlled. Also in SSA government control and interlinking in value chains was widespread. Many parastatal organizations provided both inputs to producers and purchased their outputs.[2]

---

[1] See, e.g., Kherallah et al. (2002), Rozelle and Swinnen (2004), and Swinnen and Maertens (2007) for details. "Eastern Europe" includes both Central Europe and the former Soviet Union; "SSA" is as defined in Swinnen et al. (2010).

[2] For example, the government marketing boards Agricultural and Marketing Corporation (ADMARC) in Malawi and National Agricultural Marketing Board (NAMBoard) in Zambia provided seasonal inputs to peasant farmers deducting the value of the inputs from the payment made for marketed output at harvest time. Also parastatal cotton

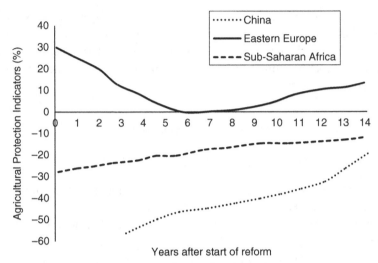

Figure 15.2. Agricultural protection indicators (API) (in %).
Source: Based on Swinnen et al. (2010), OECD (2008), and Anderson (2009).

Third, an important achievement (in historical perspective) of these systems was that they did manage to provide inputs and credit to suppliers, albeit in a costly way. Monopoly control contributed to enforcement of the interlinked contracts (as discussed in Chapter 12), but there were problems of high costs, enforcement problems with buyers (sometimes) paying with delays, and suppliers (sometimes) not repaying credit or inputs.[3]

Fourth, government control of the value chains was also used to set prices. Price setting was motivated by political objectives, so as to provide cheap food for urban markets. While price distortions were present everywhere, the nature of the distortions differed strongly across countries. Figure 15.2 presents indicators of government support and price distortions in agriculture, which show that farmers in Eastern Europe were highly subsidized prior to the reforms with indicators at around 30%. In China and SSA, farmers were strongly taxed with indicators around –30% on average in SSA and lower than –50% in China.

companies such as Companie Malienne pour le Développement du Textile (CMDT) in Mali, La Société de Développement du Coton (SODECOTON) in Cameroon, the Ghana Cotton Development Board in Ghana and the Kenyan Tea Development Cooperation provided credit and inputs to cotton farmers (Bauman, 2000; Poulton et al., 1998).

[3] Several studies conclude that state-controlled outgrower schemes were inefficient and poorly managed, while others point at successes of these systems (Bauman, 2000; Johnson and Brooks, 1983; Poulton et al., 1998; Warning and Key, 2002).

Table 15.1. *Initial conditions and reforms*

	Eastern Europe	China	Sub-Saharan Africa
Initial Conditions:			
GDP per capita (PPP$ 2000)	10,069	622	1,429
Agricultural price distortions	Subsidized	Taxed	Taxed
Reforms:	Big bang	Gradual	Mixed

Data source: World Bank (2006).

Finally, important differences between countries were their income levels at the eve of liberalization – summarized in Table 15.1. Per capita incomes were much higher in Eastern Europe ($10,069) than in SSA ($1,429) and China ($622).[4] These income differences are correlated with commodity standards and value chains. For example, in terms of their food consumption patterns, with higher incomes, consumers shift from staple foods toward higher value food items (such as fruit, vegetables, fish, and animal products) and demand higher quality and safety standards. In Eastern Europe, on average more than 70% of the total value of agricultural production consisted of food products such as fruits, vegetables, milk, and meat products; with much higher standards than in SSA and China. In SSA and China, a substantial share of agricultural production and food consumption was in very low-standard commodities such as roots, tubers and pulses, much more than in Eastern Europe.[5]

15.2.2 The Liberalization Process

Across the regions that we analyze governments reduced their intervention in price setting, leading to a reduction of distortions under the form of taxes or subsidies. Another common element was that private traders were allowed in trade, and that the monopoly status of government marketing boards and parastatal processing companies was removed.

There were differences across countries in the sequencing and the degree of implementation of the various reform elements. The main reform approach in Eastern Europe was a "big-bang" approach, which implied the simultaneous liberalization of prices and markets with the introduction of

---

[4] Incomes are expressed as GDP per capita at purchasing power parity rates in constant 2000 international dollars.

[5] Own calculations based on FAO data.

private competition.[6] At the same time property rights and companies were privatized.

In contrast, China gradually introduced the different reform components, starting in agriculture. China first transferred land rights to farmers and later administratively increased prices to reduce taxation on farmers. Only afterwards, it gradually allowed competition in other markets. This gradual reform approach in China differed from that in Eastern Europe, because control over farm prices was reduced while maintaining state control over the institutions that supplied inputs to and purchased outputs (mostly rice) from the farms.[7]

In SSA, reform strategies were a mixture.[8] In most countries, the removal of state control was not as gradual as in China but only few used a "big-bang" reform approach.[9] In many countries, reforms differed by subsector: reforms often started in basic food sectors while in export sectors – such as coffee, cocoa, cotton etc. – reform processes started later. In addition, basic food sectors were often completely liberalized while in many export sectors state control was not removed completely. State monopolies still remain in some sectors.[10]

However, despite these differences, there are two crucial common, and interrelated, aspects of the liberalization process. One is "price liberalization," meaning that the government no longer sets prices. Figure 15.2 illustrates this by showing that in all regions price distortions decreased as the assistance indicators moved closer to zero (no distortions) across all regions. The second important common element is "market liberalization," that is, the removal of state control over the structure of the commodity

---

[6]   Among these countries, there was considerable variation; see Swinnen and Rozelle (2006) for details.

[7]   The reform implementation is actually more nuanced than this "gradual process" as it is usually summarized. China's initial approach was not that different from that in Eastern Europe as it liberalized markets and allowed private traders to come in. However, the resulting turmoil on the market and the threat of reduced rice supplies for the cities induced the Chinese leaders to re-take control over the value chains. See Rozelle (1996) for a fascinating review of these policy changes and their effects.

[8]   See Akiyama et al. (2003), Kherralah et al. (2002), and World Bank (1994) for details.

[9]   For example, a big bang reform approach was launched in Nigeria in 1987 with simultaneous removal of price controls, trade restrictions and (para-) state crop procurement and input provision. A gradual approach similar to China, with first liberalization of prices and subsequently gradual removal of state monopoly, was, for example, used in the coffee sector in Cameroon and Tanzania, the cocoa sector in Cameroon, and the cotton sector in Eastern Africa. In other cases, such as the coffee sector in Uganda, the reversed sequencing was used, with first the introduction of competition and later the removal of taxes.

[10]   State monopolies still exist, most notably in the cotton sector in Western Africa (see Delpeuch and Vandeplas, 2013).

chains by allowing competition in the chain and no longer dictating trade. Despite variations, in all regions the share of the private sector increased strongly after liberalization.

Our theoretical model will integrate these common institutional characteristics, both in terms of the pre-liberalization economy and the liberalization process.[11] Interpreting these empirical observations in terms of our model will help understand the overall effects of reform and the resulting differences in economic performance.

15.3 A Model of Value Chains and Liberalization

To analyze the effects of liberalization, we introduce a few modifications to our basic model. As before, a supplier can use his inputs l together with specific inputs k provided by the buyer to produce a good that can be sold at price p_H.

We now explicitly introduce processing and transport costs, to account for efficiency effects along the value chain. The output price p_H as used in previous chapters can be interpreted as the output price net of per unit costs for processing and transport which would be incurred if the value chain was operating on the efficiency frontier. That is, we can interpret p_H as already capturing the minimum extra costs involved in producing a high-standards product and delivering it to consumers. However, firms along the value chain may not be using "best practices" in their management, and/or they may be using outdated technology. These would result in extra costs compared to the "efficient" costs. We denote these excess costs by t_m. For firms operating at the efficiency frontier, $t_m = 0$; whereas $t_m > 0$ implies that firms are incurring extra costs due to inefficiencies in management, marketing, processing, transport, and so on.

In a similar way, we take into account the role of the government in taxing or subsidizing products. To this end, we introduce a cost t_g that captures the price distortion introduced by the government, where $t_g > 0$ denotes taxes and $t_g < 0$ denotes subsidies.

---

[11] We do not discuss separately the effects of privatization. Its effects are implicit in our model. If privatization leads to more efficient management, and hence to a reduction in excess marketing costs (t_m, see further), this will lead to an increase in farm prices, with similar effects as a decrease in tax policies. This effect should lead to an increase in output and in farm incomes. However, privatization may not lead to such reduction if it perpetuates monopolistic/monopsonistic pricing. The key element is competition, which we analyze explicitly.

Given these assumptions, we now define the surplus S as the surplus for an efficient firm in a context without price distortions imposed by the government, that is, $S = p_H - l - k$. Similar to our treatment of enforcement costs in Chapter 11, we model the effect of inefficiencies t_m and government policy t_g as a subtraction from the surplus S. The actual available surplus is

$$S - t_m - t_g = p_H - l - k - t_m - t_g \tag{15.1}$$

The remainder of the theoretical model closely resembles that of Chapter 11 (apart from the fact that we again abstract away from the possibility of buyer holdup, as in Chapter 14). With perfect enforcement, the supplier and the buyer receive their outside option and a share of the surplus as determined by sharing rule β. However, contract enforcement is not perfect, and the supplier has opportunities to engage in input diversion or side selling. As a result, a self-enforcing contract must offer the supplier at least the payoff he could receive from contract breach. The resulting contract will be

$$Y^* = \max\left\{l + \beta\left(S - t_m - t_g\right); l + k - \phi; p_s - \phi\right\} \tag{15.2}$$

$$\Pi^* = p_H - t_m - t_g - Y^* \tag{15.3}$$

For the buyer to agree with the contract, $\Pi^* \geq k$ must be fulfilled; the supplier will only participate if $Y^* \geq l$. In addition, there should be enough surplus in the chain to cover the required efficiency premium. Hence, contracts will be feasible only if

$$p_H \geq p_H^{\min} = \max\left\{l + k; l + 2k - \phi;\ p_s + k - \phi\right\} + t_m + t_g \tag{15.4}$$

This is identical to the condition for feasibility established by equation (11.2), with the explicit addition of the extra costs due to inefficiencies t_m and the impact of government taxes t_g. If $p_H < l + k$, contracting would not be efficient even if the impact of t_m and t_g was zero. As before, we refer to this situation as "efficient separation." However, if $l + k \leq p_H < l + k + t_m + t_g$, there would be a surplus under nondistorted conditions, but either taxation or inefficiencies in the chain prevent an effective surplus. We refer to this situation as "distorted separation." If $p_H \geq l + k + t_m + t_g$ but smaller than $l + 2k - \phi + t_m + t_g$ or than $p_s + k - \phi + t_m + t_g$, there is no price the buyer can offer to the supplier to make him comply with the contract, and "inefficient separation" will occur.

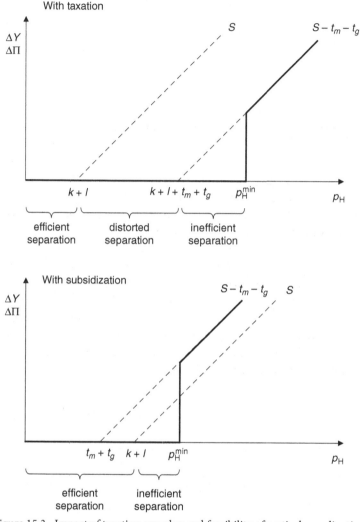

Figure 15.3. Impact of taxation on value and feasibility of vertical coordination.

Figure 15.3 illustrates these separation effects. Line S presents the surplus that could be created without inefficiencies or distortions ($t_m = t_g = 0$) and with perfect enforcement. Line $S - t_m - t_g$ represents the surplus with distortions and includes the possibility of supplier holdup, leading to an inability to enforce the contract for $p_H < l + 2k - \phi + t_m + t_g$ in case of input diversion (the case of side selling is similar).

In addition to the factors identified in Chapter 11, the feasibility of contracting thus also depends on the extent of inefficiencies in processing and marketing t_m and the level of government taxes or subsidies. A tax $t_g > 0$ or a greater degree of inefficiency $t_m > 0$ will make it harder for contracts to be feasible, whereas a subsidy $t_g < 0$ makes it more likely that contracting can occur.

15.3.1 Aggregate Output

So far, our theoretical approach has considered the relationship between an individual supplier and an individual buyer. However, to understand the aggregate effects of liberalization, it is necessary to extend our model to explain effects on aggregate output of the agricultural sector.

To this end, we now assume that there are N suppliers, each of which can produce at most one unit of the high-standards product. Moreover, we assume that the buyer faces different transaction costs for every supplier. This may be due to differences in landholding size, in experience or skill level, in distance from the contracted processor, and so on. More specifically, assume a buyer faces a transaction cost t_j in dealing with supplier j. These transaction costs are uniformly distributed between zero and T, or $t_j \sim U[0, T]$. In all other characteristics, suppliers are assumed to be identical.

The derivations in the previous section can then be interpreted as applying only to the supplier with the lowest transaction costs (i.e., $t_j = 0$). For all other suppliers, the relevant expressions become

$$Y_j^\# = \max\left\{l + \beta\left(S - t_m - t_g - t_j\right); l + k - \phi; p_s - \phi\right\} \quad (15.5)$$

$$\Pi_j^\# = p_H - t_m - t_g - t_j - Y_j^\# \quad (15.6)$$

where $\Pi_j^\#$ denotes the buyer's profit from dealing with supplier j. The expression for contract feasibility now becomes

$$p_H \geq p_{H,j}^{\min} = \max\left\{l + k; l + 2k - \phi; p_s + k - \phi\right\} + t_m + t_g + t_j \quad (15.7)$$

In this expression, $p_{H,j}^{\min}$ is the supplier-specific minimum price for supplier j. The effect of the supplier-specific transaction cost t_j on feasibility is thus similar to that of t_m or t_g.

We can rewrite this condition as $p_H \geq p_H^{\min} + t_j$ for supplier j where $p_H^{\min}$ is defined as earlier. This condition may hold for suppliers with a low enough t_j, but not for others with higher t_j. We denote by $\bar{t}_j$ the transaction cost at which the feasibility condition is binding, i.e. $p_H = p_H^{\min} + \bar{t}_j$ or $\bar{t}_j = p_H - p_H^{\min}$.

Contracts are feasible as long as $t_j < \bar{t}_j$ and no longer feasible as soon as $t_j > \bar{t}_j$. Given our assumption that transaction costs are uniformly distributed between zero and T, and given that $0 < \bar{t}_j < T$, aggregate output Q_H can be derived as a function of p_H and $p_H^{\min}$ as follows:

$$Q_H\left(p_H, p_H^{\min}\right) = \frac{\bar{t}_j}{T} N = \left(p_H - p_H^{\min}\right)\left(\frac{N}{T}\right) \quad (15.8)$$

or more explicitly,

$$Q_H = \left(p_H - \max\{l + k; l + 2k - \phi; p_s + k - \phi\} - t_m - t_g\right)\left(\frac{N}{T}\right) \quad (15.9)$$

If $p_H - p_H^{\min} = \bar{t}_j > T$, contracting is feasible for all suppliers and hence $Q_H = N$. The same factors driving feasibility will now determine the level of high-standards supply. Aggregate output increases if p_H increases, up to the point where $p_H - p_H^{\min} = T$ and the maximum level of output (N) is obtained. Aggregate output will also increase if the value of the inputs k is lower; if the supplier's reputation costs ϕ are higher, and if the opportunities for side selling are more limited (i.e., p_s is lower). Moreover, aggregate output increases if the value chain is more efficient (t_m is low) and if the government subsidizes agriculture ($t_g < 0$).

Contract enforcement under state control differs from enforcement under a market system. Monopolistic state control facilitates contract enforcement by legally ruling out competition, resulting in a lower opportunity cost l for the supplier, less options for side selling (hence a low p_s), and higher reputation costs (high ϕ).[12] These factors unambiguously make contract enforcement easier under state control. However, excess marketing costs $t_m > 0$ make enforcement more difficult, while the impact of price distortions depend on the tax regime, with taxation ($t_g > 0$) making enforcement more difficult.

As mentioned earlier, liberalization generally consisted of two main elements which we label "price liberalization" and "market liberalization." Price liberalization entails that the government no longer determines prices, and hence sets t_g closer to zero (or, in case of complete price liberalization, exactly equal to zero). Market liberalization is the removal of

---

[12] This argument is not universally valid, however. In some cases there was a political obligation for buyers to source from all suppliers in a given region, resulting in a low reputation cost ϕ.

state control over the structure of the commodity chains by allowing private trade and competition. Hence, we can analyze the effects of price and market liberalization in our model by setting $t_g = 0$ and by analyzing the effects of an increase in competition Ψ, using the insights from Chapter 12.

15.3.2 Price Liberalization

As can be seen from equations (15.5) to (15.9), price liberalization has an unambiguous impact on contract feasibility, incomes, and aggregate output. An increase in the net output price $(p_H - t_m - t_g)$ improves feasibility and incomes and raises aggregate output, while the opposite effects hold if the net output price decreases. Applied to the case of price liberalization, this implies that we expect negative effects in case the government cuts subsidies to agriculture (that is, if the government moves from $t_g < 0$ to $t_g = 0$) and positive effects in case the government removes heavy taxation on agriculture (i.e., if the government moves from $t_g > 0$ to $t_g = 0$).

15.3.3 Market Liberalization

Market liberalization was implemented by allowing private traders and buyers to enter the market and/or by privatizing and/or removing the monopoly status of the state companies. As discussed in Chapter 12, as long as contracting remains feasible, competition increases the producer's opportunity cost l and his side selling opportunities p_s, reduces his reputation cost ϕ of contract breach, and hence increases his share of the contract value. However, with increased competition between buyers, contracting may break down. The effects on contract feasibility can be analyzed by looking at the effects of competition on aggregate output as can be derived from equations (15.8) and (15.9):

$$
\begin{aligned}
\frac{\partial Q_H}{\partial \Psi} &= \left(\frac{N}{T}\right) \frac{\partial \left(p_H - p_H^{\min}\right)}{\partial \Psi} \\
&= \left(\frac{N}{T}\right) \left[\frac{\partial p_H}{\partial \Psi} - \frac{\partial p_H^{\min}}{\partial l}\frac{\partial l}{\partial \Psi} - \frac{\partial p_H^{\min}}{\partial p_s}\frac{\partial p_s}{\partial \Psi} - \frac{\partial p_H^{\min}}{\partial \phi}\frac{\partial \phi}{\partial \Psi} - \frac{\partial p_H^{\min}}{\partial t_m}\frac{\partial t_m}{\partial \Psi}\right]
\end{aligned}
\tag{15.10}
$$

where $\partial p_H^{\min} / \partial l \geq 0, \partial p_H^{\min} / \partial p_s \geq 0, \partial p_H^{\min} / \partial \phi \leq 0$ (in these three cases the effect is nonzero if the relevant constraint is binding) and $\partial p_H^{\min} / \partial t_m > 0$. We can then distinguish the following effects of market liberalization.

First, the entry of new (private) buyers on the market will have an impact on output price p_H. As discussed earlier in Chapter 12, the direction of this effect is not clear ex ante. On the one hand, the potential drive for quality differentiation under competition may put upward pressure on p_H.[13] On the other hand, if other buyers start to operate in the same market and compete on prices, p_H is likely to decline. Hence, $\partial p_H / \partial \Psi \lessgtr 0$

Second, competition between buyers will raise the supplier's opportunity cost of labor. In our model, this implies $\partial l / \partial \Psi > 0$. This will be beneficial to suppliers as long as contract enforcement remains feasible. However, as equation (15.10) shows, an increase in l is likely to make contract enforcement more difficult and hence to reduce aggregate output: $-(\partial p_H^{\min} / \partial l)\,(\partial l / \partial \Psi) \le 0$.

Third, increased competition reduces the supplier's reputation cost of contract breach ($\partial \phi / \partial \Psi \le 0$) for all the arguments set out in Chapter 12. This also enhances supplier incomes but makes contracting more difficult, leading to lower aggregate output with higher competition: $-(\partial p_H^{\min} / \partial \phi)\,(\partial \phi / \partial \Psi) \le 0$.

Fourth, competition increases the supplier's possibility for side selling $\partial p_s / \partial \Psi > 0$. Again, this increases supplier incomes as long as contracts remain feasible, but at the same time it makes contract enforcement more difficult to sustain, with negative effects on aggregate output: $-(\partial p_H^{\min} / \partial p_s)\,(\partial p_s / \partial \Psi) \le 0$.

The final effect of competition is on company management. There is an extensive literature on how competition (and privatization) changed manager and firm behavior in transition countries (Konings and Walsh, 1999; Roland, 2000). The manager's incentive for innovation and profit maximization will be stronger in a competitive environment without soft budget constraints. Improved management reduces excess processing and marketing costs, which enhances supplier incomes, contract enforcement, and aggregate output: $-\partial t_m / \partial \Psi \ge 0$.

In summary, three of the five effects of market liberalization make contract enforcement unambiguously less feasible, whereas only the possible efficiency gains (the improvements in excess processing and marketing costs) will improve contract feasibility unambiguously, ceteris paribus. While the net effect depends on the size of the different components, and is an empirical question, the theoretical results show that we can expect important constraints on output growth following market liberalization if

---

[13] Note that the "quiet life of the monopolist" hypothesis will in this setup work explicitly through t_m rather than implicitly through p_H as was the case in Chapter 12.

one takes into account the impact of liberalization on vertical coordination in value chains.

Finally, note that throughout our analysis here we assume perfect information and we focus only on output. In reality there is likely to be considerable uncertainty, and the reforms themselves may affect this uncertainty.[14] This affects behavior of the agents in the model, depending on their expectations and risk aversion. These effects may reinforce or mitigate some of the findings here.[15] However, as we have shown earlier, even with the assumption of perfect information, important contract failures may occur.

15.3.4 Implications

Our theoretical results have major implications for understanding the effects of liberalization. The output effects of price liberalization may be either positive or negative. If liberalization increases net output prices it improves contract feasibility and hence increases aggregate output; and vice versa for price decreases. The increase in competition as a result of market liberalization has ambiguous effects. To the extent that market liberalization induces more efficient forms of management, contract feasibility improves. However, increased competition may also endanger contract feasibility by improving suppliers' holdup options and reducing their reputation cost in case of contract breach. Although these factors tend to increase the income of suppliers, they make contracts more difficult to sustain. The net effect of price and market liberalization on aggregate output and supplier incomes will depend on the specific conditions of the commodity, the details of the reforms, and the magnitude of the different effects.

As we already discussed in depth in Chapter 14, contracting and output will be affected by the "value" in the value chain. To illustrate this, consider three types of commodities: low standards products which require no external inputs, and medium- and high-standards products which require external inputs. The first type of commodity will not face contract enforcement

---

[14] Both Krueger et al. (1991) for developing countries and Rozelle and Swinnen (2004) for transition countries have explained that the liberalization processes increased price volatility. Barrett (1998) analyzes output responses (and welfare) effects under uncertainty; Fafchamps (2004) and Gow et al. (2000) show how volatility may lead to more frequent contracting failures.

[15] For example, it is easy to show, based on our model, that if suppliers are risk averse, and contracts are considered more risky than alternative options, contract feasibility will be reduced. If buyers are risk-averse and third party enforcement is considered less risky than self-enforcement, more use will be made of third-party enforcement (see Chapter 11) and suppliers' payoff will be reduced.

problems because there is no interlinked contracting. The only relevant effects are the change in net output price as a result of price and market liberalization. When production requires external inputs, the theory predicts that interlinked contracting by the private sector will be easier to sustain in high-standards value chains. Therefore, for commodities that require substantive inputs, we would expect the supply response to be positively related to the quality standard of the commodity.

These arguments have important implications for the country comparison since the quality standards and input requirements of the key commodities in countries varied importantly with the countries' income level and trade structure. In richer countries both input requirements and value are higher than in poor countries. However, for specific commodities, poor countries may access rich countries' consumers by producing export crops that typically imply higher value, standards, and input requirements. In the next section we use these insights to interpret performance.

15.4 Value Chains and Liberalization Performances

We combine the insights from our model and differences in initial conditions and reform choices to offer a set of hypotheses to explain the differences in reform performances across regions (see Figure 15.1).[16]

15.4.1 Eastern Europe

In Eastern Europe, where producers were subsidized under the state-controlled system, the liberalization of prices caused a dramatic reduction in farm support: subsidies declined from 30% to almost zero (Figure 15.2). At the same time, farms and the industry were privatized. This combination caused a complete collapse of the state-controlled contracting system and with it, the provision of inputs to producers (Cungu et al., 2008; Gow and Swinnen, 1998). The effect was very strong because farms in Eastern Europe intensively used (external) inputs, which made them strongly dependent on vertical coordination for their inputs. Agricultural output and productivity declined sharply immediately after the reforms (see Figure 15.1).

This initial effect was reinforced by the land reforms, as gains from improved incentives in individual farms were initially more than offset

---

[16] The value chain effects discussed here were reinforced by differences in land reforms (see Rozelle and Swinnen, 2004).

by losses in scale economies because of the capital intensive production structure.

However, the consistent reforms in a region with relatively high incomes also induced large inflows of investments in the food chain which, in turn, induced a rapid expansion of privately organized contracting with major impacts on suppliers (Dries and Swinnen, 2004; Gow et al., 2000; World Bank, 2005). Observed contracting varies from case to case, whether it is formal or informal, written or oral, and it can vary from rather simple interlinked provision of basic inputs and trade credit to sophisticated forms of investment loans and triangular contracting structures, where written contracts between farms and processors serve as collateral for farm loans from banks.

To illustrate this, Figure 15.4 documents the extent of private sector contracting between farms and dairy processors in Eastern Europe. The vertical axis measures the share of dairy processors which provide interlinked contracts with farm assistance programs (i.e., programs that provide inputs, credit, advisory services and in some cases investment support and bank loan guarantees) to their suppliers in various countries at different points in time. Figure 15.4 clearly shows a positive correlation with both the income level of the countries (in panel a) and reform progress (in panel b).

In the mid-1990s, these investments and contracts caused a flow of inputs, capital, and technology into the farm sector – as explained by our model – and contributed to strong increases in productivity in later years of reform (e.g., Dries and Swinnen, 2004, 2010). This process started earliest and most intensively in Eastern European countries where incomes and commodity chain values were higher, and where progress in the liberalization process was faster, and later and slower in countries which were poorer and where liberalization progressed more slowly.

15.4.2 China

In China, the initial growth came from giving land rights to the rural households. Chinese farms were very labor intensive, with few external inputs, and hence benefited strongly from enhanced incentives brought about by decollectivization. This explains much of the output and productivity gains during the first years of the reforms. China also gradually adjusted prices towards market levels, thereby reducing taxation, which benefited farms.

There was much less disruption in exchange since the government remained firmly in control of the agencies buying commodities and providing inputs. In line with the analytically derived results in the model, this

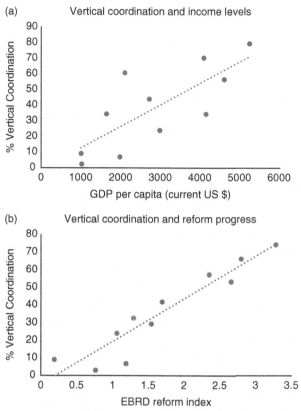

Figure 15.4. Income Levels, Reform Progress and Vertical Coordination in Eastern European Agri-Food Sectors.

Income levels and reform progress in dicators are at country level. Vertical coordination refers to the importance (expressed as share (%) of maximum) of vertical coordination in dairy chains based on surveys which were implemented in Eastern Europe (Albania, Azerbaijan, Bulgaria, Poland and Slovakia) between 1994 and 2003. For more details see Dries et al. (2009) and Swinnen et al. (2010).

reduction of taxes combined with the initial retaining of state-controlled interlinking and input provision caused a positive supply response.

The subsequent gradual introduction of competition in the food chain (by allowing suppliers to sell over-quota production and as a result traders to compete at the margin) removed inefficiencies and improved producers' income in the chains without leading to contract breaches and led to a further positive supply response.

15.4.3 Sub-Saharan Africa

As Figure 15.1 illustrates, post-liberalization growth in SSA has been lower than that of China, but initially higher than in Eastern Europe.

Liberalization caused more market disruptions in SSA than in China because the reduction in taxation was considerably less in SSA: taxation declined from 50% to around zero in China, while only from around 30% to around 10% taxation in SSA. Hence, tax reduction in SSA was only one third of that in China (see Figure 15.2). However, another important reason is that in SSA the removal of state monopolies was introduced together with price liberalization. The introduction of competition led to breakdowns in value chains, reducing access to inputs for producers in these sectors and impeding output and productivity growth.

However, value chain disruptions were still less important in SSA than in Eastern Europe because a smaller share of the SSA production was dependent on external inputs and because the degree of implementation of market liberalization was more mixed in SSA. A substantial share of SSA production, in particular staple food production, did not rely on such formal input (and output) markets, and hence suffered less from disruption. This, together with the cut in subsidies in Eastern Europe, explains why SSA's growth was initially stronger than that of Eastern Europe.

Yet in Eastern Europe growth resumed at a faster pace than in SSA because growth in the Eastern European value chains was stimulated by a massive inflow of private investment, often foreign direct investment, in agribusiness and the food industry, with strong spillover effects on suppliers through vertical coordination.

These effects have emerged at a much slower pace and much less extensively in poorer countries with more macroeconomic (and institutional) instability (see Figure 15.4). In addition to other factors (lack of infrastructure, political and economic instability), low incomes and the general low value and quality standards in SSA food chains have constrained the emergence of private sector vertical coordination and market interlinking, and thereby growth in the entire chain.

15.5 Value Chains and Variations in Commodity Sector Performance in Africa

To further document and support these arguments, we disaggregate the average growth in SSA by commodity groups. As in Chapter 14, we consider staple food crops, further disaggregated into "roots, tubers, and pulses" and

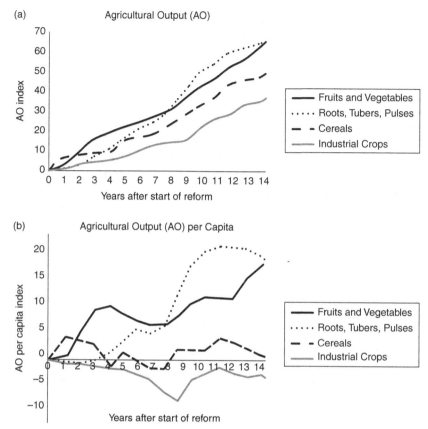

Figure 15.5. Post-reform performance by commodity in Sub-Saharan Africa.
Source: Based on Swinnen et al. (2010) and FAO data.

"cereals"; for traditional export commodities we look at "industrial crops" such as coffee, cocoa, rubber, or cotton; and for nontraditional exports we focus on "fruits and vegetables." Although these groups still include a mix of different products, commodities in a single group share many characteristics, in particular regarding the value in the commodity chain. As a result, our model predicts differences in performance between the commodity groups.

Figure 15.5 shows that fruits and vegetables and roots, tubers, and pulses have performed better than the other two groups (cereals and industrial crops). After a decade and a half of reform, the output of fruits and vegetables and roots, tubers and pulses was 70% higher than the pre-reform level. For industrial crops and cereals the output increase is substantially less: 40% and 55%, respectively. The differences are more striking when on a per capita basis: per capita output in fruits and vegetables and roots, tubers and pulses increased by 12% compared to 0% for cereals and −5% for industrial crops.[17]

These differences in performance are consistent with our value chain model. Output and productivity increases for roots, tubers, and pulses were better than average. Input requirements in this sector are generally low and therefore output growth has not been dependent on contracting. Instead, the sector benefited from liberalized prices and enhanced competition on spot markets. As external input requirements are generally higher, growth in the cereals sector has been more limited after the reforms, and new forms of private interlinked contracting did not occur in this sector because the value in the staple food chains is generally too low and competition too high to sustain it. Marketing activities have been taken over by a large amount of small private traders and are based on spot market transactions (Coulter and Poulton, 2001; Fafchamps and Minten, 2001).

The industrial crop sectors suffered from the introduction of competition and the associated collapse in state-controlled vertical coordination. They caused major disruptions in input provision to producers and led to below average output and productivity growth (despite a reduction in taxation that was much stronger than in other commodity groups). Input requirements are generally much higher than in staple foods and therefore the collapse of public input provision affected output and productivity much more – as in Eastern Europe. Unlike in Eastern Europe, however, massive private investments with contracting and input provision have not occurred in the first decade of reform in the SSA industrial crops sector, constraining a rapid recovery.

There was strong growth in fruits and vegetables. Our model suggests that this sector may have grown because of two quite different mechanisms. First, low-value fruits and vegetables production for the local market was mostly depending on labor input and benefited thus from the same effects as roots, tubers, and pulses. Second, an important – and increasing – part of the growth has come from high-standards fruits and vegetables chains for exports. This sector has grown very rapidly after the reforms. The high value in these chains has sustained post-reform private investments in this sector

[17] The lack of output growth and productivity for industrial crops in SSA is often attributed to falling world prices for these commodities. However, real producer prices for export crops went up during the 1980s in some SSA countries because the effect of price liberalization offset the effect of decreasing world market prices (Anderson and Masters, 2009; World Bank, 1994).

and the occurrence of private vertical coordination with quality upgrading, interlinking (with both large and small suppliers), and input provision to producers. A series of recent studies show how the vertical coordination mechanisms, and their spillovers and productivity growth effects, are similar to the growth mechanisms in Eastern Europe (e.g., Maertens and Swinnen, 2009; Maertens et al., 2011; Minten et al., 2009).

In summary, the different experiences of these four subsectors in SSA – which are "hidden" by the average growth rates – are consistent with our general arguments that the reliance on external inputs and the value in the value chains, which affect the endogenous emergence of exchange institutions in a liberalized environment, are crucially important to understand economic performance.

15.6 Conclusion

Over the past three decades, many poor and middle-income countries embarked on a process of liberalization of their formerly state-controlled agricultural sectors. While some countries have been successful, in others the post-liberalization performance has been disappointing.

Our interpretation emphasizes that liberalization consisted of "price liberalization," signaling the end to heavy distortions of agricultural output prices; and "market liberalization," implying an increase in competition along the value chain. Using the theoretical model developed in previous chapters, we demonstrate that price liberalization improves contract feasibility and aggregate output to the extent that it leads to a higher net price. The theoretical effects of market liberalization are more ambiguous. Improved efficiency along the value chain makes contracts more feasible, but by increasing suppliers' outside options competition may also reduce the scope for feasible contracts. The net result of these effects depends on specific conditions. This framework makes it possible to explain the observed performance differences in China, Eastern Europe, and SSA, and differences between subsectors in SSA. The observations on performance are consistent with our conjectures about the role of value chains and commodity characteristics as discussed in this chapter and in Chapter 14.

16

Standards and Value Chains with Contracting Costs: Toward a General Model

16.1 Introduction

As we have emphasized throughout the previous chapters, markets and value chains have undergone dramatic changes in recent decades. Sexton (2012) argues that "modern" markets no longer resemble the traditional textbook example of competitive spot markets, because simple spot markets are unable to cater to today's buyer needs, in particular strict requirements on quality control and supply consistency. This makes the process of supplier search and switching between suppliers particularly expensive – creating incentives for buyers to build up long-term relationships with their suppliers – and leading to an increased incidence of vertical coordination strategies, including production contracts. This is true even for agricultural markets, which are still cited in microeconomics textbooks as standard examples of competitive markets with many buyers and sellers that are small relative to the total size of the market, homogeneous products, perfect information, and perfect contract enforcement. However, as Sexton (2012: 209) points out: "I don't know of any modern agricultural market that meets all these conditions. Most don't meet any of them."

This "new architecture of modern markets" has important implications for efficiency and equity. Sexton and colleagues emphasize the role of search and switching costs associated with quality and consistency requirements. These types of transaction costs are also increasingly important in emerging and developing economies. In this book so far we have focused on imperfections in rural factor markets and poor contract enforcement institutions, giving rise to additional transaction costs and different vertical coordination strategies. This raises the question whether these different types of transaction costs and the vertical coordination strategies that are implemented in response have the same implications for efficiency and equity,

256

that is, whether the nature of the transaction costs matters. To analyze this question, this chapter develops a "general" model that integrates insights from different strands of the literature.

We develop a generalized theoretical framework accounting for quality requirements, contract-specific investments, factor market imperfections, imperfect contract enforcement institutions, and market power. As we are focusing on those transaction costs that directly derive from the contracting process, we will refer to them as "contracting costs." We explicitly consider the key characteristics of different types of contracting costs (notably search costs, training costs, monitoring costs, and input costs), and derive the implications of these characteristics for the equity and efficiency effects of vertical coordination.

This chapter is structured as follows. In the next section, we propose a framework for classification of contracting costs incurred in vertical coordination. Section 16.3 develops a general conceptual model to analyze the effects of these contracting costs. Section 16.4 shows how our model parameters influence efficiency and equity of vertical coordination; and Section 16.5 discusses what this implies for different types of contracting costs. Finally, Section 16.6 concludes the chapter.

16.2 A Classification of Contracting Costs

We extend our theoretical framework – and assess the robustness of our findings – by focusing on four types of contracting costs: search (or switching) costs incurred in the process of identifying suitable producers; the costs of training suppliers to produce high-standards commodities, which may imply the use of new technologies or complying with new standards; monitoring costs to ensure that suppliers apply the technology as has been recommended; and the costs of providing external inputs (e.g., fertilizers, credit, seeds, and/or other types of technology).[1] We focus on these because (1) they have been described as important in the literature; (2) they differ in two important characteristics, which allows to develop a classification of contracting costs along two dimensions; and (3) these dimensions importantly influence the effects of the contracting costs (as we will show). The two key dimensions are whether there are cost advantages for working

---

[1] As in the previous chapters, and like Sexton (2012), we do not consider sunk costs in processing infrastructure, but focus on supplier-specific contracting costs, by which we mean any cost the buyer needs to incur to make a transaction with a specific supplier possible. The concept of contracting costs is thus more general than the buyer's investment in inputs considered in earlier chapters.

with a repeat supplier vis-à-vis working with a potential new supplier and whether the supplier-specific investment has a value for the supplier outside of the existing contract.

16.2.1 Cost Advantage of Repeat Suppliers

Some contracting costs are the same for first-time and repeat suppliers alike, as they need to be incurred for each production cycle. This is the case for instance when the buyer is prefinancing external inputs for its suppliers. In many developing and emerging countries processors provide their suppliers under contract with seeds, pesticides, and fertilizer in crop production and feed in livestock production (e.g., Bellemare, 2012; Birthal et al., 2005; Gow et al., 2000).

This also applies to the case in which the buyer has a system in place to monitor contract compliance – for example, in the form of a set of field officers who conduct field visits on a regular basis. By means of illustration, consider the following quote from Minten et al. (2009: 1733) on monitoring in high value vegetable production in Madagascar:

> To monitor the correct implementation of the supplier contracts, the [processor] has … around 300 extension agents who are permanently on the payroll … Every extension agent, the chef de culture, is responsible for about 30 farmers. To supervise these, (s)he coordinates five or six extension assistants … that live in the village itself.… During the cultivation period of the vegetables under contract, the contractor is visited on average more than once … a week … to ensure correct production management as well as to avoid "side-selling." … 99% of the farmers say that the firm knows the exact location of the plot; 92% of the farmers say that the firm will even know … the number of plants that are on the plot. For some crucial aspects of the vegetable production process, representatives of the company will even intervene in the production management to ensure it is rightly done.

Other contracting costs are nonrecurring, and only need to be paid at the start of a collaboration between a buyer and a supplier. Working with a repeat supplier, for which these costs have already been borne, is then cheaper than contracting a new supplier. An example is search costs, which are incurred to identify a suitable supplier. For example, Sexton (2012: 215) points out that "transaction costs of engaging with repeat suppliers will likely be considerably less than transaction costs of locating and contracting with new suppliers."

Another example is training costs. A new supplier typically needs to be trained to become familiar with buyer preferences and standards, and possibly with the use of new technologies. Being trained confers a cost advantage to repeat suppliers compared to potential new suppliers.

16.2.2 Value of Investment Outside of the Contract

Another dimension of these contracting costs is their residual value to the contracted supplier outside the contract.[2] Some types of buyer investments do not have a value for the supplier beyond the existing contract. Examples include search costs and monitoring costs.

Other types of costs may have an important residual value outside of the existing contract. For example, before being applied to crops, external inputs can be diverted by the supplier for other purposes (e.g., fertilizer use for other, noncontracted, crops) or sold on the secondary market. Even after being applied to crops, external inputs convey additional value to suppliers, which may be realized outside of the contract, for instance when the contracted supplier side sells his produce to alternative buyers.

Also training costs can have a value outside of the contract, depending on the degree of specificity of the training (Becker, 1962). Training increases a supplier's human capital. This is an intangible asset that can be used in other activities and may have a long-lasting positive impact on the supplier's opportunity cost of labor.

16.2.3 Classification of Contracting Costs

Considering the two dimensions discussed above, we can classify contracting costs into four "types" – as illustrated in Table 16.1. Monitoring costs and the costs of providing external inputs are recurring costs and do not provide a cost advantage to repeat suppliers; search costs and training costs are nonrecurring and therefore do provide a cost advantage to repeat suppliers. External inputs and training have a value to the supplier outside the contract while monitoring and search costs do not.

For didactic purposes, we consider only "pure" forms of the four types of contracting costs. In reality, the boundaries between these four types are not always clear cut. Some of the contracting costs may have mixed characteristics. For example, training may be a combination of an initial

---

[2] The costs under study are all "supplier-specific" from the point of view of the buyer. Hence, once incurred, none of these costs has any residual value to the buyer outside of the current contract relationship. This would have been different if we would have considered sunk costs in infrastructure by the buyer, for example.

Table 16.1. *Values of α and γ for different types of contracting costs*

		Value outside of the contract (α)	
		$\alpha = 0$	$\alpha > 0$
Cost advantage of	$\gamma = 0$	Monitoring costs	External inputs
repeat supplier (γ)	$\gamma > 0$	Search costs	Training costs

investment at the start of a collaboration between a buyer and a supplier; supplemented by regular training sessions, possibly at the beginning of each production cycle, in which suppliers receive updates of best practices. In such case, the relative cost advantage of a repeat supplier to a new supplier depends on the relative importance of initial training sessions vis-à-vis the updates. Similarly, Dries et al. (2009) document how some of the investments in external inputs in the Eastern European dairy sector can be considered as nonrecurring investments (e.g., cheap loans for equipment and herd upgrading), while other investments, such as concentrate feed provision, are incurred for each production cycle. In this chapter, when we talk about "external inputs" we have the latter in mind, that is, those costs that are incurred for each production cycle.

16.3 The Model

We now extend the model of Chapter 11 to analyze whether and how these differences in transaction cost characteristics affect the size of the surplus which can be realized within a contract and the distribution of that surplus in contract relationships.

As in Chapter 11, to produce one unit of a high-standards product, the supplier needs to invest own labor at an opportunity cost of l. In addition, the production of high-standards agricultural products requires the buyer to initially invest resources with an opportunity cost k.

However, if a buyer has contracted with a particular supplier before, he may need to invest less. The parameter γ represents the repeat suppliers' cost advantage vis-à-vis new suppliers, so that the effective investment costs are $(1-\gamma)k$. For new suppliers, or for the case where all investments are recurring, $\gamma = 0$; for repeat suppliers where investments are entirely consisting of nonrecurring costs, $\gamma = 1$. Hence, $\gamma \in [0;1]$.

Next, we define the residual value of the investment for the supplier outside the contract as a fraction α of k, its value within the contract. The less specific these inputs are, the higher their value outside of the contract will be, that is, the higher α. If an investment does not have any value outside the contract for the supplier, $\alpha = 0$.

Parameters γ and α capture the main characteristics of complementary investments in our conceptual framework, as shown in Table 16.1. Note again that we assume "pure" forms of the four types of contracting costs.

The net surplus of the collaboration between the supplier and the buyer (i.e., the "value" in the value chain) is given by $S = p_H - l - (1 - \gamma)k$. As before, the participation constraint of the supplier is $Y \geq l$, while the buyer now requires at least $\Pi \geq (1-\gamma)k$.

16.3.1 Perfect Contract Enforcement

Under perfect enforcement, both parties will receive their disagreement payoff (i.e., the opportunity cost of their resources) plus a share of the surplus S determined by sharing rule β. Modifying the corresponding equations from Chapter 11 yields the following payoffs:

$$Y^* = l + \beta S = l + \beta\left(p_H - l - (1-\gamma)k\right) \qquad (16.1)$$

$$\Pi^* = (1-\gamma)k + (1-\beta)S = (1-\gamma)k + (1-\beta)\left(p_H - l - (1-\gamma)k\right) \quad (16.2)$$

In these equations, the asterisk again denotes the "perfect enforcement" outcome. Note in particular that the parameter α does not play a role with perfect enforcement.

16.3.2. Imperfect Contract Enforcement

To focus on the role of the different types of contracting costs, we consider only the possibility of supplier holdup through input diversion.[3] Given our previous discussion, input diversion does not necessarily imply selling physical inputs. In the case of training costs, similar opportunistic behavior can arise. Instead of applying his own labor in combination with the received training to produce high-standards goods, the supplier can use his training to earn additional income, for example, using his time and new

---

[3] Thanks to the more general specification of the input diversion option, supplier holdup through side selling can be considered a special case of input diversion (see later). As we have done in the previous two chapters, we abstract away from buyer holdup. However, it is straightforward to expand the analysis to include the same.

skills in different production activities, or by producing high-standards goods for other buyers.

However, as discussed, not all inputs lend themselves to being diverted, as some of the investments incurred by the buyer may not have a value outside of the contract. To model this, we assume that in case of input diversion the supplier can realize his opportunity cost of labor l in addition to a fraction α of k, representing the value of the buyer's investment which the supplier can realize outside the contract. The higher α, the more attractive contract breach will be. As before, we assume that contract breach results in a reputation cost ϕ for the supplier. Hence, the payoffs in case of input diversion are

$$Y_d = l + \alpha k - \phi \tag{16.3}$$

$$\Pi_d = 0 \tag{16.4}$$

A self-enforcing contract then implies that

$$Y^\# = \max\left\{l + \beta S;\, l + \alpha k - \phi\right\} \tag{16.5}$$

$$\Pi^\# = p_H - Y^\# \tag{16.6}$$

where we use the # symbol to denote the self-enforcing contract with supplier holdup, and where $S = p_H - (1-\gamma)k - 1$. The first term in the expression for supplier income $Y^\#$ is the perfect enforcement outcome Y^* (see equation 16.1). This constitutes the lower bound to supplier income under imperfect enforcement. The supplier price may be higher, however, if the supplier has an attractive option outside of the contract, once the buyer has made the required investments. In particular, if α is sufficiently high such that $\alpha k - \phi > \beta S$, the second term will bind, and supplier income $Y^\#$ will be higher than in the perfect enforcement scenario. In this case, the buyer pays an efficiency premium to the supplier:

$$\varepsilon \equiv Y^\# - Y^* = \max\{0;\, \alpha k - \phi - \beta S\} \tag{16.7}$$

As before, the self-enforcing contract will only arise if it is feasible, that is, if the "value" in the value chain is large enough to satisfy the participation constraint of both parties as well as the constraint imposed by the possibility of input diversion. This condition can be expressed as a condition on p_H as follows:

$$p_H \geq p_H^{\min} = \max\{l + (1-\gamma)k;\, l + (1-\gamma+\alpha)k - \phi\} \tag{16.8}$$

As in Chapter 11, this condition captures two major reasons for potential contract failure. First, if $p_H < l + (1-\gamma)k$, the surplus S would be negative, and there is no incentive for contract formation. Second, and more importantly, if $p_H \geq l + (1 - \gamma)k$ but $p_H < l + (1 - \gamma + \alpha)k - \phi$, the potential "value" in the value chain is positive but too small to allow the buyer to offer a price to the supplier which prevents him from diverting the inputs.

16.4 Efficiency and Equity Effects of Contracting Costs

In this section, we discuss in more detail how the different types of contracting costs affect "efficiency," that is, the total (potential) surplus and the conditions under which this surplus can be realized, and "equity," that is, the distribution of the surplus. As explained earlier, the four types of contracting costs can be identified by their values of α and γ.

16.4.1 Efficiency

The potential surplus of contracting with a repeat supplier is $S = p_H - l - (1 - \gamma)k$. As before, this implies that surplus will be greater if the output price p_H is greater or if the disagreement payoffs of the supplier (l) and of the buyer $[(1 - \gamma)k]$ are lower. Hence, potential surplus is now also increasing in γ, that is, in the cost advantage of a repeat supplier. Ceteris paribus, a higher value of γ implies that lower investment costs are incurred for the contract. The potential contract surplus is highest if a company works with repeat suppliers and if contracting costs are nonrecurring, as in the case of search costs or training costs. In this case, $\gamma = 1$, implying that after the first contracting year, the buyer does not need to spend resources on contracting anymore. The production process then only requires the deployment of the supplier's own labor at an opportunity cost l.

The potential surplus is lowest if a company works with a new supplier, or if contracting costs are fully recurring (which means that they are incurred on an annual basis), such as in the case of external input and monitoring costs. In both cases, $\gamma = 0$, which reduces the surplus S.

However, γ also affects the feasibility of the contract, as can be seen from equation (16.8). A higher value of γ reduces the minimum required price p_H^{min}, which means that the likelihood of contract formation improves. In other words, the less resources need to be invested for a transaction (for the same output), the more likely it is that a contract is feasible.

One implication is that if the price p_H declines exogenously, it is possible that starting up contracts with new suppliers (for whom $\gamma = 0$) is no longer viable while contracts with repeat suppliers (for whom $\gamma > 0$) may still be feasible.

The (potential) surplus S is not affected by the value of the contracting costs outside the contract, reflected in our model parameter α; but α does affect contract feasibility. As can be seen from equation (16.8), a higher α increases the minimum required price p_H^{min} and reduces the likelihood of contract formation by making input diversion more attractive relative to the perfect enforcement outcome. This may happen in the case where contracting costs comprise training or external inputs costs.

In contrast, if the supplier cannot put the contracting costs to any alternative use outside the contract, which means that $\alpha = 0$ (as in the case of search and/or monitoring costs), they do not create any opportunity for contract violation. In practice, if $\alpha = 0$, the contract outcome will then resemble the perfect enforcement contracting outcome, and the buyer's investment k will only affect efficiency through its impact on potential contract surplus.

16.4.2 Market Power

As can be seen from equation (16.5), supplier income $Y^{\#}$ is increasing in both γ and α, albeit through different channels. While a higher γ increases contract surplus and hence also the supplier's payoff under perfect enforcement, a higher α raises the efficiency premium (as defined by equation (16.7)) and hence also the supplier's payoff when the input diversion option binds. Hence, even if β is very low, the supplier may still receive a considerable share of total surplus if α is sufficiently high.

Interestingly, as a higher γ increases the surplus S that is shared between the supplier and the buyer, as of the second year of contracting the buyer also enjoys a higher payoff as a result of a higher γ. In contrast, a higher α will increase the efficiency premium which needs to be paid by the buyer to the supplier. This means that any increase in supplier income goes at the detriment of the buyer's payoff.

As discussed in Chapter 12, we can describing the resulting rent distribution by defining an "ex post sharing rule," defined by $\tilde{\beta} = (Y - l) / S$. Equation (12.1) expressed $\tilde{\beta}$ for the case where the supplier could hold up the buyer through input diversion. In our general model, the ex post sharing rule is given by

$$\tilde{\beta} = \max\left(\beta, \frac{\alpha k - \phi}{p_H - l - (1 - \gamma)k} \right) \tag{16.9}$$

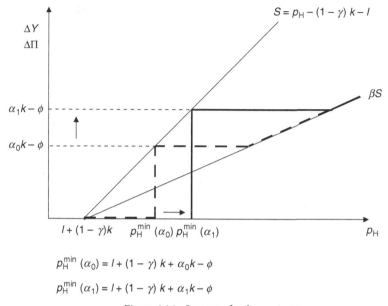

$$p_H^{min}(\alpha_0) = l + (1 - \gamma)\,k + \alpha_0 k - \phi$$

$$p_H^{min}(\alpha_1) = l + (1 - \gamma)\,k + \alpha_1 k - \phi$$

Figure 16.1. Impact of a change in α.

We see that this share is increasing in α, reflecting the fact that if α increases (and the second term in equation (16.9) is binding), part of the surplus that would otherwise accrue to the buyer, is now shifted to the supplier.

The impact of γ on $\tilde{\beta}$ is very different: if the first term in (16.9) binds, γ will not affect the ex post sharing rule. It only increases the contract surplus, which is then distributed according to the perfect enforcement sharing rule β. If the second term in equation (16.9) binds, γ will even reduce the ex post sharing rule, as the surplus increases while the supplier's payoff remains fixed at $l + \alpha k - \phi$, so that his relative share of the surplus declines.

16.4.3 Summary

Figures 16.1 and 16.2 summarize the impact of α and γ on efficiency and equity of vertical coordination. Figure 16.1 illustrates the impact of differences in α. Recall that α is an indicator for the value a supplier can realize based on the buyer's contract-specific investment outside of their joint contract. A higher α implies more benefits for a supplier from the associated (higher) efficiency premium. This is reflected in the upward shift of the horizontal line $\alpha k - \phi$. However, at the same time a higher α reduces contract feasibility. This is reflected in the enlargement of the region where contracting is not feasible.

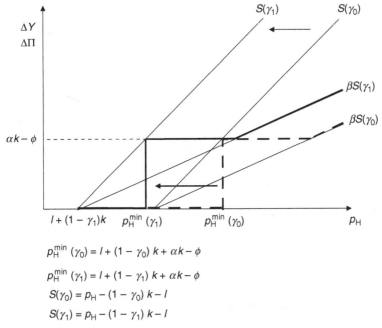

$$p_H^{min}(\gamma_0) = I + (1 - \gamma_0)\,k + \alpha k - \phi$$
$$p_H^{min}(\gamma_1) = I + (1 - \gamma_1)\,k + \alpha k - \phi$$
$$S(\gamma_0) = p_H - (1 - \gamma_0)\,k - I$$
$$S(\gamma_1) = p_H - (1 - \gamma_1)\,k - I$$

Figure 16.2. Impact of a change in γ.

Figure 16.2 illustrates the impact of γ, the cost advantage to repeat suppliers. With a higher γ (and hence lower costs), the function depicting potential surplus shifts to the left. With lower costs there is more surplus, which makes contracting easier. As a result, the "perfect enforcement" outcome is binding for a wider range of prices p_H. Moreover, the payoff for the supplier increases unambiguously.

Hence, while a higher γ improves contract feasibility by increasing the potential contract surplus, α reduces it by making holdup more attractive to the supplier. On the other hand, both γ and α may improve supplier income.

16.5 The Effect of Different Contracting Costs

We now combine these insights to study in more detail the role of different types of contracting costs.

Our analysis implies that of all the contracting cost types listed in Table 16.1, *monitoring costs* (with $\alpha = 0$ and $\gamma = 0$) offer the least scope for suppliers to benefit from contract participation. The payoff to the supplier of diverting inputs is $Y_d = I - \phi$ which is lower than his perfect enforcement payoff $Y^* = l + \beta S$ and even lower than his participation constraint. The supplier will thus always comply with the contract. However, since $\gamma = 0$, the surplus S is lower too. Thus, if contracting costs consist mainly of monitoring costs, the supplier's payoff from contracting will be lowest (ceteris paribus).

If contracting costs consist mostly of *search costs* (with $\alpha = 0$ and $\gamma > 0$), both supplier and buyer benefit compared to the case of pure monitoring costs. Since search costs offer no opportunity for input diversion to the supplier, there is again no risk of contract breach. However, in contrast with monitoring costs, search costs offer a cost advantage for a continued supplier relationship. This in turn increases total surplus and hence the payoff of buyer and supplier. The payoff to the buyer is highest in this scenario, since contract surplus is high and the buyer does not need to pay an efficiency premium to the supplier. In addition, contract feasibility with repeat suppliers is the highest in the case of search costs because of a high γ and a low α.

External input costs (with $\alpha > 0$ and $\gamma = 0$) do not offer repeat suppliers a cost advantage vis-à-vis new suppliers. As a result, contract surplus is lower. On the other hand, because α is high, suppliers can appropriate a larger share of the contract surplus given their credible threat of input diversion; at the expense of the buyer's payoff. This type of contracting cost is the least favorable to the buyer. Moreover, with a low γ and a high α also contract feasibility is lowest if contracting costs are of this type.

Finally, if contracting costs comprise *training costs* ($\alpha > 0$, $\gamma > 0$), suppliers will benefit most. The high value of α implies that the supplier will receive a high payoff, while the risk of endangering contract feasibility is lower than with contracting costs because of the cost advantage γ.

16.6 Conclusion

In this chapter we generalized the theory by accounting for quality requirements, contract-specific investments, factor market imperfections, imperfect contract enforcement institutions, and market power.

Different types of contracting costs include search costs, training costs, monitoring costs, and input costs. These different types of contracting costs can be organized by two parameters: the cost advantage of repeat suppliers and the value of the contracting costs outside of the contract for the supplier. These two parameters play an important role in determining the creation of surplus by contracting and the distribution of the surplus.

Factor market imperfections and contract breach have been analyzed in previous chapters. In the case of input costs, potentially attractive opportunities for supplier contract breach generated by the buyer's invest-ment imply that the buyer will need to pay the supplier an "efficiency pre-mium" to induce contract compliance. In the case of training costs, an additional effect comes into play, which is the efficiency effect of long-term supplier contracts, which will translate into additional benefits from con-tracting for a supplier. Both the efficiency premium and the efficiency effect reinforce each other and increase the supplier's opportunities to benefit from participation in contracts that involve substantial training. In the case of search costs, there is only the efficiency effect. This implies that repeat supplier will benefit from the cost advantage they have vis-à-vis their peers. As Sexton (2012) points out, this effect may in practice yield important benefits for suppliers of modern agricultural markets. In the case of mon-itoring costs, however, neither the equity nor the efficiency effects apply, which means that the scope for the supplier to benefit from such contracts will be more limited.

The different types of contracting cost also have an impact on contract feasibility. In short, contract feasibility with repeat suppliers will be at its best if all contracting costs are search costs; it will be at its worst if all con-tracting costs are external input costs.

Of course, in reality different types of contracting costs will be present at the same time. In modern markets, most contracts may imply search costs and training costs. Especially in high-standards production, it takes time and effort to identify capable and reliable suppliers, and these gen-erally need basic training on how to implement stringent production and process standards.

This means that, in spite of the weak "bargaining position" of small sup-pliers in negotiations with large companies, if quality matters and search and training costs are high, buyers may have strong incentives to share sur-plus with their suppliers, and suppliers will benefit from engaging in con-tract farming. The provision of external inputs is likely to differ significantly between different types of commodities and different regions, depending on credit markets and levels of development. If they are provided they may lead to additional surplus sharing with suppliers, providing an additional "efficiency premium"; but they may threaten contract feasibility at the same time.

17

General Equilibrium Effects of Standards in Value Chains

17.1 Introduction

In the previous chapters we have analyzed how various factors influence the emergence of value chains and the inclusion of different types of producers in value chains (Chapter 10) and the distribution of surplus within these value chains (Chapters 11, 12, and 16). This focus reflects the general assumption in the vast majority of studies that any benefits to smallholders from the rise of high-standards value chains could only come through their role as supplier. However, some recent studies show that, even when poor households are excluded as suppliers because of high standards, they may still benefit importantly through the labor market, that is from employment by larger firms (Maertens and Swinnen, 2009; Maertens et al., 2011). The only studies that try to measure income and poverty effects of large-scale employment find strong poverty reducing effects through labor markets for poor households involved as workers producing high-standards exports in Africa.

More generally, much of the literature (whether theoretical or empirical) has focused on partial effects. What is lacking in the debate around high-standards value chains is a consistent and comprehensive conceptual framework for capturing the multitude of effects and interpreting the partial effects observed in empirical findings. As noted, few studies include labor market effects. In addition, no studies analyze general equilibrium effects such as demand and supply spillover effects on other markets, such as staple foods, which may have very important impacts on farm income in developing countries. Measuring these effects econometrically is very difficult because annual datasets usually do not contain the necessary data on high-standards market and datasets from surveys targeted to measure impacts of the growth of high standards typically do not have sufficient information (either spatially or dynamically) to measure spillover effects on other markets. However, as emphasized by Acemoglu (2010), an understanding of general equilibrium effects is necessary because a failure to do so may lead to wrong estimates and incorrect policy conclusions.

This chapter presents a computable general equilibrium (CGE) model to identify the various mechanisms through which the introduction and growth of high standards can influence welfare and poverty. The model has both low-standards and high-standards value chains, and explicitly integrates key characteristics of many developing and emerging economies, such as capital and labor market constraints. This allows us to analyze how and through which channels the welfare of rural and urban households is affected. The model is calibrated using a Chinese dataset. A full description of the CGE model specification and its assumptions and its simulation results can be found in Xiang et al. (2012). In this chapter we limit ourselves to summarizing the basic set up of the model and its key results.

Any CGE model is necessarily sensitive to assumptions, the choice of key parameter values, and the calibration of the initial equilibrium data set (e.g., Mas-Colell et al., 1995; Shoven and Whalley, 1992). However, it is not our intention to predict the exact size of the impacts. Rather, our aim is to identify the direct and indirect channels through which the expansion of the high-standards sector may affect welfare. For these purposes, a CGE model is the natural approach.

Our application to the development of a high-standards food sector in China is particularly relevant for four reasons. First, even though China has sustained high growth rates for nearly thirty years, the food distribution system has remained laggard until very recently. However, recent years have been characterized by the rapid growth of supermarkets and some food safety scandals (Hu et al., 2004; Wang et al., 2009). This transition from a system of mainly low-standards food produced by millions of small farms (Rozelle and Swinnen, 2004) to one of high standards is only just beginning and may have substantial impacts on both producers and consumers (Mo et al., 2011). Second, despite high growth rates, an increasing inequality between wealthy and poor households becomes a more and more acute issue (Ravallion, 2001). After an initially rapid reduction in poverty rates, more recently China is facing more difficulty in reducing rural poverty (Chen and Ravallion, 2007). Ninety percent of poverty is still rural in China (World Bank, 2009). The welfare and poverty effects associated with the expansion of a high-standards food sector might therefore be very important. Third, in China, the agricultural sector alone accounted for 11.3% of gross domestic product (GDP) and almost 40% of employment in

2008 (CNBS, 2009). Including food processing activities brings the share of GDP close to 20%. Consequently, any "shocks" that impact on either agriculture or food processing have secondary economy-wide impacts. Fourth, both the agricultural commodity and factor markets are in transition. Whereas the commodity market is becoming more and more efficient (Huang and Rozelle, 2006), factor market imperfections remain important. Therefore, China provides a very interesting case for research on the interaction between the food system transition and the acute equity and poverty problem under conditions of market imperfections.

The simulation results show that the effects on poor rural households depend on a variety of factors, including the nature of the shocks leading to the expansion of the high-standards sector, production technologies, trade effects, spillover effects on low-standards markets, factor market constraints, and labor market effects. Our results demonstrate the importance of taking into account general equilibrium effects.

The next section introduces our CGE model, explaining the basic structure and assumptions behind the model as well as the empirical application using data for China. Section 17.3 contains our simulations, where we consider the two scenarios of export-led growth and domestic demand-led growth. We also discuss sensitivity analyses. Section 17.4 concludes the chapter.

17.2 Theoretical Framework and Empirical Application

Our model follows the tradition of applied general equilibrium models pioneered by Shoven and Whalley (1992), although its precise specification is more closely related to the CGE models described in de Janvry and Sadoulet (2002) and Stifel and Thorbecke (2003).

As in such canonical models, the fundamental building blocks are households, commodities, and factors. Households' income is determined through their ownership of production factors and the corresponding factor prices. Given this income and a set of prices, households maximize their utility, which leads to demands for the commodities. Firms in turn maximize profits, which leads to demands for the production factors owned by the households.

In order to incorporate the key features of standards and their linkages to the rest of the economy, we extend the basic CGE model in several dimensions. First, given that differentiated goods are important for studying the impact of standard expansion, and in line with our approach in Chapter 10, we introduce two types of vertically differentiated goods in the food sector: low-standards food and high-standards food.[1] Second, to allow for differential effects in producer welfare, we explicitly model the heterogeneity of farms. Third, to study the impact of rural credit market imperfections, which are very important in many developing countries, we introduce credit constraints for rural households. Finally, to trace the rural–urban income effects of the high-standards food expansion, an inter-regional CGE approach of Ando and Takanori (1997), Kancs (2001), and Kilkenny (1993) is adopted. Figure 17.1. summarizes the model structure. We first discuss the basic structure of our model and then discuss in detail some specific assumptions made in our analysis.

In terms of commodities, our model includes three final goods: high-standards food, low-standards food, and one good representing "other commodities."[2] Household consumption of these three commodities is modeled as a linear expenditure system subject to the household budget constraint.[3]

To study the distributional consequences between different types of consumers, we distinguish between urban households and rural households, with rural households further disaggregated into the poorest quintile and other rural households. Our model consists of four production factors: rural labor, urban labor, capital, and land. Rural households own rural labor, land, and capital; while urban households own urban labor and capital. This detailed modeling will make it possible to decompose the effects of high-standards on different subgroups of the population.

On the production side, in addition to the three final goods, we include two intermediate goods: one high-standards intermediate good used as input to produce high-standards food, and one low-standards good used as input to produce low-standards food. One can think of these as the raw agricultural inputs used by food processing firms to create processed food. The production of intermediate goods then corresponds to the production of raw agricultural products by farmers. Given that we focus on food standards, we do not include an intermediate product for the production of other commodities.

---

[1] The same extensions can also be implemented in other sectors. However, for the sake of simplicity, these extensions are not presented here.

[2] It is straightforward to expand our model to include more sectors. Given that this would add little additional insight, while unnecessarily complicating the analysis, we chose to aggregate all other economic activities under "other commodities."

[3] Linear expenditure systems are derived from a Stone–Geary utility function (Stone, 1954). This type of expenditure system is standard in the development literature (see, e.g., Lofgren et al., 2001).

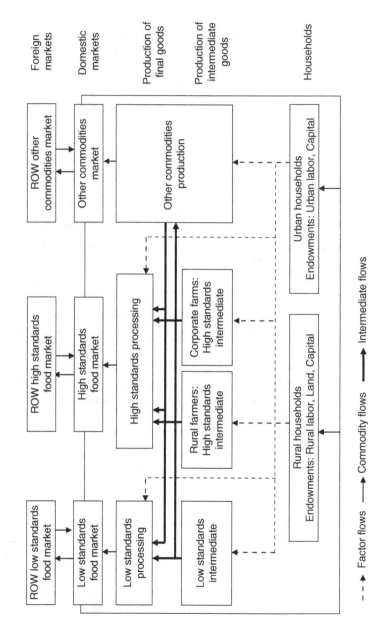

Figure 17.1. Model structure.

- - ► Factor flows   ──► Commodity flows   ━━► Intermediate flows

Foreign markets

Domestic markets

Production of final goods

Production of intermediate goods

Households

ROW other commodities market

Other commodities market

Other commodities production

Urban households
Endowments: Urban labor, Capital

ROW high standards food market

High standards food market

High standards processing

Corporate farms: High standards intermediate

Rural farmers: High standards intermediate

Rural households
Endowments: Rural labor, Land, Capital

ROW low standards food market

Low standards food market

Low standards processing

Low standards intermediate

We assume that the production of the agricultural intermediate products takes place only in the rural areas, while food processing (i.e., the production of the high-standards and low-standards food) as well as the production of the other commodities occurs in both the rural and urban areas. Accounting for the dual farm structure characteristic of many developing countries, in rural areas we make a further distinction between two types of producers of the high-standards intermediate good: rural farmers and corporate farms (which employ rural laborers).

We augment this basic structure with a number of specific assumptions. First, in order to produce the high-standards intermediate good, farms face some fixed investment costs to satisfy the requirements of high-standards production.

Second, as in previous chapters, we take into account the importance of credit constraints for rural households. To capture this, we assume (in the baseline model) that the supply of capital to rural households and corporate farms is inelastic and that the supplied capital is below their optimal capital use in high-standards production. This assumption implies that there are positive profits in high-standards agricultural production. We perform sensitivity analyses on how (the importance of) credit constraints affect the results.

Third, to decompose the aggregate labor market effect into rural and urban impacts, we model the labor market as two segmented submarkets (rural and urban labor) with different skill composition. We use iceberg migration costs to model migration between rural and urban regions, which leads to differences between wages for workers working in urban and rural regions respectively. This assumption is consistent with the observation that net wages of rural workers are often lower than urban wages, even when rural workers may migrate to urban areas. These wage differences between rural and urban workers are due to different skills of different labor types and migration costs (Stifel and Thorbecke, 2003).

Fourth, all sectors have zero pure profits as in the basic CGE model except the high-standards intermediate sector, where credit constraints may limit production capacity. Rural households' net income is the sum of their profits in high-standards farming, factor incomes and profits from corporate farms. Urban households' income is composed of factor incomes and profits from corporate farms, if any.

Our model also assumes that final goods can be traded with the rest of the world, while intermediate inputs and production factors are immobile. Finally, for simplicity we do not include government and taxes in the model.

For the empirical implementation of our model, two types of data are required: data to calibrate the model for the base year and model parameters. We obtain most of our data for the base year from the China Statistics Yearbook, the China Agriculture Yearbook, and the 2002 Input/Output Table.[4] However, there are no reliable data on the share of "high standard" commodities in total output for China.[5] Because we are primarily interested in understanding the direction, mechanisms and relative sizes of different sub-effects, we assume that high-standards production is still small (5%) and not linked to specific commodities.

Our key parameters are taken from the literature, or are calibrated within the model (see Xiang et al., 2012 for a discussion). To assess the robustness of model assumptions and parameter values, we perform extensive sensitivity analysis with respect to key assumptions. The results show that our key conclusions are robust to a reasonable range of variations in the key parameters.

17.3 Simulations

The supply and demand of all commodities, including the high-standards intermediate and food products, are determined endogenously. Therefore, we have to "induce" the expansion of the high-standards food sector through changes in exogenous variables. We consider two scenarios. First, we simulate an increase in the exogenous world price of high-standards food – a scenario that we refer to as "export-led growth." An important factor determining the welfare effects is the elasticity of transformation of high-standards food, that is, the elasticity of substitution between domestic and exported products. Therefore, we simulate the export-led growth both when the elasticity of transformation is "moderate" and when it is high (scenarios 1A and 1B). Second, we simulate an increase in domestic consumer preferences for high-standards food. By varying consumer preferences we avoid the problem of having to separate income effects from high-standards expansion from direct income growth otherwise induced by increased endowments or productivity. This scenario is referred to as "domestic demand growth." The two scenarios are related, because consumer demand

---

[4] See the online appendix to Xiang et al. (2012) for a detailed description of the data sources.

[5] Hu et al. (2004) estimated that roughly 30% of food was sold through supermarkets. Large wholesale and retail companies, as defined by the Chinese Economic Yearbook (CEYC, 2006), sold 8.7% of the total food. However, according to Wang et al. (2009), nearly all of these products came through semitraditional supply channels and production systems.

induces import growth of high-standards food with open trade. Given that trade responsiveness plays an important role, we analyze the domestic demand growth scenario with elastic imports (scenario 2A) and inelastic imports (scenario 2B).

A crucial issue in the analysis is the assumption about the technology used in the high-standards food sector in China. As explained previously, there are no precise data on the emerging high-standards sector, because the food sector is just emerging in China, and there is no consensus whether high-standards farming is relatively labor or capital intensive compared to other activities (Bijman, 2008; Miyata et al., 2007; Weinberger and Lumpkin, 2007). Therefore we first assume the same production technology, that is, factor intensities, in high-standards and low-standards farming. Subsequently, we simulate how different production technologies in high-standards farming affect the results.

17.3.1 Scenario 1: Export-Led Growth

China has continuously increased its exports of agricultural products and the ratio of agricultural trade to agricultural GDP has risen steadily (Huang et al., 2000). According to Gulati et al. (2007), an outward-looking trade policy can induce the growth of high-standards products, because the rise of high-standards product is subject to international quality standards and safety regulations.

To study the potential impact of export-led emergence of high-standards farming, we exogenously increase the world market price for high-standards food by 25%. The simulation results are reported in the first column of Table 17.1. As a consequence of the increase in the world market price of high-standards food, the domestic consumption of high-standards food declines (−1.6%) and that of low-standards food increases (+0.02%). There is a decline in imports (−27%) and growth of exports (+58%) of high-standards products. The domestic price of high-standards products increases (+13.10%) and there is a corresponding increase in production of high-standards food (+40.50%) because of growth in export demand. In turn, this increases the production of high-standards intermediate input (around 20%), and labor use increases correspondingly on all farms (around 39%) as do the returns to all rural production factors: the increase in factor prices is 0.35% for rural labor, 0.22% for capital, and 0.78% for land. As a consequence, rural household incomes increase by 0.20% and 0.17% (for poor and other households, respectively). Urban households lose (−0.17%), as their wage increase from increased employment in high-standards food processing is more than offset by higher consumer prices.

Table 17.1. *Simulation results (percentage change comparing with baseline)*

	Export-Led		Domestic Demand	
	Sim 1A	Sim 1B	Sim 2A	Sim 2B
Aggregate effects				
Real GDP	−0.04	−0.06	−0.00	−0.00
Gini coefficient	−0.31	−0.54	−0.04	−0.07
Consumption				
Low-standards food	0.02	0.04	−0.01	−0.01
High-standards food	−1.60	−2.51	13.38	13.24
Other commodities	0.03	0.05	−0.04	−0.04
Output of final commodities				
Low-standards food	−0.02	−0.04	−0.00	−0.01
High-standards food	40.50	64.41	6.35	12.96
Other commodities	−0.08	−0.14	−0.01	−0.03
Import volume				
Low-standards food	1.07	1.85	−0.15	−0.05
High-standards food	−27.11	−8.72	18.77	13.53
Other commodities	0.16	0.29	−0.07	−0.05
Export volume				
Low-standards food	−0.44	−0.75	0.05	0.01
High-standards food	58.05	146.82	3.99	6.26
Other commodities	−0.29	−0.49	0.04	0.01
Domestic consumer price				
Low-standards food	0.35	0.60	−0.05	−0.01
High-standards food	13.10	22.29	1.56	2.59
Other commodities	0.27	0.47	−0.06	−0.04
Farm gate price				
Low-standards product	0.38	0.66	−0.04	−0.01
High-standards product	24.01	40.68	3.46	5.60
Factor price				
Rural labor	0.35	0.60	−0.05	−0.02
Urban labor	0.20	0.34	−0.07	−0.05
Land	0.78	1.33	0.03	0.10
Capital	0.22	0.38	−0.06	−0.05
Poorest rural households				
Profit from high-standards farming	0.12	0.21	0.02	0.03
Factor income	0.07	0.13	0.01	0.02
Labor	0.03	0.05	0.01	0.01
Land	0.05	0.08	0.01	0.01
Total income	0.20	0.35	0.03	0.05

(continued)

Table 17.1 (*continued*)

	Export-Led		Domestic Demand	
	Sim 1A	Sim 1B	Sim 2A	Sim 2B
Other rural households				
Profit from high-standards farming	0.12	0.22	0.02	0.03
Factor income	0.04	0.08	0.01	0.01
Labor	0.02	0.04	0.00	0.01
Land	0.05	0.09	0.01	0.01
Capital	−0.03	−0.05	−0.00	−0.01
Total income	0.17	0.30	0.03	0.04
Urban households				
Total income	−0.17	−0.29	−0.02	−0.03

Source: Authors' simulation (see Xiang et al., 2012).
Notes: All simulations shown here assume identical technology in the high-standards and low-standards sector.
Scenario 1: World price of high-standards food increases by 25%. Simulation 1A: Elasticity of transformation of high-standards food is low. Simulation 1B: Elasticity of transformation of high-standards food is large.
Scenario 2: Urban households' preference for low-standards food decreases by 25%. Simulation 2A: Import is elastic. Simulation 2B: Import is inelastic.

The income effects are relatively small. The first reason for this is that the high-standards sector is small in the model so that changes have relatively limited effects on aggregate. Therefore, the effects will be larger if the high-standards sector grows larger in the future. Given that this is a theoretical exercise, what matters are the mechanisms and the relative sizes of the effects.

The second reason is a relatively limited "pass-through" of world market effects to the domestic market in scenario 1A. A comparison with scenario 1B shows that these effects depend strongly on the elasticity of transformation between domestic and exported products. With a higher elasticity, the increase in domestic high-standards prices in scenario 1B is much larger: the price of domestic high-standards food is higher (+22% instead of +13%) as is the increase in the (farm gate) price of high-standards intermediate goods (+40% instead of +24%). The output response is stronger both for high-standards food (+64% instead of +40%) and high-standards farm products (more than 28% compared to less than 21% on all farms). Labor use on high-standards farms increases considerably more (by more than 58%) and the income effects for rural households are almost twice as high: +0.35% compared to +0.20%.

The aggregate effects on growth and inequality are reflected in changes in GDP and in the Gini coefficient. Real GDP declines by −0.04% to −0.06%. The growth in rural incomes with increasing international high-standards prices is more than offset by urban consumer losses in terms of total growth. However, inequality reduces: the Gini coefficient declines by −0.31% to −0.54%. With (richer) urban consumers losing and (poorer) rural households gaining, the income gap between both decreases.

17.3.2 Scenario 2: Domestic Demand Growth

We now simulate the effect of a change in consumer preferences for high-standards products. Such change may come gradually or with shocks. The demand for high-standards food will normally increase gradually with rising incomes (Gale and Huang, 2007). However, in developing countries markets are often exposed to shocks, such as the scandal in the dairy sector of China in 2008 (Mo et al., 2011; Xinhua Net, 2008). Such shocks could trigger sharp shifts in preferences.

Scenario 2A simulates the effect of increasing consumer preferences for high-standards food by exogenously increasing the minimum consumption of high-standards food of urban households.[6] As shown in Table 17.1, the reported results are rather different from the export-led growth scenario. Now the substitution between low-standards and high-standards food leads to an increase in high-standards food consumption (+13.38%) but a decline in low-standards food consumption (−0.01%). Most of this increased consumption comes from increased imports of high-standards food (+18.77%). Domestic production of high-standards food (+6.35%) and high-standards intermediate products (+2.78% to +3.07%) increase less, while low-standards production decreases. Because of the high share of low-standards production, this reduces nominal returns to the rural factors: labor (−0.05%) and capital (−0.06%), except land (+0.03%). Because the individual price indices for rural households decrease more (due to falling low-standards food prices), the real effects on returns to factors are positive (+0.01% for both poorest and other rural households). Profit effects are also positive (+0.02% for both). As a result, the real incomes of all rural households increase. Notice that the household income changes reported in Table 17.1 reflect the real income effects, which are measured

---

[6] Given that we are working with a linear expenditure system, demand consists of a "non-discretionary" and a "discretionary" component (Savard, 2005). In other words, a part of demand is independent of prices and income, which is why we refer to it here as the "minimum consumption."

by household-specific price indices. For example, while the factor price of rural labor declines by 0.05% in simulation 2A, the factor income from labor for the poorest household increases by 0.01% because their price index decreases more than the wage rate, as low-standards food prices (which make up a large share of their expenditures) decline by 0.05%. This is less the case for richer households that spend more on high-standards food whose price increases by 1.56%.

Again these results are strongly influenced by the trade effects. This can be seen from comparing the results with scenario 2B where we simulate the same exogenous change in preferences but with less elastic imports. In this case, the domestic producers benefit more from the increased demand for high-standards food by domestic consumers. High-standards producers benefit more because more of the increased domestic demand now comes from domestic production; low-standards producers benefit more because the price of low-standards farm products falls less due to lower substitution. The increase in the domestic high-standards food price is almost twice as high (+2.59% compared to +1.56%) and the fall in low-standards food prices is much less (–0.01% compared to –0.05%) as there is less substitution by consumers. Rural households, including the poor, benefit considerably more: their income increase is now 0.05% instead of 0.03%, that is, almost double.

The simulation results indicate that there is no net impact on real GDP as the fall in urban consumer incomes is exactly offset by the gains in rural producer incomes at the aggregate level. This also leads to a reduction in inequality (the Gini coefficient declines by around 0.05%): with (richer) urban consumers losing and (poorer) rural households gaining, the income gap between both reduces.

17.3.3 Sensitivity Analyses

To test the robustness of our results, we performed several sensitivity analyses, looking at the role of technology, credit constraints, and investment costs. We briefly summarize the main results.

Rural households will benefit more if the technology used in high-standards farming is more labor intensive. This effect is strongest for the poorest. As the poor's main production factor is their family labor, they will benefit more the more this factor is used in the high-standards production and vice versa.

If credit is more easily accessible for all the farms (i.e., credit constraints are relaxed for all farms simultaneously) income effects for rural households may be different for the poorest and the other (somewhat better off) rural households. The "other" rural households, who have more access to non-labor assets, benefit from reduced credit constraints. In contrast, the poorest rural households may actually lose from the reduction of credit constraints for all farms. The reason is that they face stronger competition from other rural households and corporate farms who benefit relatively more from capital cost reductions after credit constraints for all of them are relaxed. Hence, the impact on rural households depends not only on general changes in credit market constraints (e.g., by falling interest rates) but also by the relative effects across the different farm types.

Not surprisingly, our simulations show that in particular the poorest farmers are negatively affected by higher investment costs.

In summary, sensitivity analyses are consistent with intuition: poor farms whose main assets are labor are most likely to gain if the high-standards products can be produced with labor intensive technologies and less likely if the investment requirements are higher. The impact of capital market constraints depends on the distribution of these constraints across farms.

17.4 Conclusion

In this chapter we used a structural CGE model to analyze the income, poverty, and equity effects of an expansion of high-standards food production. Our model takes into account rural factor market imperfections and distinguishes between rural and urban households and different types of farms.

A first observation is that the effects of an increase in the high-standards sector have different effects on rural and urban households. Because rural households are poorer, they consume less high-standards food. A price increase for high-standards food (whether as the result of increased exports or increased domestic demand) will thus hurt urban consumers more than rural consumers. In our simulations, rural households are net beneficiaries of an increase in the high-standards economy, as the combined effect of changes in the prices of factors they own and of goods they consume is a net gain in real income. Because rural households are poorer than urban households, the effect is to reduce poverty and inequality. The poverty and inequality effects of changes in food prices thus crucially depend on whether households are "net consumers" or "net producers," an observation consistent with recent analyses of the effects of high food prices on poverty in developing countries more generally (Swinnen, 2011; Swinnen and Squicciarini, 2012).

For rural households, the poverty-reducing effects of an increase in the high-standards economy depend crucially on the following factors.

First, export-led growth in the high-standards economy has a bigger impact than a domestic demand-driven expansion. An increase in domestic high-standards food consumption will partly lead to greater imports, which means the growth of the domestic high-standards sector (and hence the positive income effects for rural producers) will be correspondingly lower.

Second, the elasticity of substitution between domestic and foreign high-standards products plays an important role. If domestic consumers consider these goods to be highly substitutable, an increase in domestic demand will mostly result in higher imports, which do not benefit rural households. Likewise, if on the production side there is a high elasticity of substitution between foreign and domestic high-standards food, an increase in the world price of high-standards food will lead to a much higher increase in the domestic price of high-standards food.

Third, the technology used in high-standards production matters. If high-standards production is more intensive in those factors that rural households own, the poverty effects of increased high-standards production will be correspondingly larger.

Fourth, lower investment costs help rural households, but relaxing credit constraints may have ambiguous effects on poverty; the poorest households may lose from a reduction in credit constraints as they face more competition from other producers.

Fifth, spillover effects on other markets need to be taken into account. An increase in domestic demand for high-standards food can imply a substitution away from low-standards food and a decrease in the price of low-standards food. Since poor rural households depend importantly on low-standards production and consumption, they may benefit or lose from such spillover effects.

The general equilibrium approach as presented here is best seen as a complement, rather than a substitute, for partial equilibrium analyses. As with any CGE approach, our model is limited by the many assumptions that have to be made in specifying equations and their calibration with the data. Partial equilibrium analyses, such as the ones presented in the previous chapters, can shed light on the role of specific elements in isolation, such as scale economies, spillover effects, technology transfer, skill heterogeneity, various transaction costs, vertical coordination, contracting, and so forth. Although partial equilibrium analysis has the benefit of providing a clear understanding of the role of a single factor, our general equilibrium analysis shows how the overall welfare effects of standards on poor rural households are determined by many factors and a variety of mechanisms throughout the economy.

References

Acemoglu, D. (2010). "Theory, General Equilibrium and Political Economy in Development Economics." NBER Working Paper 15944. Cambridge, MA: National Bureau of Economic Research.

Ackerman, F., Stanton, E. A., Roach, B., and Andersson, A.-S. (2008). "Implications of REACH for Developing Countries." *European Environment* 18(1): 16–29.

Aghion, P., Bloom, N., Blundell, R., Griffith, R., and Howitt, P. (2005). "Competition and Innovation: An Inverted-U Relationship." *The Quarterly Journal of Economics* 120(2): 701–728.

Aghion, P., Griffith, R., and Howitt, P. (2006). "Vertical Integration and Competition." *American Economic Review: Papers and Proceedings*, 96(2): 97–102.

Akerlof, G. A. (1970). "The Market for 'Lemons': Quality Uncertainty and the Market Mechanism." *Quarterly Journal of Economics* 84(3): 488–500.

Akiyama, T., Baffes, J., Larson, D. F., and Varangis., P. (2003). "Commodity Market Reforms in Africa. Some Recent Experience." World Bank Policy Research Working Paper No. 2995. Washington, DC: The World Bank.

Allen, D. W., and Lueck, D. (1998). "The Nature of the Farm." *The Journal of Law and Economics* 41(2): 343–386.

Amacher, G. S., Koskela, E., and Ollikainen, M. (2004). "Environmental Quality Competition and Eco-labeling." *Journal of Environmental Economics and Management* 47(2): 284–306.

Anderson, K. ed. (2009). *Distortions to Agricultural Incentives: A Global Perspective, 1955 to 2007.* London: Palgrave Macmillan and Washington, DC: The World Bank.

Anderson, K., Damania, R., and Jackson, L. (2004). "Trade, Standards, and the Political Economy of Genetically Modified Food." World Bank Policy Research Working Paper 3395. Washington, DC: The World Bank.

Anderson, K., and Masters, W. (2009). *Distortions to Agricultural Incentives in Africa.* Washington, DC: The World Bank.

Anderson, K., Rausser, G., and Swinnen, J. (2013). "Political Economy of Public Policies: Evidence from Distortions to Agricultural and Food Markets." *Journal of Economic Literature* 51(2): 423–477.

Andersson, C., Chege, C., Rao, E., and Qaim, M. (2015). "Following Up on Smallholder Farmers and Supermarkets in Kenya." *American Journal of Agricultural Economics*, forthcoming.

Ando, A., and Takanori, S. (1997). "A Multi-regional Model for China Based on Price and Quantity Equilibrium." In M. Chatterji (ed.), *Regional Science Perspectives for the Future*. London: Macmillan.

Andreoni, J. (1989). "Giving with Impure Altruism: Applications to Charity and Ricardian Equivalence." *Journal of Political Economy* 97(6): 1447–1458.

Ansell, C., and Vogel, D., eds. (2006). *What's the Beef?* Cambridge, MA: MIT Press.

Arora, A., Bhaskar, A., Minten, B., and Vandeplas, A. (2011). "Opening the Beer Gates: How Liberalization Caused Growth in India's Brewery Market." In J. Swinnen (ed.), *The Economics of Beer*, 308–332. Oxford: Oxford University Press.

Arora, S., and Gangopadhyay, S. (1995). "Toward a Theoretical Model of Voluntary Overcompliance." *Journal of Economic Behavior and Organization* 28: 289–309.

Arthur, W. B. (1989). "Competing Technologies, Increasing Returns, and Lock-in by Historical Events." *The Economic Journal* 99: 116–131.

Augier, P., Gasiorek, M., and Lai Tong, C. (2005). "The Impact of Rules of Origin on Trade Flows." *Economic Policy* 20(43): 567–623.

Azzam, A., and Pagoulatos, E. (1990). "Testing Oligopolistic and Oligopsonistic Behaviour: An Application to the U.S. Meat-Packing Industry." *Journal of Agricultural Economics* 41(3): 362–370.

Bacon, C. (2005). "Confronting the Coffee Crisis: Can Fair Trade, Organic and Specialty Coffee Reduce Small-Scale Farmer Vulnerability in Northern Nicaragua?" *World Development* 33(3): 497–511.

Bagwell, K., and Staiger, R. W. (2001). "Domestic Policies, National Sovereignty and International Economic Institutions." *Quarterly Journal of Economics* 116(2): 519–562.

Bajari, P., and Tadelis, S., (2001). "Incentives versus Transaction Costs: A Theory of Procurement Contracts." *RAND Journal of Economics* 32(3):387–407.

Baldwin, R. (1970). *Non-Tariff Distortions in International Trade*. Washington, DC: Brookings Institution.

(2001). "Regulatory Protectionism, Developing Nations and a Two-Tier World Trading System." In K. Maskus and J. S. Wilson (eds.), *Quantifying the Impact of Technical Barriers to Trade: Can It Be Done?*, 59–93. Ann Arbor: Michigan University Press.

Baldwin, R., and Krugman, P. (1989). "Persistent Trade Effects of Large Exchange Rate Shocks." *Quarterly Journal of Economics* 104: 635–654.

Baltzer, K. (2011). "Minimum Quality Standards and International Trade." *Review of International Economics* 19(5): 936–949.

Bardhan, P. (1989). *The Economic Theory of Agrarian Institutions*. Oxford: Clarendon Press.

Bardhan, P., and Udry, C. (1999). *Development Microeconomics*. Oxford: Oxford University Press.

Barla, P. (2000). "Firm Size Inequality and Market Power." *International Journal of Industrial Organization* 18(5): 693–722.

Barrett, C. (1998). "Immiserized Growth in Liberalized Agriculture." *World Development* 26(5): 743–753.

Barrett, C., and Yang, Y. (2001). "Rational Incompatibility with International Product Standards." *Journal of International Economics* 54 (1): 171–191.

Barrett, S. (1994). "Strategic Environmental Policy and International Trade." *Journal of Public Economics* 54: 325–338.

Barrientos, S., Gereffi, G., and Rossi, A. (2011). "Economic and Social Upgrading in Global Production Networks: A New Paradigm for a Changing World." *International Labour Review* 150: 319–340.

Battigalli, P., and Maggi, G. (2003). "International Agreements on Product Standards: An Incomplete-Contracting Theory." NBER Working Paper 9533. Cambridge, MA: National Bureau of Economic Research.

Bauman, P. (2000). "Equity and Efficiency in Contract Farming Schemes: The Experience of Agricultural Tree Crops." Working Paper 139. London: Overseas Development Institute.

Becker, G. S. (1962). "Investment in Human Capital: A Theoretical Analysis." *Journal of Political Economy* 70 (5): 9–49.

Beghin, J., Disdier, A., Marette, S., and Van Tongeren, F. (2012). "Welfare Costs and Benefits of Non-Tariff Measures in Trade: A Conceptual Framework and Application." *World Trade Review* 11(3): 356–375.

Beghin, J., and Li, Y. (2013). "The Political Economy of Food Standard Determination: International Evidence from Maximum Residue Limits." Working Paper No. 13011. Ames: Iowa State University Department of Economics.

Beghin, J., Maertens, M., and Swinnen, J. (2015). "Non-Tariff Measures and Standards in Trade and Global Value Chains." *Annual Review of Resource Economics*, forthcoming.

Belke, A., and Göcke, M. (1999). "A Simple Model of Hysteresis in Employment under Exchange Rate Uncertainty." *Scottish Journal of Political Economy* 46(3): 260–286.

Bell, C. (1988). "Credit Markets and Interlinked Transactions." In H. Chenery and T. Srinivasan (eds.), *Handbook of Development Economics*, 763–830. Amsterdam: North Holland.

Bellemare, M. F. (2012). "As You Sow, So Shall You Reap: The Welfare Impacts of Contract Farming." *World Development* 40 (7): 1418–1434.

Benfica, R., Tschirley, D., and Sambo, L. (2002). "The Impact of Alternative Agro-industrial Investments on Poverty Reduction in Rural Mozambique." Research Report No. 51E. Republic of Mozambique: Ministry of Agriculture and Rural Development, Directorate of Economics.

Bernheim, B. D., and Whinston, M. D. (1986). "Menu Auctions, Resource Allocation, and Economic Influence." *Quarterly Journal of Economics* 101(1): 1–31.

Besley, T., and Ghatak, M. (2007). "Retailing Public Goods: The Economics of Corporate Social Responsibility." *Journal of Public Economics* 91(9): 1645–1663.

Bhagwati, J. (1982). "Directly Unproductive, Profit-Seeking (DUP) Activities." *Journal of Political Economy* 90(5): 988–1002.

Bijman, J. (2008). "Contract Farming in Developing Countries: An Overview." Working Paper. Wageningen University.

Binkley, J., Canning, P., Dooley, R., and Eales, J. (2002). "Consolidated Markets, Brand Competition, and Orange Juice Prices." *Agriculture Information Bulletin No.* 747-06, USDA-ERS.

Binkley, J., and Connor, J. M. (1998). "Grocery Market Pricing and the New Competitive Environment." *Journal of Retailing* 74: 273–294.

Binswanger, H. P., and Rosenzweig, M. R. (1986). "Behavioural and Material Determinants of Production Relations in Agriculture." *Journal of Development Studies* 22(3): 503–539.

Birthal, P. S., Joshi, P. K., and. Gulati, A. (2005). "Vertical Coordination in High-Value Food Commodities: Implications for Smallholders." MTID Discussion Paper No. 85. Washington DC: Markets, Trade and Institutions Division, International Food Policy Research Institute.

Blanchflower, D., Oswald, A., and Sanfey, P. (1996). "Wages, Profits and Rentsharing." *Quarterly Journal of Economics* 111(1): 227–252.

Blandford, D., and Fulponi, L. (1999). "Emerging Public Concerns in Agriculture: Domestic Policies and International Trade Commitments." *European Review of Agricultural Economics* 26(3): 409–424.

Bockstael, N. (1984). "The Welfare Implications of Minimum Quality Standards." *American Journal of Agricultural Economics* 66(4): 466–471.

Boldrin, M., and Levine, D. K. (2004). "The Case Against Intellectual Monopoly." The Lawrence Klein Lecture. *International Economic Review* 45: 327–350.

(2008). *Against Intellectual Monopoly*. Cambridge: Cambridge University Press.

Bolwig, S., Gibbon, P., and Jones, S. (2008). "The Economics of Smallholder Organic Contract Farming in Tropical Africa." *World Development* 37(6): 1094–1104.

Bonnet, C., and Requillart, V. (2012). "Sugar Policy Reform, Tax Policy and Price Transmission in the Soft Drink Industry." TRANSFOP Working Paper 4. Working Paper of the Transparancy of Food Pricing Project, supported by the Seventh Framework Programme of the European Commission.

Boom, A. (1995). "Asymmetric International Minimum Quality Standards and Vertical Differentiation." *The Journal of Industrial Economics* 43(1): 101–119.

Borjas, G. J., and Ramey, V. A. (1995). "Foreign Competition, Market Power and Wage Inequality." *Quarterly Journal of Economics* 110(4): 1075–1110.

Bredahl, M., Schmitz, A., and Hillman, J. (1987). "Rent Seeking in International Trade: The Great Tomato War." *Journal of Agricultural Economics* 69(1): 1–10.

Brenton, P., and Manchin, M. (2002). "Making the EU Trade Agreements Work. The Role of Rules of Origin." CEPS Working Document 183. Brussels: Centre for European Policy Studies.

Brom, F. W. A. (2000). "Food, Consumer Concerns, and Trust: Food Ethics for a Globalizing Market." *Journal of Agriculture and Environmental Ethics* 12: 127–139.

Budd, J. W., Konings, J., and Slaughter, M. J. (2005). "Wages and International Rent Sharing in Multinational Firms." *Review of Economics and Statistics* 87(1): 73–84.

Cadot, O., de Melo, J., and Olarreaga, M. (2004). "Lobbying, Counterlobbying, and the Structure of Tariff Protection in Poor and Rich Countries." *World Bank Economic Review* 18(3): 345–366.

Cattaneo, O., Gereffi, G., and Staritz, C., eds. (2010). *Global Value Chains in a Postcrisis World: A Development Perspective*. Washington, DC: The World Bank.

Chang, H., and Griffith, G. (1998). "Examining Long-run Relationships Between Australian Beef Prices." *Australian Journal of Agricultural Economics* 42: 369–387.

Chen, M. X., and Mattoo, A. (2008). "Regionalism in Standards: Good or Bad for Trade? *Canadian Journal of Economics* 41(3): 838–863.

Chen, S., and Ravallion, M. (2007). "Absolute Poverty Measures for the Developing World, 1981–2004." *Proceedings of the National Academy of Sciences of the USA* 104: 16757–16762.

Chen, Z. (2003). "Dominant Retailers and the Countervailing Power Hypothesis." *The RAND Journal of Economics* 34(4): 612–625.

China Economy Yearbook Committee (CEYC). (2006). *China Economy Yearbook*. Beijing: China Economy Yearbook Committee.

China National Bureau of Statistics (CNBS). (2009). *China Statistical Yearbook* Beijing: China Statistics Press.

Clarke, R., Davies, S., Dobson, P., and Waterson, M. (2002). *Buyer Power and Competition in European Food Retailing*. Cheltenham, U.K.: Edward Elgar.

Colen, L., Maertens, M., and Swinnen, J. (2012). "Private Standards, Trade and Poverty: GlobalGAP and Horticultural Employment in Senegal." *The World Economy* 35 (8): 1073–1088.

Commander, S., ed. (1989). *Structural Adjustment & Agriculture: Theory and Practice in Africa and Latin America*. London: James Currey.

Competition Commission. (2000). "Supermarkets: A Report on the Supply of Groceries from Multiple Stores in the United Kingdom." Available at www.competition-commission.org.uk.

Compte, O., Jenny, F., and Rey, P. (2002). "Capacity Constraints, Mergers and Collusion." *European Economic Review* 46: 1–29.

Conning, J. (2000). "Of Pirates and Moneylenders: Product Market Competition and the Depth of Lending Relationships." Working Paper. Williamstown, MA: Department of Economics, Williams College.

Cooper, D. (2003). "Findings from the Competition Commission's Inquiry into Supermarkets." *Journal of Agricultural Economics* 54(1): 127–143.

Cooper, R., and Ross, W. (1985). "Product Warranties and Double Moral Hazard." *Rand Journal of Economics* 16(1): 103–113.

Copeland, B. R. (1990). "Strategic Interaction among Nations: Negotiable and Non-negotiable Trade Barriers." *Canadian Journal of Economics* 23(1): 84–108.

Costa-Font, M., Gil, J. M., and Traill, W. B. (2008). "Consumer Acceptance, Valuation of and Attitudes Towards Genetically Modified Food: Review and Implications for Food Policy." *Food Policy* 33: 99–111.

Costinot, A. (2008). "A Comparative Institutional Analysis of Agreements on Product Standards." *Journal of International Economics* 75(1): 197–213.

Cotterill, R. W. (1986). "Market Power in the Retail Food Industry: Evidence from Vermont." *Review of Economics and Statistics* 68: 379–386.

   (1999). "Continuing Concentration in Food Industries Globally: Strategic Challenges to an Unstable Status Quo." Food Marketing Policy Center Research Report 49. Storrs: Department of Agricultural and Resource Economics, University of Connecticut.

Cotterill, R. W., and Harper, C. D. (1995). "Market Power and the Demsetz Quality Critique: An Evaluation for Food Retailing." Research Report No. 29. Storrs: Food Marketing Policy Center, University of Connecticut.

Coulter, J., and Poulton, C. (2001). "Cereal Market Liberalization in Africa." In T. Akiyama, J. Baffes, D. F. Larson, and P. Varangis (eds.), *Commodity Market Reforms: Lessons of Two Decades*. Washington, DC: The World Bank.

Cowan, R. (1990). "Nuclear Power Reactors: A Study in Technological Lock-in." *Journal of Economic History* 50: 541–567.

Crampes, C., and Hollander, A. (1995). "Duopoly and Quality Standards." *European Economic Review* 39: 71–82.

Cross, R., and Allan, A. (1988). "On the History of Hysteresis." In R. Cross (ed.), *Unemployment, Hysteresis and the Natural Rate Hypothesis*, 26–38. Oxford: Basil Blackwell.

Cungu, A., Gow, H., Swinnen, J., and Vranken, L. (2008). "Investment with Weak Contract Enforcement: Evidence from Hungary during Transition." *European Review of Agricultural Economics* 35(1): 75–91.

Curtis, K., McCluskey, J., and Swinnen, J. (2008). "Differences in Global Risk Perceptions of Biotechnology and the Political Economy of the Media." *International Journal of Global Environmental Issues* 8(1&2): 79–89.

Curtis, K., McCluskey, J., and Wahl, T. (2004). "Consumer Acceptance of Genetically Modified Food Products in the Developing World." *AgBioForum* 7(1& 2): 69–74.

Czubala, W., Shepherd, B., and Wilson, J. S. (2009). "Help or Hindrance? The Impact of Harmonized Standards on African Exports." *Journal of African Economies* 18(5): 711–744.

Darby, M., and Karni, E. (1973). "Free Competition and the Optimal Amount of Fraud." *Journal of Law and Economics* 16(1): 67–88.

David, P. A. (1985). "Clio and the Economics of QWERTY." *American Economic Review* 75: 332–337.

Davidson, J., Halunga, A., Lloyd, T. A., McCorriston, S., and Morgan, C. W. (2012). "Explaining UK Food Price Inflation." TRANSFOP Working Paper 1. Working Paper of the Transparancy of Food Pricing Project, supported by the Seventh Framework Programe of the European Commission.

De Janvry, A., and Sadoulet, E. (2002). "World Poverty and the Role of Agricultural Technology: Direct and Indirect Effects." *Journal of Development Studies* 38: 1–26.

Delgado, C. L. (1999). "Sources of Growth in Smallholder Agriculture in Sub-Saharan Africa: The Role of Vertical Integration of Smallholders with Processors and Marketers of High-Value Added Items." *Agrekon* 38(1): 165–189.

Delpeuch, C., and Vandeplas, A. (2013). "Revisiting the 'Cotton Problem' – A Comparative Analysis of Cotton Reforms in Sub-Saharan Africa." *World Development* 42: 209–221.

Demont, M., and Rizzotto, A. C. (2012). "Policy Sequencing and the Development of Rice Value Chains in Senegal." *Development Policy Review* 30(4): 451–472.

Demsetz, H. (1973). "Industry Structure, Market Rivalry, and Public Policy." *Journal of Law and Economics* 16(1): 1–9.

Dercon, S., and Christiaensen, L. (2007). "Consumption Risk, Technology Adoption, and Poverty Traps: Evidence from Ethiopia." World Bank Policy Research Working Paper No. 4257. Washington, DC: The World Bank.

D'Haese, M., and Van Huylenbroeck, G. (2005). "The Rise of Supermarkets and Changing Expenditure Patterns of Poor Rural Households: Case Study in the Transkei Area, South Africa." *Food Policy* 30(1): 97–113.

Dhillon, A., and Rigolini, J. (2006). "Development and the Interaction of Enforcement Institutions." Working Paper. University of Warwick.

Dillemuth, J., Frederick, S., Parker, R., Gereffi, G., and Appelbaum, R. (2011). "Traveling Technologies: Societal Implications of Nanotechnology through the Global Value Chain." *Journal of Nano Education* 3(1–2): 36–44.

Dimitri, C., Tegene, A., and Kaufman, P. R. (2003). "U.S. Fresh Produce Markets: Marketing Channels, Trade Practices, and Retail Pricing Behavior." Agricultural Economic Report Nr. 825, ERS. Washington, DC: U.S. Department of Agriculture.

Dixit, A. (1980). "The Role of Investment in Entry Deterrence." *The Economic Journal* 90: 95–101.

(1989a). "Entry and Exit Decisions under Uncertainty." *Journal of Political Economy* 97(3): 620–638.

(1989b). "Hysteresis, Import Penetration, and Exchange Rate Pass-through." *Quarterly Journal of Economics* 104(2): 205–228.

Djankov, S., La Parto, R., Lopez-de Silanes, F., and Shleifer, A. (2003). "Courts." *Quarterly Journal of Economics* 118(2): 453–517.

Dobson, P. W., Clarke, R., Davies, S., and Waterson, M. (2001). "Buyer Power and Its Impact on Competition in the Food Retail Distribution Sector of the European Union." *Journal of Industry, Competition and Trade* 1(3): 247–281.

Dobson, P. W., and Waterson, M. (1997). "Countervailing Power and Consumer Prices." *The Economic Journal* 107(441): 418–430.

Dolan, C., and Humphrey, J. (2000). "Governance and Trade in Fresh Vegetables: The Impact of UK Supermarkets on the African Horticulture Industry." *Journal of Development Studies* 37(2): 147–176.

Dong, D., and Saha, A. (1998). "He Came, He Saw, (and) He Waited: An Empirical Analysis of Inertia in Technology Adoption." *Applied Economics* 30: 893–905.

Dorward, A., Chirwa, E., Kelly, V. A., Jayne, T. S., Slater, R., and Boughton, D. (2008). "Evaluation of the 2006/07 Agricultural Input Subsidy Programme, Malawi." Final report. Food Security Collaborative Working Paper No. 97143. Ann Arbor: Department of Agricultural, Food and Resource Economics, Michigan State University.

Downs, A. (1957). *An Economic Theory of Democracy*. New York: Harper.

Doyle, C., and Inderst, R. (2007). "Some Economics on the Treatment of Buyer Power in Antitrust." *European Competition Law Review* 28: 210–219.

Dries, L., Germenji, E., Noev, N., and Swinnen, J. (2009). "Farmers, Vertical Coordination, and the Restructuring of Dairy Supply Chains in Central and Eastern Europe." *World Development* 37 (11): 1742–1758.

Dries, L., and Swinnen, J. (2004). "Foreign Direct Investment, Vertical Integration and Local Suppliers: Evidence from the Polish Dairy Sector." *World Development* 32(9): 1525–1544.

Dries, L., and Swinnen, J. (2010). "The Impact of Interfirm Relationships on Investment: Evidence from the Polish Dairy Sector." *Food Policy* 35 (2): 121–129.

Dye, R. (1985). "Costly Contract Contingencies." *International Economic Review* 26(1):233–250.

Ederington, J. (2001). "International Coordination of Trade and Domestic Policies." *American Economic Review* 91(5): 1580–1593.

Elbasha, E. H., and Riggs, T. L. (2003). "The Effects of Information on Producer and Consumer Incentives to Undertake Food Safety Efforts: A Theoretical Model and Policy Implications." *Agribusiness* 19(1): 29–42.

Emons, W. (1988). "Warranties, Moral Hazard, and the Lemons Problem." *Journal of Economic Theory* 46: 16–33.

Esterhuizen, D. (2010). "Grain and Feed Quarterly Update." Global Agricultural Information Network, USDA Foreign Agricultural Service, July 20.

Eswaran, M., and Kotwal, A. (1985). "A Theory of Two-Tier Labor Markets in Agrarian Economies." *American Economic Review* 75(1):162–177.

European Commission. (2009). "A Better Functioning Food Supply Chain in Europe. Communication from the Commission to the European Parliament, the Council, the European Economic and Social Committee and the Committee of the Regions." Brussels: European Commission.

Evgeniev, E., and Gereffi, G. (2008). "Textile and Apparel Firms in Turkey and Bulgaria: Exports, Local Upgrading and Dependency." *Economic Studies* 17(3): 148–179.

Fafchamps, M. (2004). *Market Institutions in Sub-Saharan Africa: Theory and Evidence.* Cambridge, MA: MIT Press.

Fafchamps, M., and B. Minten (2001). "Property Rights in a Flea Market economy." *Economic Development and Cultural Change* 49: 229–267.

Falck-Zepeda, J. B., Traxler, G., and Nelson, R. G. (2000). "Surplus Distribution from the Introduction of a Biotechnology Innovation." *American Journal of Agricultural Economics* 82: 360–369.

FAO. (2009). *The State of Food Insecurity in the World 2009. Economic Crises - Impacts and Lessons Learned.* Rome: FAO.

FAOSTAT. (2014). FAOSTAT online database. http://faostat.fao.org. Rome, Italy: Food and Agriculture Organization of the United Nations.

Farrell, J., and Saloner, G. (1985). "Standardization, Compatibility, and Innovation." *RAND Journal of Economics* 16(1): 70–83.

Farris, P. W., and Ailawadi, K. L. (1992). "Retail Power: Monster or Mouse?" *Journal of Retailing* 68(4): 351–369.

Figuié, M., and Moustier, P. (2009). "Market Appeal in an Emerging Economy: Supermarkets and Poor Consumers in Vietnam." *Food Policy* 34: 201–217.

Fischer, R., and Serra, P. (2000). "Standards and Protection." *Journal of International Economics* 52(2): 377–400.

Flynn, J., Slovic, P., and Mertz, C. K. (1993). "Decidedly Different: Expert and Public Views of Risks from a Radioactive Waste Repository." *Risk Analysis* 13(6): 643–648.

Frederick, S., and Gereffi, G. (2011). "Upgrading and Restructuring in the Global Apparel Value Chain: Why China and Asia Are Outperforming Mexico and Central America." *International Journal of Technological Learning, Innovation and Development* 4(1/2/3): 67–95.

Fulponi, L. (2006). "Private Voluntary Standards in the Food System: The Perspective of Major Food Retailers." *Food Policy* 31: 1–13.

(2007). "The Globalization of Private Standards and the Agri-Food System." In J. F. M. Swinnen (ed.), *Global Supply Chains, Standards, and the Poor,* 19–25. Wallingford, Oxfordshire: CABI Publications.

Fulton, M., and Giannakis, K. (2004). "Inserting GM Products into the Food Chain: The Market and Welfare Effects of Different Labelling and Regulatory Regimes." *American Journal of Agricultural Economics* 86(1): 42–60.

Gabre-Madhin, E., Fafchamps, M., Kachule, R., Soule, B. G., and Kahn, Z. (2001). "Impact of Agricultural Market Reforms on Smallholder Farmers in Benin and Malawi." Final Project Report, Vol. 2. Washington, DC: International Food Policy Research Institute.

Gabszewicz, J. J., and Thisse, J.-F. (1979). "Price Competition, Quality and Income Disparities." *Journal of Economic Theory* 20: 340–359.

Galbraith, J. K. (1952). *American Capitalism: The Concept of Countervailing Power.* Boston: Houghton Mifflin.

Gale, F., and Huang, K. (2007). "Demand for Food Quantity and Quality in China." *Economic Research Report.* No. 32. Washington, DC: U.S. Department of Agriculture.

Gardner, B. (2003). "U.S. Food Quality Standards: Fix for Market Failure or Costly Anachronism?" *American Journal of Agricultural Economics* 85(3): 725–730.

Gawande, K., and Krishna, P. (2003). "The Political Economy of Trade Policy: Empirical Approaches." In E. Kwan Choi and James Harrigan (eds.), *Handbook of International Trade*, 213–250. Oxford: Blackwell Publishing.

Genicot, G., and Ray, D. (2006). "Bargaining Power and Enforcement in Credit Markets." *Journal of Development Economics* 79: 398–412.

Gereffi, G., Humphrey, J., and Sturgeon, T. (2005). "The Governance of Global Value Chains." *Review of International Political Economy* 12(1) : 78–104.

Gergely, N. (2010). "The Cotton Sector of Côte d'Ivoire." Africa Region Working Paper Series No. 130a. Washington, DC: The World Bank.

Giannakas, K., and Yiannaka, A. (2008). "Market and Welfare Effects of Second-Generation, Consumer-Oriented GM Products." *American Journal of Agricultural Economics* 90(1): 152–171.

Gibbon, P. (2003). "Value-Chain Governance, Public Regulation and Entry Barriers in the Global Fresh Fruit and Vegetable Chain into the EU." *Development Policy Review* 21(5/6): 615–625.

Giné, X., Goldberg, J., and Yang, D. (2012). "Credit Market Consequences of Improved Personal Identification: Field Experimental Evidence from Malawi." *American Economic Review* 102(6): 2923–2954.

GlobalGAP. (2014). THE GLOBALG.A.P. DATABASE. www.globalgap.org.

Glover, D., and Kusterer, K. (1990). *Small Farmers, Big Business. Contract Farming and Rural Development*. London: Macmillan.

Göcke, M. (2002). "Various Concepts of Hysteresis Applied in Economics." *Journal of Economic Surveys* 16(2): 167–188.

Golan, E., Krissoff, B., Kuchler, F., Calvin, L., Nelson, K., and Price, G. (2004). "Traceability in the U.S. Food Supply: Economic Theory and Industry Studies." Agricultural Economic Report No. 830. Washington, DC: Economic Research Service, U.S. Department of Agriculture.

Golan, E., Kuchler, F., and Mitchell, L. (2001). "Economics of Food Labeling." *Journal of Consumer Policy* 24: 117–184.

Goldberg, P. K., and Pavcnik, N. (2007). "Distributional Effects of Globalization in Developing Countries." *Journal of Economic Literature* 45(1): 39–82.

Goodwin, B., and Holt, M. (1999). "Price Transmission and Asymmetric Adjustment in the US Beef Sector." *American Journal of Agricultural Economics* 81: 630–637.

Govereh, J., Jayne, T. S., and Nyoro, J. (1999). "Smallholder Commercialization, Interlinked Markets and Food Crop Productivity: Cross-country Evidence in Eastern and Southern Africa." Working Paper. Ann Arbor: Michigan State University.

Gow, H., Streeter, D., and Swinnen, J. (2000). "How Private Contract Enforcement Mechanisms Can Succeed Where Public Institutions Fail: The case of Juhocukor a.s." *Agricultural Economics* 23(3): 253–265.

Gow, H., and Swinnen, J. (1998). "Agribusiness Restructuring, Foreign Direct Investment, and Hold-Up Problems in Agricultural Transition." *European Review of Agricultural Economics* 25(4):331–350.

  (2001). "Private Enforcement Capital and Contract Enforcement in Transition Countries." *American Journal of Agricultural Economics* 83(3): 686–690.

Greif, A. (2006). *Institutions and the Path to the Modern Economy: Lessons from Medieval Trade.* Cambridge University Press.

Grethe, H. (2007). "High Animal Welfare Standards in the EU and International Trade – How to Prevent Potential 'Low Animal Welfare Havens'"? *Food Policy* 32(3): 315–333.

Grossman, G. M., and Helpman, E. (1994). "Protection for Sale." *American Economic Review* 84(4): 833–850.

(1995a). "Trade Wars and Trade Talks." *Journal of Political Economy* 103(4): 675–708.

(1995b). "The Politics of Free-Trade Agreements." *American Economic Review* 85(4): 667–690.

(2001). *Special Interest Politics.* Cambridge and London: MIT Press.

(2005). "Outsourcing in a Global Economy." *Review of Economic Studies* 72: 135–159.

Gulati, A, Minot, N., Delgado, C., and Bora, S. (2007). "Growth in High-Value Agriculture in Asia and the Emergence of Vertical Links with Farmers." In J. F. M. Swinnen (ed.), *Global Supply Chains, Standards and the Poor.* Wallingford, Oxfordshire: CABI Publishing.

Gulati, S., and Roy, D. (2007). "How Standards Drive Taxes: The Political Economy of Tailpipe Pollution." *The B.E. Journal of Economic Analysis & Policy* 7(1): 1–23.

Guy, C., Bennison, D., and Clarke, R. (2004). "Scale Economies and Superstore Retailing: New Evidence from the UK." *Journal of Retailing and Consumer Services* 12(2): 73–81.

Hall, L., Schmitz, A., and Cothern, J. (1979). "Beef Wholesale-Retail Marketing Margins and Concentration." *Econometrica* 46: 195–300.

Hausman, J., and Leibtag, E. (2007). "Consumer Benefits from Increased Competition in Shopping Outlets: Measuring the Effect of Wal-Mart." *Journal of Applied Econometrics* 22(7): 1157–1177.

Headey, D. (2011). "*Was the Global Food Crisis Really a Crisis? Simulations Versus Self-Reporting.*" Washington, DC: Development Strategy and Governance Division, International Food Policy Research Institute.

Heckelei, T., and Swinnen, J. (2012). "Introduction to the Special Issue of the World Trade Review on Standards and Nontariff Barriers in Trade." *World Trade Review* 11 (3): 353–355.

Henson, S. (2004). "National Laws, Regulations, and Institutional Capabilities for Standards Development." Paper presented at World Bank training seminar on Standards and Trade, Washington, DC.

(2006). "The Role of Public and Private Standards in Regulating International Food Markets." Paper prepared for the IATRC Summer Symposium "Food Regulation and Trade: Institutional Framework, Concepts of Analysis and Empirical Evidence," Bonn, Germany, May 28–30.

Henson, S., and Hooker, N. H. (2001). "Private Sector Management of Food Safety: Public Regulation and the Role of Private Controls." *International Food and Agribusiness Management Review* 4: 7–17.

Henson, S., and Humphrey, J. (2010). "Understanding the Complexities of Private Standards in Global AgriFood Chains as They Impact Developing Countries." *Journal of Development Studies* 46/9: 1628–1646.

Henson, S., and Jaffee, S. (2007). "The Costs and Benefits from Compliance with Food Safety Standards for Exports by Developing Countries: The Case of Fish and

Fishery Products." In J. F. M. Swinnen (ed.), *Global Supply Chains, Standards and the Poor*. Wallingford, Oxfordshire: CABI Publishing.

Hicks, J. R. (1935). "Annual Survey of Economic Theory: The Theory of Monopoly." *Econometrica* 3(1): 1–20.

Hillman, A. (1982). "Declining Industries and Political-Support Protectionist Motives." *American Economic Review* 72 (5): 1180–1187.

(1989). *The Political Economy of Protection*. London: Taylor & Francis.

Hillman, A., and Ursprung, H. W. (1988). "Domestic Politics, Foreign Interests, and International Trade Policy." *American Economic Review* 78(4): 719–745.

Hoban, T. J., and Kendall, P. A. (1993). *Consumer Attitudes about Food Biotechnology*. Raleigh, NC: North Carolina Cooperative Extension Service.

Hobbs, A. L., Hobbs, J. E., Isaac, G. E., and Kerr, W. A. (2002). "Ethics, Domestic Food Policy and Trade Law: Assessing the EU Animal Welfare Proposal to the WTO." *Food Policy* 27(5–6): 437–454.

Hobbs, J. E. (2010). "Public and Private Standards for Food Safety and Quality: International Trade Implications." *The Estey Centre Journal of International Law and Trade Policy* 11(1): 136–152.

Hoekman, B. (2013). "Adding Value." *Finance & Development* 50(4): 22–24.

(2014). *Supply Chains, Mega-Regionals and Multilateralism: A Road Map for the WTO*. London: CEPR Press.

Hoff, K., and Stiglitz, J. E. (1998). "Moneylenders and Bankers: Price-Increasing Subsidies in a Monopolistically Competitive Market." *Journal of Development Economics* 55: 485–518.

Holm, T., Loy, J.-P., and Steinhagen, C. (2012). "Cost Pass-through in Differentiated Product Markets: A Disaggregated Study for Milk and Butter." TRANSFOP Working Paper 6. Working Paper of the Transparancy of Food Pricing Project, supported by the Seventh Framework Programe of the European Commission.

Horn, H. (2006). "National Treatment in the GATT." *American Economic Review* 96(1): 394–404.

Horn, H., Maggi, G., and Staiger, R. W. (2010). "Trade Agreements as Endogenously Incomplete Contracts." *American Economic Review* 100(1): 394–419.

Hossain, F., Onyango, B., Schilling, B., Hallman, W., and Adelaja, A. (2003). "Product Attributes, Consumer Benefits and Public Approval of Genetically Modified Foods." *International Journal of Consumer Studies* 27: 353–365.

Hu, D., Reardon, T., Rozelle, S., Timmer, P., and Wang, H. (2004). "The Emergence of Supermarkets with Chinese Characteristics: Challenges and Opportunities for China's Agricultural Development." *Development Policy Review* 22: 557–586.

Huang, J., and Rozelle, S. (2006). "The Emergence of Agricultural Commodity Markets in China." *China Economic Review* 17:266–280.

Huang, J., Rozelle, S., and Zhang, L. (2000). "WTO and Agriculture: Radical Reforms or the Continuation of Gradual Transition." *China Economic Review* 11: 397–401.

Huang, J., Wu, Y., Zhi, H., and Rozelle, S. (2008). "Small Holder Incomes, Food Safety and Producing, and Marketing China's Fruit." *Applied Economic Perspectives and Policy* 30(3):469–479.

Humphrey, J. (2007). "The Supermarket Revolution in Developing Countries: Tidal Wave or Tough Competitive Struggle?" *Journal of Economic Geography* 7(4): 433–450.

Humphrey, J., McCulloch, N., and Ota, M. (2004). "The Impact of European Market Changes on Employment in the Kenyan Horticulture Sector." *Journal of International Development* 16(1): 63–80.

Jaffee, S. (1994). "Contract Farming in the Shadow of Competitive Markets: The Experience of Kenyan Horticulture." In P. D. Little, and M. J. Watts (eds.), *Living under Contract: Contract Farming and Agrarian Transformation in Sub-Saharan Africa*, 97–139. Madison: University of Wisconsin Press.

Jaffee, S., and Henson, S. (2005). "Agro-food Exports from Developing Countries: The Challenges Posed by Standards." In M. A. Aksoy and J. C. Beghin (eds.), *Global Agricultural Trade and Developing Countries*, 91–114. Washington, DC: The World Bank.

Jayne, T. S., Chapoto, A., and Govereh, J. (2010). "Grain Marketing Policy at the Crossroads: Challenges for Eastern and Southern Africa." In A. Sarris and J. Morrison (eds.), *Food Security for Africa: Market and Trade Policy for Staple Foods in Eastern and Southern Africa*. Cheltenham, U.K.: Edward Elgar.

Jayne, T. S., and Jones, S. (1997). "Food Marketing and Pricing Policy in Eastern and Southern Africa: A Survey." *World Development* 25(9): 1505–1527.

Jeanneret, M., and Verdier, T. (1996). "Standardization and Protection in a Vertical Differentiation Model." *European Journal of Political Economy* 12(2): 253–271.

Johnson, D.G., and Brooks, K. M., eds. (1983). *Prospects for Soviet Agriculture in the 1980s*. Bloomington: Indiana University Press.

Josling, T., Roberts, D., and Orden, D. (2004). *Food Regulation and Trade: Toward a Safe and Open Global System*. Washington, DC: Institute for International Economics.

Kalaitzandonakes, N., Marks, L. A., and Vickner, S. S. (2004). "Media Coverage of Biotech Foods, and Influence on Consumer Choice." *American Journal of Agricultural Economics* 86(5): 1238–1246.

Kancs, D. (2001). "Predicting European Enlargement Impacts: A Framework of Interregional General Equilibrium." *Eastern European Economics* 39: 31–63.

Kaplinsky, R. (2004). "Competition Policy and the Global Coffee and Cocoa Value Chains." Paper prepared for the United Nations Conference for Trade and Development, May.

Katz, M., and Shapiro, C. (1985). "Network Externalities, Competition and Compatibility." *American Economic Review* 75(3): 424–440.

Kaufman, P. R., and Handy, C. R. (1989). "Supermarket Prices and Price Differences: City, Firm, and Store-Level Determinants." Technical Bulletin No. 1776. Washington, DC: Commodity Economics Division, Economic Research Service, U.S. Department of Agriculture.

Key, N., and Runsten, D. (1999. "Contract Farming, Smallholders, and Rural Development in Latin America: The Organization of Agroprocessing Firms and the Scale of Outgrower Production." *World Development* 27(2): 381–401.

Kherallah, M., Delgado, C., Gabre-Madhin, E., Minot, N., and Jonson, M. (2002). *Reforming Markets in Africa*. Baltimore and London: The John Hopkins University Press.

Kherallah, M. (2000). "Access of Smallholder Farmers to the Fruits and Vegetables Market in Kenya." Washington, DC: International Food Policy Research Institute, mimeo.

Kilkenny, M. (1993). "Rural/Urban Effects of Terminating Farm Subsidies." *American Journal of Agricultural Economics* 75: 968–980.

Kirchhoff, S. (2000). "Green Business and Blue Angels: A Model of Voluntary Overcompliance with Asymmetric Information." *Environmental and Resource Economics* 15: 403–420.

Klein, B., Crawford, R. G., and Alchian, A. A. (1978). "Vertical Integration, Appropriable Rents, and the Competitive Contracting Process." *Journal of Law and Economics* 21(2): 297–326.

Klein, D. B. (1992). "Promise Keeping in the Great Society: A Model of Credit Information Sharing." *Economics and Politics* 4(2): 117–136.

Kleiner, M. (2000). "Occupational Licensing." *Journal of Economic Perspectives* 14(4): 189–202.

Kolk, A. (2005). "Corporate Social Responsibility in the Coffee Sector: The Dynamics of MNC Responses and Code Development." *European Management Journal* 23(2): 228–236.

Konings, J., and Walsh, P. (1999). "Disorganization in the Process of Transition: Firm-Level Evidence from Ukraine." *Economics of Transition* 7(1): 29–46.

Kranton, R., and Swamy, A. V. (2008). "Contracts, Hold-Up, and Exports: Textiles and Opium in Colonial India." *American Economic Review* 98(3): 967–989.

Krueger, A. B. (1996). "Observations on International Labor Standards and Trade." NBER Working Paper 5632. Cambridge, MA: National Bureau of Economic Research.

Krueger, A. O. (1974). "The Political Economy of the Rent-seeking Society." *American Economic Review* 64(3): 291–303.

Krueger, A. O., Schiff, M., and Valdés, A. (1988). "Agricultural Incentives in Developing Countries: Measuring the Effect of Sectoral and Economy-wide Policies." *World Bank Economic Review* 2(3): 255–272.

Krueger, A. O., Schiff, M., and Valdés, A. (1991). *The Political Economy of Agricultural Pricing Policy*, Vol. 1: *Latin America*, Vol. 2: *Asia*, and Vol. 3: *Africa and the Mediterranean*. Baltimore: Johns Hopkins University Press for the World Bank.

Krugman, P. R. (1987). "Is Free Trade Passé?" *Journal of Economic Perspectives* 1(2): 131–144.

Kühn, K.-U. (2002). "Closing Pandora's Box? Joint Dominance after the Airtours Judgement." In *The Pros and Cons of Merger Control: Swedish Competition Authority*, 39–61, Stockholm.

(2004). "The Coordinated Effects of Mergers in Differentiated Products Market." The John M. Olin Center for Law & Economics Working Paper Series, 34. Ann Arbor: University of Michigan Law School.

Lamm, R. M. (1981). "Prices and Concentration in the Food Retailing Industry." *The Journal of Industrial Economics* 30(1): 67–78.

Langinier, C., and Babcock, B. (2008). "Agricultural Production Clubs: Viability and Welfare Implications." *Journal of Agricultural & Food Industrial Organization* 6(1): 1–31.

Lapan, H. E., and Moschini, G. (2004). "Innovation and Trade with Endogenous Market Failure: The Case of Genetically Modified Products." *American Journal of Agricultural Economics* 86(3): 634–648.

(2007). "Grading, Minimum Quality Standards, and the Labeling of Genetically Modified Products." *American Journal of Agricultural Economics* 89(3): 769–783.

Larsen, M. N. (2002). "Is Oligopoly a Condition of Successful Privatization? The Case of Cotton in Zimbabwe." *Journal of Agrarian Change* 2: 185–205.

Larson, B. (2003). "Eco-labels for Credence Attributes: 'Ihe Case of Shade-grown Coffee." *Environment and Development Economics* 3: 529–547.

Latouche, K., Rainelli, P., and Vermersch, D. (1998). "Food Safety Issues and the BSE Scare: Some Lessons from the French Case." *Food Policy* 23(5): 347–356.

Lawrence, R. Z. (1996). *Regionalism, Multilateralism, and Deeper Integration.* Washington, DC: The Brookings Institution.

LeClair, M. S. (2002). "Fighting the Tide: Alternative Trade Organizations in the Era of Global Free Trade." *World Development* 30(6): 949–958.

Leland, H. E. (1979). "Quacks, Lemons, and Licensing: A Theory of Minimum Quality Standards." *Journal of Political Economy* 87(6): 1328–1346.

Lindbeck, A., and Snower, D. J. (1986)."Wage Setting, Unemployment and Insider-Outsider Relations." *American Economic Review* 73: 235–239.

Lloyd, T., McCorriston, S., Morgan, W., Rayner, A., and Weldegebriel, H. (2009). "Buyer Power in UK Food Retailing: A 'First-Pass' Test." *Journal of Agricultural & Food Industrial Organization* 7(1): Article 5.

Lofgren, H., Harris, R. L., and Robinson, S. (2001). "A Standard Computable General Equilibrium (CGE) Model in GAMS." Discussion Paper No. 75. Washington, DC: Trade and Macroeconomics Division, International Food Policy Research Institute.

Loureiro, M. L. (2003). "GMO Food Labelling in the EU: Tracing 'the Seeds of Dispute.'" *EuroChoices* 2(1): 18–22.

Lusk, J. L., and Briggeman, B. C. (2009). "Food Values." *American Journal of Agricultural Economics* 91(1): 184–196.

Lustgarten, S. H. (1975). "The Impact of Buyer Concentration in Manufacturing Industries." *The Review of Economics and Statistics* 57(2): 125–132.

Lutz, S., Lyon, T. P., and Maxwell, J. W. (2000). "Quality Leadership when Regulatory Standards Are Forthcoming." *Journal of Industrial Economics* 48: 331–348.

MacLeod, W. B. (2006). "Reputations, Relationships and the Enforcement of Incomplete Contracts." IZA Discussion Paper No. 1978, Bonn, Germany.

Macours, K., and Swinnen, J. (2000a). "Causes of Output Decline during Transition: The Case of Central and Eastern European Agriculture." *Journal of Comparative Economics* 28(March): 172–206.

(2000b). "Impact of Reforms and Initial Conditions on Agricultural Output and Productivity Changes in Central and Eastern Europe, the Former Soviet Union, and East Asia." *American Journal of Agricultural Economics* 82(5): 1149–1155.

(2002). "Patterns of Agrarian Transition." *Economic Development and Cultural Change* 50(2): 365–395.

Maertens, M., Colen, L., and Swinnen, J. (2011). "Globalization and Poverty in Senegal: A Worst Case Scenario?" *European Review of Agricultural Economics* 38: 31–54.

Maertens, M., Minten, B., and Swinnen, J. (2012). "Modern Food Supply Chains and Development: Evidence from Horticulture Export Sectors in Sub-Saharan Africa." *Development Policy Review* 30(4): 473–497.

Maertens, M., and Swinnen, J. (2007). "Standards as Barriers and Catalysts for Trade, Growth, and Poverty Reduction." *Journal of International Agricultural Trade and Development* 4(1): 47–62.

(2009). "Trade, Standards and Poverty: Evidence from Senegal." *World Development* 37(1): 161–178.

Magee, S., Brock, W., and Young, L. (1989). *Black Hole Tariffs and Endogenous Policy Theory: Political Economy in General Equilibrium.* Cambridge and New York: Cambridge University Press.

Maggi, G., and Rodríguez-Clare, A. (1998). "The Value of Trade Agreements in the Presence of Political Pressures." *Journal of Political Economy* 106(3): 574–601.

(2007). "A Political-Economy Theory of Trade Agreements." *American Economic Review* 97(4): 1374–1406.

Marcoul, P., and Veyssiere, L. (2010). "A Financial Contracting Approach to the Role of Supermarkets in Farmers' Credit Access." *American Journal of Agricultural Economics* 92(4): 1051–1064.

Marette, S., and Beghin, J. C. (2010). "Are Standards Always Protectionist?" *Review of International Economics* 18(1): 179–192.

Marion, B. W., Heimforth, K., and Bailey, W. (1993). "Strategic Groups, Competition, and Retail Food Prices." In R. W. Cotterill (ed.), *Competitive Strategy Analysis in the Food System* 179–199. Boulder, CO: Westview Press.

Marx, A., Bécault, E., and Wouters, J. (2012a) "Private Standards in Forestry. Assessing the Legitimacy and Effectiveness of the Forest Stewardship Council." In A. Marx, M. Maertens, J. Swinnen, and J. Wouters (eds.), *Private Standards and Global Governance: Legal and Economic Perspectives*, 60–97. Cheltenham, U.K.: Edward Elgar.

Marx, A., Maertens, M., Swinnen, J., and Wouters, J., eds. (2012b). *Private Standards and Global Governance: Legal and Economic Perspectives.* Cheltenham, U.K.: Edward Elgar.

Mas-Colell, A., Whinston, M., and Green, J. (1995). *Microeconomic Theory.* New York: Oxford University Press.

Mason, N., Jayne, T. S., Donovan, C., and Chapoto, A. (2009). "Are Staple Foods Becoming More Expensive for Urban Consumers in Eastern and Southern Africa? Trends in Food Prices, Marketing Margins, and Wage Rates in Kenya, Malawi, Mozambique, and Zambia." MSU International Development Working Paper No. 98. Ann Arbor: Department of Agricultural, Food and Resource Economics, Department of Economics, Michigan State University.

Matsuyama, K. (1990). "Perfect Equilibria in a Trade Liberalization Game." *American Economic Review* 80(3): 480–492.

Maxwell, J. W. (1998). "Minimum Quality Standards as a Barrier to Innovation." *Economics Letters* 58(3): 355–360.

McCluskey, J., Grimsrud, K., Ouchi, H., and Wahl, T. I. (2003). "Consumer Response to Genetically Modified Food Products in Japan." *Agriculture and Resource Economics Review* 32(2): 222–231.

McCluskey, J., and Swinnen, J. (2004). "Political Economy of the Media and Consumer Perceptions of Biotechnology." *American Journal of Agricultural Economics* 86(5): 1230–1237.

McCluskey, J., and Winfree, J. (2009)."Pre-empting Public Regulation with Private Food Quality Standards." *European Review of Agricultural Economics* 36(4): 525–539.

McCorriston, S., Morgan, C., and Rayner, A. J. (1998). "Processing Technology, Market Power and Price Transmission." *Journal of Agricultural Economics* 49(2): 185–201.

McCorriston, S., Morgan, C., and Rayner, A. J. (2001). "Price Transmission: The Interaction Between Market Power and Returns to Scale." *European Review of Agricultural Economics* 28(2): 143–159.

McCorriston, S., and Sheldon, I. (1996). "The Effects of Vertical Markets on Trade Policy Reform." *Oxford Economic Papers* 48: 664–672.

Mérel, P., and Sexton, R. (2012). "Will Geographical Indications Supply Excessive Quality?" *European Review of Agricultural Economics* 39(4): 567–587.

Messinger, P. R. and Narasimhan, C. (1995). "Has Power Shifted in the Grocery Channel?" *Marketing Science* 14(2): 189–223.

Meyer, J., and von Cramon-Taubadel, S. (2004). "Asymmetric Price Transmission: a Survey." *Journal of Agricultural Economics* 55(3): 581–611.

Michelson, H., Reardon, T., and Perez, F. (2012). "Small Farmers and Big Retail: Trade-offs of Supplying Supermarkets in Nicaragua." *World Development* 40(2): 342–354.

Minder, R. (2007). "Trade Warning over 'Green' Product Standards." *Financial Times*, 21 September 21, 2007.

Minot, N. (2012). "Food Price Volatility in Africa: Has It Really Increased?" Discussion Paper No. 01239. Washington, DC: International Food Policy Research Institute.

Minot, N., and Ngigi, M. (2004). "Are Horticultural Exports a Replicable Success Story? Evidence from Kenya and Côte d'Ivoire." EPTD/MTID Discussion Paper. Washington, DC: International Food Policy Research Institute.

Minten, B. (2008). "The Food Retail Revolution in Poor Countries: Is It Coming or Is It Over?" *Economic Development and Cultural Change* 56: 767–789.

Minten, B., Randrianarison, L., and Swinnen, J. (2009). "Global Retail Chains and Poor Farmers: Evidence from Madagascar." *World Development* 37(11): 1728–1741.

Minten, B., and Reardon, T. (2008). "Food Prices, Quality, and Quality's Pricing in Supermarkets versus Traditional Markets in Developing Countries." *Review of Agricultural Economics* 30(3): 480–490.

Minten, B., Vandeplas, A., and Swinnen, J. (2011). "Regulations, Brokers, and Interlinkages: The Institutional Organization of Wholesale Markets in India." *Journal of Development Studies* 48(7): 864–886.

Mitchell, L. (2001). "Impact of Consumer Demand for Animal Welfare on Global Trade." In A. Regmi (ed.), *Changing Structure of Global Food Consumption and Trade*, 80–89. Agriculture and Trade Report WRS-01-1. Washington, DC: Market and Trade Economics Division, Economic Research Service, U.S. Department of Agriculture,.

Miyata, S., Minot, N., and Hu, D. (2007). "Impact of Contract Farming on Income: Linking Small Farmers, Packers and Supermarkets in China." Discussion Paper 742. Washington, DC: International Food Policy Research Institute.

Mo, D., Huang, J., Jia, X., Luan, H., Rozelle, S., and Swinnen, J. (2012). "Checking into China's Cow Hotels: Have Policies Following the Milk Scandal Changed the Structure of the Dairy Sector?" *Journal of Dairy Science* 95(5): 2282–2298.

Mookherjee, D., and Ray, D. (2002). "Contractual Structure and Wealth Accumulation." *American Economic Review* 92(4): 818–849.

Moschini, G. (2008). "Biotechnology and the Development of Food Markets: Retrospect and Prospects." *European Review of Agricultural Economics* 35(3): 331–356.

Moschini, G., Menapace, L., and Pick, D. (2008). "Geographical Indications and the Competitive Provision of Quality in Agricultural Markets." *American Journal of Agricultural Economics* 90(3): 794–812.

Motta, M. (1993). "Endogenous Quality Choice: Price versus Quantity Competition." *The Journal of Industrial Economics* 41(2): 113–131.

Muller, A., and van Tulder, R. (2006). "A 'rough guide' to Partnerships for Development." Utrecht, the Netherlands: Expert Centre for Sustainable Business and Development Cooperation and Inter-Church Organization for Development Cooperation (ICCO).

Mussa, M., and Rosen, S. (1978). "Monopoly and Product Quality." *Journal of Economic Theory* 18(2): 301–317.

Nash, J. (1953). 'Two-Person Cooperative Games." *Econometrica* 21(1):128–140.

Negash, M., and Swinnen, J. (2013). "Biofuels and Food Security: Micro–evidence from Ethiopia." *Energy Policy* 63: 963–967.

Nelson, P. (1970). "Information and Consumer Behaviour." *Journal of Political Economy* 78(2): 311–329.

Neven, D., Reardon, T., Chege, J., and Wang, H. (2006). "Supermarkets and Consumers in Africa: The case of Nairobi, Kenya." *Journal of International Food & Agribusiness Marketing* 18(1/2): 103–123.

Newmark, C. M. (1990). "A New Test of the Price-Concentration Relationship in Grocery Retailing." *Economics Letters* 33: 369–373.

Ngeleza, G. K., and Robinson, E. J. Z. (2013). "Cartels and Rent Sharing at the Farmer-Trader Interface: Evidence from Ghana's Tomato Sector." *Journal of Agricultural and Food Industrial Organization* 11(1): 1–16.

Nickell, S. (1999). "Product Markets and Labour Markets." *Labour Economics* 6: 1–20.

Noev, N., Dries, L., and Swinnen, J. (2009). "Institutional Change, Contracts, and Quality in Transition Agriculture: Evidence from the Bulgarian Dairy Sector." *Eastern European Economics* 47(4): 62–85.

North, D. C. (1990). *Institutions, Institutional Change, and Economic Performance.* New York: Cambridge University Press.

Oates, W. E. (1972). *Fiscal Federalism.* New York: Harcourt Brace Jovanovich.

OECD. (2001). "Agricultural Policies in Emerging and Transition Economies: Special Focus on Non-tariff Measures." Paris: Organisation for Economic Co-operation and Development.

OECD. (2008). "Producer and Consumer Support Estimates." OECD Database 1986–2007. Paris: Organisation for Economic Co-operation and Development.

Ogilvie, S. (2014). "The Economics of Guilds." *Journal of Economic Perspectives* 28(4): 169–192.

Olson, M. (1965). *The Logic of Collective Action: Public Goods and the Theory of Goods.* Cambridge, MA: Harvard University Press.

Otsuki, T., Wilson, J. S., and Sewadeh, M. (2001). "Saving Two in a Billion: Quantifying the Trade Effect of European Food Safety Standards on African Exports." *Food Policy* 26(5): 495–514.

Peltzmann, S. (1977). "The Gains and Losses from Industrial Concentration." *Journal of Law and Economics* 20(2): 229–263.

Pennings, J. M. E., Wansink, B., and Meulenberg, M. T. G. (2002). "A Note on Modeling Consumer Reactions to a Crisis: The Case of the Mad Cow Disease." *International Journal of Research in Marketing* 19: 91–100.

Peter, J. P., and Ryan, M. J. (1976). "An Investigation of Perceived Risk at the Brand Level." *Journal of Marketing Research* 13: 184–188.

Petersen, M. A., and Rajan, R. G. (1995). "The Effect of Credit Market Competition on Lending Relationships." *Quarterly Journal of Economics* 110(2): 407–443.

Platteau, J.-P. (2000). *Institutions, Social Norms and Economic Development*. London: Routledge.

Pollak, R. A. (1985). "A Transaction Cost Approach to Families and Households." *Journal of Economic Literature* 23(2): 581–608.

Porter, G., Phillips-Howard, K. (1994). "Outgrower Barley Cultivation on the Jos Plateau, Nigeria: A Case Study of Agricultural Innovation." *The Geographical Journal* 160(3): 319–327.

Poulton, C. (1998). "Cotton Production and Marketing in Northern Ghana: The Dynamics of Competition in a System of Interlocking Transactions." In: A. Dorward, J. Kydd, and C. Poulton (eds.), *Smallholder Cash Crop Production under Market Liberalisation: A New Institutional Economics Perspective*, 56–112. Wallingford, Oxfordshire: CABI Publishing.

Poulton, C., Dorward, A., and Kydd, J. (2010). "The Future of Small Farms: New Directions for Services, Institutions, and Intermediation." *World Development* 38:1413–1428.

Poulton, C., Dorward, A., Kydd, J., Poole, N., and Smith, L. (1998). "A New Institutional Economics Perspective on Current Policy Debates." In A. Dorward, J. Kydd, and C. Poulton (eds.), *Smallholder Cash Crop Production under Market Liberalisation: A New Institutional Economics Perspective*. Wallingford, Oxfordshire: CABI Publishing.

Poulton, C., Gibbon, P., Hanyani-Mlambo, B., Kydd, J., Maro, W., Nylansted-Larsen, M., Osorio, A., Tschirley, D., and Zulu, B. (2004). "Competition and Coordination in Liberalized African Cotton Market Systems." *World Development* 32(3): 519–536.

Poulton, C., Kydd, J., and Dorward, A. (2006). "Overcoming Market Constraints on Pro-Poor Agricultural Growth in Sub-Saharan Africa." *Development Policy Review* 24(3): 243–277.

Pray, C., Oehmke, J. F., and Naseem, A. (2005). "Innovation and Dynamic Efficiency in Plant Biotechnology: An Introduction to the Researchable Issues." *AgBioForum* 8(2/3), 52–63.

Puffert, D. (2002). "Path Dependence in Spatial Networks: The Standardization of the Railway Track Gauge." *Journal of Economic History* 39: 282–314.

Rao, E. J. O., Brümmer, B., and Qaim, M. (2012). "Farmer Participation in Supermarket Channels, Production Technology, and Efficiency: The Case of Vegetables in Kenya." *American Journal of Agricultural Economics* 94(4): 891–912.

Rao, E. J. O., and Qaim, M. (2011). "Supermarkets, Farm Household Income, and Poverty: Insights from Kenya." *World Development* 39(5): 784–796.

Rapsomanikis, G. (2011). "Price Transmission and Volatility Spillovers in Food Markets." In A. Prakash (ed.), *Safeguarding Food Security in Volatile Global Markets*, 144–170. Food and Agriculture Organization of the United Nations.

Rashid, S., and Negassa, A. (2011). "Policies and Performance of Ethiopian Cereal Markets." Ethiopia Strategy Support Program II Working Paper 21. Addis Abada,

Ethiopia: International Food Policy Research Institute and Ethiopian Development Research Institute.

Ravallion, M. (2001). "Growth, Inequality and Poverty: Looking Beyond Averages." *World Development* 29: 1803–1815.

Raynolds, L. (2004). "The Globalization of Organic Agro-food Networks." *World Development* 32:725–743.

Reardon, T., Barrett, C., Berdegué, J., and Swinnen, J. (2009). "Agrifood Industry Transformation and Small Farmers in Developing Countries." *World Development* 37(11): 1717–1727.

Reardon, T., and Berdegué, J. (2002). "The Rapid Rise of Supermarkets in Latin America: Challenges and Opportunities for Development." *Development Policy Review* 20(4): 317–334.

Reardon, T., Codron, J. M., Busch, L., Bingen, J., and Harris, C. (1999). "Global Change in Agrifood Grades and Standards: Agribusiness Strategic Responses in Developing Countries." *International Food and Agribusiness Management Review* 2(3): 421–435.

Reardon, T., and Farina, E. (2002). "The Rise of Private Food Quality and Safety Standards: Illustrations from Brazil." *International Food and Agricultural Management Review* 4: 413–421.

Reardon, T., and Hopkins, R. (2006). "The Supermarket Revolution in Developing Countries: Policies to Address Emerging Tensions Among Supermarkets, Suppliers and Traditional Retailers." *The European Journal of Development Research* 18(4): 522–545.

Reardon, T., and Timmer, P. (2012). "The Economics of the Food System Revolution." *Annual Review of Resource Economics* 4: 225–264.

Reardon, T., Timmer, P., Barrett, C., and Berdegué, J. (2003). "The Rise of Supermarkets in Africa, Asia, and Latin America." *American Journal Agricultural Economics* 85(5): 1140–1146.

Rey, P., and Vergé, T. (2008). "The Economics of Vertical Restraints." In *Handbook of Antitrust Economics*, 353–390. Cambridge, MA: MIT Press.

Richards, T. J., and Patterson, P. M. (2003). "Competition in Fresh Produce Markets: An Empirical Analysis of Marketing Channel Performance." USDA Contractor and Cooperator Report No. 1. USDA/ERS. Washington, DC: U.S. Department of Agriculture.

Ritson, C., and Mai, L. W. (1998). "The Economics of Food Safety." *Nutrition and Food Science* 5: 253–259.

Roberts, D. (1999). "Analyzing Technical Barriers to Trade in Agricultural Markets." *Agribusiness: An International Journal* 15: 335–354.

Rodrik, D. (1995). "Political Economy of Trade Policy." In G. M. Grossman and K. Rogoff (eds.), *Handbook of International Economics*, 1st, Vol. 3, 1457–1494. Amsterdam: Elsevier.

Roe, B., and Sheldon, I. (2007). "Credence Good Labeling: The Efficiency and Distributional Implications of Several Policy Approaches." *American Journal of Agricultural Economics* 89(4): 1020–1033.

Roland, G. (2000). *Transition and Economics: Politics, Markets, and Firms*. Cambridge, MA: MIT Press.

Ronnen, U. (1991). "Minimum Quality Standards, Fixed Costs, and Competition." *RAND Journal of Economics* 22(4): 490–504.

Rozelle, S. (1996). "Gradual Reform and Institutional Development: The Keys to Success of China's Agricultural Reforms." In J. McMillan and B. Naughton (eds.), *Reforming Asian Socialism: The Growth of Market Institutions*, 197–220. Ann Arbor: University of Michigan Press.

Rozelle, S., and Swinnen, J. (2004). "Success and Failure of Reform Insights from the Transition of Agriculture." *Journal of Economic Literature* 42: 404–456.

Ruotsi, J. (2003). "Agricultural Marketing Companies as Sources of Smallholder Credit in Eastern and Southern Africa: Experiences, Insights and Potential Donor Role." Rome, Italy: International Fund for Agricultural Development, Eastern and Southern Africa Division.

SABMiller (2011). "Farming Better Futures." Available at www.sabmiller.com (accessed January 14, 2015).

Salop, S. C. (1979). "A Model of the Natural Rate of Unemployment." *The American Economic Review* 69(1): 117–125.

Salop, S. C., and Scheffman, D. T. (1983). "Raising Rival's Costs." *The American Economic Review Papers and Proceedings* 73(2): 267–271.

Sanyal, P., and Ghosh, S. (2013). "Product Market Competition and Upstream Innovation: Evidence from the U.S. Electricity Market Deregulation." *The Review of Economics and Statistics* 95(1): 237–254.

Savadori, L., Savio, S., Nocotra, E., Rumiati, R., Finucane, M., and Slovic, P. (2004). "Expert and Public Perception of Risk from Biotechnology." *Risk Analysis* 24: 1289–1299.

Savard, L. (2005). "Poverty and Inequality Analysis within a CGE Framework: A Comparative Analysis of the Representative Agent and Microsimulation Approaches." *Development Policy Review* 23: 313–331.

Schipmann, C., and Qaim, M. (2011). "Modern Food Retailers and Traditional Markets in Developing Countries: Comparing Quality, Prices, and Competition Strategies in Thailand." *Applied Economic Perspectives and Policy* 33(3): 345–362.

Schleich, T. (1999). "Environmental Quality with Endogenous Domestic and Trade Policies." *European Journal of Political Economy* 15(1): 53–71.

Schmidt, S. K. (2007). "Mutual Recognition as a New Mode of Governance." *Journal of European Public Policy* 14(5): 667–681.

Schuster, M., and Maertens, M. (2013). "Do Private Standards Create Exclusive Supply Chains? New Evidence from the Peruvian Asparagus Export Sector." *Food Policy* 43: 291–305.

Setboonsarng, S., Leung, P. S., and Cai, J. (2006). "Contract Farming and Poverty Reduction: The Case of Organic Rice Contract Farming in Thailand." In J. Weiss and H. A. Khan (eds.), *Poverty Strategies in Asia: A Growth Plus Approach*, 266–300. Asian Development Bank Institute and Cheltenham, U.K.: Edward Elgar.

Sexton, R. J. (2012). "Market Power, Misconceptions, and Modern Agricultural Markets." *American Journal of Agricultural Economics* 95(2): 209–219.

Sexton, R. J., Sheldon, I., McCorriston, S., and Wang, H. (2007). "Agricultural Trade Liberalization and Economic Development: The Role of Downstream Market Power." *Agricultural Economics* 36: 253–270.

Sexton, R. J., and Zhang, M. (1996). "A Model of Price Determination for Fresh Produce with Application to California Iceberg Lettuce." *American Journal of Agricultural Economics* 78(4): 924–934.

    (2001). "An Assessment of the Impact of Food Industry Market Power on US Consumers." *Agribusiness* 17(1): 59–79.

Sexton, R. J., Zhang, M., and Chalfant, J. A. (2005). "Grocery Retailer Behavior in Perishable Fresh Produce Procurement." *Journal of Agricultural & Food Industrial Organization* 3(1): 1–23.

Shaked, A., and Sutton, J. (1982). "Relaxing Price Competition through Product Differentiation." *Review of Economic Studies* 49(1): 3–13.

Shapiro, C. (1983). "Premiums for High Quality Products as Returns to Reputations." *Quarterly Journal of Economics* 98(4): 659–680.

    (1986). "Investment, Moral Hazard, and Occupational Licensing." *Review of Economic Studies* 53(5): 843–862.

Sharma, R. (2011). "Review of Changes in Domestic Cereal Prices during the Global Price Spikes." Food and Agriculture Organization of the United Nations.

Sheldon, I. (2012). "North-South Trade and Standards: What Can General Equilibrium Analysis Tell Us?" *World Trade Review* 11(3): 376–389.

Shepherd, R., Hedderley, D., Howard, C. and Frewer, L. J. (1998). "Methodological Approaches to Assessing Risk Perception Associated with Food-Related Risks." *Risk Analysis* 18: 95–102.

Shervani, T. A., Frazier, G., and Challagalla, G. (2007). "The Moderating Influence of Firm Market Power on the Transaction Cost Economics Model: An Empirical Test in a Forward Channel Integration Context." *Strategic Management Journal* 28: 635–652.

Shoven, J., and Whalley, J. (1992). *Applying General Equilibrium*. New York: Cambridge University Press.

Simpson, J. (2011). *Creating Wine. The Emergence of a World Industry, 1840–1914*. Princeton, NJ: Princeton University Press.

Singh, S. (2005). *Political Economy of Contract Farming in India*. New Delhi: Allied Publishers.

Smith, G. (2009). "Interaction of Public and Private Standards in the Food Chain." OECD Food, Agriculture, and Fisheries Working Papers No. 15. Paris: OECD Publishing.

Smith, L., Stockbridge, M., and Lohano, H. (1999). "Facilitating the Provision of Farm Credit: The Role of Interlocking Transactions between Traders and Zamindars in Crop Marketing Systems in Sindh." *World Development* 27 (2): 403–418.

Smith, P. (1991). "The Butterfly Effect." *Proceedings of the Aristotelian Society* 91: 247–267.

Snyder, C. M. (2008). "Countervailing Power." In S. N. Durlauf, and L. E. Blume (eds.), *The New Palgrave Dictionary of Economics*, 2nd ed. London: Palgrave Macmillan. The New Palgrave Dictionary of Economics Online. Palgrave Macmillan April 1, 2015. www.dictionaryofeconomics.com/article?id=pde2008_C000538.

Spence, M. (1975). "Monopoly, Quality and Regulation." *Bell Journal of Economics* 6: 417–429.

    (1976a). "Product Differentiation and Welfare." *American Economic Review* 66: 407–414.

    (1976b). "Product Selection, Fixed Costs, and Monopolistic Competition." *Review of Economic Studies* 43(2): 271–235.

(1977). "Entry, Capacity, Investment and Oligopolistic Pricing." *Bell Journal of Economics* 10: 1–19.

Staiger, R. W., and Tabellini, G. (1987). "Discretionary Trade Policy and Excessive Protection." *American Economic Review* 77(5): 823–837.

Stephenson, S. M. (1997). "Standards, Conformity Assessment and Developing Countries." Washington, DC: The World Bank.

Stevenson, T. (2008). "I Have Six Billion Euros. Who Will Give Me Twelve?" WinePages. com. Available at http://www.wine-pages.com/guests/tom/champagne-expansion. htm (accessed December 23, 2013).

Stifel, C., and Thorbecke, E. (2003). "A Dual-Dual CGE Model of an Archetype African Economy: Trade Reform, Migration and Poverty." *Journal of Policy Modeling* 25: 207–235.

Stockbridge, M., Smith, L., and Lohano, H. R. (1998). "Cotton and Wheat Marketing and the Provision of Pre-harvest Services in Sindh Province, Pakistan." In A. Dorward, J. Kydd, and C. Poulton (eds.), *Smallholder Cash Crop Production Under Market Liberalization: A New Institutional Economics Perspective*, 177–239. Wallingford, Oxfordshire: CABI Publishing.

Stone, R. (1954). "Linear Expenditure System and Demand Analysis: An Application to the Pattern of British Demand." *The Economic Journal* 64: 511–527.

Stringer, C. (2006). "Forest Certification and Changing Global Commodity Chains." *Journal of Economic Geography* 6: 701–722.

Sturgeon, T., Memodovic, O., Van Biesebroeck, J., and Gereffi, G. (2009). "Globalisation of the Automotive Industry: Main Features and Trends." *International Journal of Technological Learning, Innovation and Development* 2(1–2): 7–24.

Sturgeon, T., Van Biesebroeck, J., and Gereffi, G. (2008). "Value Chains, Networks and Clusters: Reframing the Global Automotive Industry." *Journal of Economic Geography* 8(3): 297–321.

Sturm, D. M. (2006). "Product Standards, Trade Disputes, and Protectionism." *Canadian Journal of Economics* 39(2): 564–581.

Subervie, J., and Vagneron, I. (2013). "A Drop of Water in the Indian Ocean? The Impact of GlobalGap Certification on Lychee Farmers in Madagascar." *World Development* 50: 57–73.

Sutton, J. (2001). "Rich Trades, Scarce Capabilities: Industrial Development Revisited." Keynes Lecture, Proceedings of the British Academy.

Suwa-Eisenmann, A., and Verdier, T. (2002). "Reciprocity and the Political Economy of Harmonization and Mutual Recognition of Regulatory Measures." CEPR Discussion Paper 3147. London: Centre for Economic Policy Research (CEPR).

Svejnar, J. (1986). "Bargaining Power, Fear of Disagreement, and Wage Settlements: Theory and Evidence from US Industry." *Econometrica* 54(5): 1055–1078.

Swinnen, J. (2006). *The Dynamics of Vertical Coordination in Agro-food Chains in Europe and Central Asia: Case Studies*. Washington, DC: The World Bank.

Swinnen, J., ed. (2007). *Global Supply Chains, Standards and the Poor*. Wallingford, Oxfordshire: CABI Publishing.

(2008). *The Perfect Storm*. Brussels: Centre for European policy studies (CEPS).

Swinnen, J. (2011). "The Right Price of Food." *Development Policy Review* 29 (6): 667–688.

Swinnen, J., Dries, L., Negash, M., and Vandemoortele, T. (2010). "Consumers and EU Agricultural and Food Policies." In A. Oskam, G. Meester, and H. Silvis (eds.),

EU Policy for Agriculture, Food and Rural Areas, 255–264.Wageningen Academic Publishers.

Swinnen, J., Knops, L., and Van Herck, K. (2013). "Food Price Volatility and EU Policies." In P. Pinstrup-Andersen (eds.), *Food Price Policy in an Era of Market Instability: A Political Economy Analysis*. Helsinki, Finland: United Nations University World Institute for Development Economics Research.

Swinnen, J., and Maertens, M. (2007). "Globalization, Privatization, and Vertical Coordination in Food Value Chains of Transition and Developing Countries." *Agricultural Economics* 37(2): 89–102.

(2014). "Finance Through Food and Commodity Value Chains in a Globalized Economy." In D. Köhn, (ed.), *Finance for Food. Towards New Agricultural and Rural Finance*. Berlin and Heidelberg: Springer Science+Business Media.

Swinnen, J., McCluskey, J., and Francken, N. (2005). "Food Safety, the Media and the Information Market." *Agricultural Economics* 32(1): 175–188.

Swinnen, J., and Rozelle, S. (2006). *From Marx and Mao to the Market: The Economics and Politics of Agricultural Transition*. Oxford: Oxford University Press.

Swinnen, J., Sadler, M., and Vandeplas, A. (2007). "Contracting, Competition, and Rent Distribution in Supply Chains: Theory and Empirical Evidence from Central Asia." In J. Swinnen (ed.), *Global Supply Chains, Standards, and the Poor*. Wallingford, Oxfordshire: CABI Publishing.

Swinnen, J., and Squicciarini, P. (2012). "Mixed Messages on Prices and Food Security." *Science* 335(6067): 405–406.

Swinnen, J., and Vandemoortele, T. (2008). "The Political Economy of Nutrition and Health Standards in Food Markets." *Review of Agricultural Economics* 30(3): 460–468.

(2012). "Trade and the Political Economy of Standards." *World Trade Review* 11(3): 390–400.

Swinnen, J., and Vandeplas, A. (2010). "Market Power and Rents in Global Supply Chains." *Agricultural Economics* 41(1): 109–120.

(2011). "Rich Consumers and Poor Producers: Quality and Rent Distribution in Global Value Chains." *Journal of Globalization and Development* 2(2): 1–28.

Swinnen, J., Vandeplas, A., and Maertens, M. (2010). "Liberalization, Endogenous Institutions, and Growth: A Comparative Analysis of Agricultural Reforms in Africa, Asia, and Europe." *World Bank Economic Review* 24 (3): 412–445.

Sykes, A. O. (1995). *Product Standards for Internationally Integrated Goods Markets*. Washington, DC: The Brookings Institution.

Tandon, S., Landes, M., and Woolverton, A. (2011). "The Expansion of Modern Grocery Retailing and Trade in Developing Countries." Economic Research Report No. 122. Washington, DC: Economic Research Service, U.S. Department of Agriculture.

Thilmany, D. D., and Barrett, C. B. (1997). "Regulatory Barriers in an Integrating World Food Market." *Review of Agricultural Economics* 19(1): 91–107.

Tian, H. (2003). "Eco-labelling Scheme, Environmental Protection, and Protectionism." *Canadian Journal of Economics* 36(3): 608–633.

Timmer, P. (1986). *Getting Prices Right: The Scope and Limits of Agricultural Price Policy*. Ithaca, NY: Cornell University Press.

Tirole, J. (1988). *The Theory of Industrial Organization*. Cambridge, MA: MIT Press.

Traub, L. N., and Jayne, T. S. (2006). "Opportunities to Improve Household Food Security through Promoting Informal Maize Marketing Channels: Experience from Eastern Cape Province, South Africa." MSU International Development Working Paper No. 85. Ann Arbor: Department of Agricultural Economics, Michigan State University.

Tschirley, D., Abdula, D., and Weber, M. T. (2005). "Toward Improved Marketing and Trade Policies to Promote Household Food Security in Central and Southern Mozambique." Paper prepared for the FANRPAN conference "Toward Improved Maize Marketing and Trade Policies in the Southern Africa Region," June 21–22, 2005, South Africa.

Tschirley, D., Ayieko, M., Hichaambwa, M., Goeb, J., and Loescher, W. (2009a). "Modernizing Africa's Fresh Produce Supply Chains without Rapid Supermarket Takeover: Towards a Definition of Research and Investment Priorities." Paper presented at the ILRI-AGRA workshop "Towards Priority Actions for Market Development for African farmers," Nairobi, May 15–17.

Tschirley, D., Poulton, C., and Labaste, P., eds. (2009b). "Organization and Performance of Cotton Sectors in Africa: Learning from Reform Experience." Washington, DC: The International Bank for Reconstruction and Development/The World Bank.

Unnevehr, L. (2000). "Food Safety Issues and Fresh Food Product Exports from LDCs." *Agricultural Economics* 23(3): 231–240.

Valletti, T. M. (2000). "Minimum Quality Standards under Cournot Competition." *Journal of Regulatory Economics* 18(3): 235–245.

Van Herck, K., Swinnen, J., and Deconinck, K. (2012). "How the East Was Won: Supply Chain Restructuring in the Eastern European Beer Market." *German Journal of Agricultural Economics* 61: 213–222.

van Tongeren, F., Beghin, J., and Marette, S. (2009). "A Cost-Benefit Framework of the Assessment of Non-Tariff Measures in Agro-Food Trade." OECD Food, Agriculture and Fisheries Working Papers, 21. Paris: OECD Publishing.

Verbeke, W., and Ward, W. (2001). "A Fresh Meat Almost Ideal Demand System Incorporating Negative TV Press and Advertising Impact." *Agricultural Economics* 25: 359–374.

Verpoorten, M., Arora, A., Stoop, N., and Swinnen, J. F. M. (2013). "Self-Reported Food Insecurity in Africa during the Food Price Crisis." *Food Policy* 39: 51–63.

Veyssiere, L. (2007). "Strategic Response to GMOs by GM-free Countries." *European Review of Agricultural Economics* 34(3): 365–392.

Vigani, M., and Olper, A. (2013). "GM-free Private Standards, Public Regulation of GM Products and Mass Media." LICOS Discussion Paper 331/2013, Leuven, Belgium.

Vogel, D. (1995). *Trading Up: Consumer and Environmental Regulation in a Global Economy*. Cambridge, MA: Harvard University Press.

(2003). "The Hare and the Tortoise Revisited: The New Politics of Consumer and Environmental Regulation in Europe." *British Journal of Political Science* 33: 557–580.

Vogel, D., and Swinnen, J., eds. (2011). *Transatlantic Regulatory Cooperation: The Shifting Roles of the EU, the US and California*. Cheltenham, U.K.: Edward Elgar.

Von Cramon-Taubadel, S. (1998). "Estimating Asymmetric Price Transmission with the Error-Correcting Representation." *European Review of Agricultural Economics* 25: 1–18.

Von Schlippenbach, V., and Teichmann, I. (2012). "The Strategic Use of Private Quality Standards in Food Supply Chains." *American Journal of Agricultural Economics* 94/5: 1189–1201.

Wang, H., Dong, X., Rozelle, S., Huang, J., and Reardon. T. (2009). "Producing and Procuring Horticultural Crops with Chinese Characteristics: The Case of Northern China." *World Development* 37(11): 1791–1801.

Wang, X., Tadesse, H., and Rayner, T. (2006). "Price Transmission, Market Power and Returns to Scale: A Note." University of Nottingham Discussion Papers in Economics No. 06/07.

Wangwe, S., and Lwakatare, M. (2004). "Innovation in Rural Finance in Tanzania." Paper prepared for the Third Annual Conference on Microfinance, Arusha, March 15–17.

Ward, C. (2010). "Assessing Competition in the U.S. Beef Packing Industry." *Choices* 25(2): 1–7.

Warning, M., and Key, N. (2002). "The Social Performance and Distributional Consequences of Contract Farming: An Equilibrium Analysis of the Arachide de Bouche Program in Senegal." *World Development* 30(2): 255–263.

Weatherspoon, D., Cacho, J., and Christy, R. (2001). "Linking Globalization, Economic Growth and Poverty: Impacts of Agribusiness Strategies on Sub-Saharan Africa." *American Journal of Agricultural Economics* 83 (3): 722–729.

Weatherspoon, D., and Reardon, T. (2003). "The Rise of Supermarkets in Africa: Implications for Agrifood Systems and the Rural Poor." *Development Policy Review* 21(3): 333–356.

Weinberger, K., and Lumpkin, T. A. (2007). "Diversification into Horticulture and Poverty Reduction: A Research Agenda." *World Development* 35: 1464–1480.

Weldegebriel, H. T. (2004). "Imperfect Price Transmission: Is Market Power Really to Blame?" *Journal of Agricultural Economics* 55: 101–114.

Wilkie, W. L., Desrochers, D. M., and Gundlach, G. T. (2002). "Marketing Research and Public Policy: The Case of Slotting Fees." *Journal of Public Policy & Marketing* 21(2): 275–288.

Williamson, O. E. (1981). "The Economics of Organization: The Transaction Cost Approach." *American Journal of Sociology* 87(3): 548–577.

(2002). "The Theory of the Firm as Governance Structure: From Choice to Contract." *Journal of Economic Perspectives* 16(3): 171–195.

Wilson, S. J., and Abiola, V. (2003). *Standards and Global Trade: A Voice for Africa.* Washington, DC: The World Bank.

Winfree, J. A., and McCluskey, J. J. (2005). "Collective Reputation and Standards." *American Journal of Agricultural Economics* 87(1): 206–213.

Wohlgenant, M. K. (2001). "Marketing Margins: Empirical Analysis." In B. Gardner and G. Rausser (eds.), *Handbook of Agricultural Economics*, Vol. 1, 934–970. Amsterdam: Elsevier.

World Bank. (1994). *Adjustment in Africa: Reforms, Results and the Road Ahead.* Washington, DC: The World Bank.

World Bank. (2005). *The Dynamics of Vertical Coordination in Agrifood Chains in Eastern Europe and Central Asia. Implications for Policy Making and World Bank Operations.* Washington, DC: The World Bank.

World Bank. (2006). "World Bank Development Indicators." data.worldbank.org/indicator. Washington, DC: The World Bank.

World Bank. (2007). *World Development Report 2008: Agriculture for Development.* Washington, DC: The World Bank/New York: Oxford University Press.

World Bank. (2009). "From Poor Areas to Poor People: China's Evolving Poverty Reduction Agenda –An Assessment of Poverty and Inequality in China." Poverty Reduction and Economic Management Department Report Washington, DC: The World Bank.

World Trade Organization (WTO). (2012). *World Trade Report 2012: Looking beyond International Co-operation on Tariffs: NTMs and Services Regulation in the XXIst Century.* Geneva, Switzerland: WTO.

World Trade Organization (WTO). (2014a). Committee on Sanitary and Phytosanitary Measures. "Overview Regarding the Level of Implementation of the Transparency Provisions of the SPS Agreement." – Note by the Secretariat – Revision 7.

World Trade Organization (WTO). (2014b). Committee on Technical Barriers to Trade. "Nineteenth Annual Review of the Implementation and Operation of the TBT Agreement. Note to the Secretariat."

Wouters, J., and Geraerts, D. (2012). "Private Standards and the World Trade Organization: Some Legal Considerations." *World Trade Review* 11(3): 479–489.

Xiang, T., Huang, J., Kancs, d'A., Rozelle, S., and Swinnen, J. (2012). "Food Standards and Welfare: General Equilibrium Effects." *Journal of Agricultural Economics* 63(2): 223–244.

Xinhua Net. (2008). "Rolling Report on Sanlu Babies and Infants Milk Powder Event" (in Chinese). Available at http://news.xinhuanet.com/newscenter/2008-09/12/content_9935963.htm (accessed March 1, 2009).

Xiong, B., and Beghin, J. (2013). "Aflatoxin Redux: Does European Aflatoxin Regulation Hurt Groundnut Exporters from Africa?" *European Review of Agricultural Economics* 40(5): 895–895.

Yeager, M. (1981). *Competition and Regulation: The Development of Oligopoly in the Meat Packing Industry.* Greenwich, CT: JAI Press.

Yeung, R. M. W., and Morris, J. (2001). "Food Safety Risk: Consumer Perception and Purchase Behaviour." *British Food Journal* 103(3): 170–186.

Yu, C., and Connor, J. M. (2002). "The Price-Concentration Relationship in Grocery Retailing: Retesting Newmark." *Agribusiness* 18(4): 413–426.

Zanardi, M. (2004). "Antidumping Law as a Collusive Device." *The Canadian Journal of Economics* 37(1): 95–122.

Index

Acemoglu, D., 34n1, 270
Aflatoxins, 50, 66
Africa
  commodity characteristics in, 234
  comparative perspective of commodity
    characteristics
    overview, 221, 224
    non-traditional export crops, 223–224
    staple food crops, 221–222
    traditional export crops, 222–223
  food exports from, 4, 50
  income, effect on high standards
    economy, 148
  liberalization in
    overview, 9, 235
    liberalization process, 240
    non-traditional export crops and,
      252–255
    performance, analysis of, 252
    pre-liberalization economy, 239–241
    staple food crops and, 252–255
    traditional export crops and, 252–255
    variations in performance, 237, 252–255
  market power in, 207
  price transmission in, 208n2
  production structure in, 159–160
  staple food crops in, 220n1
  supermarkets in, 142–143
  third party contract enforcement in, 180
  value chains in, 235
  vertical coordination in, 162–163
Aghion, P., 195n1
Agricultural Marketing Service
    (USDA), 68n2
Agriculture, scale economies in, 149n5–150
Ailawadi, K.L., 198

Akerlof, G.A., 12
Akiyama, T., 240n8
Aldi (retail store), 198
Amacher, G.S., 16, 17, 101
American Meat Institute, 78n4–79
Anderson, K., 13, 16–17, 18, 37, 50,
    51n5, 57, 74
Andersson, C., 5n8
Ando, A., 272
Andreoni, J., 69
Animal welfare, private standards
    regarding, 78–79, 78n4
Ansell, C., 72
Asia
  commodity characteristics in, 234
  contract farming in, 4n6–5
  food exports from, 4
  liberalization in, 192
  vertical coordination in, 162–163
Asymmetric information
  modeling of standards and, 12–16, 12n1
  private standards reducing, 77–78
Azzam, A., 198

Babcock, B., 125
Bajari, P., 181
Baldwin, R., 4n4, 62n10, 63, 99n2
Baltzer, K., 13, 16–17, 18, 50n2
Bardhan, P., 171n13–172
Barla, P., 198
Barrett, C., 18, 49n1, 248n14
Becker, G.S., 34n1
Beef
  hormones in, 53
  traceability standards, 77n1
Beghin, J., 4n4, 16–17, 50n3, 51

Noev, N., 4n6
Non-tariff barriers (NTBs), 49
Non-traditional export crops
  comparative perspective, 223–224
  implications for value chain governance,
    233–234
North, D.C., 163n2
NTBs (Non-tariff barriers), 49

Occupational licenses, 8, 122–123
Office Internationale des Epizooties, 64
Oligopoly, private standards in, 95–96
Olper, A., 79
Olson, M., 34n1
Organic food, 68
Otsuki, T., 50, 50n3
Outsiders. *See* Inclusion or exclusion of
  producers in value chains
Over-standardization
  in political economy model of standards,
    35, 41–42
  protectionism and, 51

Pagoulatos, E., 198
Pakistan, market power in, 206
Pareto improvement, vertical coordination
  and, 166
Pareto inefficiency, market concentration and,
    194–195
Patterson, P.M., 197n4, 198
Pennings, J.M.E., 69, 72n4
Perfect foresight assumption, 103n10–104
Persson, T., 34n1
Peter, J.P., 69
Philip Morris (supplier), 196
Platteau, J.-P., 163n2
Poland
  contract farming in, 4n6
  production structure in, 150
Policy persistence in dynamic model
  of standards, 98–99, 110, 113,
    118–119, 121
Political economy model of standards
  overview, 6, 7, 34–35, 45–46
  "anti-standard coalitions" in developing
    countries, 35, 42–44
  comparative statics, 35, 39–41, 48
  Cournot-Nash equilibrium and, 46
  economic structure and, 35–37
  first order condition, proof of, 38n6, 47
  information, impact on development,
    35, 44–45

international trade and, 52, 56–57
media, impact on development, 35, 44–45
over-standardization in, 35, 41–42
perception of standards, impact on
  development, 35, 44–45
political equilibrium in, 35, 37–39
political structure and, 35, 37–39
producers, inclusion in or exclusion
  from (*See* Inclusion or exclusion of
  producers in value chains)
"pro-standard coalitions" in developed
  countries, 35, 42–44
public regulations and, 34n1, 51n5
social optimum in, 35–37
truthfulness of contribution schedules,
  proof of, 37–38, 37n5, 46
under-standardization in, 35, 41–42
Political equilibrium
  consumer surplus and, 37–39
  in dynamic model of standards
    constant and different consumer
      preferences, 107–113
    constant and identical consumer
      preferences, 105–107
    temporary differences in consumer
      preferences, 114–118
  geographical indications and, 130
  inclusion or exclusion of producers in value
    chains and (*See* Inclusion or exclusion
    of producers in value chains)
  integration of risk and externalities
    and, 70–73
  international trade and, 52, 56–57
  in political economy model of standards,
    35, 37–39
  quality standards and, 71, 72–73
  safety standards and, 70–72
  social and environmental standards
    and, 71, 72
Poulton, C., 207, 221, 231
Precautionary principle, 97–98
Price liberalization, 240, 246
Price setting as institutional characteristic of
  pre-liberalization economies, 238
Price transmission
  overview, 9, 192, 208–210, 219
  in Africa, 208n2
  consumer price shocks, effect of, 219
  in developing countries, 208
  efficiency discounts, 218n7
  efficiency premiums, 218n7
  empirical evidence, 208n2, 210n4

Transaction costs (*cont.*)
  fixed per supplier, 157–158
  fixed per unit of input, 157–158
  inclusion in economy, 156–157, 158
  size of economy, 156
  international trade and, 57
  market concentration and, 195
Traub, L.N., 230n8
Turkmenistan, market power in, 206

Udry, C., 171n13–172
Uganda
  liberalization process in, 240n9
  staple food crops in, 222n2
  traditional export crops in, 223
Under-standardization
  in political economy model of standards,
    35, 41–42
  protectionism and, 51
Unilever (supplier), 196, 196n3
United Egg Producers, 78n4–79
United Kingdom
  British Retail Consortium (BRC), 80
  Competition Commission, 197, 198
  food industry in, 198
  "mad cow" disease and, 71
  retail concentration in, 196n3, 197, 198
United Nations Food and Agriculture
    Organization, 68n2, 208n2
United States
  Agricultural Marketing Service
    (USDA), 68n2
  Agriculture Department, 68n2, 195
  food industry in, 195, 198
  GM food
    comparative advantage regarding, 57
    public perception of, 44–45
  precautionary principle in, 97–98
  retail concentration in, 197n4, 198
  SPS Agreement notifications, 2
Ursprung, H.W., 51n5
Uruguay Round (1994), 63–65
Uzbekistan, market power in, 206

Valletti, T.M., 11, 13, 16, 17, 51
Value, vertical coordination and
  buyer holdup, self-enforcing contracts
    with, 175
  supplier holdup, self-enforcing contracts
    with, 172–173
  two-sided holdup, self-enforcing contracts
    with, 176–177

Value chains
  in Africa, 235
  in Central Europe, 235
  commodity characteristics and
    (*See* Commodity characteristics)
  contracting costs and
    (*See* Contracting costs)
  debate regarding, 3–5
  in Eastern Europe, 235
  general equilibrium effects (*See* General
    equilibrium effects)
  globalization and, 1
  high standards economy (*See* High
    standards economy)
  inclusion or exclusion of producers in
    (*See* Inclusion or exclusion of
    producers in value chains)
  in Latin America, 235
  liberalization and (*See* Liberalization)
  market power and (*See* Market power)
  price transmission and (*See* Price
    transmission)
  producers, inclusion in or exclusion
    from (*See* Inclusion or exclusion of
    producers in value chains)
  vertical coordination and (*See* Vertical
    coordination)
Vandemoortele, T., 13, 16–17, 68
Vandeplas, A., 207
Van Huylenbroeck, G., 197
van Tongeren, F., 16–17
Verdier, T., 13, 49n1
Verpoorten, M., 208n2
Vertical coordination
  overview, 8, 162–164, 191–192
  in Africa, 162–163
  in Asia, 162–163
  buyer holdup, self-enforcing contracts with,
    173–176
    overview, 164
    efficiency discounts, 174
    feasibility under, 175–176
    incentive compatibility constraints,
      168n12
    rent distribution under, 174
    value under, 175
  commodity characteristics and, 221
  in developing countries, 164–165
  in Eastern Europe, 162–163
  efficiency and equity effects of development
    overview, 164, 185–186, 192
    aggregate effect, 189–191